DOUBLEDAY
CELEBRATES
100 YEARS OF
EXCELLENCE

The
Best
of

1997

Edited and with an Introduction by
Phillip Lopate

The Anchor Essay Annual

Anchor Books/Doubleday
New York London Toronto Sydney Auckland

AN ANCHOR BOOK
PUBLISHED BY DOUBLEDAY

a division of Bantam Doubleday Dell Publishing Group, Inc.
1540 Broadway, New York, New York 10036

ANCHOR BOOKS, DOUBLEDAY, and the portrayal of an anchor are
trademarks of Doubleday, a division of Bantam Doubleday Dell
Publishing Group, Inc.

Book design by Cheryl L. Cipriani

The Anchor Essay Annual
Vol. 1
ISSN 1093-7005

ISBN 0-385-48413-5

Co

ntents

Phillip Lopate

Introduction

Are we living through a resurgence of the essay?

Depends whom you talk to. Writers increasingly love the form; booksellers have their doubts; magazine editors find essays quite useful in a pinch; book review assigners often consider collections of the stuff a pain. But essays have become ubiquitous, as part of the general boom in nonfiction prose.

When you think about it, essays are everywhere: they turn up in the costumes of personal memoir, humorous sketch, diatribe, speech, prose poem, vignette, philosophical treatise; in performance pieces, comic books and on the radio; in specialty journals covering everything from gardening to foreign affairs; in the many new essay anthologies organized around a topic, as well as the collected essays of individual authors. One reason, besides naked ambition, that I accepted Anchor Books' invitation to have me edit in the coming years their new essay annual (a companion volume to their long-established fiction book, *O. Henry Prize Stories*) was that I wanted to reflect more of that cornucopic variety in my selections.

I've envisioned an essay annual that would differ from the

others in drawing not only from periodicals but from books and unpublished manuscripts; not only from the present but a few rediscoveries from the past as well; not only from the United States but from the international literary scene. Not the "best" (whatever *that* means) of one calendar year, necessarily—but a lively, cosmopolitan mix; not a salon of blue-chip names but a conversation among absorbing, obstreperous voices.

To arrive at a few dozen memorable essays I have had to read myself bleary-eyed. Of course I skimmed. Often I would pick up a magazine and find nothing but journalism: celebrity interviews, muckraking exposés, travel guides, perfectly realized on their own terms, mind you, but not what I'd call a real *essay* among them.

How can you tell a first-rate essay? I am tempted to repeat what St. Augustine said about Time: "When no one asks what it is, I know what it is; if someone asks me, I don't know." All I can say is that I was looking for a certain density of thought. A living voice. A text that would surprise me and take me through a mental adventure.

Admittedly, I've been drawn to the analytical, the wry, the self-aware. To me there is no room for naïfs or solemn primitives in the essay; it's a performance of extreme sophistication, the argument rising or falling on the basis of verbal nuance, persona pirouette, exposure of unconscious contradiction in oneself and others. There are many think pieces that make a reasonable point but then continue to hammer away; they don't turn against themselves enough. Still other essays wander into a glade of pastoral appreciation where there's no tension, the stakes seem insufficient. I was on the lookout for the pleasure a mind takes in finding its way through a dangerous thicket.

Anyone who reads the prose of a calendar year cannot help but be aware of trends. The presidential campaign inspired a million written words on political strategy, gay marriage, welfare reform. Most have already faded, and deserved to fade; but, considering how many great English essays of the eighteenth and nineteenth centuries were occasioned by party partisanship, I was on the alert for something about politics with the capacity to generalize the issues wittily or broadly enough to go beyond the merely topical. Christopher Hitchens's "Against Lesser Evilism" does that; though I happen to disagree with his conclusions, I admire his cool, intransigent rhetoric.

Another trend involved a defense of reading, and a concomitant fear of computers (see Lynne Sharon Schwartz's and Andrei Codrescu's able pieces). The body and sexuality continued to exercise critically minded essayists (such as Jean Baudrillard and Daniel Harris), while race, multiculturalism and issues involving the Other remained a richly worrying preoccupation (see Richard Rodriguez, James McPherson, Pascal Bruckner, Hilton Als).

In what is now dubbed the Age of Memoir, we have been inundated with half-lives, stopping before forty, that feature one or two sensational chapters and then give way to a sense of letdown. All the more valuable seems the memoir-essay: here all the juice of a *Bildungsroman* is compressed into a vivid, self-reflective tale (see Emily Fox Gordon, Cynthia Ozick, Vivian Gornick and Thomas Larson), minus the padding.

For me, there is nothing quite like the beauty of a worldly, meditative and amply mature sensibility going about its bee-like business of constructing meaning. The Irish master, Hubert Butler, in "Little K," perpetrates what might be called an "everything-essay," weaving together the personal, historical and tragically universal; the veteran Edward Hoagland surprises us with his digressions and shifts in geography; the Continental experience of an Aldo Buzzi offers prose caviar to the reader; while our late, lamented Diana Trilling walks thoughtfully and magisterially around her portrayed subject, reviving old controversies, until she has rendered him in three shrewd dimensions.

Finally, the majority of these pieces champion an uneasy complexity and contradiction, just as they refuse glib accommodations. To keep desire alive, concludes Jean Baudrillard, "One should not be reconciled with one's body, nor with oneself, one should not be reconciled with the other, one should not be reconciled with nature, one should not reconcile male and female, nor good and evil." Many of the essayists included here echo this opposition to easy answers, and help increase our capacity to face the unreconciled.

Emily Fox Gordon

Mockingbird Years

When I was eighteen my parents were faced with a problem: What to do with a sullen, disorganized daughter who had failed to graduate from high school and who had returned home to Washington D.C., wrists bandaged, from an extended stay with her boyfriend's mother in Indianapolis. They took me in tow to the psychiatrist I'd been seeing off and on through my high school years, who recommended that I spend some time in a "therapeutic environment." He suggested Austen Riggs, a hospital in Stockbridge, Mass. where patients—none of them too sick, he reassured us—were free to come and go, and where I might spend some months away from the immediate source of my confusion, the boyfriend and his mother.

I stayed at Riggs for three years, one as an inpatient, two as an outpatient, living in apartments with various roommates. These were years I should have been in college, and they were so empty and aimless that when I remember Riggs now my mind pans around the corridors of the big comfortable patient residence, the Inn, as we called it, and in my imagination it is absolutely uninhabited. I drift through the central hall, and into the dining room, where the fruit bowl and the iced tea urn rested on a polished sideboard, replenished by the staff at regular intervals. I cross the hall to the living room with its twelve couches, grand piano and tall windows hung with flowered chintz curtains. Then I withdraw to the wide central hall and approach the reception desk below the great curving central staircase, and wander in memory through the back door to the grounds, where deck chairs were arrayed in pairs under the trees. I skim by the volleyball and tennis courts and across the parking lot behind the medical building, where patients met with therapists, past the patient-run, staff-supervised nursery school and the greenhouse.

Riggs was an anachronistic institution even then. (I often wonder what it's like there now; the patients are a lot sicker, I'm told, and they stay for shorter periods of time.) The population was very young, very bored. There were a few middle aged people there, but we younger ones tended to avoid them. They looked baggy and defeated, truly sad in a way we sensed had more to do with life than diagnostic categories. Years later, when I actually went to college, I read *The Magic Mountain* in a seminar, and I felt I had a certain advantage over the other students. How well my Riggs experience prepared me to understand the convalescent languors of the tuberculosis patients, reclining on their deck chairs, blankets draped over their knees, eyes fixed on the middle distance. Now, whenever I see one of those chairs, the white-painted wooden Adirondack type which seem to show up in soft-focus lithographs on the walls of so many doctors' offices, I feel a familiar jelly-limbed ennui.

My suicidal gesture had been feeble, a few swipes with a pair of nail scissors. I knew when I arrived at Riggs that I was quite sane and only mildly sick; I had no business being there. But I had no business anywhere else either—no diploma, no prospects and no ambitions.

I arrived excited; going to Riggs was the fulfillment of an adolescent fantasy. The status of mental patient would invest me with significance. The frantic little act which landed me there had been my entree to a process; life would work on me in this particularly colorful way, and who knew what might happen? Riggs had a special interest for me because by coincidence I had spent some time hanging around there at age fifteen, when I visited the home of my friend Caroline, whose father was the financial manager of the institution. We had recently seen the movie *David and Lisa,* and we were smitten with the romance of madness. I think we believed that if we cultivated dissociation we would become as beautiful as Lisa; our complexions would turn luminous, our faces grow expressive hollows, our hair lie flat and glossy. We spent our days edging cautiously around the grounds, taking drags on shared cigarettes and muttering "a touch can kill," hoping to be noticed by the patients, drawn into their glamorous orbit by the magic of proximity. The patients frustrated us by staying indoors, their windows open to the July breezes, playing "Mockingbird" on their stereos. We heard this song constantly, from multiple windows under which we passed, and for us its refrain became the perverse anthem of mental illness:

> Mock, yeah!
> Ing, yeah!
> Bird, yeah!
> Yeah, yeah!
> Mock-ing-bird!

When the psychiatrist in Washington recommended that I be sent to Riggs, I quivered inwardly, afraid to blow it all by showing my pleasure, and the moment I got home and free of my parents I called Caroline long-distance. "Guess what?" I whispered. "Guess where I'm going?" Caroline was going to college, but I was going to Riggs, and I knew by the envy in her voice that I had double-trumped her.

At community meetings patients sat crosslegged on couches, or lay sprawled on the carpet, and were encouraged to ventilate their feelings by the nurses and a small, round-eyed man, a non-doctor whose function I couldn't understand at first, a kind of professional gadfly and controversialist. Years later I found a category for him; he was a proto-facilitator, perhaps the first of his kind to emerge from the fledgling family-systems school of psychiatry.

These meetings, meals and therapy sessions were the only real structure of our days. We were assigned tasks, called "work-jobs," in the mornings, but most patients slept through the hour reserved for them. It felt a little gratuitous to spend an hour sponging down baseboards when that hour was being charged to one's account. The issues of work-jobs and D.N.R., or Day-Night Reversal (this was the late sixties, and already we were using acronyms: Riggs was both anachronistic and ahead of its time) were the staples of discussion at community meet-ings—not so much discussion, really, as nagging and resistance. The nurses and the proto-facilitator kept after us. Why couldn't we take pride in our environment? Could we get to the bottom of this, please? The patients sank deeper into silence and into the contorted positions young bodies assume in shamed repose.

The essential passivity of life at Riggs, a life lived to be examined in therapy, worked against the staff's attempts to get us to clean up after ourselves and keep sensible hours. The domestic staff in the Inn, the nurses and Richard, operated at cross-purposes with the therapists, those austere beings in the big white building across the way who received us singly in their offices and were seen in the Inn only when a patient was having what the nurses called an "upset," with the accent on the first syllable of the word, late at night. The therapists viewed our sloth as symptomatic, and we all tacitly understood that any attempt to expunge what was symptomatic in our be-havior was anti-therapeutic. The therapists were the radicals, the staff the exponents of *realpolitik*. The conflict between these factions was never open, and perhaps it was never a real one, but rather a deliberately engineered tension, a therapeutic master-plan, a good-cop, neutral-cop ploy. But even if that were true, I know that like most master-plans it was often lost sight of, even by its designers.

Not all of us were essentially normal late adolescents. Some were seriously depressed, not just sluggish. Some were harmlessly odd, like L., a lapsed seminarian who carried on a constant internal debate about the supremacy of the papacy. He would emerge from his room to keep a running score on the blackboard above the mailboxes—L. 24, Pope 17. Some of the elderly outpatients seemed beyond hope. The parameters of their worlds shrank as they aged; their compulsiveness stiffened. Never quite accepted by the townspeople, they shuffled up and down Main Street, stopping for the lunch special at the drugstore, ducking into the library for a nap.

A few patients were mad. I can think of two in the early days of my stay there; one somehow got her hands on an antique cannon, fiddled with it to make it operational and fired it out of her bedroom window. She also pulled a gun on her therapist, made him plead for his life. The other, a young man who could have doubled for Charles Manson, stuffed hard boiled eggs into his rectum and laid them publicly, dropping his pants and squatting in the hallway.

Still, making allowance for the effects of idleness and boredom, most Riggs patients were much like people in the outside world. Graduate students, for example, don't seem much saner as a group, or even much happier. The striking difference between Riggs patients and comparable young people living outside was that Riggs patients were richer. I believe I came from the least wealthy family of any patient while I was there.

My mother delivered me to Riggs. She spent the first night with me in the local guest house. We were shown into our room, with its flounced twin beds and space heater, its view of Stockbridge's famous main street, the one painted by Norman Rockwell. She closed the door and took her flask from her purse. "I guess the sun's over the yardarm," she said.

The next morning was frosty and bright; we said goodbye in the parking lot of the therapy building, and she alarmed me by bursting into tears, very uncharacteristic behavior. "Goodbye my dear," she said, and clutched me. The sun bounced off the lenses of her dark glasses and blazed in the car windshields. I remember staring over her shoulder blankly, eager to see her go, eager to get started.

I was led from office to office in the warren of small rooms in the basement of the therapy building, tested and interviewed by five or six of the psychiatrists on staff. I was given the standard Wechsler Intelligence Quotient test for adults. (What is the Koran? What does the following quotation mean: "A single swallow does not a summer make?" Assemble these blocks so that the result exactly reproduces the pattern in this booklet. Tell me a story which explains this picture—a boy stands at the head of the stairs, a broken violin in his hand. A man stands over him.) I was given a Rorschach, a Personality Inventory. When I hesitated, the examiner leaned back in his chair, drummed the desk with his thumbs, took a furtive look at his stopwatch. "Take your time," he said.

After my diagnostic workup was complete I was the subject of a full-dress staff conference in which my prognosis was discussed and my treatment plan drawn up. I think I may have been the last patient at Riggs to be brought into her own conference. The custom was dropped, probably because it had an unenlightened, nineteenth-century feel to it.

I remember entering that room, led in by a nurse, shown to a chair at the head of a polished oval table that seemed to me the size of a fishing boat. The nurse withdrew. Seated there, looking down the rows of faces which looked back inquiringly into mine, I was visited with an impulse to say "Perhaps you gentlemen were wondering why I called you all together today." That made me smirk inappropriately. "Emily," said one of the doctors, "I'm interested in this detached feeling you described in your interview—that floating, disengaged sensation. Are you feeling that way right now?"

"I guess I am," I said, and I lifted my lowered eyes to

hazard a smile at the assembled doctors. They smiled back encouragingly, and at that moment I felt a desolate certainty that now there would be no backing out. Now I had left home for good.

I was a hog for attention and welcomed nearly any kind, but the doctors' questions, the nurses' charting of my moods and actions, all this had the feel of the speculum about it.

Within a few months, though, the staff's vigilance had dissipated, and I took my place among the other patients, lounging on the leather sofas in the entrance hall, ashtray balanced on my knee, running my eyes over back issues of *Horizon*. I learned to scorn the activities Riggs offered, ceramics and woodworking in the Shop, repotting plants in the greenhouse. I learned to pretend that I hated the food, which was actually the best institutional food I had ever eaten, or ever have since. My adjustment was quick and unproblematic.

I was assigned to a therapist, a research psychologist. I learned later that I was only his second clinical patient. He was a man in his middle thirties, amiable, earnest, eager. He had a spade-shaped, high-cheekboned, luminous face—a beautiful face, really—which sat at an odd angle to his neck, a disc facing up rather than out, and he stood rocked forward on his toes, his shoulders so hunched they were nearly level with his ears. My adolescent sensors instantly registered something alien and slightly goony in his aspect, and I never fully accepted him. Now I understand him better; experience has provided me with a context into which I can place him. He came from the Bronx, a *yeshiva bucher* from a Yiddish-speaking household. When I think of him now, I put a yarmulke on his balding head and append Hassidic curls to his temples, and I see his face as a throwback to visionary and ecstatic ancestors.

I was re-tested a year after I arrived, and my I.Q. had declined significantly—how much, my therapist wouldn't tell me. He would only say the test results were "disappointing." My diagnosis was altered. Now my anxiety neurosis had become a "schizoid personality disorder with borderline trends." This is a bad diagnosis, and an insulting one, I've been told since, but at the time I rather liked the sound of "borderline trends." It made me think of a stylish flourish, an extra, like piping on a jacket or whitewall tires on a car.

Apathy wasted us. I had been a failure as a student, but I had always read voraciously. At Riggs I stopped. We lost our normal adolescent interest in sex—for the most part, at least. We hung out in groups, but we tended not to form real friendships; we saw one another as fundamentally inaccessible, three quarters submerged. We wore kimonos and hair curlers, jeans and slippers as we padded around the Inn—half dressed, half-there. News of the Vietnam War protests reached us; we crowded into the patient library where the record player was kept to listen to *Blonde on Blonde, Music from Big Pink* and *Abbey Road,* but still we felt wistfully peripheral. The great countercultural storm was rising, but far away from us. Actually, to the degree that a therapeutic view of life has been a legacy of the sixties, we seem in retrospect to have been an advance guard. But at the time we viewed ourselves as the last of the stragglers.

Many of us got worse rather than better, and for some, getting worse was dangerous. By the time some patients ran out of money, and this was bound to happen eventually, even to the multi-million dollar trustfunders, their parents and doctors had come to view them as too debilitated to go back into the world. Instead they moved on to state institutions, where sometimes they stayed for life.

My therapist became inappropriately attached to me. Our meetings were charged with feeling, every session seemed to end in an epiphany. But it was Dr. Schiffer's eyes that beaded with tears, not mine. My parents, we acknowledged in therapy, had rejected and abandoned me. I had known this for years, but pretended it was a revelation because I found his emotion too gratifying not to play on. At the same time I felt itchy and uncomfortable, instantly sated with his love, made queasy by it. I'm not sure whether this was because I felt myself to be in bad faith or whether I was unaccustomed to this kind of moony empathy, this cherishing pity. I was not the kind of young girl a lot of men fell in love with. And I always felt that the object of Dr. Schiffer's love was not me, but some phantasmal waif who only half-inhabited the chair in which I sat.

"Thank you," I would say as we paused at the door of his office at the end of an hour. "No, thank *you*," Dr. Schiffer said. I had opened up the world of feeling for him, he told me. The years of charts and statistics and rat mazes were over for him now. We began to take walks on autumn days. Dr. Schiffer taught me to drive and accompanied me when I took my driving test. I taught him to smoke cigarettes.

Around the time when Dr. Schiffer's wife was due to deliver a baby, I became an outpatient. Dr. Schiffer began to appear at my door. One evening we drank a lot of wine, he and my roommate and I, and we all took a tipsy walk after dinner. Dr. Schiffer put his arm around my waist. This was the first physical contact between us, and the only, but it changed things unalterably. I woke the next morning charged with a theatrical anger and teased by doubts about its legitimacy.

In therapy I remained mostly silent after this incident, and glared. Dr. Schiffer became frantic. He told me one day that he had spent the morning weeping in his parked car on a farm road in Lenox, one of the routes we often took on our drives. Hearing this confession puffed me up with scorn like a blowfish. I was thrilled and enraged. Inwardly, I felt some alarm at this reaction; it seemed partly out of my control. My disgust at Dr. Schiffer had something to do with the way his clammy feelings for me entwined with professional ambition— at my second staff conference he presented our work together as a new way of doing therapy in which the therapist makes himself vulnerable, fully embraces his own transference, drops his therapeutic distance. A triumph, except for my unfortunate deterioration, documented in testing. But that was easily finessed with the familiar psychoanalytic rationalization that explains an increase in symptoms as a necessary precursor to a breakthrough. As for my baleful new diagnosis; that was drawn from the testing. Having forsworn objectivity in his dealings with me, Dr. Schiffer took no part in it.

I was witnessing the final collapse of adult authority, and my anger was a cover for fear. But it also served to conceal a kind of sexual frustration. I think my semi-conscious thought process went something like this: if I'm going to do something so extreme and destructive as to have an affair with my married therapist, I want him to be so powerful, so seductive, that my culpability is washed away. I want his passion to overcome me and leave me blameless. But Dr. Schiffer's feeling for me was more emotional than sexual, more tender than passionate. I could feel a smug slackness in the arm that encircled my waist, tentativeness in his dangling fingers as they brushed against my hip, and it made me mad. I never fully acknowledged this to myself at the time. But let me give my former self the highly qualified credit she deserves; my self-suspicion was like a thready, persistent extra pulse.

I began an unsystematic search for a new therapist, approaching doctors who looked sympathetic and explaining guardedly that I felt I would do better with somebody more experienced than Dr. Schiffer. The answer was always the same: this is an issue to be worked out in therapy.

I I

The new Director arrived, startling us all with his appearance. He was tall and boney, with a comic villain's brilliantined black hair and a waist that seemed to begin six inches below his lantern jaw. He wore cowboy boots and string ties, and he brought with him a bevy of beautiful psychotic young girls from the hospital he had directed in Washington, D.C. He was a swashbuckler, a florid, impulsive personality. Going crazy is an occupational risk for therapists who work with psychotics, and the new director was famous for his hands-on treatment: if the patient crawled under a bed, the story went, he crawled under too, and conducted the session right there.

But those girls! They were like a team of NBA all-stars trooping in to watch a Junior College practice. They quickly showed us their tricks; one inserted needles in the pupils of her eyes; another plastered her face with chalky makeup and walked around the Inn with her eyes closed and arms extended, a kabuki somnambulist. A third became a member of my therapy group (Subgroup C), and she enlivened the proceedings by screaming at unpredictable intervals, full-throated operatic screams that lasted for fifteen seconds. The arrival of these girls precipitated an avalanche of competitive upsets among the patients, and the nurses had their hands full for a few months. Then these patients, too, "settled in," being human as well as mad.

Dr. Leslie Farber had come to Riggs with the new administration. He was an old friend of the director, who lured him with promises of time to spend on his writing. I first saw him when he visited our community meeting, which began with the usual nagging by the nurses and Richard about the work jobs left undone, the unwholesome hour at which most of the inpatients had gone to bed, followed by the usual silence, and then the dribble of patient complaints. Sue M., the lanky Floridian, wanted to know why scrambled eggs could not be substituted for the food offered at every meal, not just breakfast. Howard Z., a new patient housed in the East Wing of the Inn complained that trucks making early morning deliveries to the kitchen were waking him.

Diana D. spoke next, from her crosslegged position on the floor, leaning forward from the waist, arching her neck and gesturing extravagantly. Diana's speaking style was expressive and tormented. She would make a stab at saying something, fail, erase the air with flailing palms, cover her face with her hands and rock back and forth on her haunches, then try again.

Today she said: "I . . . I don't feel very good about this, but I'm just so uncomfortable. I don't think this is something I can say."

"We're listening, Diana," said Richard. "We want to hear what you have to say."

"It's the outpatients," Diana finally blurted. "The outpatients are making me depressed. Especially John Haviland. I wish he didn't have to come into the Inn. I wish he didn't have to eat with us. He's so depressing, the way he eats." John Haviland, wearing a soiled windbreaker, looked up from the piano bench by the window. He was a little man with a built-up shoe. He was often the object of imitations by the late-night crew in the patient kitchen; stuffing a roll of toilet paper down the front of one's pants and locking one knee helped to evoke his off-center lumpiness and his fractured gait. "When they're around, the older ones, I feel like that's how I'm going to end up, and I don't want to have to look at that. I don't really think I should have to."

I had been stealing looks at Dr. Farber, who sat quietly in the wing chair by the fireplace. I had noted that he was slightly plump, balding and middle-aged, with an elfin-Semitic face and an air of masculine elegance that none of his constituent physical parts accounted for. (Later I learned from him how he felt about his embodiment: "a fat little Jewish dentist," he said, quoting a former patient.) In the silence after Diana's remarks I slid my eyes in his direction again and saw on his face an unmistakable expression of shocked contempt. His eyebrows were arched, his lip curled, his nostrils distended.

This look jolted me. I knew instantly that Dr. Farber was a different kind of being than the other therapists. His was not the neutral watchfulness I had become so used to; he judged, and revealed his judgment. This was striking enough, but it was really just the first layer of my reaction. I think I also sensed, if obscurely, that he was a person whose way of looking at the world—unlike that of any therapist I had encountered—was integrated with, and undetachable from, his self.

I learned later that Dr. Farber was well known not only in

psychoanalytic circles, but in the wider intellectual world as well. He was a maverick, humane and cultivated, who challenged his colleagues to confront what the science of psychology had refused to acknowledge—the inextinguishable presence of will in human behavior.

In one of his essays Dr. Farber wrote of the therapist who is like a man who has spent decades building a splendid mansion, a great complex multi-storied edifice with wings flung out in every direction. But when the man has finally completed his dream house he settles contentedly into a shack next door. So in his view the house of psychoanalysis was impressive but unfit for human habitation.

Dr. Farber's face, its expression that afternoon, was a life-lesson for me, the first I had received since I willingly immured myself at Riggs, a very dense, impacted lesson which I would spend years absorbing and have yet to learn completely.

I made an appointment with Dr. Farber immediately, and once seated in his office I wasted no time in blurting out the story of Dr. Schiffer and the driving lessons and the baby Mrs. Schiffer had just given birth to and the arm around my waist and his tears. I felt some terror as I spoke; Dr. Farber's dour expression was not encouraging. He heard me out without interruption, though, and when I was finished he agreed it would be impossible for me to continue in therapy with Dr. Schiffer. Which doctors on the staff would I consider compatible? I didn't really know, I said. They seemed kind of indistinguishable from one another. Would he, Dr. Farber, take me on as a patient? No, he said; his docket was already full. We sat in silence for a few minutes.

Next Dr. Farber startled me by asking what I thought of Washington, D.C. He had just come from there, he said, and he had noticed a Washington address in my file. I stalled, floundered. What could this question mean? Finally I said that I liked Washington, although it was kind of a weird city. He nodded gravely. It is kind of weird, and I like it too, he said. He added that he was having some trouble adjusting to Stockbridge. Did anybody actually work around here, or were the townspeople all models for Norman Rockwell? I laughed explosively. A joke!

We went on to talk about other subjects. Poetry: did I like John Crowe Ransom, a special enthusiasm of his? Yes, I did, I replied, although I had never read or heard of John Crowe Ransom. Dr. Farber stubbed out his Camel and propelled himself headlong out of his chair so abruptly that for a moment I feared he was having a seizure. He rummaged in one of the cardboard boxes that surrounded his desk—he was still unpacking his library—and drew out a book. He tossed it to me, and I caught it two-handed. Take it, he said. You can return it when you come back to talk to me next week. He moved to the door and opened it. What about therapy? I asked, rising from my seat. Do without therapy for a while, he said, ushering me out. Just come back next week and we'll talk.

My father was understandably outraged when he learned that I had gone without therapy for three weeks. Just talking, he shouted over the phone, at eighty dollars a day? Just chatting? He handed the receiver to my mother.

I read the Ransom anxiously, preparing myself to be quizzed, but when I awkwardly got out of my chair to give back the book—even the simplest physical transactions between patient and therapist made me self-conscious—Dr. Farber took it, opened and leafed through it, reading passages aloud in his fine deep voice, smiling, shaking his head in confounded admiration. "The curse of hell upon the sleek upstart," he read,

> That got the Captain finally on his back
> And took the red red vitals of his heart
> And made the kites to whet their beaks clack clack.

(I copy these lines from the same Vintage paperback Dr. Farber threw at me twenty-six years ago, one of many books he loaned me which I never returned.) Involuntarily, in a burst of delight, I clapped my hands and repeated "clack clack." I blushed. Dr. Farber smiled his odd, wounded smile and we lapsed into a long, for me unnerving, appreciative silence.

I was desperately eager to please Dr. Farber, but the open-endedness of our arrangement made me so anxious that my conversational timing was thrown off. I sensed that he was wavering in his refusal to accept me as a patient, that I was being auditioned, and the more urgently I wished to pass this obscure test, the more clumsy and aggressive my efforts to win him became. Too shy and fearful of rejection to plead, I some-times veered off into truculence, imposed my own attention-demanding silences. I wanted to talk about Dr. Schiffer, my parents, myself. So we talked about these things, but in a novel kind of way. I told him the particulars of the mess that had precipitated my suicidal gesture—the boyfriend and his mother, the train ride from Indianapolis to Washington when I lay in a roomette and wept myself sick. And instead of inviting me to continue with a receptively neutral psychoanalytic si-lence, he forthrightly responded with an anecdote from his own life. He told me about the breakup of his first marriage, the car trip he took from San Francisco to New York, driving for eigh-teen hours a day and collapsing in roadside motels for six. I hung on these stories, these amazing offerings, but when they ended I lapsed into panic. What now? How was I to respond? And could any response be adequate? I wanted to lift Dr. Far-ber's confidences out of the hour, out of their contextual bed-ding, and take them home with me to gnaw on in private, ex-tract all the nourishment to be had from them.

Did I like Joanne Woodward? This one came from way out in left field. Did I? I asked myself, and rummaged franti-cally in the underused opinion-forming sector of my mind. Finding no ready-made response I asked myself what movies I had seen in which Joanne Woodward appeared. I knew I'd seen some, but my memory was clouded and roiled with anxiety. I called up an image of Joanne Woodward's face. "Yes," I said, "it's her face I like. It's plain and handsome at the same time.

It's very direct." Yes, said Dr. Farber, with gratifying emphasis. That's the thing about her, all right. And we went on to talk about Joanne Woodward movies, a few of which, now that I had relaxed, bobbed up naturally onto the surface of my recollection.

> Thus does the despairer appear before us to ask that most extraordinary and truly diabolical question—especially when addressed to a psychotherapist—"is there any good in talking?" After this, we may recover our composure and succeed in engaging him imaginatively, so that real talk, does, after all, begin to come about. Despite his absolute certainty of a few moments before that even momentary relief from the torment of despair was no longer possible, his despairing self-absorption may yield to forthright interest in the subject at hand, a yielding which goes beyond mere distraction. Relief has, in spite of everything, actually been granted him; his despairing certainty has been exposed to the real world of discourse and proved false. We might even say that a minor miracle has occurred. What are we to answer then, when, as the hour nears its end, our patient or friend, preparing to take his leave, turns to us and asks, "But haven't you something *useful* to say to me—something I can use after I leave here?" If there is an answer to this question, it has not occurred to me.

This passage comes from Dr. Farber's essay "Despair and the Life of Suicide," and it describes exactly the experience of therapy—or friendship; for him the two were inseparable—with Dr. Farber. "The real world of discourse": this is where we are all free to live when we live outside of systems, but I had lived inside one for a long time. Years of psychotherapy (I started at age eleven) had made me smoothly practiced at collapsing into my components, exposing them for convenient inspection on cue. I had learned to "assume the position" so automatically that Dr. Farber's requirement that I come to our talks as pulled together as possible—ready to exercise judgment, to make distinctions, to listen and respond, to view myself first as a moral and then a psychological being, most importantly, to tell the truth; the high value he placed on tact, empathy, intellectual substance, wit—all this bewildered me at first. It bewildered me later too. In fact, it bewilders me now all over again, having lived for nearly fifteen years after Dr. Farber's death in a culture that has become saturated with therapy, in a world which has become a hospital.

The patient or friend in this passage is in despair, for Dr. Farber a very specific state, which he vividly describes and carefully documents as a drastic spiritual condition which presents its sufferer with an opportunity for redemption (not recovery) at the same time that it provides "fertile soil" for the "intrigues of suicide." What bothers me when I read this passage is a nagging sense that I never was the patient or friend of whom Dr. Farber speaks here. "[D]espair seems to afflict only those whose relation to life is a serious and potentially responsible one," he remarks later in his essay. While I hope I was "potentially responsible," I don't believe I was "serious" in the way that Dr. Farber's hypothetical friend was serious. Despair was not my condition; neediness was. In fact, from my perspective now, in middle age, the story of my attachment to Dr. Farber would seem more likely drawn from the annals of Primatology than from Philosophy or Theology (the latter, really, was Dr. Farber's stomping ground). It seems plain to me now that while I felt the purest and most ardent admiration for him that I had ever felt for anybody, I was also an unprotected young female trying to find refuge in the care of a "silverback," a dominant male.

Dr. Farber was extremely sedentary; his idea of exercise was to fumble energetically for his lighter when it fell between the cushions of his red leather chair. Now that they had moved to the country, his wife persuaded him to buy a bike and ride it to Riggs in the morning. He fell off the bicycle almost immediately, cracked a rib and broke an arm.

He sat uncomfortably upright, twisted to shield his injured right side from collisions with the arm of his chair, lighting his innumerable cigarettes one-handedly. He looked miserable. After a few minutes of halting monologue I reverted to the politeness I had been taught in early childhood and suggested he go home. He thanked me, and we broke the session off.

The next week he greeted me with warmth. His arm was still in a sling, but he looked much better. At the end of the hour he announced almost casually that a space had opened up and he would, after all, be able to take me on as a patient.

Dr. Farber insisted that I have a final, civil talk with Dr. Schiffer. I protested that I was too angry at Dr. Schiffer to speak to him. Dr. Farber suggested that I consider the connection between guilt and anger. I countered with genuine indignation that Dr. Schiffer was far more guilty than I. Dr. Farber allowed that, and observed that the greater guilt did not completely mitigate the lesser. I made the appointment and spent an hour with Dr. Schiffer, the details of which I can't remember. I think he cried, and I do remember walking into his office with the sullen air of a child forced by adults to apologize. Now I want to say to my former self: you didn't need to apologize, you dolt! You needed to ask to see the baby pictures, and to say goodbye.

I had come to view guilt as a noxious psychic by-product, something to be gotten rid of in the interests of health. It took me a while to grasp that Dr. Farber's idea was different: for him guilt was a state which must be acknowledged and, only if possible, expiated. Farber believed that people have real moral claims on one another, and that a full honoring of each of these claims is always impossible. Guilt—some of it a permanent burden—is thus inevitable. For Dr. Farber, guilt was a moral, not a psychological, category.

Dr. Farber's attitude toward me was never the "unconditional positive regard" with which therapists are charged to view their patients. His regard was highly qualified and partial, and it was as real as rock.

III

I studied for and passed my G.E.D. certification. I took a few night classes at the local community college. I began to read again, mostly books loaned to me by Dr. Farber— Goncharov's *Oblomov* (appropriate for me), Martin Buber's *I and Thou,* which I still fail to appreciate, poems by Randall Jarrell and Phillip Larkin. I got a summer job in the kitchen of a summer camp. "Girl, we've got to teach you to *work,"* said the cook, and I quit after a few weeks.

I also began to get myself in trouble with alcohol and bad companions. When night fell we could be found at the Stockbridge Inn, known to regulars as Simmy's, drinking beer and waiting to be picked up. Simmy's was full of local characters, pool-players laid off from their jobs at G.E., reprobates thrown out of their houses by their wives, glumly stewing at the bar, low-life freeriders on the sexual revolution, buying us drinks and dragging a *carpe diem* line.

I became promiscuous, and I confessed my promiscuity to Dr. Farber. I think I told him about every encounter. His response was surprisingly muted. Again? he would say. Once he called me a "female jerk." He got truly angry only when the man in question was married.

Why did I behave like this? I can think of psychoanalytic explanations: perhaps I was "acting out" the unconscious feelings that Dr. Schiffer's seductiveness had aroused in me, or, more likely, punishing myself for having rejected him and having won Dr. Farber as a protector. I can think of obvious explanations: I was bored, and getting picked up was fun.

I tried out my hypotheses on Dr. Farber. His response was to cut me off. "I'm not interested in that," he would say. His approach, as always, seemed to steer a slalom course around the casual markers I had put in place. Instead he turned the discussion to my drinking, and drinking in general. We talked about the coarsening of feeling, the blurring of distinctions and the deadening of thought that habitual drunkenness brings about. He also talked about the joy of another kind of non-habituated drinking. Stop the bad kind of drinking, he advised me, so that you can regain the good kind. You were meant, he told me during one of those talks, for the conscious life.

I carry that around with me still, and also the "female jerk" remark. One negative, one positive, they were both his gifts of confirmation.

Then I got pregnant, not by one of my Simmy's pick-ups, but as a result of a brief re-encounter with another patient who had been my boyfriend for a summer.

I had skipped a period, felt sick in the mornings, but I refused to acknowledge my condition until one of the nurses, a local woman with a pungent sense of humor, whacked me on the rear as I stood serving myself in the Riggs dining room and made some remark about eating for two. Then I panicked.

A Pittsfield gynecologist confirmed my condition. There are certain circumstances in which bringing a pregnancy to term may not be advisable, he told me. Do what you can do on your own, and call me in two weeks if you haven't had any luck. Perhaps they can help you at Riggs. I wonder now why I didn't take this as a veiled and provisional assurance that he would give me an abortion (then illegal). That was surely what he meant. Instead, I put emphasis on his instruction to "do what I could."

When Dr. Farber asked me if I wanted my parents told I said *no*. I did tell two of my in-patient friends about the pregnancy, though, and soon everybody knew. The Director barged into Dr. Farber's office and demanded that my parents be called immediately. The institution would be liable, he insisted, for anything that happened to me. He picked up the phone receiver. Dr. Farber grabbed it away from the Director, he later told me, and a physical struggle ensued. The image of a wrestling match between that aging Mutt and Jeff pair seems hilarious to me now, and Dr. Farber's part in it heroic.

Dr. Farber reported to me that the Director had suggested a therapeutic abortion. This would require Dr. Farber's assent, and his signature on a document attesting to my unfitness to bear and raise a child. Dr. Farber explained his refusal carefully; he could not arrange the abortion because he could not agree with such a statement. I nodded, barely listening. He had raised my hopes and dashed them, but I felt no resentment, no reaction except an acceleration of panic.

I spent a week on the phone, following leads, being scolded long-distance by abortion activists for my past failure to get involved in the issue. Finally I was instructed to dial a New York number, to wait until the phone was picked up and to give my number and area code to the silent person at the end of the line, then to wait for a call. I followed these instructions; the phone rang and a deep, emphysematous male voice told me to be at the Port Authority bus terminal, standing by the third phone booth at the Forty-second Street entrance, carrying six hundred dollars in cash at a certain time and date the following week.

I got the money from the ex-boyfriend, and the two friends in whom I had confided drove me to New York. I waited at the designated place until I was approached by a little man in a green suede feathered cap, who beckoned me out of the terminal and into the back of a limousine, where I was soon joined by an engaged couple from Teaneck. We were all blindfolded and driven to some place in the Bronx (my friends, I learned later, were following in their car). I waited in the parked limousine while the couple were ushered into a building. They emerged a half hour later, the girl walking a little unsteadily, the boy shielding her solicitously with his arm.

Then it was my turn to follow the little man up the back stairs, to shake hands solemnly with "Dr. Adams," to lie down on my back on the linoleum table in a kitchen furnished as sparely as a stage-set while five or six radios blared, all tuned to different stations, a crude wall of sound. It was over soon, and I was given pads and an envelope full of antibiotics, and allowed to go.

I was delighted to see my friends waiting for me at the end of the block, waving and jumping. They had spent the time eating a late lunch at a nearby Chinese restaurant, and they had saved me an eggroll.

Later that evening I stood dialing Dr. Farber's Stockbridge number, up to my wobbly ankles in sawdust in the back of a West Village bar and steakhouse, full of Brandy Alexanders and Demerol. Dr. Farber's wife answered and handed the phone immediately to Dr. Farber. "You're all right?" he said. I heard his wife whisper "Thank God!" in the background. Years later, when I got to know her well, she told me that Dr. Farber had spent hours that day in acute anxiety, pacing back and forth in his study.

I launched into a description of my experience, but he cut me off. "Tell me later. You really feel all right?" I feel *fine* I said, and I did. I was celebrating my passage through a rite; my friends were treating me with respect and solicitude; the adventure had ended safely and I was high as a kite. At the end of the conversation I said something like "You're really a great guy!" or perhaps "I love you!" I don't remember.

Many of the things Dr. Farber said have acted on me much later with a "time-release" effect. Only a few years ago, some time after Dr. Farber's death, I realized what Dr. Farber meant by his refusal to endorse a therapeutic abortion for me. At the time I had dismissed it, if I thought about it at all, as adult boilerplate, the kind of carefully worded refusal every adolescent recognizes. Now I realized, *he really meant it.* Let me put it another way; he did not refuse to sign this statement because of a legalistic moral scrupulousness (i.e., he could not say that I would *not* turn out to be a fit parent). He refused to sign it because he believed I was able, even then, to bear and raise a child.

Living in the world has been hard enough for me without the complication of what then was called an illegitimate child. I'm retrospectively relieved that I had an abortion. I cannot imagine myself in one of my many chaotic apartments, feeding and rocking and changing a baby. Apparently Dr. Farber could, though, and perhaps he was right. But whether or not he was right doesn't matter; what does is his faith in me, which took me some twenty years to appreciate, or perhaps to accept.

Was Dr. Farber acting out of an anti-abortion agenda? He was, after all, a religious man, a private and non-observant but passionate believer. Was his refusal to endorse a therapeutic abortion an attempt to influence me? No. He was an anti-ideologue, and no manipulator. He took the crisis of my pregnancy far more seriously than I did; he understood it as a true dilemma, and he showed a respect for me which I perhaps did not deserve by allowing it to be mine.

Have I found myself, now that I am older and the mother of a living child, capable of guilt about that abortion? Not really. I find I can't advance very far along the path of speculation about alternative fates for that dead fetus who would now be twenty-five without backing up in confusion. The voice of the conceptus is too faint, too garbled and muted by the distance of time and the crosscutting static of possibility for me to hear it clearly. He is no more apparent to me than Dr. Farber's God.

I am just as needy now as then. But perhaps by now I've also become the serious friend—the despairer—of whom Dr. Farber wrote. This is the question that continues to haunt me: what would Dr. Farber make of me now? How would he judge the person I've become?

My third staff conference came and went. "They made you sound like a little machine," Dr. Farber reported, "a little machine that could barely make it to the bathroom."

Things were jumping at the Inn under the new regime, plenty of upsets, angry contention in the community meetings. Dr. Farber waved it all away with a gesture of disgust. For the most part, it didn't interest him. He was an enthusiastic gossip, though, and sometimes he would find some piece of exhibition-istic lunacy diverting. He loved the story about the patient (the same one who laid eggs in the hallway) who shaved his head bald except for one sideburn and then felt so delighted with himself that he jumped up and down on his bed until it col-lapsed.

Dr. Farber began to complain about Stockbridge. I hate this place, he said. I hate this goddamned maple sugar Norman Rockwell tourist-infested place where you can't find a decent corned beef sandwich. He announced that he was moving to New York, where he would set up a private practice and con-tinue his writing. "If you don't believe I'm going," he said, quoting some old blues lyric, "just count the days I'm gone."

You're welcome to come along, he told me. Or perhaps that was my idea. At any rate, all three of us who were his patients at Riggs packed up and followed him to New York, as if on a dare. He beckoned, and we were sprung.

Margaret Talbot

Les Très Riches Heures de Martha Stewart

Every age gets the household goddess it deserves. The '60s had Julia Child, the sophisticated French chef who proved as permissive as Dr. Spock. She may have proselytized for a refined foreign cuisine from her perch at a Boston PBS station, but she was always an anti-snob, vowing to "take a lot of the la dee dah out of French cooking." With her madras shirts and her penumbra of curls, her 6'2" frame and her whinny of a voice, she exuded an air of Cambridge eccentricity—faintly bohemian and a little tatty, like a yellowing travel poster. She was messy and forgiving. When Julia dropped an egg or collapsed a soufflé, she shrugged and laughed. "You are alone in the kitchen, nobody can see you, and cooking is meant to be fun," she reminded her viewers. She wielded lethal-looking kitchen knives with campy abandon, dipped her fingers into crème anglaise and wiped her chocolate-smeared hands on an apron tied carelessly at her waist. For Child was also something of a sensualist, a celebrant of appetite as much as a pedant of cooking.

In the '90s, and probably well into the next century, we have Martha Stewart, corporate overachiever turned domestic superachiever, Mildred Pierce in earth-toned Armani. Martha is the anti-Julia. Consider the extent of their respective powers. At the height of her success, Child could boast a clutch of bestselling cookbooks and a *gemütlich* TV show shot on a single set. At what may or may not be the height of her success, here's what Stewart can claim: a 5-year-old magazine, *Martha Stewart Living,* with a circulation that has leapt to 1.5 million; a popular cable TV show, also called "Martha Stewart Living" and filmed at her luscious Connecticut and East Hampton estates; a dozen wildly successful gardening, cooking and lifestyle books; a mail-order business, Martha-by-Mail; a nationally syndicated news-paper column, "Ask Martha"; a regular Wednesday slot on the "Today" show; a line of $110-a-gallon paints in colors inspired by the eggs her Araucana hens lay; plans to invade cyber-space—in short, an empire.

Julia limited herself to cooking lessons, with the quiet implication that cooking was a kind of synecdoche for the rest of bourgeois existence; but Martha's parish is vaster, her field is all of life. Her expertise, as she recently explained to *Mediaweek* magazine, covers, quite simply, "Beautiful soups and how to make them, beautiful houses and how to build them, beautiful children and how to raise them." (From soups to little nuts.) She presides, in fact, over a phenomenon that, in other realms, is quite familiar in American society and culture: a cult, devoted to her name and image.

In the distance between these two cynosures of domestic life lies a question: What does the cult of Martha mean? Or, to put it another way, what have we done, exactly, to deserve her?

If you have read the paper or turned on the television in the last year or so, you have probably caught a glimpse of the WASPy good looks, the affectless demeanor, the nacreous perfection of her world. You may even know the outlines of her story. Middle-class girl from a Polish-American family in Nutley, New Jersey, works her way through Barnard in the early '60s, modeling on the side. She becomes a stockbroker, a self-described workaholic and insomniac who by the '70s is making six figures on Wall Street, and who then boldly trades it all in . . . for life as a workaholic, insomniac evangelist for domesticity whose business now generates some $200 million in profits a year. (She herself, according to the *Wall Street Journal,* makes a salary of $400,000 a year from Time Inc., which generously supplements this figure with a $40,000 a year clothing allowance and other candies.) You may even have admired her magazine, with its art-book production values and spare design, every kitchen utensil photographed like an Imogen Cunningham nude, every plum or pepper rendered with the loving detail of an eighteenth-century botanical drawing, every page a gentle exhalation of High Class.

What you may not quite realize, if you have not delved deeper into Stewart's oeuvre, is the ambition of her design for living—the absurd, self-parodic dream of it. To read Martha Stewart is to know that there is no corner of your domestic life that cannot be beautified or improved under careful tutelage, none that should not be colonized by the rhetoric and the discipline of quality control. Work full time though you may, care for your family though you must, convenience should never be your watchword in what Stewart likes to call, in her own twee coinage, "homekeeping." Convenience is the enemy of excellence. "We do not pretend that these are 'convenience' foods," she writes loftily of the bread and preserves recipes in a 1991 issue of the magazine. "Some take days to make. But they are recipes that will produce the very best results, and we know that is what you want." Martha is a kitchen-sink idealist. She scorns utility in the name of beauty. But her idealism, of course, extends no further than surface appearances, which makes it a very particular form of idealism indeed.

To spend any length of time in Martha-land is to realize that it is not enough to serve your guests homemade pumpkin soup as a first course. You must present it in hollowed-out, hand-gilded pumpkins as well. It will not do to serve an Easter ham unless you have baked it in a roasting pan lined with, of all things, "tender, young, organically-grown grass that has not yet been cut." And, when serving a "casual" lobster and corn dinner al fresco, you really ought to fashion dozens of cunning little bamboo brushes tied with raffia and adorned with a chive so that each of your guests may butter their corn with something pretty.

To be a Martha fan (or more precisely, a Martha adept) is to understand that a terracotta pot is just a terracotta pot until you have "aged" it, painstakingly rubbing yogurt into its dampened sides, then smearing it with plant food or "something you found in the woods" and patiently standing by while the mold sprouts. It is to think that maybe you could do this *kind* of thing, anyway—start a garden, say, in your scruffy backyard—and then to be brought up short by Martha's enumeration, in *Martha Stewart's Gardening*, of forty-nine "essential" gardening tools. These range from a "polesaw" to a "corn fiber broom" to three different kinds of pruning shears, one of which—the "loppers"—Martha says she has in three different sizes. You have, perhaps, a trowel. But then Martha's garden is a daunting thing to contemplate, what with its topiary mazes and state-of-the-art chicken coop; its "antique" flowers and geometric herb garden. It's half USDA station, half Sissinghurst. And you cannot imagine making anything remotely like it at your own house, not without legions of artisans and laborers and graduate students in landscape design, and a pot of money that perhaps you'll unearth when you dig up the yard.

In *The Culture of Narcissism,* Christopher Lasch describes the ways in which pleasure, in our age, has taken on "the qualities of work," allowing our leisure-time activities to be measured by the same standards of accomplishment that rule the workplace. It is a phenomenon that he memorably characterizes as "the invasion of play by the rhetoric of achievement." For Lasch, writing in the early '70s, the proliferation of sex-advice manuals offered a particularly poignant example. Today, though, you might just as easily point to the hundreds of products and texts, from unctuous home-furnishings catalogs to upscale "shelter" magazines to self-help books like *Meditations for Women Who Do Too Much,* that tell us exactly how to "nest" and "cocoon" and "nurture," how to "center" and "retreat," and how to measure our success at these eminently private pursuits. Just as late-nineteenth-century marketers and experts promised to bring Americans back in touch with the nature from which modern industrial life had alienated them, so today's "shelter" experts—the word is revealingly primal—promise to reconnect us with a similarly mystified home. The bourgeois home as lost paradise, retrievable through careful instruction.

Martha Stewart is the apotheosis of this particular cult of expertise, and its most resourceful entrepreneur. She imagines projects of which we would never have thought—gathering dewy grass for our Easter ham, say—and makes us feel the pressing need for training in them. And she exploits, brilliantly, a certain estrangement from home that many working women feel these days. For women who are working longer and longer hours at more and more demanding jobs, it's easy to think of home as the place where chaos reigns and their own competence is called into doubt: easy to regard the office, by comparison, as the bulwark of order. It is a reversal, of course, of the hoary concept of home as a refuge from the tempests of the marketplace. But these days, as the female executives in a recent study attested, the priority they most often let slide is housekeeping: they'll abide disorder at home that they wouldn't or couldn't abide at the office. No working couple's home is the oasis of tranquility and Italian marble countertops that Martha-ism seems to promise. But could it be? Should it be? Stewart plucks expertly at that chord of doubt.

In an era when it is not at all uncommon to be cut off from the traditional sources of motherwit and household lore—when many of us live far from the families into which we were born and have started our own families too late to benefit from the guidance of living parents or grandparents—domestic pedants like Martha Stewart rightly sense a big vacuum to fill. Stewart's books are saturated with nostalgia for lost tradition and old moldings, for her childhood in Nutley and for her mother's homemade preserves. In the magazine, her "Remembering" column pines moralistically for a simpler era, when beach vacations meant no television or video games, just digging for clams and napping in hammocks. Yet Stewart's message is that such simplicity can only be achieved now through strenuous effort and a flood of advice. We might be able to put on a picnic or a dinner party without her help, she seems to tell us, but we wouldn't do it properly, beautifully, in the spirit of excellence that we expect of ourselves at work.

It may be that Stewart's special appeal is to women who wouldn't want to take their mother's word anyway, to babyboomer daughters who figure that their sensibilities are just too different from their stay-at-home moms', who can't throw themselves into housekeeping without thinking of their kitchen as a catering business and their backyards as a garden show. In fact, relatively few of Martha's fans are housewives—72 percent of the subscribers to *Martha Stewart Living* are employed outside the home as managers or professionals—and many of them profess to admire her precisely because she isn't one, either. As one such Martha acolyte, an account executive at a Christian radio station, effused on the Internet: "[Stewart] is my favorite independent woman and what an entrepreneur! She's got her own television show, magazine, books and even her own brand of latex paint. . . . Martha is a feisty woman who settles for nothing less than perfection."

For women such as these, the didactic faux-maternalism of Martha Stewart seems the perfect answer. She may dispense the kind of homekeeping advice that a mother would, but she does so in tones too chill and exacting to sound "maternal," singling out, for example, those "who will always be too lazy" to do her projects. She makes housekeeping safe for the professional woman by professionalizing housekeeping. And you never forget that Stewart is herself a mogul, even when she's baking rhubarb crisp and telling you, in her Shakeresque mantra, that "It's a Good Thing."

It is tempting to see the Martha cult purely as a symptom of anti-feminist backlash. Though she may not directly admonish women to abandon careers for hearth and home, Stewart certainly exalts a way of life that puts hearth and home at its center, one that would be virtually impossible to achieve without *somebody's* full-time devotion. (Camille Paglia has praised her as "someone who has done a tremendous service for ordinary women—women who identify with the roles of wife, mother, and homemaker.") Besides, in those alarming moments when Stewart slips into the social critic's mode, she can sound a wee bit like Phyllis Schlafly—less punitive and more patrician, maybe, but just as smug about the moral uplift of a well-ordered home. Her philosophy of cultivating your own walled garden while the world outside is condemned to squalor bears the hallmarks of Reagan's America—it would not be overreading to call it a variety of conservatism. "Amid the horrors of genocidal war in Bosnia and Rwanda, the AIDS epidemic and increasing crime in many cities," Stewart writes in a recent column, "there are those of us who desire positive reinforcement of some very basic tenets of good living." And those would be? "Good food, gardening, crafts, entertaining and home improvement." (Hollow out the pumpkins, they're starving in Rwanda.)

Yet it would, in the end, be too simplistic to regard her as a tool of the feminine mystique, or as some sort of spokesmodel for full-time mommies. For one thing, there is nothing especially June Cleaverish, or even motherly, about Stewart. She has taken a drubbing, in fact, for looking more convincing as a businesswoman than a dispenser of milk and cookies. (Remember the apocryphal tale that had Martha flattening a crate of baby chicks while backing out of a driveway in her Mercedes?) Her habitual prickliness and Scotchguard perfectionism are more like the badges of the striving good girl, still cut to the quick by her classmates' razzing when she asked for extra homework.

Despite the ritual obeisance that Martha pays to Family, moreover, she is not remotely interested in the messy contingencies of family life. In the enchanted world of Turkey Hill, there are no husbands (Stewart was divorced from hers in 1990), only loyal craftsmen, who clip hedges and force dogwood with self-effacing dedication. Children she makes use of as accessories, much like Parisian women deploy little dogs. The books and especially the magazine are often graced with photographic spreads of parties and teas where children pale as waxen angels somberly disport themselves, their fair hair shaped into tasteful blunt cuts, their slight figures clad in story-book velvet or lace. "If I had to choose one essential element for the success of an Easter brunch," she writes rather menac-ingly in her 1994 *Menus for Entertaining*, "it would be chil-dren." The homemade Halloween costumes modeled by wee lads and lasses in an October 1991 issue of *Martha Stewart Living* do look gorgeous—the Caravaggio colors, the themes drawn from nature. But it's kind of hard to imagine a 5-year-old boy happily agreeing to go as an acorn this year, instead of say, Batman. And why should he? In Marthaland, his boyhood would almost certainly be overridden in the name of taste.

If Stewart is a throwback, it's not so much to the 1950s as to the 1850s, when the doctrine of separate spheres did allow married or widowed women of the upper classes a kind of power—unchallenged dominion over the day-to-day function-ing of the home and its servants, in exchange for ceding the public realm to men. At Turkey Hill, Stewart is the undisputed chatelaine, micromanaging her estate in splendid isolation. (This hermetic pastoral is slightly marred, of course, by the presence of cameras.) Here the domestic arts have become ends in themselves, unmoored from family values and indeed from family.

Stewart's peculiar brand of didacticism has another nine-teenth-century precedent—in the domestic science or home economics movement. The domestic scientists' favorite reci-pes—"wholesome" concoctions of condensed milk and canned fruit, rivers of white sauce—would never have passed Martha's muster; but their commitment to painstakingly elegant presen-tation, their concern with the look of food even more than its taste, sound a lot like Stewart's. And, more importantly, so does their underlying philosophy. They emerged out of a tradition:

the American preference for food writing of the prescriptive, not the descriptive, kind, for food books that told you, in M.F.K. Fisher's formulation, not about eating but about what to eat. But they took this spirit much further. Like Stewart, these brisk professional women of the 1880s and '90s believed that true culinary literacy could not be handed down or casually absorbed; it had to be carefully taught. (One of the movement's accomplishments, if it can be called that, was the home ec curriculum.)

Like Stewart, the domestic scientists were not bent on liberating intelligent women from housework. Their objective was to raise housework to a level worthy of intelligent women. They wished to apply rational method to the chaos and the drudgery of housework and, in so doing, to earn it the respect accorded men's stuff like science and business. Neither instinct, nor intuition, nor mother's rough-hewn words of advice would have a place in the scientifically managed home of the future. As Laura Shapiro observes in *Perfection Salad,* her lively and perceptive history of domestic science, the ideal new housewife was supposed to project, above all, "self-sufficiency, self-control, and a perfectly bland façade." Sound familiar?

It is in their understanding of gender roles, however, that the doyennes of home ec most closely prefigure Marthaism. Like Stewart, they cannot be classified either as feminists or traditionalists. Their model housewife was a pseudo-professional with little time for sublimating her ego to her husband's or tenderly ministering to his needs. She was more like a factory supervisor than either the Victorian angel of the home or what Shapiro calls the courtesan type, the postwar housewife who was supposed to zip through her chores so she could gussy herself up for her husband. In Martha's world, too, the managerial and aesthetic challenges of "homekeeping" always take priority, and their intricacy and ambition command a respect that mere wifely duties never could. Her husbandless hauteur is rich with the self-satisfaction of financial and emotional independence.

❈   ❈   ❈

In the end, Stewart's fantasies have as much to do with class as with gender. The professional women who read her books might find themselves longing for a breadwinner, but a lifestyle this beautiful is easier to come by if you've never needed a breadwinner in the first place. Stewart's books are a dreamy advertisement for independent wealth—or, more accurately, for its facsimile. You may not have a posh pedigree, but with a little effort (okay, a lot) you can adopt its trappings. After all, Martha wasn't born to wealth either, but now she attends the weddings of people with names like Charles Booth-Clibborn (she went to his in London, the magazine tells us) and caters them for couples named Sissy and Kelsey (see her *Wedding Planner,* in which their yacht is decorated with a "Just Married" sign).

She is not an American aristocrat, but she plays one on TV. And you can play one, too, at least in your own home. Insist on cultivating only those particular yellow plums you tasted in the Dordogne, buy your copper cleaner only at Delherin in Paris, host lawn parties where guests come "attired in the garden dress of the Victorian era," and you begin to simulate the luster of lineage. Some of Stewart's status-augmenting suggestions must strike even her most faithful fans as ridiculous. For showers held after the baby is born, Martha "likes presenting the infant with engraved calling cards that the child can then slip into thank you notes and such for years to come." What a great idea. Maybe your baby can gum them for a while first, thoughtfully imprinting them with his signature drool.

The book that best exemplifies her class-consciousness is *Martha Stewart's New Old House,* a step-by-step account of refurbishing a Federal-style farmhouse in Westport, Connecticut. Like all her books, it contains many, many pictures of Martha; here she's frequently shown supervising the work of plasterers, carpenters and other "seemingly taciturn men." *New Old House* establishes Stewart's ideal audience: a demographic niche occupied by the kind of people who, like her, can afford to do their kitchen countertops in "mottled, gray-green, hand-honed slate from New York state, especially cut" for them. The cost of all this (and believe me, countertops are only the beginning) goes unmentioned. If you have to ask, maybe you're not a Martha kind of person after all.

In fact, Stewart never seems all that concerned with reassuring her readers of their ability to afford such luxuries or their right to enjoy them. She's more concerned with establishing her own claims. Her reasoning seems to go something like this: the houses that she buys and renovates belong to wealthy families who passed them down through generations. But these families did not properly care for their patrimony. The widowed Bulkeley sisters, erstwhile owners of Turkey Hill, had let the estate fall "into great disrepair. All the farms and outbuildings were gone. . . . The fields around had been sold off by the sisters in 2-acre building lots; suburbia encroached." The owner of the eponymous New Old House was a retired librarian named Miss Adams who "had little interest in the house other than as a roof over her head. Clearly a frugal spirit, she had no plans to restore the house, and she lived there until she could no longer cope with the maintenance and upkeep of the place. The house was in dire need of attention, and since no other family member wanted to assume responsibility, Miss Adams reluctantly decided to sell her family home. I wanted very much to save the Adams house, to put it to rights, to return its history to it, to make it livable once again."

It's a saga with overtones of Jamesian comedy: a family with bloodlines but no money is simultaneously rescued and eclipsed by an energetic upstart with money but no bloodlines. The important difference—besides the fact that Martha is marrying the house, not the son—is that she also has taste. And it's taste, far more than money, she implies, that gives her the right to these splendid, neglected piles of brick. Unlike the "frugal" Misses Bulkeley, she will keep suburbia at bay; unlike the careless Miss Adams, she would never resort to "hideous rugs" in (yuck) shades of brown. They don't understand their own houses; she does, and so she *deserves* to own their houses. But leave it to Martha to get all snippy about these people's aesthetic oversights while quietly celebrating their reversion to type. They're useful to her, and not only because their indifference to decor bolsters her claim to their property. Like the pumpkin pine floors and original fixtures, these quaintly cheeseparing New Englanders denote the property's authenticity.

The fantasy of vaulting into the upper crust that Martha Stewart fulfilled, and now piques in her readers, is about more than just money, of course. Among other things, it's about time, and the luxurious plenitude of it. Living the Martha way would mean enjoying a surfeit of that scarce commodity, cooking and crafting at the artisanal pace her projects require. Trouble is, none of us overworked Americans has time to spare these days—and least of all the upscale professional women whom Stewart targets. Martha herself seemed to acknowledge this when she told *Inside Media* that she attracts at least two classes of true believers: the "Be-Marthas," who have enough money and manic devotion to follow many of her lifestyle techniques, and the "Do-Marthas," who "are a little bit envious" and "don't have as much money as the Be-Marthas."

To those fulsome categories, you could surely add the "watch Marthas" or the "read Marthas," people who might consider, say, making their own rabbit-shaped wire topiary forms, but only consider it, who mostly just indulge in the fantasy of doing so, if only they had the time. There is something undeniably soothing about watching Martha at her absurdly time-consuming labors. A female "media executive" explained the appeal to Barbara Lippert in *New York* magazine: "I never liked Martha Stewart until I started watching her on Sunday mornings. I turn on the TV, and I'm in my pajamas, still in this place between sleep and reality. And she's showing you how to roll your tablecloths in parchment paper. She's like a character when she does her crafts. It reminds me of watching Mr. Green

Jeans on Captain Kangaroo. I remember he had a shoebox he took out that was filled with craft things. There would be a close-up on his hands with his buffed nails. And then he would show you how to cut an oaktag with a scissor, or when he folded paper, he'd say: 'There you go, boys and girls,' and it was very quiet. It's like she brings out this great meditative focus and calm."

The show does seem strikingly unfrenetic. Unlike just about everything else on TV, including the "Our Home" show, which follows it on Lifetime, it eschews Kathy Lee-type banter, perky music, swooping studio shots and jittery handheld cameras. Instead there's just Martha, alone in her garden or kitchen, her teacherly tones blending with birdsong, her recipes cued to the seasons. Whimsical recorder music pipes along over the credits. Martha's crisply ironed denim shirts, pearl earrings, and honey-toned highlights bespeak the fabulousness of Connecticut. Her hands move slowly, deliberately over her yellow roses or her Depression glasses. Martha is a Puritan who prepares "sinful" foods—few of her recipes are low-fat or especially health-conscious—that are redeemed by the prodigious labors, the molasses afternoons, involved in serving them. (She preys upon our guilt about overindulgence, then hints at how to assuage it.) Here at Turkey Hill, time is as logy as a honey-sated bumblebee. Here on Lifetime, the cable channel aimed at baby-boom women, Martha's stately show floats along in a sea of stalker movies, Thighmaster commercials and "Weddings of a Lifetime" segments, and by comparison, I have to say, she looks rather dignified. Would that we all had these *très riches heures.*

But if we had the hours, if we had the circumstances, wouldn't we want to fill them with something of our own, with a domestic grace of our own devising? Well, maybe not anymore. For taste is no longer an expression of individuality. It is, more often, an instrument of conformism, a way to assure ourselves that we're living by the right codes, dictated or sanctioned by experts. Martha Stewart's "expertise" is really nothing but another name for the perplexity of her cowed consumers. A life-style cult as all-encompassing as hers could thrive only at a time when large numbers of Americans have lost confidence in their own judgment about the most ordinary things. For this reason, *Martha Stewart Living* isn't really living at all.

David Mamet

The Diner

There is an old and probably true story of Hollywood. A Producer is hired and comes, at the end of the day, to report to his betters. He informs on several writers: "I hung around outside the Writers Building for a quarter of an hour, and they didn't write a word."

Writing, in my experience, consists of long periods of hanging out, punctuated by the fugue of remorse at the loss of one's powers and wonder at occasional output in spite of that loss.

Writing, to stretch it, is to hanging out as degustation is to the art of cooking.

I hear, as do we all, of those people who spend eight to ten hours a day at their typewriters, and I think, has no one told them of the Nap?

In this Puritan country we have never truly had the Club, and the last decades have seen the erosion unto disappearance of its American descendants the Barbershop and the Pool Hall, sparing only—in those more fortunate and generally small-town venues—the Coffeeshop.

Those who have not experienced the glow engendered on

one's entering the coffeeshop and having the server inquire, "The Usual?" are poor indeed.

For who wants to stay home? We know, for good or ill, that we belong there; the comfort of domesticity may be great indeed, but it is not convivial.

No, the Idle-Hour, Coffee-Corner, Coffee-Cup, where even the stranger may still find himself addressed as "Hon"— that is the place for me.

We've seen and may still see the white-shirted confraternity of movers and shakers at their sacred table in the window of a morning, settling the business of the town. We've seen the waitress chatting up the trucker, the pair having their fight, and the couple previously believed happily married to others holding their first preternaturally innocent conclave.

In larger towns we've seen the budding writer at his or her table, frowning into the notebook; and in the cities themselves, the actor and actress with their flimsy scripts—outsiders all, at home in the diner, coffeeshop, café.

Where *else* would one go? The Lounge seems to have degenerated into the Sports Bar, that is, a spot one can go to watch television.* That is not hanging out; no: We cannot say it. It is a portrayal of leisure in the face of suspected societal disapprobation. This is not hanging out—it is performance as alternative to anomie.

To hang out is to proclaim and endorse our need for leisure and autonomy. How about that. That frantic and forced consumerism of the Sports Bar will not do; neither what has become the muddled and tense obsequiousness of that proclaiming itself the Restaurant. No. You've got to sit there and eat that greasy sandwich.

There you sit with your beautiful plastic-covered menu. If it's breakfast time (stretched by the familiar local dispensation to eleven or even one o'clock; or perhaps our coffeeshop proclaims its hospitality with that most liberal phrase, "Breakfast

---

* I exempt the bar of the Ritz Carlton, in New York, its dispensation due to the merit of its avatar, Norman; and the Twin Anchors, in Chicago, "Positively no dancing."

Served All Day"—that Danton of proclamations, somehow superior even to the cognate "We Never Close")—if, I say, it is breakfast time, we sit and we peruse the card, *although* we know not only its contents but our election from them; for we do not require the information, we relish the privilege.

"I can have whatever I sodding want," we think. "I have but to bid them, and it will appear. Well, in fact, do you know what? I will have eggs." We then continue, do we not, to specify their preparation, and that of their appurtenances, in detail. And the server stands by. Is he or she testy or short with our self-indulgence? To the contrary. They portray their zeal in transcription of our merest whim; and the alacrity of the subsequent repair to the kitchen speaks not of censure for our narcissism but of the desire to be about our service.

Now, isn't that better than the smarmy "Is everything all right?"—that ritualized Restaurant extortion?

And where else is the writer to go? The libraries seem to be closing; there's very little public transportation; one cannot write at home, for those we love might there confound our occupation with Sitting Around and suggest we fix the shower rod.

No. We've got to write, to read, and, to do so, to get out of the house and to get into the coffeeshop. The Olympia at Pike's Market in Seattle; Jeff's Laugh-Inn at the foot of Lincoln Avenue, Chicago; the Athens Diner, Twenty-third and Ninth, New York; Early World, on San Vicente; the Bon Vivant, on Broadway; Rainbow Sweets, Route Two, Marshfield, Vermont; the River Run Café in Plainfield.

We may stop on the way, at the shoe store, bookstore, gun shop, or cosmetics or notions counter, as our tastes command, but we must go in the end to the diner. We, readers and writers, must hang out.

But can we take our computers there? Thankfully not. Yes, I understand that they are portable; but this, like many another diversion, its portability notwithstanding, is best indulged in the home. Please, do not write on them in the Café.

A friend and I were strolling through the West Village

streets where for years he and I, both together and separately, had lived in the cafés. Reading, writing, trying to look deep and attractive. At times succeeding. And there, in the correct posture, elbow on the table, head on the hand, correctly shaking the head in disappointment, we saw the Young Writer.

And yes, the hand supporting the head held a cigarette; and yes, he wore a turtle, or mock-turtle, sweater; and yes, he was unshaved; and yes, and yes infinitely but for this: He shook his head not at a coffee-stained notebook, no, but, you have guessed it, at a computer.

We could not credit it. We looked at one another for that brief instant conveying "I thought that it would last out my day," and then we walked slowly on.

I have hung out at Schwab's Drugstore and watched the actors singing each to each. Likewise at the old Imperial Gardens on Sunset, and similarly there glassed the Writers and the Brits. I hung out at the bar at the Old (but not the *old* Old) Second City and saw Nelson Algren there; and at that of John and Jim Belushi, the Blues Brothers Bar of memory.

I was privileged to frequent the Carnegie Deli of old, and was there invited regularly to join the luncheon club of Paddy Chayefsky, Bob Fosse, Ulu Grosbard, and Herbie Gardner; with Henny Youngman at his wonted Shotgun table, over-by-the-door.

And what better place to read? When I was young the Penguin book was British green, and its appearance in the back pocket of another's jeans was quite as much the Grand Hailing Sign of fellow feeling as was the Volkswagen on the road.

I recall the early sixties and Hyde Park, Chicago; Fifty-seventh Street and the Medici Café, where, barely teenagers, we sat all night and drank spiced hot cider, or iced coffee, and heard the folk music on WFMT and read the Penguin novel, and fretted or mooned over young loves—habits that seem to've stayed with me through this much of a lifetime and that instruct me that the young fellow with his computer has the same right to his callow exertions as I did to mine; and may he be blessed to continue happy in the dilatory habit in the Cafés of et cetera . . .

And may the Automobile disappear (except, of course, for yours and mine), and the Main Street and the Marketplace reemerge with their cafés and lead us back to their pleasures of reading, writing, gossip, mutual observation, and whatever else, if such there be, that makes the world go round.

Vivian Gornick

The Catskills Remembered

I have never been able to think of the old Catskill Mountains hotel circuit as the actual setting for all those borscht belt jokes. For me, a college student waitressing in the late fifties, the Catskills was a wild place, dangerous and exciting, where all the beasts were predatory, none pacific. The years I spent working in those hotels were my introduction to the brutishness of function, the murderousness of fantasy, the isolation inflicted on all those living inside a world organized to provide pleasure. It's the isolation I've been thinking about lately—how remarkably present it was, crude and vibrant, there from the first moment of contact.

I walked into Stella Mercury's employment agency one afternoon in the winter of my freshman year at City College. Four men sat playing cards with a greasy deck, chewing gum methodically, never looking up once. The woman at the desk, fat and lumpy with hard eyes and a voiceful of cigarette wheeze, said to me, "Where ya been?" and I rattled off a string of hotels. "Ya worked all those places," she said calmly. "Ain't the human body a mah-h-vellous thing, ya don't look old enough to have worked half of 'em." I stood there, ill with fear that on the one hand she'd throw me out and on the other she'd give me a job, and assured her that I had. She knew I was lying, and I knew that she knew I was lying, but she wrote out a job ticket anyway. Suddenly I felt lonely inside the lie, and I begged her with my eyes to acknowledge the truth between us. She didn't like that at all. Her own eyes grew even harder, and she refused me more than she had when I'd not revealed open need. She drew back with the ticket still in her hand. I snatched at it. She laughed a nasty laugh. And that was it, all of it, right there, two flights above Times Square, I was in the mountains.

That first weekend in a large glittering hotel filled with garment district salesmen and midtown secretaries, weaving clumsily in and out of the vast kitchen all heat and acrimony (food flying, trays crashing, waiters cursing), I gripped the tray so hard all ten knuckles were white for days afterward, and every time I looked at them I recalled the astonishment I'd felt when a busboy at the station next to mine stuck out his fist to a guest who'd eaten three main dishes and said, "Want a knuckle sandwich?" But on Sunday night when I flung fifty single dollar bills on the kitchen table before my open-mouthed mother there was soft exultancy, and I knew I'd go back. Rising up inside this brash, moralistic, working-class girl was the unexpected excitement of the first opportunity for greed.

I was eighteen years old, moving blind through hungers whose force I could not grasp. Unable to grasp what drove me, I walked around feeling stupid. Feeling stupid I became inept. Secretly, I welcomed going to the mountains. I knew I could do this hard but simple thing. I could enter that pig-eyed glitter and snatch from it the soft, gorgeous, fleshy excitement of quick money. This I could master. This, I thought, had only to do with endurance; inexhaustible energy; and that I was burning up with.

The summer of my initiation I'd get a job, work two weeks, get fired. "You're a waitress? I thought you said you were a waitress. What kinda waitress sets a table like that? Who you think you're kidding, girlie?" But by Labor Day I *was* a waitress and a veteran of the first year. I had been inducted into an underclass elite, a world of self-selected Orwellian pariahs for whom survival was the only value.

At the first hotel an experienced waiter, attracted by my innocence, took me under his wing. In the mountains, regardless of age or actual history, your first year you were a virgin and in every hotel there was always someone, sentimental as a gangster, to love a virgin. My patron in this instance was a twenty-nine-year-old man who worked in the post office in winter and at this hotel in summer. He was a handsome vagrant, a cunning hustler, what I would come by the end of the summer to recognize as a "mountain rat."

One night a shot rang out in the sleeping darkness. Waiters and waitresses leaped up in the little barracks building we shared at the edge of the hotel grounds. Across the wide lawn, light filled the open doorway of one of the distant guest cottages. A man stood framed in the light, naked except for a jockstrap. Inside the barracks people began to laugh. It was my handsome protector. He'd been sleeping with a woman whose gambler husband had appeared unexpectedly on a Thursday night.

The next day he was fired. We took a final walk together. I fumbled for words. Why? I wanted to know. I knew he didn't like the woman, a diet-thin blonde twenty years older than himself. "Ah-h-h," my friend said wearily. "Doncha know nothing, kid? Doncha know what I am? I mean, whaddaya think I am?"

At the second hotel the headwaiter, a tall sweating man, began all his staff meetings with, "Boys and girls, the first thing to understand is, we are dealing with animals." He stood in the dining-room doorway every morning holding what I took to be a glass of apple juice until I was told it was whiskey neat. "Good morning, Mrs. Levine," he'd nod affably, then turn to a busboy and mutter, "That Holland Tunnel whore." He rubbed my arm between his thumb and his forefinger when he hired me and said, "We'll take care of each other, right, kid?" I nodded, thinking it was his way of asking me to be a responsible worker.

My obtuseness derailed him. When he fired me and my friend Marilyn because he caught us eating chocolate tarts behind an alcove in the dining room he thundered at us, his voice hoarse with relief, "You are not now waitresses, you never were waitresses, you'll never *be* waitresses."

At the third hotel I had fifty dollars stolen from me at the end of a holiday weekend. Fifty dollars wasn't fifty dollars in the mountains, it was blood money. My room was crowded with fellow workers, all silent as pallbearers. The door racketed open and Kennie, a busboy who was always late, burst into the room. "I heard you had money stolen!" he cried, his face stricken. I nodded wordlessly. Kennie turned, pulled the door shut, twisted his body about, raised his arm and banged his fist, sobbing, against the door. When I said, "What are *you* getting so excited about?" he shrieked at me, "Because you're a waitress and a human being! And I'm a busboy and a human being!" At the end of the summer, four more robberies having taken place, the thief was caught. It was Kennie.

At the fourth hotel the children's waiter was a dedicated womanizer. A flirtatious guest held out on him longer than usual, and one morning I saw this waiter urinate into a glass of orange juice, then serve it to the woman's child with the crooning injunction to drink it all up because it was so-o-o good.

At the fifth hotel I served a woman who was all bosom from neck to knee, tiny feet daintily shod, smooth plump hands beautifully manicured, childish eyes in a painted face. When I brought her exactly-three-minute eggs to the table she said to me, "Open them for me, dear. The shells burn my hands." I turned away, to the station table against the wall, to perform in appropriate secrecy a task that told me for the first but certainly not the last time that here I was only an extension of my function. It was the Catskills, not early socialist teachings at my father's knee, that made me a Marxist.

One winter I worked weekends and Christmas at a famous hotel. This hotel had an enormous tiered dining room and was run by one of the most feared headwaiters in the mountains. The system here was that all newcomers began at the back of the dining room on the tier farthest from the kitchen. If your work met with favor you were moved steadily toward the center, closer to the kitchen doors and to the largest tips which came not from the singles who were invariably placed in the back of the room but from the middle-aged manufacturers, club owners, and gangsters who occupied the tables in the central tiers, cutting a wide swath as though across a huge belly between the upper and lower ends of the dining room.

As the autumn wore on I advanced down the tiers. By Christmas I was nearly in the center of the room, at one of the best stations in the house. This meant my guests were now middle-aged married couples whose general appearance was characterized by blond bouffants, mink stoles, midnight-blue suits, and half-smoked cigars. These people ate prodigiously and tipped well.

That Christmas the hotel was packed and we worked twelve hours a day. The meals went on forever. By the end of the week we were dead on our feet but still running. On New Year's Eve at midnight we were to serve a full meal, the fourth of the day, but this was to be a banquet dinner—that is, a series of house-chosen dishes simply hauled out, course by course—and we looked forward to it. It signaled the end of the holiday. The next morning the guests checked out and that night we'd all be home in our Bronx or Brooklyn apartments, our hard-earned cash piled on the kitchen table.

But a threatening atmosphere prevailed at that midnight meal from the moment the dining room doors were flung open. I remember sky blue sequined dresses and tight mouths, satin cummerbunds and hard-edged laughter, a lot of drunks on the vomitous verge. People darted everywhere and all at once, pushing to get at the central tables (no assigned seats tonight), as though, driven from one failed part of the evening to another here, at last, they were going to get what *should* come through for them: a good table in the famous dining room during its New Year's Eve meal.

The kitchen was instantly affected: it picked up on atmosphere like an animal whose only survival equipment is hyperalertness. A kind of panicky aggression seemed to overtake the entire staff. The orderly lines that had begun to form for the first appetizer broke almost immediately. People who had grown friendly, working together over these long winter weekends, now climbed over each other's backs to break into the line and grab at the small round dishes piled up on the huge steel tables.

I made my first trip into the kitchen, took in the scene before me, and froze. Then I took a deep breath, inserted myself into a line, held my own against hands and elbows pushing into my back and ribs, and got my tray loaded and myself out the kitchen doors. I served the fruit cup quickly and, depending on my busboy to get the empties off the tables in time, made my anxious way back into the kitchen for the next course which, I'll not forget as long as I live, was chow mein. This time I thought violence was about to break out. All those people, trays, curses being flung about! And now I couldn't seem to take a deep breath: I remained motionless just inside the kitchen doors. Another waitress, a classmate from City College, grabbed my arm and whispered in my ear, "Skip the chow mein, they'll never know the difference. Go on to the next course, there's nobody on the line over there." My heart lifted, the darkness receded. I stared at her. Did we dare? Yes, she nodded grimly, and walked away. It didn't occur to either of us to consider that she, as it happened, had only drunken singles at her tables who of course wouldn't know the difference, but I had married couples who wanted everything that was coming to them.

I made my first mistake. I followed my classmate to the table with no line in front of it, loaded up on the cold fish, and fought my way out the nearest kitchen door. Rapidly, I dealt out the little dishes to the men and women at my tables. When I had finished and was moving back to my station table and its now empty tray, a set of long red fingernails plucked at my upper arm. I looked down at a woman with coarse blond hair, blue eyelids surrounded by lines so deep they seemed carved, and a thin red mouth. "We didn't get the chow mein," she said to me.

My second mistake. "Chow mein?" I said. "What chow mein?" Still holding me, she pointed to the next table where chow mein was being finished and the cold fish just beginning to be served. I looked at her. Words would not come. I broke loose, grabbed my tray, and dived into the kitchen.

I must have known I was in trouble because I let myself be kicked about in the kitchen madness, wasting all sorts of time being climbed over before I got the next dish loaded onto my tray and inched myself, crablike, through the swinging doors. As I approached my station I saw, standing beside the blond woman, the headwaiter, chewing a dead cigar and staring glumly in my direction. He beckoned me with one raised index finger.

I lowered my tray onto the station table and walked over to him. "Where's the chow mein?" he asked quietly, jerking his thumb back at my tables, across the head of the woman whose blue-lidded eyes never left his face. Her mouth was a slash of narrow red. Despair made me simple.

"I couldn't get to it," I said. "The kitchen is a madhouse. The line was impossible."

The headwaiter dropped his lower lip. His black eyes flickered into dangerous life and his hand came up slowly to remove the cigar stub from between his teeth. "You couldn't *get* to it?" he said. "Did I hear you right? You said you couldn't get to it?" A few people at neighboring tables looked up.

"That's right," I said miserably.

And then he was yelling at me, "And you call yourself a waitress?"

A dozen heads swung around. The headwaiter quickly shut his mouth. He stared coldly at me, in his eyes the most extraordinary mixture of anger, excitement, and fear. Yes, fear. Frightened as I was, I saw that he too was afraid. Afraid of the blond woman who sat in her chair like a queen with the power of life and death in her, watching a minister do her awful bidding. His eyes kept darting toward her, as though to ask, All right? Enough? Will this do?

No, the unyielding face answered. Not enough. Not nearly enough.

"You're fired," the headwaiter said to me. "Serve your morning meal and clear out."

The blood seemed to leave my body in a single rush. For a moment I thought I was going to faint. Then I realized that tomorrow morning my regular guests would be back in these seats, most of them leaving after breakfast, and I, of course, would receive my full tips exactly as though none of this had happened. The headwaiter was not really punishing me. He knew it, and now I knew it. Only the blond woman didn't know it. She required my dismissal for the appeasement of her lousy life—her lined face, her hated husband, her disappointed New Year's Eve—and he, the headwaiter, was required to deliver it up to her.

For the first time I understood something about power. I stared into the degraded face of the headwaiter and saw that he was as trapped as I, caught up in a working life that required *someone's* humiliation at all times.

The summer I turned twenty-one I graduated both from City College and from the Catskills. It was an apotheosis that summer, that hotel: no one and nothing seemed small, simple, or real. The owners were embezzling the place, the headwaiter was on the take, the cook gave us food poisoning. The viciousness between busboys and waiters was more unrestrained than I had ever seen it and the waitresses were required to mingle, that is, show up in the casino at night and "dance" with the male guests, as the headwaiter leeringly put it.

The staff was filled with people I had worked with before, and two old friends were there as well: Marilyn of "you're not now waitresses" fame and Ricky, the waitress who had advised me to forget the chow mein. We three roomed together in a tiny barracks room inside of which was jammed four cots, four

small chests of drawers, two narrow closets, and two rickety
bedside tables.

The fourth bed in our room was occupied by Marie, a
stranger to us in every way. From the moment I saw her sitting
on the edge of her bed removing her stockings as Marilyn and I
came in from the first lunch meal of an early June weekend I
knew she was not like us. I knew it from the way she was taking
off her stockings. Our hands would have torn quickly at the
stocking, pulling it off in one swift gesture, hers moved slowly
over leg and stocking together; the motion they made was one
that prolonged the moment rather than telescoped it, the expression on her face sensual not impatient.

She was tall and thin, one of those women with narrow
shoulders, small breasts, a high waist and long legs who, even
when she gains weight, looks slim: the kind of body that is
never stylish, always alluring. Her hair, as unfashionable as her
body, was a long red frizz that clung in Botticelli curls about
her face and forehead and straggled down her back in a ragged
ponytail. The eyes were large, the nose bony, the skin milk
white. Her mouth, easily her most distinctive feature, was long
with deep creases in the lips. ("Ravaged" was the word that,
with an unexpected thrill, came into my head.) We all smoked,
but she chain-smoked. Those lips came with a cigarette between them.

The three of us were twenty-one, Marie was twenty-five.
We were students, she was an out-of-work actress. We were old
hands in the mountains, she was a novice. We lived at home
with our working-class families, she came from a middle-class
family with whom she had severed relations. She was an unknown: I could not imagine her before she came among us and
I could not imagine her after she'd leave us. No, I take that
back. It wasn't that I couldn't imagine her, it was that it didn't
occur to me to imagine her.

In the mountains only that which caused blunt outrage or
open despair (bad tips, an intractable busboy, unhappy sex, a
strained back) attracted deeper attention. If someone was not
directly responsible for anger or misery the instinct to speculate

was not aroused. Like the dining room furniture, the kitchen heat, or the heavy trays, people were simply "there," part of a vast set against which we moved without nuance or dimension.

The waiter at the station next to mine that summer was another social oddity: Vinnie Liebowitz, an ambitious pre-med student whose name wasn't Liebowitz at all, it was Lentino. But as Vinnie said, "Who could make out in the Catskills with a name like Lentino?" and making out was what Vinnie was all about.

Vinnie was a smart, well-organized waiter who while not expansive was not excessively guarded either. A once dedicated seducer of women, he had never been driven by the intense need to score that dominated all sexual transactions in the mountains. He thought of himself as having a tender rather than a fierce appetite for the act of love.

In his second year in the mountains Vinnie had met Carol, a girl whose conventional good looks matched his own to an uncanny extent: same chiseled features, same large brown eyes and dense black hair, same thin, self-regarding body. Vinnie had pursued Carol madly. She had expertly beckoned and avoided him. By the end of that summer they were engaged. The plan was to marry after Vinnie's first year in medical school.

Vinnie and Carol had not slept together and were not going to until their wedding night. In this, the third summer of engagement, their passionate necking sessions had become regulated, and they found themselves absorbed by the more mature considerations of life; such as, where they would make their future home (Brooklyn or Long Island), the kind of furniture they would have, number of babies, location of summer and winter vacations. Vinnie was sometimes baffled as to how it was that his entire life seemed settled at the age of twenty-two, but he was working class from Brooklyn and Carol was a princess from Forest Hills. Without her, he often said, he'd have spent the rest of his life pumping gas in Brownsville.

All this I knew because that summer Carol and her parents were guests at a hotel fifteen miles from ours where my boyfriend Danny was working as a busboy, and two or three times a week Vinnie (the only waiter with a car) drove over to see Carol and took me along. This boyfriend of mine was also a medical student and a man of good-natured appetite as well. Danny loved sex, food, jazz, and memorizing medical textbooks. He also thought he loved me. And sometimes I thought the same. Together, we'd been meeting the needs of the moment for more than a year now.

The summer wore on in an exhaustion that came early and stayed late. By the end of July, young and healthy as we were, tiredness began dissolving collectively into all of us. People fell asleep sitting on the toilet, or standing on line in the kitchen, or taking a shower. One afternoon Marilyn got down on her hands and knees to retrieve a shoe that had been kicked under her cot; no sooner was her head parallel with the floor than her body forgot why it was there, and she fell asleep.

I don't think any of us ever felt lonely. Hot, angry, bored, weary yes, but lonely? No. Partly it was that punishing physical labor precludes every kind of reflectiveness, including the one out of which loneliness arises; partly it was that we lived in a mob scene, and the absence of solitude obscures the issue. But even at the time neither condition seemed fully to explain our uniform disallowance of this particular emotion.

One morning at seven o'clock, as I was walking from the barracks to the kitchen door, I stopped to smell the air on the great hotel lawn. The moment was lovely: clear and sensual. Buried in the early morning cool was the growing heat that would spread itself hour by hour across the sexy summer day. I felt pierced to the heart. There were other ways to spend this day! Other lives to live, other people to be. I did then what was never done: I began to daydream. I saw myself standing in the same morning light somewhere else, under a great shade tree of a kind we didn't have in the mountains. Beside me, on the grass, sat a group of strangers—graceful, beautiful, intelligent— animated by clever talk and sophisticated laughter. They invited me to join them, even made a place for me on the grass. I longed to sit down. I felt that I *knew* these people, that I belonged among them. Suddenly and without warning, a space seemed to open between me and the image in my mind. The space lengthened into a road. It was clear that I would have to walk the road, step by step, to get to my people. The movie in my mind stopped running. I could not *see* myself on the road. I could not imagine the steps, taken one by one, that were necessary to close the gap between me and the people I was daydreaming. Inside, I began to congeal. Then all inner movement ceased. I stood on the lawn and stared at my own dumb longing. Desolation crowded in. I was lonely.

I remember that I wrenched myself then from the loneliness. It frightened me. I had felt myself pitching forward, as though about to lose my balance. And balance, I knew, was everything. I looked around me at the lawn, the buildings, the parking lot, this small, tight world where function was all, and I had learned to operate supremely well (avoid gross humiliation and control the limits of surrender). All I had to do was look straight ahead, keep my mouth shut, and my balance intact. Life, I thought grimly, whatever its size or composition, depends on walking the straight and narrow of the moment. I turned away from my own daydream and walked through the kitchen door.

Yet everything seemed harder than ever that summer. The tips were bad, the cook was a sadist, and we had to steal more meat, fruit, and milk than usual. The mountains were always one long siege of vitamin deprivation. No one ever wanted to feed the help; the agony on an owner's face if his eye fell on a busboy drinking orange juice or eating a lamb chop was palpable. One night a waiter was fired because the maitre d' tore open his bulging shirt as he was leaving the dining room and found two steaks lying flat against his naked chest. Six or eight of us watched from our stations. No one spoke, no one moved. What made things worse in this instance was that many of us knew the maitre d' was out to fire this waiter because he had refused to kick back.

The headwaiter was a Hungarian Jew with a despairing sense of class: life had dealt him a blow by making him end his working years in the mountains. A vain handsome man, all brushed white hair, manicured hands, and sky blue suits to match the color of his eyes, he perspired constantly and, if taken by surprise, his eyes rolled in his head. He often began staff meetings with a hysterical denunciation of these rumors about pay-offs that his enemies (and don't think for a minute he didn't know who *they* were) were spreading. Most of us sat at these meetings genuinely baffled by such ravings, but some of us nodded our heads in vigorous sympathy for the injustices suffered by the sweating madman who paced the floor in front of us. Those of us who were baffled were indeed in the dark, those of us who were nodding were regularly handing over 10 percent of our tips to be assured a full station each week.

In mid-August fifteen people came down with food poisoning. The huskiest waiters in the hotel were clutching their stomachs and heaving into their busboys' dish bins. One of them vomited all night, another was delirious for twelve hours, a third drooled up green bile. The barracks took on the hushed atmosphere of an epidemic ward. When we discovered that the source of the food poisoning had been a dinner made up of turkey wings the cook suspected of having gone bad one of the waitresses broke. The cook had been making her life miserable, grabbing at her, taunting her, and now, her body racked with diarrhetic convulsion, she demanded and gained entry to the owner's office. He sat behind his desk. Beside him stood his son and the bell captain. The waitress began to speak. She told her story of weariness and harassment and then described in detail how those poisoned were suffering. She demanded the dismissal of the cook. The owner stared into a space somewhere between her shoulder and the door. "Get this cunt outta here," he announced to the air. Stunned, the waitress allowed herself to be led, as though blind, from the office. In the barracks she told what had happened. Some of us were silent, some of us cursed, some turned quickly away. Needless to say, no one did anything.

My visits to Danny were, during these days, a consolation. I was grateful to him for providing me with a means of escape from the hotel. It was not only being with Danny that made going to see him important, it was everything about the visit itself—hurrying to get out of the dining room on the nights I knew we were traveling, climbing into Vinnie's car with the smell of summer stronger than when I was going nowhere, driving through the dark silent countryside behind the sweep of headlights beyond which the familiar daytime roads and hotels had become almost mysterious.

The night was invariably rich, dark, sweet, shot through with a kind of lit-from-within intensity. The smell of wet earth came up through grass, trees swayed in a warm wind, molecules of excitement gathered in the clear mountain air. Sitting close together on the front seat of his ten-year-old Chevy, Vinnie and I were both infected by the atmosphere.

Aroused in each other's presence, we hardly ever thought we were being aroused by each other, yet this closeness, which blossomed only on the ride out never on the way back, began to accumulate a peculiar life. We never spoke of it, and certainly we did not bring it back with us to the hotel. Nonetheless, I felt its influence. Sometimes, something ordinary came into unexpected relief and suddenly the familiar would seem threatening. I'd feel a shock to the system, and I'd find myself flashing on the ride out with Vinnie.

Take Marilyn and the butcher, for instance. This butcher, a good-looking ex-Marine, was a true primitive: murderous when crossed, slavishly loyal when done a good turn. In his lexicon Marilyn had done him a good turn by bestowing the gift of her virginity on him, and his devotion knew no bounds. He assured her daily he would steal and kill for her.

Marilyn, of course, had a hard time concentrating on Thomas's adoration as her virginity had been an obstacle to "getting on with it," and she was grateful to Tom for relieving her of its burdensomeness. The most hardened mountain rat participated in a fear of virginity, and every one of them had drawn back from the taint of Marilyn's purity. Thomas also had drawn back but she had been able to persuade him that her feeling for him was so deep it would be a sin *not* to. To this argument he finally assented and thereafter treated Marilyn worshipfully, her capacity for such deep feeling, coupled with the contradictory reference to sin, having become confused in him with religious experience.

Thomas appeared regularly in our room after dinner and while Marilyn lay back on her bed, still in her work clothes, he would sit dreamily stroking her lower leg. As he did so the secret smile that seemed perpetually on Marilyn's mouth these days deepened and, beneath the dirty white uniform, a long delicate shudder moved visibly down the length of her beautiful midriff and flat belly. She had become sleek as a bird-eating cat since she'd begun making love, and almost as remote.

One afternoon I came into the room after the lunch meal and saw the *Times* lying on Marilyn's bed. Surprised, as we never got the papers, I said, "Where'd this come from?" Marilyn followed my eyes to the bed. "Oh, Tom left it here this morning," she said. My eyebrows went up. "Thomas reads the *Times?*" I asked. Marilyn's face turned a dull red. "He does *now,*" she said. Her eyes came up level with mine. We looked at each other for a long suspended moment. Then we both began to howl.

Suddenly I felt gripped with anxiety, and in my mind's eye I saw me and Vinnie riding through the night toward who, what, I didn't know. But this, me and Marilyn laughing over Thomas, it frightened me. Something vicious here, something fearful and sacrificial. My heart pressed on my ribs.

Three weeks before Labor Day Vinnie and I climbed into the Chevy one night and took off. We'd been late getting out of the dining room, and now Vinnie was driving fast. As he raced along the road he could drive in his sleep, I babbled at him a tale of dining-room fatigue having to do with a guest I'd spilled hot liquid on three meals in a row. The story had a point, and I was reaching it. Vinnie leaned forward over the wheel, his fine black eyebrows pressing closer together over the bridge of his thin straight nose, his wonderfully dark eyes narrowed with concentration. Just as I was about to deliver the punch line, the car swerved sharply to the right of the road and came to an abrupt halt.

Vinnie turned to me. Even in the dark I could see how white his face had become. His eyes were a film of misery. We stared at one another.

"I can't stand it anymore," he whispered.

"Stand what?" I whispered back.

"I want her," he moaned.

"Carol, you mean?"

"No. Marie!"

"Marie?" I repeated.

"Yes."

"Marie from our hotel?"

"Yes!"

"But you're engaged to Carol," I explained.

"I know!" he cried. "Don't you think I know that? Don't you think I say to myself every day and every night, You've got Carol. Carol who loves you, Carol who's a thousand times better looking than she is, a thousand times sharper, nicer, more terrific in every way. But it doesn't do any good. I want *her*. And it's tearing me apart!"

I could feel my eyes growing large in the dark. "How long has this been going on?" I asked, my voice nakedly curious.

"Weeks," he said, slumping back against the seat. He stared bleakly out the window. "It feels like years but I guess it's really only weeks."

"Does she know?"

"I'm not sure. I think so. But I'm not sure."

"You mean you've never said anything to her?"

"Christ, no. To begin with, I couldn't believe this was happening to me, and then . . ." The color was returning to his cheeks. "I was confused and ashamed. Jesus Christ. Marie! She's not good-looking, she's older than me, she's like no one I ever knew." His voice broke. "I mean sometimes she really looks like hell." He stopped talking. I waited. When he spoke again his voice was soft and steady. "I don't know how it started," he said. "One day I was just aware of her. Aware of her in the kitchen. Aware of her in the dining room. Aware of her in the barracks. Aware of her. Once we both reached into the silverware pail at the same time. My hand touched hers and I felt like I'd been burned. I was so surprised. I didn't know what it meant. After that I'd find myself looking for her in the dining room. And all this time I'm saying to myself, Vinnie you crazy? What's goin' on here? Remember Carol? The girl you love. The girl you're gonna marry. The best-looking girl in the mountains. What *is* this? But it didn't do any good. Every day I'd find myself thinking about *her*. More and more. Not exactly thinking about her, just *feeling* her, feeling her presence, and then I couldn't take my eyes off her when she was anywhere near me." He struck his forehead with his balled-up right hand and fell forward over the wheel. "She *must* know," he groaned. "I can't figure out how come everybody doesn't know. I feel like it's written all over my face all the time."

"It's not," I said drily.

His long speech had given me time to absorb what he was saying, but I too kept repeating to myself, Marie? Carol is so beautiful, so right in every way. What has *Marie* got to do with anything? I could not take it in. Handsome, pre-med Vinnie Liebowitz, with this life all mapped out, wanting Marie who in no way belonged. It was crazy, nuts, exciting. That was another thing I couldn't take in: I was excited by Vinnie's confession of desire for Marie.

"I feel better for having told you," Vinnie smiled wanly. "You don't mind, do you? I mean, you're not sorry I told you, are you?"

"Of course not," I said briskly, not knowing what I felt. "But we'd better go now. They'll be waiting for us."

Vinnie's eyes clouded over. He nodded at me and turned the key in the ignition. The car climbed back onto the road. In twenty minutes we were pulling into the driveway of Carol and Danny's hotel.

I remember lying in Danny's arms that night fantasizing

about Vinnie and Marie. I saw them locked together, thrashing wildly, their faces contorted with pain, their bodies in fever. My own body was so coiled with tension that Danny's pleasure was greatly heightened, and he suggested we might be falling in love anew. I said nothing. I could hardly hear his voice, my attention had wandered so far from the man I was lying with. It was a relief, two hours later, to be back in the car where burning interest could be openly pursued. The ride home was spent with me pumping Vinnie about Marie, and he plunging eagerly into his tale of illicit desire.

After that night our rides took on new meaning. Vinnie's obsession had touched something secret in him, and a strain of wildness had flared in us both. When I had daydreamed my beautiful people, the clever ones, the ones I couldn't reach on my own, the fantasy had made me lonely. But now, daydreaming Vinnie and Marie, there rose up in me a hunger so open and so acute it sent me into a trance. Reckless, sweet, compelling, it became a dream that settled in the groin. Vinnie's desire became all desire, his urgency all urgency, his necessity a drama we could, neither of us, get enough of. I felt released into complicity, about what I did not know. I only knew that the atmosphere inside the car had become rich with secrecy. He talked, and I fed him questions. My questions extended the obsession, deepened the drama. Some live, fluid movement went streaking through our furtive exchange. A wave of hidden promise rose and fell in the speeding dark, and rose again. I wanted to go on riding it forever.

I could imagine for him what I could not imagine for myself, and often what I imagined felt alarming: hard, bright, insistent. This was the exact opposite of my lonely daydream. This was all appetite and acquisition; what triggered everyone around me. It appalled and excited me. I remember once flashing on the woman who'd gotten me fired that long ago New Year's Eve. Suddenly I could feel her mean hungriness moving inside me. I wanted Vinnie to get what he wanted the way she had wanted to get . . . what? What was it exactly that she *had* wanted to get? At this point my thoughts went fuzzy, but the feeling remained: hard and bright. The trance deepened. Nothing seemed to matter then, only that desire be gratified.

One night we got into the car and Vinnie said to me, "Talk to her." I fell toward him as though I'd been slapped and had involuntarily jerked the wrong way. "What do you mean, talk to her? And say what?" He was silent, his handsome face white and drawn. "Tell her how I feel," he said. "I can't do it, I just can't do it. And you could. I mean, you're a girl, you live with her, you're sort of friends. You could explain it to her. Ask her to meet me after the meal tomorrow night. Just that. Nothing else. She's got nothing to be afraid of. Tell her that. I won't hurt her, I won't ask her to do anything she doesn't want to do. I just want to talk to her." He brightened up. "That's all," he repeated. "I just want to talk to her. She's got nothing to be afraid of. Nothing. I swear it."

My heart began to pound. I slept beside Marie every night but she was not as real to me in the flesh as she was here in the car, a conjured vision, the shared object of Vinnie's overexcited anguish. I stared at him. I yearned to remain as we were, locked together inside the nighttime confessional of the car, and I think he did too. I saw that he was afraid yet he felt compelled to act, to move into consequence.

He lifted his head high in the darkened car, his eyes pinpoints of dilated light, his jawline a throb of conjested strain. Then his head dropped forward over his smooth, beautiful neck. Humbled by need, he had become unbearably handsome.

"I'll talk to her," I said.

The next morning as we were stumbling around getting ready for breakfast I asked Marie to meet with me after the meal. She looked quizzically at me, but I remained silent. "Sure," she said quietly. We each turned back into ourselves, finished dressing, and tore out of the room.

Four hours later Marie and I walked through the dining room doors together for the first time that summer and headed wordlessly for the pool. This was a "singles" hotel; at 10:30 in the morning, we knew, there would be no one lying on the painted concrete beside the chlorine blue water. As we walked I glanced at Marie's bare legs. They were scruffy looking, in need of a shave. For the thousandth time I thought, "Why her? Why does he want her?"

We sat down on the lower ends of two lounge chairs, uneasy in our occupancy (we never used guest facilities), and faced each other across the black-and-white expanse of our morning uniforms. Marie seemed not tense but alert, her long narrow body waiting, her bony face a smooth mask. Suddenly I was overcome with confusion. Why was I about to speak of intimate matters for one stranger with another stranger? I did then what I always did in confusion, became self-righteous.

"I wanted to talk to you about Vinnie," I said crisply.

Marie's mouth tightened. Her hands, lying quietly against her thighs, now met in her lap and she twisted them together. "I knew it," she said, her voice soft with resignation.

"You *knew* it? How?"

"Come *on*," she said impatiently.

"He'd like to see you," I went on.

"No," she said. "I won't."

"You won't? What do you mean you won't?" This I had not considered. "Why not? He just wants to see you. To talk. That's all. He just wants to talk to you."

"There's nothing to talk about."

"How can you say that? There's everything to talk about."

"Not as far as I'm concerned."

"For God's sake. He's suffering. Doesn't that mean anything to you?"

"No. Why should it?"

"It's *you* he wants!"

"No, he doesn't."

"What do you mean, he doesn't?"

"He doesn't know me at all," she said. "How can he want me? It's not *me* he wants."

"Who is it then?" I was stupefied.

"Don't you know anything?" she said softly. "It's never you they want."

She looked down at her hands. I looked out at the pool. The sun climbed high in the late morning sky. I felt drowsy. A warm yellow fog filled my head. Years seemed to pass.

Marie looked up. I looked over at her. My head cleared instantly. It was true, I knew nothing, but the anxiety in that face! I saw how isolated she was, alone in the words she had just spoken. Not one of us could have said what she had said, and she knew it. My heart went out to her.

"I won't see him," she said. "That's final."

My heart came back to me. Vinnie! Handsome Vinnie wouldn't get what he wanted and needed. I felt like slapping her. Who was *she* to deny *him*. She was nothing, no one, a name, a face, a body to which hunger had become attached. If I had put out my hand to touch her then I'm sure I would have felt glass, that's how unreal she was to me.

"Besides," she was saying brightly (she had just remembered something useful), "I couldn't. Even if I wanted to. There's somebody else."

"Somebody else?" My eyes shot open. "Where? In the city?"

"No. Here."

"Here? Who is it?"

"Eddie," she said.

"Who's Eddie?" I said.

"The bell captain."

"The *bell* captain?" I said and stared at her anew. The hierarchy of association was so strict in the mountains that if you were a waiter you had nothing to do with chambermaids or bellhops. (Marilyn's affair with the butcher was a matter of desperate dispensation.)

"Yes," she said, face flushed, head at a defiant tilt.

I didn't know what to do next.

"Is he nice?" I asked idiotically.

"No," the laugh was short and sharp. "But we understand each other," she said evenly.

I turned away from her and looked out again at the chemically colored water, the painted concrete, the striped deck chairs.

"It's all so disgusting," Marie said softly.

We rose without another word. I headed for the barracks, she headed for the side of the main building. For the first time I realized that she spent less time in the room between meals than any of the rest of us; Eddie lived just off the lobby.

That night Vinnie didn't see any of the people around him until he was crashing into them. I know he didn't remember any of his orders because his guests were yelling at him. Women who had loved him in the morning were now turning hurt, betrayed eyes on him as he forgot their special requests repeatedly and their husbands, feeling unmanned by the inability to control the quality of the service, threatened to become ugly. But Vinnie's gaze was fixed in space, his upper teeth nipping distractedly at his lower lip. No external threat could touch him. The next night he said he didn't feel well and would not be going to see Carol as usual. He spoke with exaggerated politeness: he knew he knew my name but for the moment it had escaped him.

Time seemed to expand and contract abnormally for days after that exchange, speeding up and slowing down for no discernable reason, as in a dream. In another minute the Labor Day weekend had arrived, and the season was about to end.

On Sunday, all day, the entire barracks seemed shrouded in a kind of convalescent inertness that contrasted strongly with the usual racketing-about that went on in our common hallway from six in the morning until midnight. The summer had, all at once, wound down with no resolution of the conflicts that had set the racket in motion. Abruptly, our agitation was ended. Now we were hanging on, waiting only to get sprung. The evening meal passed with less friendliness than ever before, many of us gone in spirit already. Faces were cool, guarded, remote. Vinnie's face, especially, was beyond reach.

Yet our bodies demonstrated a remarkable stylishness that night, arrived at with an energy fed, as never before, by the

defensive cool. Trays were carried with the elegance of a
dancer's control, the grace and skill of motion long ceremonial-
ized. We were masters now, in possession of an art. Behind the
seamless skill, well behind it, our sealed over young hearts.

At eleven o'clock that night Ricky and I sat on our beds,
talking quietly, the room half pulled apart with our just begun
packing. Outside our door hallway toilets flushed, sink faucets
went on and off, rides were being arranged for. Suddenly, there
was a muffled explosion against the wall behind our beds, and
then everything was happening at once: the sound of furniture
being flung, bodies thrown, a man's voice shouting, a woman's
crying; waiters and waitresses running down the hall past the
sinks nearly to the toilets, skidding to a stop, crowding into an
open doorway, me and Ricky pushing forward with the rest;
there inside, the chaos of cots half overturned, a bureau nearly
pulled down, toilet things floating in the bedclothes as though
on a shipwrecked sea, Vinnie in his black pants and sleeveless
undershirt (muscles flexed, eyes glazed) and Marie, crouched in
the far corner of the room, her uniform hanging in ripped
shreds, clutching at her naked breasts, arms and neck covered
with scratches already turning purple, her frizzy hair stringy
with sweat, her crushed mouth twitching.

We stood there: cold with curiosity. No one looked at
Vinnie. Everyone stared at Marie. She was in solitary. Waves of
emotion came off her: hot and silent. It was her loneliness she
was sending out. Her wise, humiliated loneliness. ("It's never
you they want.") We looked at her out of our flat, young faces
without pity or regret. She sat there, waiting. Her eyes flickered
dully from one to another of us. They came to rest on me. I felt
my own confusion—hard, mean, insistent—welling up.

"You asked for it," I said, and turned away.

But I have continued to look at her, for years and years.
Her bony, knowing face still floats past me as she sits crouched
in memory, forever trapped in that room with me, her keeper
in the doorway, standing there upon a ground of brutish innocence that in more than thirty years has not given way, only

shifted position many times over as I struggle ineptly to take in the meaning of her loneliness.

It was a world predicated on blind hunger: everything depended on the blindness. It took hard work to remain unknowing. Those of us who didn't manage it went into quarantine. Those of us who did required someone's humiliation at all times.

Mary Gaitskill

Revelation

I did not have a religious upbringing and I count that a good thing; almost everyone I know who has had one appears to have suffered for it. I know there are exceptions, but when I think of "religious upbringing," I think of the two little girls I once walked home with in the fourth grade who, on hearing that I didn't believe that Jesus was the Son of God, began screaming, "There's a sin on your soul! You're going to hell!" I think of my friend who, as a kid, was repeatedly exorcised in her mother's fundamentalist church and who still has nightmares about it at forty-five. I think of a thirteen-year-old boy I recently met who told me he believes that God will punish his sexually active classmates by giving them AIDS. I think of watching *The Exorcist* in theaters and seeing adult moviegoers jump up and stumble toward the exits, retching and/or weeping with fear.

My mother, to her credit, told me that "God is love" and that there is no hell. But I don't think I quite believed her. Even though I have very little conscious religious anxiety, since childhood, I periodically have had dreams that suggest otherwise; dreams of hooded monks carrying huge, grim crosses in processions meant to end in someone's death by fire, drowning, or quartering. Of endless liturgies by faceless choirs to faceless parishioners in cavernous dark churches. Of trials, condemnations, sacrifices, and torture. I have no idea where this stuff comes from. Horror movies and creeping cultural fear are obvious sources, but my unconscious has taken these images in with such kinetic intensity and conviction that mere suggestion doesn't seem to be the culprit. When I wake from these dreams, it is with terror.

When I was twenty-one, I became a born-again Christian. It was a random and desperate choice; I had dropped out of high school and left home at sixteen, and while I'd had some fun, by twenty-one, things were looking squalid and stupid. My boyfriend had dumped me and I was living in a rooming house and selling hideous rodium jewelry on the street in Toronto, which is where the "Jesus freaks" approached me. I had been solicited by these people before and usually gave them short shrift, but on that particular evening I was at a low ebb. They told me that if I let Jesus into my heart right there, even if I just said the words, that everything would be okay. I said, all right, I'll try it. They praised God and moved on.

Even though my conversion was pretty desultory, I decided to pray that night. I had never seriously prayed before, and all my pent-up desperation and fear made it an act of furious psychic propulsion that lasted almost an hour. It was a very private experience that I would find hard to describe; suffice to say that I felt I was being listened to. I started going to a bleak church that had night services and free meals, and was attended heavily by street people and kids with a feverish, dislocated look in their eyes. And, for the first time, I started reading the Bible. For me, it was like running into a brick wall.

I was used to reading, but most of it was pretty trashy. Even when it wasn't, the supple, sometimes convoluted play of modern language entered my mind like radio music—then, of course, there was the actual radio music, the traffic noise, the continual onrush of strangers through the streets I worked, the slower shifting movements of friends, lovers, alliances, the jabber of electricity and neon in the night. All of which kept my mind and nervous system in a whipsawed condition from which it was difficult to relate to the Bible. "The earth was without form and void; and darkness was on the face of the deep. And the Spirit of God was hovering over the face of the waters. Then God said let there be light and there was light." I couldn't even appreciate the beauty of the words. The phrases seemed like big dumb swatches of form imposed on something swift-moving and endlessly changeable. The form was mute, huge, and absolutely immobile. It made me feel I was being smothered. One clergyman after another would quote from it so intensely, as if its big majestic opaqueness was meaningful in and of itself, and I would try to at least feel the meaning if I couldn't comprehend it. But all I felt was that persistent sense of truncation, the intimation of something enormous and inchoate trying to squeeze through the static form of written words.

This feeling became most intense when I read the Revelation. The Revelation is the most cinematic and surreal part of the Bible—it's a little like a horror movie, which is probably why it was relatively easy for me to take in. It certainly confirmed my free-floating fear. It seemed terribly real to me; I would walk out into the streets, amid the big buildings in which commerce ground forward, and I would feel the violence, the lies, the fornication, and so on pitching and heaving under the semblance of order. The air would crackle with the unacknowledged brutality of human life, and I would feel acutely all the small, stupid betrayals and lies I committed every day, both against myself and others. The angels with their seven stars and their lamp stands, the beast with his seven heads and ten horns—the static imagery was terrifying and senseless to me, and yet all the more convincing for it. I could imagine angels and beasts looming all about us, invisible because of our willful stupidity, our refusal to see the consequences of our actions, our little petty vanities. Their stars and lamp stands and horns seemed like peculiar abstractions on the page, but, I feared, when the horses came down, with their fire and teeth and snake tails, their reality would be all too clear. I lay in my bed and prayed, trying to convince myself of God's love, but, in the face of such mayhem, my prayers seemed a rag in a typhoon.

Besides, I couldn't help but think it was a little harsh. Locusts, malignant sores, scorpions, fire, men "gnawing their tongues" with pain—I knew people were horrible, but even in my youth I could also see that most people did the best they could. Even as angry and fearful and disappointed as I was, I knew I wouldn't torture people in such a way, and I didn't see how I could be more compassionate than God. I was moved when I read, in First Corinthians 13: "Love suffers long and is kind; love does not envy; love does not parade itself, is not puffed up; does not behave rudely, does not seek its own, is not provoked, thinks no evil, does not rejoice in iniquity, but rejoices in truth; bears all things, believes all things, hopes all things, endures all things. Love never fails." But I also remember thinking that, well, yes, and love is not pathologically cruel, either.

The fury of Revelation sometimes made my compassion feel weak and mealy-mouthed, but my reservations were not only humanitarian. I was more perturbed by what to me was the mechanical quality, not just of Revelation, but of the whole Bible. You had to worship God in exactly a certain way, according to certain prescriptions—and Revelation hinted that the rules set out in, say, the Ten Commandments, were only one tiny piece of a vast schema in which human ambivalence was not a factor.

I had a dream which was not about the Bible but which embodied my consternation about it. In the dream I lived in a house with several other people. We could not get out of the house and our relationships with each other had been preordained, regardless of feeling. Our actions were controlled by masters whom we never saw. One day a man came to visit us, ostensibly for lunch. He was very polite and even friendly, and we were also friendly with him. But it was understood that he was one of the people who controlled us, and the atmosphere was one of pure dread. During lunch, when one of the men of the house suddenly attacked and killed one of the household cats, we knew it was because our visitor had somehow made him do it. I couldn't hide my horror completely and our visitor looked at me a moment and then said, referring to the mangled body of the cat, "That's what I'm going to do to you one day." I understood him to mean that he was going to rape me, and I said, "But I'm married," not because it mattered to me, but because I knew that the only thing that mattered to him was his laws. Then I became too angry to go along with this and I added, "Even though I don't respect my husband." Very threateningly—after all, it's part of the law that we love our spouses—the visitor asked, "Do you have sex with your husband?" I answered yes, and it was clear from my tone that I did so only in order to obey the law. "That's good," said the visitor, "because your husband is a very intelligent man." This was a strange moment because there was such a sense of approval for the fact of my husband's intelligence, but it had nothing to do with the man he was; rather the approval was all for an idea of an intelligent man and a dutiful wife paying him the homage of sex. The hellish thing was, it was true. Even though I didn't love my dream husband, I considered him intelligent. And so I said, "Yes, he is very intelligent." I said it for complicated reasons. Partly to please the visitor, whom I was afraid of, but more to make some emotional contact with him by invoking a concept he had codified as law, and making him see that I respected intelligence too. The way he looked at me when I said this was also complicated. It was a look of respect for my miserable loyalty to my husband, for my detached admiration for his mind. It was a look that appreciated my humanity, but would only give it a tiny space to breathe, a look a torturer might give a victim who had just expressed a sentiment the torturer considered noble, but that would not prevent torture from taking place.

This prison-house seemed to me our human state, the circumstances of our birth into families not of our choosing, and our inability to free ourselves from psychological patterns learned before we can decide for ourselves. The visitor seemed

like the God in the Bible who is kind only as long as you adhere
to the rules, and who will sometimes decide to punish you
anyway. God doesn't afflict Job because of anything Job has
done, but because he wants to prove a point to Satan. When,
for example, the angel in Revelation criticizes the church of
Pergamos for having members who "hold the doctrine of the
Nicolaitanes, which thing I hate," we as readers aren't required
to know what this doctrine is or why God hates it or what we
might think of it if we knew what it was—that is all irrelevant.
And on a larger scale, all our complicated feelings and con-
flicted impulses about, say, sex are irrelevant. If it's outside
marriage it's bad, period.

My conversion lasted only about six months. I was still
calling myself a Christian when I took a GED and returned to
Michigan to attend community college, but I gradually let it go.
I began to write seriously for the first time in my life and I used
my passion in telling stories instead of saying prayers.

Twenty years later, I am sympathetic with my first assessment;
to me, the Bible still has a mechanical quality, a refusal to brook
complexity that feels brutal and violent. There has been a
change, however. When I look at Revelation now, it still seems
frightening and impenetrable, and it still suggests a fearful, in-
exorable order that is unknowable by us, in which our earthly
concerns matter very little. However, it no longer reads to me
like a chronicle of arbitrarily inflicted cruelty. It reads like a
terrible abstract of how we violate ourselves and others and
thus bring down endless suffering on earth. When I read "And
they blasphemed God of heaven because of their pain and their
sores, and did not repent of their deeds," I think of myself and
dozens of other people I've known or know who blaspheme life
itself by failing to have the courage to be honest and kind. And
how we then rage around and lash out because we hurt. When
I read "fornication," I no longer read it as a description of sex
outside marriage: I read it as sex done in a state of psychic
disintegration, with no awareness of one's self or one's partner,
let alone any sense of honor or even real playfulness. I still

don't know what to make of the doctrine of the Nicolaitanes, among other things, but I'm now inclined to read it as a writer's primitive attempt to give form to his moral urgency, to create a structure that could contain and give ballast to the most desperate human confusion.

I'm not sure how to account for this change. I think it mainly has to do with gradually maturing and becoming more deeply aware of my own mechanicalness and my own stringent limitations in giving form to immense complexity—something writers understand very well. It probably has to do with my admittedly dim understanding of how apparently absolute statements can contain an enormous array of meaning and nuance without losing their essential truth. And it has to do with my expanded ability to accept my own fear, and to forgive myself for my own mechanical responses to things I don't understand. In the past, my compassion felt inadequate in the face of Revelation because my compassion was small—perhaps immature is a better word—and conditional. I could not accept what I read there because it did not fit my idea of how life should be, even though I could feel the truth of it in my psyche. Now I recognize, with pain, a genuine description of how hellish life can be, and how even God can't help us because we won't allow it. Paradoxically, I find that the more you accept the pain and fear inherent in human experience, the greater your compassion can become, until finally it is no longer merely your compassion but a small part of the greater love epitomized in the Bible as Jesus.

To me, these realizations don't mean I have arrived at a point of any real knowledge; they are simply interesting as small markers of my development. I imagine that twenty years from now, when I read the Revelation I will once again see it the same, yet differently. I am looking forward to it.

Christopher Hitchens

Against Lesser Evilism

"Whenever A and B are in opposition to each other," wrote George Orwell in 1945, in "Through a Glass, Rosily," "anyone who attacks or criticizes A is accused of aiding and abetting B." He added: "It is a tempting maneuver, and I have used it myself more than once, but it is dishonest." Orwell lived and wrote in a period when the pressure on intellectuals to "take sides" was ostensibly much more palpable than it is now, and when with that pressure came a surreptitious invitation to moral blackmail: the element that tells thinking people that the less adventurous the use they make of their ratiocinative capacity, the better. When the big decision has already been taken, what need of paltry misgivings? Who desires to be called a wavering intellectual dilettante when grand enterprises are on foot, and when the engine of destiny has gone to all the trouble of revving itself up?

In our time, of course, the great question has become more banal. It is most commonly stated as the theory and practice of the "lesser evil." And, as argued in its conventional form, it has become worn as smooth as a stone. Thus A will exhort B, how can you vote for Clinton when . . . (list of betrayals and

depredations follows) and B replies, without the slightest re-
hearsal, do you suppose that the right wing (taxonomy of depredations and fell intentions ready to hand) would be preferable?
And that's the whole exchange. And not just in a nutshell either, since the amount of time and of mental effort expended is
usually less than it has taken me to set it down. However, as
Prince Hamlet once exclaimed, one may be confined in a nutshell and still count oneself a king of infinite space. Folded
inside the "lesser evil" argument, there is a worthwhile confrontation waiting to be enacted. The smooth stone can become
an effective projectile, to be employed with care by either an-
tagonist.

If one divides the contending parties into the purists and
rejectionists on the one hand, and the pragmatists and lesser-
evilists on the other, one can discover at once that neither really
means what they say. Out of respect for Orwell, and for the
sake of sheer convenience, let us call these respective debaters
A and B for now. A does not really maintain that it makes *no*
difference which party wins the election. It must be agreed for
one thing that no outcome is identical to any other. Nor does A
usually like to argue that it would be better for "the other side"
to win, because it is that "other side" that anchors the concept
of "lesser evil" to begin with. (There used to be a subset of A,
which said with contempt that the worse things were, the better. *Tanto pio, tanto meglia,* as the Italian Red Brigades once
happily intoned. But this faction no longer exists for our pur-
poses.) Thus, B starts with the advantage of being able to address A in pitying tones, as if A had a lesson still to learn from
that great moral tutor, "the real world." Yet B would never be
caught arguing in favor of permanent one-party rule, in the real
world or any other. One-party rule does not work in practice or
in principle. Why, then, does B argue that it is *always* better for
the Democratic party to win an election, whether congressional
or presidential, and that it always has been better? If the "lesser
evil" argument is not an axiom, it is nothing. It cannot be true
only some of the time, without losing all or most of its force.
Furthermore, surely B would generally scorn anyone whose

vote was, so to speak, mortgaged in advance. How can you be an autonomous and free citizen if your franchise is pledged to one machine, without conditions, whatever happens in the course of the election or in the conduct of the argument?

Let us try some "real world" applications. I'll select mine only from what was going on in the newspapers while I was writing this essay. Elections and campaigns were underway in Israel, Italy, Bosnia-Herzegovina, Russia, and the United States. An example, first, from each of the four overseas ones:

• In the closing days of the Israeli election campaign, where nobody but a fool would claim that there was "no difference" between the two main coalitions, Shimon Peres undertook a campaign of ruthless bombing and strafing in southern Lebanon. Some hundreds of thousands of refugees were created as a matter of policy, and some hundreds of innocent civilians were, in "collateral" manner, deprived of life and limb. It was, I thought, slightly too easily said by American and Israeli pundits that this could be overlooked as a hard-headed electoral test of Peres's "toughness" (surely sufficiently demonstrated already) on the "security" issue. Amos Perlmutter, a rather hawkish Israeli pundit, observed to me that if the problem was the bases of Hezbollah then Peres could have sent a commando expedition to deal with them, so to speak, selectively. This point, though it left untouched the larger issue of Israel's right to be in occupation of southern Lebanon in the first place, was at least congruent with Perlmutter's second point, which was that the actual collective punishment had increased support for Hezbollah and stored up future trouble, while exposing Israeli soldiers to the temptation to commit crimes against the defenseless. I think we may take it that this same advice was available to Peres. So, what is wrong with the following factual assertion: "Shimon Peres, leader of a party that is a member of the Socialist International, ostentatiously killed and scattered the civilians of another country in order to protect himself from domestic criticism and to guard a personal and electoral flank?"

If A had said this, then B might have replied (as the Clinton-Gore administration indeed did) that one had to bear in mind the "peace process" and the dangers of a Netanyahu victory. Yet there *was* a Netanyahu victory, and who can say that, by echoing Netanyahu on the fetish of "security" in this way, Peres did not (subjectively and yes, "objectively") assist in bringing this about?

Let's keep score. The As would have made a correct moral point and been able to claim that in doing so they had not undermined their "own" side. The Bs would have sat on their hands morally, or perhaps applauded something very questionable indeed, and seen their own side defeated not with honor but instead with ignominy. Clintonoid score: uncritically pro-B, but retaining the power (and the readiness) to shift to Netanyahu in any case.

• In Italy, a ramshackle coalition of Stalinist, Eurocommunist, liberal, and centrist forces narrowly outpointed an opportunist alliance of neofascist, fascist, clerical, separatist, and conservative parties. What's not to like about that? True, the left put forward a mediocre candidate of conciliation to "reassure" waverers. True, also, the left will now have to impose an "austerity" budget. True, perhaps, that the next time around the right will be led by the neofascist Gianfranco Fini, who will run against the austerity program and possibly win. Not much alternative here: the balance of forces is too equal. Factual statement: "The As accepted the logic of the Bs, who accepted most of the logic of their right-wing opponents, who were glad to be out of power in a crisis period." Clintonoid score: neutral. Had already said that they did not object to the presence of neofascists in government (a postwar European first).

• In Bosnia-Herzegovina, the Dayton accords created conditions where those parties would do best that represented a one-nation, one-religion, one-leader ideology—very much in accordance with the partitionist spirit of the accords themselves. Only one leader of one party in one post-Yugoslav republic stood both for democracy as the end as well as the means, and for multi-ethnic pluralism as the system as well as the goal. This was Haris Siladzic, at different times prime minister and foreign minister, and now leader of the Party of Bosnia-Herzegovina. He had separated himself from the ruling SDA (Party of Democratic Action) under whose colors the war of liberation had largely been fought. In June 1996, campaigning near Bihac, he was attacked by an Islamist mob, loyal to the ruling party, and beaten to the ground with an iron bar. Most reports from the region ignored this "incident," since the electoral "process" was seen as a referendum or plebiscite on a pre-arranged decision to divide Bosnia into three one-party and one-religion cantons. A vote for Siladzic, in this discourse, was a wasted vote and a romantic gesture, an inconvenience to the pragmatists and realists who said, indignantly, that war was the "only alternative" to their peace plan—which had itself, be it noted, grown out of a war they had licensed.

Difficult to score this one as between A and B, since As and Bs had taken different and similar positions on the war and on partition. But a definite defeat for those who opposed both ethnic partition and the use of force to achieve it. Clintonoid score: indifferent to the war at the first; favorable to partition throughout; most inclined to think of all ruling-party signatories to Dayton (Milosevic, Tudjman, and Izetbegovic) as the only "players" worth bothering about. Very hard, however, to classify Izetbegovic versus Siladzic as in any intelligible sense as the "lesser evil." It could only be true if those with the power to decide such things decided to make it so.

• In the instance of Russia, what is wrong with the following factual assertion: "With Boris Yeltsin, the United States worked tirelessly to assure the political triumph of a drunken, moribund, authoritarian war criminal"? Nothing, as a matter of fact, except when we do our patriotic duty and "consider the alternatives." When compounded of the elements of renascent Stalinism and chauvinism, this argument from alternatives has the hoped-for effect of a Medusa's head. It turns all criticism into stone. And in such a petrified landscape, who has time or permission to notice the other "alternatives"? Sergei Kovalev, for example, who inherited the mantle of Andrei Sakharov and who resigned as Yeltsin's human rights *responsable* over the butchery in Chechnya. Or a host of other citizens and rights groups who, once their ruling enemy was defined as indispensable vis à vis their more traditional enemy, found all the oxygen sucked out of their atmosphere. ("You don't like our Boris? Surely you're not saying you really want a return to the past.")

Once Yeltsin had become "our" man, moreover, there is no guarantee that he would not have been defended just as dogmatically against a *more* democratic opponent. It's been known to happen in American foreign policy. Yeltsin was, for example, given great latitude to protect and defend Slobodan Milosevic lest any affront to the Serbs increase his own difficulties with Orthodox and irredentist types. And even Milosevic has benefited in his time from being a "lesser evil," indeed continues to do so. So let us at least, as we pay our regular rental to pragmatism, be honest. Let us admit that we know what the price is going to be. Once secure in his position as a "lesser" evil, Yeltsin is free to be more and more "great" an evil, if not indeed greater. This ratchet-like rule will apply in other comparable situations.

The As were right in many ways this time, in predicting early that Yeltsin would turn out to be a bully and a demagogue and a chauvinist. The Bs could hardly be expected to give up their point that there were worse demagogues and chauvinists around. Clintonoid score: they endorsed Yeltsin whether he was a bully and demagogue and chauvinist or not, and thus have a large share in his crimes as well as his comparative and marginal advantages.

Now let us see how this macro-argument plays out in the case of Clinton and the left. And here is a micro-example. David Mixner is well-known in both gay and liberal Democratic circles as a highly effective activist and organizer. He was a major fund-raiser for the Clinton administration. During the last election, he "delivered" large sums of money and large quantities of votes to the Clinton ticket, making this the first presidential election in which the organized "gay vote" played a distinctive role. The campaign pledge to lift the ban on homosexuals serving in the military was the high-profile *quid* for this *quo*, and enjoyed wide public sympathy. No need to rehearse what happened to that. Mixner nonetheless continued his loyal efforts on behalf of the administration. His reward, last June, was a presidential announcement that, as soon as the "Defense of Marriage Act" could be rammed through both houses, Clinton was impatient to sign it. Faced with such an undignified willingness to capitulate to the Christian Right before battle had even been joined, Mixner spoke bitterly of "an ugly, vicious act" and "one of the most immoral things I've ever seen him [Clinton] do." But, as he made haste to tell Michael Kelly of the *New Yorker*, he was still intending to vote for Clinton this fall. "Politically, he did the right thing. They made a correct calculation that they could do this to us and get away with it."

Here, stated in its full masochistic form, is the very essence of "lesser evilism." If it were a doctrine, instead of a reflex or a dogma, it would be a doctrine without limits. Try rephrasing it. "We have already made the decision that they can do this to us and get away with it. We have made this decision known in advance. *Ergo* they can and will get away with it."

In four short years, Clinton has made himself both the patron and the serf of corporate America, and not just "presided" over the national polarization of power and wealth and income, but actively sponsored it. He has advertised himself as the candidate of capital punishment, and his crime and terrorism bills have cut great roads through civil liberty and habeas corpus. He has awarded the military-industrial complex a heavier share of the national budget than it even had the nerve to demand. He has fired or abandoned, with contempt, any members of his government, or any nominees for government service, who come under the least attack from the right. He has made the morals of the underclass into the touchstone issue, holding the poor accountable for their conduct in a way that he would never dare to do with his rich campaign donors. He has proposed the dumping of a half-century-old commitment to provide a welfare minimum for all American children. He has dissipated a once-dynamic consensus in favor of national health care. Absurd insinuations from the GOP to the contrary, there is every reason to suppose that Clinton has fully internalized all the regnant assumptions of power in America, and that a second term would see all these tendencies become more full blown. And until August, his re-election strategy was being crafted by a paid-up Republican strategist, Dick Morris, who cut his teeth working for Jesse Helms. Evidently, the calculation had been made that Clinton "can do this to us and get away with it."

Now, if all this were being done by Bush or Dole, it might or might not be more thorough and brutal. But one thing can be stated with confidence. It would be meeting with *opposition*. I had the most remarkable conversation recently with Senator Daniel Patrick Moynihan. In a speech on the proposed welfare compromise—the one that pitches perhaps a million children off the support rolls—he had asked what had happened to the dozens of well-organized lobbying groups who usually watch out for the interests of the poor and neglected. They had fallen silent. They were shuffling their feet. They had demobilized. "I had *to shame* them," said the original begetter of "welfare reform." Much the same could be said about civil libertarians and the crime and terrorism bills, and about labor and African-American forces across the board. We are, albeit in a "soft" way, back in the petrified world of party-mindedness, where Democratic centralism brooks no disunity and where dissenters are accused of "giving ammunition to the enemy" or weakening the united front. I would not undertake to say for certain whether this state of affairs qualifies as "lesser," because the "lesser" is an assumption at once unprovable and unfalsifiable. But I can certainly recognize it as "evil," for all the good that does me. And I think that the examples, of Mixner and of welfare "reform," are sufficient refutation of a certain line popular among left-liberals. Let us have a "two-track" strategy, say these master tacticians. Let us vote for Clinton on Tuesday, and mobilize independently of, and if necessary against, him on Wednesday. Not only do the arguments that sustain the first have a tendency to militate against the second, but so do the habits of mind and patterns of behavior.

It might be objected that there is no reason *in principle* (and therefore, no reason in practice) why one cannot chant the above slogan and succeed in having it both ways. But it will be found, both in practice and in principle, that all euphemisms and all compromises and all adaptations exact their toll. For one thing, this is not a four-yearly excruciation. It goes on, as does the campaign process, all the time. Once concede that you are with party B, and that's all anyone wants to know about you. The hundred-and-one local, regional, and "mid-term" pressures will replicate themselves across the board, and allow less freedom of choice rather than more. Well—since we are after all speaking of brute practicalities—*cui bono?* Oh dear, it turns out that the beneficiary will always be the person who takes the party-line argument in deadly earnest. So, just this once, let's give the benefit of the doubt to Marion Barry or Richard Daley or Edwin Edwards. Do you suppose that they worry about the exquisiteness of your calibration? Do you imagine that in a bottom-line argument, you can out-bottom-line them? The onus here is on those who hold the contrary opinion. When, in fact, did they ever multiply the difficulties of a supposedly friendly incumbent, or potentially friendly candidate, under this flag?

To take the classic instance of opposition politics, is it not the case that many liberals and even leftists (and even *Dissent*niks) were inclined to hang back about the Vietnam war and about civil rights, for no better reason than that a possibly friendly White House might be upset? Might not the Mississippi delegation have been seated at the Democratic convention a little earlier if the Democratic party had been out of power? I don't claim to know the answer (though I think I can guess it) but I do remember how the arguments went and I hate to see them being so smoothly recycled. This brings us smack up against the ironies of history. Irony is marketed at a

discount these days. The last time I can remember it being
deployed at full strength was during the gubernatorial election
in Louisiana in 1992. The above-mentioned Edwin Edwards, a
high-octane fraud and poseur and captive of the special interests, was the Democratic standard-bearer against David Duke.
Well, that should have been an easy enough call—if you could
forget the role of people like Edwards in recruiting populist
support for a person like Duke in the first place. Anyway, the
anti-Duke activists in New Orleans and Baton Rouge, and
many tougher spots, came up as they had to with the disarming
slogan: "Vote For the Crook. It's Important." To this declension
we have all come, by degrees that were invisible until they
became explicit. Hurray for all those who brought us to this
pass, and will bring us to narrower ones.

Ironies of history are not just conversation points. Should
it not concern us that the other side knows when to lose? Just
be Newt Gingrich for a moment. Do you suppose that he wants
Bob Dole to become president? I have heard his acolytes snick-
ering to the contrary these past two years. His entire power of
patronage and placemanship demands a Democrat in the
White House. And what about Bill Clinton? Why do we imagine so automatically that he desires the return of a Democratic
Congress? His whole "take-off" as a re-electable president began with the eclipse of his own party in White House and
Senate. I hate to say it (all right, I don't actually *hate* to say it)
but it's a bad day when *Commentary* magazine shows a superior grasp of the ironies. Reviewing the near destruction of the
Democratic party in the July 1996 issue, the intelligent conservative Daniel Casse had this to say:

> In the shadow of November 1994, what few could have
> predicted was that the ousting of the Democratic ma-
> jorities in both houses of Congress would turn out to
> be, for the President, a liberating experience. . . .
> Since January of this year, the President has appeared
> bent not only on imitating but on seizing on the Re-

publican agenda . . . Far from trying to rebuild the
party, Clinton is trying to decouple the presidential engine from the congressional train. He has learned how
the Republicans can be, at once, a steady source of
new ideas and a perfect foil.

Anyone who wishes to play the old "lesser evil" board
game after considering the above had best put himself in the
position of his smartest opponent. Time spent in that way is
seldom wasted.

If the purely pragmatic ingredient of lesser evilism were
any good, it would surely appeal to those who make a virtue
precisely of their pragmatism: the conservative Democrats and
right-wing Lib-Lab types. Yet these forces, whenever faced
with a turn in the party that they do not care for, are always
ready to jettison lesser evilism. "Democrats for Nixon" did so
well, in fact, that it became the building block for the Democratic Leadership Council and eventually for the Clinton candi-
dacy itself, just in nice time to sound the "lesser evil" alarm for
everybody else. Those "social democrats" who fled the Labour
party in the face of Thatcherism, and who ensured Thatcherism's success at two subsequent general elections, have now
made their peace at a high price and been readmitted to a
Labour party that brooks no criticism *at all* from the left. The
Tony Blair "project" depends, after all, on a clear unity against
the Tory foe. So . . . not in front of the *goyim,* if you please.

There is an enduring legend, among those foot soldiers
who always stayed loyal (to generals who found them expend-
able), that it was the left that secured Nixon's original victory in
1968. In that year, with the country ruined by an imperialist
war and with the gains of the civil rights movement callously
flung away and with a state-sponsored campaign against dissent
in full swing, some people actually did say that they would not
vote for a man, Hubert Humphrey, who was directly complicit
in all this. The revolt was more one of moral revulsion than of

political principle but it did at least say out loud what is supposed never to be said—that there is a limit of decency beyond which one should not allow oneself to be pushed. The self-correcting mechanism of emotional coercion temporarily broke down, or at least faltered. And as it happened, the Democratic ticket was narrowly defeated that year. But it wasn't the fault of the few isolated rejectionists. The leadership had spent the preceding four years steadily destroying the basis for reformist politics and consciously crushing opposition within the party itself. On the eve of the vote, furthermore (as we suspected then, and has been attested since in the memoirs of Clark Clifford and H. R. Haldeman), the Johnson-Humphrey forces came into possession of information that might have made the difference. They discovered an unethical and probably illegal back channel between Nixon and the South Vietnamese junta. Pull out of the Paris peace talks at the last minute, said Nixon and Kissinger to their friends, and Saigon will get a better deal from the Republican victors. Humphrey personally decided not to go public with this devastating intelligence, according to Clifford, because it would do such damage to bipartisan civility. So power takes care of itself, and as for the birds . . . well, they can always chirrup "lesser evil" in tones of surprised relief. But if the two-party collusion is the evil itself, then the birds will have to learn a new song.

"Consider the alternatives." Not a bad mantra, when you come really to reflect upon it. We should all, always, be considering the alternatives. That's what we engage in politics to do. The argument from the lesser evil, however, has become a different sort of mantra; one designed precisely to *quench* the consideration of alternatives. There is an undistributed middle in the lesser-evil syllogism, and a rather indigestible one at that. It suggests that we are not responsible for what we *do* vote for, only for what we vote against. It is therefore morally shady. It commits us in advance to underwrite those who have an objective quite different from our own, and methods entirely different. It places a guard upon the tongue, and upon the exercise of critical intelligence. It is both ahistorical and unhistorical. It is not even useful as a tactical resort (which is just as well, since it can be so simply grasped as to make any op-ed amateur into a master strategist). Those in power in our present politics already possess, by way of excuses and self-justifications, an *embarasse de richesse.* It is not our task to devise, on their behalf, further evasions.

Diana Trilling

Goronwy—and Others:
A Remembrance of England

When late in 1979 the news reached me that Goronwy Rees had died in London, I had not seen him for a long time, more than six years, other than for the two or three hours we had spent together on his visit to America four years earlier, shortly before my husband died, nor had he and I, or he and Lionel, been in correspondence since we had last been in England six years earlier. On the occasion of his brief stop-over in New York—he was here for only a weekend—the two of us, Goronwy and I, met for a quiet lunch, after which he came to our apartment to make his farewell to Lionel. Lionel died not many days later and in a forthcoming issue of *Encounter* magazine, the distinguished Anglo-American journal to which Goronwy contributed a monthly column, he published a moving memorial to his American friend.

There was of course no reason for Goronwy's not having simply explained to me why he was in New York for only so short a time when he at last—at long last—got to this country and why his stay in New York followed a similarly brief visit to San Francisco. His daughter, Jenny Rees, has now published in England a biography of her father, *Looking for Mr. Nobody,* and from her careful reconstruction of his movements I learn that in 1975 Goronwy visited the United States, also Canada and Australia, as part of a quick overview of the Dalgety Enterprises about which he had been commissioned to write a book. He hurried the visit because his wife Margie was now gravely ill and he wanted to get back to her as fast as possible.

But why did he himself not make this explanation to me? The answer, I fear, is all too obvious. Secrecy was Goronwy's habit and nourishment. Like a familiar perfume, it announced and trailed him. In Jenny Rees's memory of her family, mystery had always pervaded the Rees household. In fact, it was in order to discover what her parents hid from their children and from the world—it was a Secret so portentous that it is regularly capitalized in her book—that she undertook her research into her father's life.

From the start of our acquaintance with Margie and Goronwy, I had the sense, not of Goronwy alone but of the pair of them, that there was something they withheld from us, an aspect of their thought or experience which, though it undoubtedly had its original reference to Goronwy rather than Margie, had come to color not only his state of being but hers as well. While one would not have thought to describe Goronwy as a silent person, he seemed always to be on guard in conversation. He was the author of several volumes of memoirs, yet he employed the medium more for the statement of ideas or, as in the case of *A Chapter of Accidents,* to correct the troubling historical record than for self-exploration. Even his column for *Encounter* was signed with only the initial "R," as if, by keeping the whole of his name from view, he was himself shielded. And indeed this was in some part the case. In America, even regular readers of *Encounter* were little aware of him as a figure in the literary life of our time and as for his reputation in England— well, in England he was always recognized less for his critical accomplishment than for his association with the notorious Cambridge spies, Guy Burgess, Donald Maclean, Kim Philby and Anthony Blunt, in particular his long-time friend Guy Burgess.

Goronwy was himself not a Cambridge man nor was he, like Burgess and Burgess's co-conspirators, a product of the British public schools. He was Welsh, the son of a well-known theologian, and had attended a grammar school in Cardiff. His university was "the other place," Oxford, which he attended on scholarship. Oxford had also been his father's university. At Oxford he took a First and on graduation won a much-coveted junior fellowship at All Souls. But the academic promise he had shown as a student was not to be realized: he gave up his All Souls fellowship to travel on the Continent and try his hand at fiction. Although he published several novels, he was never successful as a fiction writer. On his return to England, until he joined the army in the late summer of 1939, he earned a precarious living in various branches of the higher journalism. Early in the war, he met and married Margie with whom he fathered a family of five children. In the early Fifties, he returned to Oxford as Estates Bursar at All Souls, a position from which he was recalled to his native Wales to become Principal of University College at Aberystwyth.

It was while Rees was in his Aberystwyth post that he effectively ruined his career. Whether because he was in need of money—he usually was—or because he was driven for patriotic reason to alert Britain to the presence of Soviet spies at high levels of British government, he published a series of articles in which he revealed the traitorous activities of Guy Burgess. He had been an intimate of Burgess for many years, ever since they had come to know each other while Burgess was still a Cambridge undergraduate and Goronwy had just taken up his fellowship at All Souls. Whatever his motive in making the disclosure, he could not have chosen a less fortunate vehicle for it. His series of six articles appeared in a popular British weekly, *People*. They were unsigned but their author was immediately recognized. By now Burgess's involvement in Soviet espionage was of course widely known: it was five years since, together with Donald Maclean, he had fled the country. Actually, only a short time before the appearance of Rees's series, he had surfaced in a television interview in Moscow. The punishment meted out to Rees for his revelations about his friend was nevertheless prompt, cruel and lasting. He was forced to resign his position at Aberystwyth. More, he was permanently ostracized by his old acquaintances at Oxford and by the British intellectual establishment. As late as 1964, when Lionel and I came to Oxford for Lionel to take up his year's appointment as Eastman Professor, Goronwy was still "received" at his old university by only two friends from the past, John Sparrow, then head of All Souls, and the renowned intellectual historian, Sir Isaiah Berlin.

It is plain that E. M. Forster was not alone among the educated British in believing that as between betraying one's country and betraying a friend, it was far preferable to betray one's country. In response to Rees's exposure of the already self-exposed Burgess, the noted Oxford classicist Maurice Bowra proposed that a stand of Judas trees be planted in Rees's name. No one proposed that the traitorous Guy Burgess be similarly dishonored.

Maurice Bowra was homosexual, as was Guy Burgess. On his first meeting with Goronwy, Burgess had made a homosexual advance which Goronwy pleasantly rejected—even at this early age, Goronwy was already an accomplished womanizer (that lovely English word). E. M. Forster, too, was homosexual and there is small doubt but that there was an element of sexual kinship in the unwillingness of so many of Burgess's associates to be troubled by his treason: Goronwy's exposure of Burgess bore all too closely upon Britain's homosexual community. The Cambridge spy ring had come into existence in the Thirties when in Britain, as in America, the economic depression was at its height and when Communism on the Soviet model was being embraced by many of its best-educated and idealistic young people as the sole remedy for the glaring failures of capitalism. It was also a period in which homosexuality, widespread though it might be in practice, was harshly condemned in British social custom and law. The left-wing British homosexual could well feel that his sexual preference made him an alien in his own country and that to betray Britain to the Soviet Union, far from being an act of treason, was an act of hope.

In the years of our friendship with the Reeses—they extended from 1964 until 1973, when we were last in England—neither Margie nor Goronwy ever spoke of Guy Burgess to us or alluded to the Aberystwyth incident. Other than to speak of the Hiss-Chambers case, a subject to which Goronwy recurred with some persistence, we indeed spoke very little of politics. I nonetheless assumed—and I am sure that Lionel did, too—that politics were not only important to Goronwy but the ground in which was planted at least one root of his romantic adventurousness. I recall, for instance, that after one of his inquiries about Chambers, I proposed to Lionel, and not in entire frivolity, that perhaps Goronwy had himself once been a spy.

What we did speak about with the Reeses now escapes me. What, after all, does one talk about as one moves from acquaintance to friendship with someone one has newly met? What is it that initiates or bolsters the relationship, separating it from the more ordinary of one's social encounters, those which make up the everyday content of our lives but fail to give them their substance or shine?

Eventually, someone other than Goronwy or Margie did tell us of the Aberystwyth publication. This could not but have happened since every knowledgeable Briton knew about it. It would turn out, however, that this was not the Secret which inspired Goronwy's daughter to launch her researches. With the collapse of the Soviet Union, the files of Soviet Intelligence were slowly becoming accessible to foreign scholars and in 1993 a respected British historian of espionage, John Costello, writing in collaboration with Oleg Tsarev, a former Colonel in the KGB who had become Historical Consultant to the new Russian Foreign Intelligence Service, published a volume called *Deadly Illusions* which disclosed that Goronwy, once so much at pains to publicize the treason of others, had himself been a Soviet agent. In studying her father's life, it was the truth or untruth of this charge that Jenny set out to investigate.

If true, this was the upper-case Secret, the mystery of mysteries, which had shadowed the Rees household.

We were introduced to Goronwy by Fred Warburg of the English publishing firm of Secker & Warburg. Fred had for some time been Lionel's British publisher and he was about to become mine as well. In literary circles in New York he was chiefly known as the publisher and friend of George Orwell. While this gave him literary distinction, it also brought him political distrust: left-wing intellectuals have never been able to comprehend how anyone with Orwell's supposedly liberal principles could also be so firm and vocal an anti-Communist. To most people this obviously meant that in making the claim to liberalism Orwell was sailing under false colors.

Warburg frequently came to New York on book-buying trips and sometimes Lionel and I had had a drink or dinner with him. He was a tall, handsome man with a long, narrow face, olive-skinned, with bold aquiline features. His tailoring was almost too impeccable; in a careless world it drew attention to itself. What I was particularly impressed by in him was his air of good breeding, as it would once have been called; everything about him, not only the way he dressed but the way he sat or walked, the way he handled himself in conversation, was testimony to his unimpeachable upbringing. Late in life, he would publish an autobiography, *A Gentleman's Profession*. Its title was embarrassingly appropriate: Fred was nothing if not a gentleman-publisher. Plainly, his marriage to the obstreperous Pamela was his single bid for freedom from the rigid rules of behavior in which he had been reared and in which he was otherwise still bound.

Until our invitation to dinner at Fred's flat in London, neither Lionel nor I had met his French-born wife, Pamela de Bayou, as she was known in the offices of Secker & Warburg where, though her name didn't appear as a member of the firm, she exerted a considerable influence in its operations. There was no trace of foreign accent in Pamela's speech, and if it weren't for her French name, one would not easily have guessed her birth. It was also difficult to determine her age; her air of shrewdness made her seem older than she probably was. While she was not in any conventional sense pretty, she had the assurance of a woman accustomed to the attention of men. That Fred doted on her was not to be missed though in her company he was measurably less a person than when we had met him alone. She was his challenge to decorum but the thief of his authority.

One hadn't to be in Pamela's company for long to become aware of the pleasure she took in outraging the proprieties. Not long ago I spoke of her to a friend in America who had been one of Fred's early authors. "Pamela de Bayou," he chuckled. "What a terror! I remember the first time I met her. The three of us were having dinner together and she opened the conversation by saying that she had had an awful day. She had lost her tampon. Inside her. She screamed this unlikely story so loudly that everyone in the restaurant was looking at her!"

We were staying in a hotel in London's West End and took a cab to the Warburgs'. They lived on a modest street a short distance beyond Regents Park in a building some six or eight storeys tall. The dull, unbroken façade which their apartment house presented to the street labeled it "modern," in the style which in the Sixties had begun to replace the traditional architecture of London. The Warburgs lived on an upper floor and to reach their flat we had to entrust ourselves to a lift so tiny that we felt that we were being propelled skyward in a coffin.

It was a small party they had put together for us, two other couples in addition to them and ourselves: Goronwy and Margie Rees and the playwright John Osborne and his then wife Penelope Gilliatt. In the interval before the other guests gathered, the Warburgs proudly took us out on the strip of balcony which bordered their sitting-room—one looked down on a dim spread of scrubby field, dotted here and there with a low-lying house and a scattering of trees. Awaiting the other guests I sipped my pre-dinner sherry and pondered the width of ocean that separated the publishing life of England from that of the United States. Where, I wondered, was an American publisher who would be as content as Warburg with his small show of worldly success: his three-room apartment and his scrap of a view?

I had not been in England since early childhood and I was being regularly surprised in my first confrontation with the differences between our two countries. We shared a language and a substantial portion of our cultural heritage, but then what? Lionel and I could not have been more cordially welcomed than by the people we were meeting, yet strange barriers rose between us which didn't have to be perceived as in any way hostile for us to experience them as divisions to be noted, and a chasm bridged. Later, after living in Oxford for several months, Lionel and I would go on holiday to France or Holland or Italy: we would find it strange that in these other countries we were more at home than with our new British acquaintances. Long ago, H. G. Wells had mocked the idea of national traits, dismissing them as governess talk, the unexamined formulations of the nursery, but how, other than as tokens of national character, was one to explain the reiterated appearance of patterns of speech and conduct so distinct from our own, the prevailing taste, for instance, for self-dramatization which seemed to impel the British, even in their most commonplace occupations, choosing, say, a tomato at the greengrocer's or cashing a check at the local bank, to wring the last bit of theater from these prosaic routines or, at another and more troubling extreme of social habit, the readiness of the English to forget their still-recent war and forgive the enemy, as if the contest had indeed been only a game and their bombed-out city its playing field? In 1964 a mere twenty years had elapsed since Hitler's defeat. The scars which the blitz had left upon London were still visible. The fact that flowers bloomed in the craters which still marred some of the less prominent streets of London didn't camouflage their wartime origin. Yet we heard no mention of the war from anyone in England and it would constitute for Lionel and me a vitalizing return to reality to visit in Amsterdam and be at once taken to the home of Anne Frank and to the synagogue which, whatever the intent of the Nazis, still so solidly stood its ground.

The Warburgs' dinner wasn't the most stirring entertainment one might have anticipated. Ironically, for this occasion it was the French-born Pamela who produced what little drama the evening offered. "The English are the dirtiest people in the world," she proclaimed as we gathered at the table. She looked around at her guests invitingly, soliciting contradiction. As a shocker, it was a distant second to her lost tampon. No one ventured a reply. The remark lay on the table like a flattened balloon.

The Osbornes were not really aloof from the rest of us but they were quiet guests. They did their conversational duty but it was clear that they were not eager celebrants of the occasion. It struck me that they were perhaps disappointed in the company which the Warburgs had provided for them and were sitting out the time until they could go elsewhere more to their taste.

While the Reeses were quiet as well, they managed to communicate even more than that they were enjoying the evening: a flattering deference to the company in which they found themselves. There was a grace in their social behavior which, together with the straightforward intelligence in everything they said, made me hope that our introduction was a prelude to further acquaintance.

Initially, I was more drawn to Margie than to Goronwy Rees but this soon altered as I grew to like them equally. Margie Rees had surely been a very pretty girl. Even now, in her mid-forties, she was effortlessly appealing. She had a small, mobile face with regular features and a quick generous smile, and she moved with an unconscious grace. I especially liked her manner of speech, her gently-chiding voice. In her speech there was a colloquialism not of her own time, more of the Twenties than the Thirties or Forties. In America it would have been realized that she had first appeared in the pages of F. Scott Fitzgerald. As I came to know her better, I would often think how lucky Fitzgerald would have been if, in what we like to call "real life," he had had Goronwy's Margie as his wife instead of his unfortunate Zelda.

Goronwy Rees was probably the most attractive man I have ever met—I soon learned that a crowded calendar of sexual conquests attested to his power with women. At the time we met, he was already in his mid-fifties but he was still slim and lithe, quick-moving. His face was at once boyish and, like that of the poet Auden, deeply furrowed by experience. I forget the color of his eyes but not their probing inquisitiveness. It would always be a question whether what he was searching out was one's good will or its opposite, one's suspiciousness and doubt of him. His smile was frequent and brilliant but ultimately lacking in mirth. I do not mean that it was a mechanical smile, a mere twitch of the lips. It was full and pleasing, dangerously so. But it was gone as fast as it had appeared, like a curtain which rises for an instant to reveal a scene of joy, only in the next instant to fall abruptly, robbing us of our happy illusion.

I remember little of our talk this first night of our meeting with the Reeses, not much else than Lionel's and my antiphonal account of the curious occurrence in our taxi as we had been driving to the Warburgs' earlier that evening. Our cab had been halted by a traffic light and another cab had drawn up alongside of us. It appeared to be driven by a friend of our driver; the two men greeted each other familiarly and our driver called out: "the Warburgs." To this mention of our destination the other driver nodded appreciatively. What Lionel and I couldn't understand was how our driver knew whom we were visiting. Giving him the address to which we wished to be taken, Lionel had mentioned only a street and number, not a name; and even if he overheard us speaking of the Warburgs, why did our driver want to share this information with his friend?

Pamela supplied the answer. We had undoubtedly been driven by the same cabbie who, with her encouragement, had submitted a novel to her. It was a promising subject for a work of fiction, was it not? Pamela inquired brightly of us. Life as seen through the eyes of a London cab driver? But the manuscript had now been submitted and she would have to write him a note of rejection. She would give the disappointed author the name of a rival publishing house to which he could send his book, she concluded naughtily.

Throughout her explanation Warburg regarded his wife with unwavering admiration and when, some months later, Goronwy would tell me of his old affair with Pamela, I would retrieve, as from a computer, this expression on Warburg's face, this declaration of his unfaltering love. Why, I asked myself then and still ask, why an affair with Pamela of all people, and why had Goronwy made this intimate disclosure to me? "She had the softest skin of any woman I had ever known," he assured me in response to my unasked question and added, unnecessarily: "All over." Boo! I replied silently. The discovery of his wife's infidelity, Goronwy told me, had all but destroyed the Warburgs' marriage and Fred's life. Broken-hearted, he had packed to leave but Pamela had managed to hold him back. The affair had ended and she and Fred had once more become their old devoted selves.

Together, there was now no hint of constraint between Fred and Goronwy, nor any visible flutter of excitement on Pamela's side beyond the stir which, I was already gathering, she always created around her. And Margie? What about Margie? Dear gentle Margie would seem to be well-practiced in the art of sustaining her marriage, keeping its surface unmarred, its depths unroiled.

We didn't again see the Reeses with the Warburgs but in the next months we often came down to London from Oxford and now and then met Fred and Pamela for lunch or a drink. On one such visit, the Warburgs took us to lunch at the Athenaeum, Fred's club in London. It may no longer be so but at the time the Athenaeum didn't permit women in its main dining room; women had to be entertained in the adjacent Annex. Whether it was Fred or Pamela who chose it as our place to meet for lunch, Pamela had of course to have approved it. Had she chosen it just because it would allow her to make a fuss?

"Isn't this ridiculous?" she shrilled from the top of the

flight of stairs leading from the door of the Annex to the crowded room in which members dined with their female guests and where Fred and Lionel and I were waiting for her. "Do we women have to put up with this?" In 1964 Pamela's feminist fervor was precocious; women's liberation had just begun to make itself known in England. She meant to provoke whoever heard her in the room at the foot of the stairs and several of the people in the large dining area did in fact look up questioningly. But no one gave any sign of disturbance. As for Fred, as always Fred beamed. Another time when we came to London from Oxford and saw the Warburgs, I heard Pamela tell a captive audience that she had once sat next to Thomas Mann at table and that the famous German author had spent most of the meal with his hand up her skirt.

In the few weeks remaining before we moved from London to Oxford, we saw the Reeses several times, either in their casual comfortable home or at the Old St. James's House, the hotel in London's West End to which we had been recommended by friends in New York. Sadly, I learn that it no longer exists. The Reeses were charmed by the Old St. James's House. They especially responded to something disreputable about it, or not so much disreputable as illicit. Neither of them had heard of our hotel before we asked them to meet us there one late afternoon for a drink.

The Old St. James's House was a group of four-storey brownstones—or it may have been redstones—thrown together at the end of a small dead-end street off St. James's Street and it didn't at all look like a hotel. I assume that all the guests occupied suites, as we did. Ours was a suite on the ground floor and it consisted of a large bedroom, a bath, and a good-sized sitting-room, furnished with sofa, easy chairs, tables, and a giant sideboard equipped with an imposing array of glassware, whiskey glasses, sherry glasses, wine glasses, brandy glasses, champagne glasses. Although the sideboard could supply neither plates nor cutlery, the hotel offered a limited range of food which was served at any hour of the day or night. Yet there was no sign of hotel staff other than the chambermaid who tidied for us each morning and then disappeared and a towering male porter on twenty-four-hour duty, a great hulk of a man who filled the cage-like office in the lobby near the hotel's front door. At night, still in his dowdy uniform, his jacket unbuttoned at the throat, he slept on the office floor. The door of the hotel was locked at ten each evening; if we returned at a later hour than this, the porter would rouse himself and ill-naturedly let us in. There were times when as many as three Rolls Royces were lined up at the curb, none with a chauffeur. Their owners had no doubt come in from the country for a day of innocent errands in London but there were other enticing possibilities to account for their presence.

Over the next months, my hope that we would become friends with the Reeses was steadily realized. Or was it? We did indeed see Margie and Goronwy more frequently than anyone else we knew in London or Oxford but today, as I look back upon the relationship, the never-to-be-answered question recurs to me, whether friendship is ever really possible where people are not joined by a common past. Were we ever friends, I wonder now, with any of the people who comprised our social circle in England or did they simply represent for us a series of pleasant ports of call on our journey away from home, while we represented for them no more than a temporary change in their social landscape, new faces at the old table? I come even to question whether one can ever go beyond congeniality with people of a country other than one's own. Where people haven't grown up together, the newcomer hasn't an assigned place in the social scheme of things. The loyalty among friends which is so much prized by the British has been built over the centuries, brick by precious social brick. It is their most personal and particular expression of class solidarity.

No doubt because of his Welsh background, Goronwy seems to have been more aware than most of the stratifications of class in the England of his time. He addresses this in the early pages of *A Chapter of Accidents,* the memoir he published in 1972 in which he recalls his Oxford experience and his loneliness and sense of apartness from the other students. One evening, he tells us, he was invited to play bridge by some neighbors in his hall. "Very early in the evening," he writes, "I realized that they had so much in common in the way of social background, education, mutual friends and shared experiences that they were able to talk in a kind of conversational shorthand in which a large part of their meaning was unspoken and suppressed. . . . Later, I learned to recognize this . . . as a rather topsy-turvy kind of politeness, which assumes that whatever is known to themselves is known equally to all and has no need of explanation."

How much the disapprobation which later in life would be directed to Rees because of the Aberystwyth incident was due to the fact that he was an outsider, not native to the privileges he acquired through his Oxford education, is difficult for an American to determine with certainty. It may be that Americans are abnormally sensitive to the class structure of British society, but I suspect that his treatment would have been measurably less harsh had Goronwy been writing from within rather than from outside the magic circle of authenticated birth. To this day, I note a discomforting social awareness in virtually any public mention of him. As late as 1994, the British reviewer of Jenny Rees's biography of her father in the *Times Literary Supplement* found it important to record that Rees was "the first state-educated Welshman to be elected to All Souls."

Goronwy's mother died just as he was graduating from Oxford; her loss considerably reduced the pleasure he would otherwise have taken in his First. He writes about her with much affection in *A Chapter of Accidents,* fondly recalling her domestic dutifulness and her missionary devotion to her community. Somewhat more moderately, he also reports his love and respect for his theologian father. Oxford had been the elder Rees's university, too, but no one could have made less claim to the place or been less claimed by it—so far as Goronwy's father can be said to have been shaped by Oxford, he might have taken his degree by correspondence. Back in

Wales, he became one of its outstanding churchmen, a passionate preacher, first in Aberystwyth, then in Cardiff, greatly concerned with the working lives of the Welsh miners. From his father Goronwy had his early training in the progressive politics which he took with him to Oxford and which, through most of the Thirties, announced itself in his commitment to Marxism.

At Oxford, surrounded as he was by the privileged youth of England, Goronwy never ceased to yearn for the simplicity and warmth of his boyhood home, the quiet evenings in his Cardiff parlor, alone with his parents at their books. Inevitably, he took with him into adulthood the lesson of his parents' high-mindedness and their sense of social responsibility. For the whole of his life, this man who would be so widely scorned for his Aberystwyth publication carried within him, whether he was pursuing the parental instruction or seeming to do violence to it, the heavy legacy of parental principle. Even where he plainly flouted the stern "Calvinistic Methodism" (as Jenny calls it) of his upbringing, it continued to make the armature of his moral being.

But I stop myself. This is my view of Goronwy. It is not the view of others who knew him.

I had to sit at the side of Margie Rees as she maneuvered her car on the hazardous highway between Oxford and London in order to have a first intimation of her practical competence and, just so, I had to learn a great deal more about her than was to be gathered from a casual first meeting—indeed, I had finally to see her from the vantage of my present-day knowledge of Goronwy's difficult life—to have some measure of her bravery and dedication as his enduring partner. Today, I think of Margie as no less than a domestic heroine, making her decent home and raising her five children on what was always so insufficient and undependable an income; coping with her husband's infidelities, whatever their extent and however much she came to hear of them; most daunting of demands upon her courage and resilience, managing as she did the consequences of the Aberystwyth incident and Goronwy's tangled relationship with Guy Burgess. If the miracle of Goronwy Rees lay in his having recognized Margie's quality and chosen her as his wife, the miracle of Margie Rees was the grace she brought to her life with a husband who became virtually an official object of public condemnation, someone from whom the people they met at dinner parties drew back their moral skirts.

Margie knew nothing of self-pity. Her gallantry declared itself only as good manners. Her valiant nature served her well: as far back as when we first met, she was already battling the cancer from which she eventually died. This no doubt made for the note of wry fatality which one soon discerned at the edge of her quiet liveliness. I'm sure she died bravely. She died in the summer of 1976, not long after Lionel died. We last saw her in the late spring of 1973. This final time that we were together, she gave me a gift of two little blue and white porcelain fish which I keep on my desk. My hand rests on them now as I write of her.

Gossip is everywhere its own sweet pastime. Although we heard only so minimally of the Aberystwyth scandal, we had been living in Oxford no more than a few months when we learned—I don't now remember from whom—of Goronwy's famous affair with Rosamond Lehmann. Where Goronwy's affair with Pamela Warburg was of relatively recent vintage, the affair with Lehmann was the well-advertised adventure of his youth—it dated from before his marriage. In this affair it was only Lehmann, eight years Goronwy's senior and already married, who was adulterous. Yet as the story was recounted to us, Goronwy was made to seem, even at this early stage of his career, a practiced and conscienceless seducer.

When Goronwy and Rosamond Lehmann met, Lehmann had already published an unusually successful first novel, *Dusty Answer*. She was also a widely-acclaimed beauty. Indeed, I remember from my own young womanhood my admiration for her photograph on the cover of that book, the tranquil, unsmiling face (as I then saw it), with its wide, calm brow; the patrician poise of the head; the finely-chiseled cheeks and chin and the delicately-lined mouth. Today, I leaf through an improbable

English publication, *Rosamond Lehmann's Album*, a pictorial survey of her life, and I not only marvel that such a volume should have been commercially published but I am stupefied that I once thought this image a model of female loveliness. Did the young women of my generation really envy a beauty this blank, this lacking in spirit? Somewhere, wherever it is that people live their lives of feeling, the woman in these photographs had to have been out of reach, or not worth reaching for.

It had been a legendary encounter, the meeting of Lehmann and Rees, and it was reported to me in sunlit detail. On a fine summer afternoon they had both of them been guests at Bowen's Court, the home in Ireland of the novelist Elizabeth Bowen. Rosamond Lehmann was chatting with others of the company in Bowen's sitting-room when the garden doors opened and in came Goronwy. He was barefoot—so went the reverential account—and wore light linen trousers. The sleeves of his shirt were rolled to the elbow and the shirt was Byronically open at the throat. A soft curl of hair fell carelessly over his forehead. Across the sitting-room floor, the beautiful young Rosamond and the beautiful younger Goronwy looked into each other's eyes and fell in love. It was in Rosamond's, not Elizabeth's, bed that Goronwy spent that night—or have I neglected to mention that, according to my informant, Goronwy was Bowen's lover at this time? The walls of the house were not sufficiently solid to keep this hidden from their hostess. There was left to Bowen only such solace as she might one day find in recreating Rees—so it is said—in the character of the repugnant Eddie in her best-known work of fiction, *The Death of the Heart*.

Many years have now passed since I first read this work of Elizabeth Bowen's and on the earlier reading I seem wholly to have missed what now strikes me as its most salient but least attractive feature, its author's bald assumption of the natural superiority of her class. Nowhere does the book challenge Bowen's right, conferred upon her by her own elevated social location, to pass condescending and even dismissive judgment upon those of her characters who happen to be less fortunately situated in the world than herself. The book is undeniably gifted. Few novelists since Dickens have matched Bowen's ability to capture atmosphere—I still feel in my nostrils the wet salt air which blows in from the ocean at the seaside resort where much of her narrative unfolds. And although her Portia, the book's sixteen-year-old protagonist, is much too "fine" for my taste or credence, Bowen's portrayal of the other adolescents in her story is unerringly skillful.

Today, I find it highly unconvincing that Bowen's Eddie is in any sense a portrait of the youthful Goronwy Rees. Bowen was a mature woman, ten years his senior, when she knew Goronwy—he apparently had a penchant for women older than himself. It is unimaginable to me that she would have taken an Eddie, so callow and small-minded, into her home and life. While it may be that at twenty-three, Eddie's age in the novel, Goronwy was in fact a seducer and even a scamp, we know that he was also a developed intelligence, the winner of a First at Oxford and of a highly-valued junior fellowship at All Souls. His youthful distinction of mind is surely not to be confused with the cheap cleverness of an Eddie. We may easily understand that Goronwy at twenty-three would have been attracted to a mature distinguished woman like Bowen, but it defies good sense to suppose that he would have amused himself, as Eddie does, with the love of a child. Bowen's Portia is not an intellectual prodigy, far from it, nor is she a sexual prodigy, a Lolita. She is not presented to us by her author as at all a perverse sexual preference of Eddie's. She is Bowen's notion of virtuous girlhood.

Elizabeth Bowen was living in Oxford during our first year there and we were often at the same Oxford functions. She was an imposing presence in the University community. It was forbidden to smoke at High Table in the Oxford colleges; Bowen alone violated this rule. No one dared to intervene. I watched her light up between courses at dinner at Magdalen; anxious but wordless, the Principal fetched her an ashtray. I was myself then still a compulsive smoker and I envied Bowen her boldness and wished that I could command the deference which she could rely upon. It was difficult for me to associate someone of her weightiness with the roguish boy lover, Eddie.

As I think of this strange trio, Bowen, Lehmann and the youthful Goronwy, my mind returns to silly, noisy Pamela de Bayou, who never achieved the worthy place in English life accorded to these other celebrated women. John Costello, historian of Soviet espionage in Britain, apparently never thought to interview Fred Warburg's wife about her possible acquaintance among the English spies, but we can feel fairly certain that, if he had, she would never have been tempted, like Rosamond Lehmann, to denounce Rees as a liar. She was not moved, like Bowen, to avenge herself upon her former lover and leave us so reductive a portrait of him. Pamela might say whatever came into her foolish head about anyone or anything but never, so far as I know, did she speak at all of Goronwy. On his behalf she practiced an unaccustomed discretion. Once their affair had ended, she maintained an amiable acquaintanceship with her old lover. Hers was a living heart.

There is nothing of this, nothing of Pamela Warburg or Elizabeth Bowen, no mention of Rosamond Lehmann, though the path of her life certainly at many points crossed that of Guy Burgess, in Goronwy's *A Chapter of Accidents*. His memoir is not so much a backward glance over the whole range of his personal and professional experience as a careful recreation of his central drama, his relationship with Burgess. What usually most engages us in autobiography are its opening pages where the author returns to his early years and shares with us his first knowledge of the universe into which he was so fatedly delivered, but though Goronwy's volume deals in adequate detail with his boyhood in Wales and his undergraduate years at Oxford, these are not the heart of the autobiographical matter.

The purpose of *A Chapter of Accidents* is obvious: it provides Rees with the opportunity to tell his side of the famous Aberystwyth story, beginning with the history of his friendship with Burgess and culminating in his exposure of his friend's

activity as a Communist agent. As it works out, the early sections of the book constitute a kind of character reference for
the man who made so disastrous a choice as Goronwy's at Aberystwyth. They assure the reader that this person whom the
world has accused of lies and disloyalty is by birth and upbringing well-certified for honor and good faith.

Goronwy and Burgess first met in Oxford as guests of
Felix Frankfurter, the future Supreme Court Justice who at the
time was an American visiting professor at the University. That
the two brilliant young men were at once drawn to each other
cannot surprise us. Burgess promptly made a homosexual advance to Goronwy; it was declined. Burgess was untroubled by
the refusal. They shared a youthful idealism which expressed
itself in their left-wing politics. At Cambridge, Burgess was a
ripening revolutionary; Goronwy had brought with him to Oxford his father's socialist preference. In the next few years their
paths diverged: Goronwy was travelling on the Continent, writing fiction. But in the mid-Thirties they found themselves living
near each other in London and fell to drinking together at the
same pub or spending their evenings together at Burgess's flat
on Bentinck Street.

Burgess's Bentinck Street dwelling is now famous in London's social history. By all report, it was a sordid affair. Burgess
drank inordinately and lived in filth. He apparently subsisted on
a diet of dried fish and garlic; unrefrigerated, this smelly mash
sat on one of his windowsills. Yet such was his power of mind
and personality that he had no difficulty in bringing the world
to his door, the luminaries of English society no less than a
range of unsavory characters who were present either as an aid
in his undercover political activities or in response to his indiscriminate sexual appetite. Some years later, Malcolm Mugger-
idge, that most finicky of observers, would describe the scene:

> There we found . . . a whole revolutionary *Who's
> Who*. It was the only time I ever met Burgess; and he
> gave me a feeling such as I have never had from any-
> one else, of being morally afflicted in some way. His

very physical presence was, to me, malodorous and sinister. . . . There was not so much a conspiracy gathered round him as just decay and dissolution. It was the end of a class, of a way of life; something that would be written about in history books, like Gibbon on Heliogabalus with wonder and perhaps hilarity, but still tinged with sadness, as all endings are.

According to *A Chapter of Accidents,* it was on an evening in 1936 that Guy Burgess abruptly revealed to Goronwy that he had been a Comintern agent ever since he had come down from Cambridge. He proposed that Goronwy become his fellow-conspirator. Goronwy tells us that he declined the invitation. In this conversation, as a final seductive stroke, Burgess identified for Goronwy one of his, Burgess's, most illustrious partners in espionage: swearing Goronwy to solemnest secrecy, he told him that Anthony Blunt, who was already in 1936 highly regarded as an art historian and critic, was also a Communist agent. It could be that Burgess was very drunk when he made his dangerous disclosure. But more likely he was employing the mention of Blunt as his trump card in the attempt to entice Rees into his spy ring. If someone as respectable and respected as Blunt could spy for the Soviet Union, why should Goronwy hesitate?

Blunt is not identified as this co-conspirator in Goronwy's memoir; no name is supplied for Burgess's partner in spying. Apparently, even as late as 1972, when *A Chapter of Accidents* was published, Goronwy was still intent upon keeping his old promise not to reveal Blunt's part in the Cambridge spy ring. (Actually, however, he had broken this vow almost immediately after he had made it by repeating Burgess's revelation to Rosamond Lehmann, who was then his lover.) But obviously Rees had other reason than the honoring of an old promise for not publicly divulging what Burgess had told him about Blunt. Except for Burgess's word, he had no evidence with which to support an accusation of treason against Blunt and to make the charge without proof would put him at gravest legal and social risk. In the close to forty years since Burgess's mention of Blunt's name as a member of the Cambridge group, Blunt's public eminence had rocketed: he was not only a world-re-nowned historian of art but he was now Keeper of the Queen's Pictures and an intimate of the Palace. Not until Margie had died and Goronwy was himself approaching death would he make public mention of what he had for so long privately known about Blunt. In 1977, recounting what was presumed to be his "whole story" to a British journalist, Andrew Boyle, Goronwy finally made his public accusation of Blunt. Boyle, as it happened, was already on Blunt's trail as a spy.

Today, what is probably most significant for us about *A Chapter of Accidents* is the absence of all suggestion that Goronwy himself, in this period of his involvement with Burgess, also spied for the Soviet Union, whether in response to Burgess's invitation or on his own or other initiative. In fact, in nothing which Goronwy ever wrote does he offer the slightest hint that he was himself a Comintern agent. He readily acknowledges in his memoir that through most of the Thirties he was a Marxist and a Communist sympathizer, but he gives no indication that his revolutionary involvement ever went beyond that of a fellow-traveler—spying was never his own occupation, only the occupation of others. He firmly declares that with the signing of the Nazi-Soviet Pact in the late summer of 1939, he became permanently disaffected with Communism. This no one has of course questioned.

In his youthful travels on the Continent, the grim actuality of Nazism had been lastingly impressed upon Goronwy and he never wavered in his hatred and fear of fascism. He was more than commonly alert to the threat to England which was posed by Chamberlain's appeasement of Hitler at Munich. Forever after the Pact, he was a patriot. In England as in America, however, it is now a long time since patriotism has earned the respect of intellectuals. Love of country is all but ceded to the side of reaction. Even where the patriot is not thought to be politically retrograde, he is assumed to be ungenerous and a creature of convenient moral accommodation.

A Chapter of Accidents moves briskly over the war years and Goronwy's rise in the army from an early volunteer in the Welsh Fusilliers, posted to the docks of Liverpool, to a Lieutenant Colonel on the staff of Field Marshal Montgomery. In this high post he was privy to top military secrets, including Allied plans for the landings in Normandy. The fact that despite his sensitive wartime position, Goronwy continued to frequent the Bentinck Street flat and to drink with Burgess and the riffraff whom Burgess collected around him is, for me, the most disturbing feature of his memoir and of his life. It was early in the war that he had met and married Margie. Margie, too, became friendly with Burgess—he was named godfather to one of the Reeses' sons.

And yet Rees reports in *A Chapter of Accidents* that he was never certain that Burgess had told him the truth when he said that he was a Comintern agent, nor was he convinced that if Burgess had once been a spy, he had continued in this traitorous activity during and after the war. The reader is bound to find such naivete difficult to credit. Day in and day out, before the war, during the war, after the war, the two men engaged in constant political talk. It is hard to suppose that Goronwy drew no conclusions from Burgess's strange associations or from his many shifts in declared political opinion. How could it not have occurred to Rees that behind his various masquerades Burgess pursued the underground assignment to which he had confessed?

However, nothing of Goronwy's historical past, nothing of his political past, entered into our early acquaintance with him and Margie. Even the fact that this attractive couple seemed not to be welcome among their old Oxford friends didn't intrude into our relationship. At most, it left us mildly puzzled.

No matter how well-informed American visitors may be in the history and literature of England, they rarely know as much about that country as the average educated Englishman knows about America. An Englishman's command of past and present American culture and custom is like a natural extension of his schooling in the history of his own country. Goronwy's store of information about the political culture of the United States in recent decades, particularly in the sphere which we in our country now refer to as "cultural politics," that area of our political discourse which bears most directly upon ideas and principles and upon the moral life of the nation, never failed to astonish me.

At the time we met the Reeses, almost twenty years had elapsed since the publication of Lionel's novel, *The Middle of the Journey,* yet Goronwy had this document of American cultural politics at his fingertips. He spoke of Lionel's book as if it had been published only yesterday. He was especially interested in the character of Gifford Maxim. At home, it was generally known of Lionel's novel that Maxim was based upon Whittaker Chambers, Lionel's college acquaintance who had now become famous in the trials that followed his charge that Alger Hiss, an official in the American State Department, had, like Chambers himself, been a Soviet agent. The real-life source of Lionel's fictional character made, I felt, an odd topic for such a reiteration of interest on Goronwy's part, yet Goronwy was apparently magnetized by it. Again and again, he returned to questioning Lionel: How well had he known Chambers? In college? After college? When had he first discovered that Chambers was a Soviet spy and how had this information come to him? Had Lionel liked Chambers? Had he trusted him? What did he know of Chambers's life before joining the Communist Party? After he left the Party? Did Lionel feel that Chambers had been treated fairly by the American intellectual community? It was soon clear that the importance which Lionel's novel had for Rees had little to do with its merit as a work of fiction and all to do with Rees's interest in the original of this one of its characters.

Throughout these interrogations, it was only Chambers of whom Goronwy inquired, never Hiss with whom Chambers's name was now so inexorably linked. There were now of course a number of people in England, as in America, who believed that Hiss was innocent of the accusation which Chambers had brought against him, but Goronwy was not among them. Implicit in all his references to Chambers was the opinion—it was ours as well—that Chambers had been telling the truth when he accused Hiss as he did and that Hiss had spied for the Soviet Union. It was not debate about Hiss's guilt or innocence which moved Rees to question Lionel. On this point his mind was settled. What he sought from Lionel was personal information about Chambers, of a kind which was not contained in Lionel's book.

As I reconstruct these conversations in the light of the present-day charge against Goronwy, that he, too, like the members of the Cambridge group, Burgess and Philby and the rest, spied for the Soviet Union, they necessarily take on new meaning. I realize that in Chambers's burdened life Goronwy recognized a parallel to his own much-burdened life and something of this must even have communicated itself to me at the time because, as I say, I suggested to Lionel that, like Chambers, Goronwy may once have been an agent of the Soviet Union, or perhaps a British agent, or both. But Lionel was not inclined to speculation of this sort and I soon dropped the subject.

Actually, in some important part I shared Lionel's reluctance to see Goronwy as a figure in this dark political program of our century. I preferred to think of him as reckless in love rather than in politics, a romantic rather than an ideological adventurer. Yet considering the fact that he was the most attractive man I ever met, it is strange that he was never, for my imagination, an object of direct sexual interest. One evening he and I were alone together at our London hotel while we waited for Margie and Lionel, each engaged elsewhere, to join us. Goronwy was restless; he moved about the room nervously. This was unusual for him. He was not a person who was uncomfortable in his skin. He went to the window and drew aside the heavy draperies; for several moments he stood looking out on our quiet street. Perhaps he was counting the Rolls Royces at our curb. Without turning, he said quietly: "This is where I would have taken you if we had met when we were younger." I made no reply; none was required of me. It was a seduction without an invitation and until I came to write this recollection of our friendship, I had not again thought of it.

Today, there is still something unnatural to me in having to think of Goronwy as only secondarily a charming and intelligent friend and first as a member of his radical generation, someone who so easily but calamitously overstepped the line between Communist fellow-traveling and disloyalty to his country. Whittaker Chambers had similarly breached this thin wall and similarly destroyed his life. Lionel had been at college with Chambers but I scarcely knew him—until, all unexpectedly, he had one day appeared at our apartment to see me. His purpose was to solicit my help in his spying operation. (I have in several places written about this encounter.) He wanted me to receive mail for him. In spy parlance, I was to be his mail drop. I said "no" to his request but I am not convinced that I deserve any great moral credit for the decision. Had the scene been enacted six months earlier, it might have had an opposite outcome. I was approaching the end of what had been almost a year-long commitment to the Communist cause; my disenchantment was about to be translated into a lifelong opposition to the Soviet despotism. Although it had never occurred to me to join the Communist Party, I had been for these past months a devoted adherent of its principles and program and if Chambers had approached me earlier I am far from certain that I would have refused. Treason and even illegalities less extreme than treason are not my moral style and my taste for risk is sadly limited to the life of discourse, yet I recall my bumbling delay in replying to Chambers and the throb of pride which ran through me because he thought me worthy to be part of his conspiracy.

In the years that followed our first stay in Oxford, Lionel and I were frequently back and forth to England and often in the company of the Reeses. Goronwy never spoke of Guy Burgess or Aberystwyth. He reserved to himself many areas of his experience: he never referred to his Welsh boyhood or his travels on the Continent; he never mentioned his novels or his having been an editor of the *Spectator;* he made no mention of having been Estates Bursar at All Souls or of his having been sent to Germany at the end of the war to help in the administration of that conquered country. Even on innocent themes he talked around large gaps, as one might walk around holes in an otherwise solid pavement.

Had it not been for the publication of Costello and Tsarev's *Deadly Illusions,* the case against Rees might have remained what it had always been for the English intellectual establishment: Rees was the man who had so contemptibly betrayed a friend. But this was only the lower-case secret which had had such major consequences for him. It was an uppercase Secret which, as Jenny tells us, had always hung over the Rees household and it was this Secret which she set out to uncover. In her book she lifts the veil on what Margie and Goronwy had for the whole of their marriage struggled to conceal: far back in the Thirties, before the war and even before he had met Margie, Goronwy had briefly been a Comintern agent. He had not stayed long in Stalin's service, probably less than a year. With the Nazi-Soviet Pact, he had become forever disillusioned with Communism. Poor hectored, guilty Goronwy! His long, wearying effort to bury his moment of error had failed.

In the spring of 1965, Norman Mailer published his novel *An American Dream* in England and came to London for its publication. Beverly, his wife at the time, accompanied him. Norman and I had long been friends and I invited him and his wife to visit us in Oxford. Would he like a party, I asked him on the telephone, or would he prefer that we simply have a few people in for dinner? He chose the latter and in reply to my inquiry whether there was anyone whom he would especially like to meet, proposed Iris Murdoch—he had always been interested in her work. We could seat eight people at our dining table in the Eastman house, the residence which accompanied Lionel's appointment, and to the Mailers and ourselves we added Iris Murdoch and her husband, John Bayley, and Margie and Goronwy Rees. The Reeses and the Mailers would stay the night.

I had met Iris Murdoch on several occasions during our Oxford year; like Elizabeth Bowen, she was a notable presence in the university community. She had once asked me to lunch in London but I had found myself as little comfortable in her orderly company as with her disorderly novels. What, I wondered, was this bright-eyed rosy-cheeked woman, so seemingly down to earth and wholesome, up to with these fictional extravagances of hers? Where, in the actual living of her life, did she fit into the rousing universe of her fantasy?

I discovered no answer to these questions in our lunch together. She took me to a family-style Italian restaurant in Soho and over lunch questioned me about my family background and upbringing. I was flattered by her interest in my life but it also made me feel oddly childish. It occurred to me that she might be planning to put me in a novel. That didn't happen.

Within short distance of Oxford there is the town of Cowley. It is importantly devoted to the manufacture of motor cars. As early as the Sixties, Cowley had a supermarket or its simulacrum. Each week I was driven there by an Oxford acquaintance, a young American woman married to an Oxford don. Otherwise, I did my shopping in Oxford's covered market.

By American standards the Cowley supermarket was a modest enterprise; it was in no way as colorful as the covered market on Oxford's High Street. But I welcomed any change in my domestic routine. I was amused by the astonishment with which the young women at the checkout counters regarded my heavily-loaded cart—they looked at it suspiciously, almost fearfully, as if its abundance portended the return of the American army. In reality, ours was a frugal table compared to the meals which we were served by our new Oxford friends. The English were not only more lavish in their hospitality than I was accustomed to in America; they seemed to have a different relation to food. They were more open in their appreciation of what they ate and drank and made a virtually pagan ritual of the appearance of seasonal foods such as strawberries or raspberries.

Obedient to local custom, I served an extra course at our

dinner for Mailer. Poor Mailer! This prolonged our time at table and his suffering. He sat at my right, with Iris Murdoch at his right, and I was able to eavesdrop on their conversation. His anticipated meeting with Murdoch was far from turning out as he must have hoped. She seemed not to understand Mailer's concern with the theater. He had for some time wanted to make his Hollywood novel, *The Deer Park*, into a play and expectably he inquired of Murdoch about her recent achievement in bringing her fiction to the stage. What part, he asked, had she herself had in transforming *A Severed Head* into a play? Was it she who had done most of the dramatization or had this been the work of J. B. Priestley, her collaborator? The tone of his inquiry was entirely respectful. It was clear, if only to me, that he was merely looking for information which might be useful to him in his own attempt to write for the theater. But Murdoch apparently found his questions intrusive and even impertinent. She answered him so cuttingly that at last he turned to me, grinning but red-faced, and drew a finger across his throat. His was the severed head.

But rescue was not yet to be his. Returning to his conversational duty, he quit the subject of playwriting, only to plunge into the yet darker pit of philosophy. When Mailer had spoken to Murdoch of the theater, her rebuff had been unwarrantedly harsh. Now, with considerably more justification, the annihilation was total. Mailer's quixotic fictional representation of the human condition might merit critical disapproval but in the wide range of his work he had regularly demonstrated his capacity to master various fields of technical learning. It required no special training in philosophy, however, to be aware of his miscomprehension of Existentialism, a philosophical doctrine to which he made frequent reference in his writing. Repeatedly in his work he used the word "existential" when he had it in mind to indicate that something was actual or pertained to his experience. Iris Murdoch taught philosophy and had written a definitive book on Existentialism. As I overheard Mailer at my table moving ever more inescapably to his philosophical doom, I wished that I could warn him: Stay off that subject! He at last realized his mistake. He was manly in defeat. "I give up," he announced to Murdoch. "You're the champ!"

Dinner over, I was finally able to bring Mailer and Goronwy together in the sitting room. They seemed to like each other at once: each must instinctively have perceived in the other the hard core of venturousness which lay beneath the surface of his social amiability. I suspect that each of them sensed of the other that he had lived, and perhaps still lived, at what Mailer so admiringly calls the cutting edge of experience. For the remainder of the evening, the two men sat apart from the rest of us, talking prodigiously and drinking prodigiously. Except for a slight thickening of their laughter and a glistening on the brow, neither of them exhibited any effect of the drink. Murdoch and her husband went home early, as soon as politeness allowed. Only now does it occur to me that she may have vented on Mailer some of the annoyance which she had felt at finding herself at dinner with the infamous Rees.

The next morning, Lionel and I and our houseguests had a long, lazy breakfast and then the Reeses drove the Mailers back to London—which is to say that Margie drove Goronwy and the Mailers back to London. It had to have been as astonishing to Mailer as to Lionel and me that Goronwy didn't drive and was content to be driven everywhere by his wife. To look at him, one would suppose that Goronwy sailed, skied, flew his own plane.

With Margie at the wheel and Beverly at her side, Goronwy and Norman had sat in the back, talking. Later Mailer told me that on their drive back to London, Goronwy had repeated to him a remark of mine, that to an American man his car was an extension of his masculinity. Was this so, Goronwy wanted to know of Mailer, and Mailer assured him that it was. The Reeses deposited the Mailers at their London hotel. So far as I know, they never saw each other again, nor did either of them ever inquire of me about the other.

I could wish to have heard what Mailer and Goronwy talked about so absorbedly that evening in our Oxford sitting room. It was not about espionage, of that I can be fairly certain, but how fascinated Mailer would have been had he been granted a glimpse of the business of spying as Goronwy knew of it through his association with the Cambridge group or even through his own direct involvement. Mailer had spent his writing life as a conjurer of the subversive and forbidden. Yet, in sum, his was of course more a universe of personal than political rebellion. The closer he had drawn to what was meant to be the reality of left-wing revolution, as in his second novel, *Barbary Shore*, the more he was lost in allegory. In *Barbary Shore*, the novel which followed his commanding entrance upon the literary world, he had indeed broached the subject of political treason. But he had been far from penetrating its ignoble actuality: Mailer's spy novel is about the hunt for "a little object" which holds the key to the political future of the democracies; its villain is the FBI in sinister alliance with fascism. Such fictional conspirators as Mailer offers us in *Barbary Shore* would consort but poorly with Goronwy's friend on Bentinck Street or with Burgess's scholarly associate, Sir Anthony Blunt.

Other than his continuing readiness to accept each day as independent of what lay either behind or ahead of it, there was little to connect the author of *Barbary Shore* with the Mailer we introduced to Rees. For the Mailer I knew and read, life was not an accretion of experience; it was a progression of un-linked happenings, without any necessary or integral sequence or consequence. His skewed notion of the existential might well have this as its source. The Mailer who wrote *Barbary Shore* had long since yielded place to a newer Mailer, a creature of the newer day. It was his lack of a footing in history that made Mailer so much a man of his own country and century: life was for him always of the present moment, never the total of its moments.

But nothing could have been more the opposite of Goronwy and I wondered if the two men had intuitively recognized this difference which divided them and which, while it allowed them the pleasantest of passing encounters, could promise no future friendship. The British Goronwy was a captive of history. He had no present other than as a sequence or consequence of the past and a foretaste of the future. Like no American life I have known, his was a life heavy with history, tragic with history.

Guy Burgess fled England in 1951. (In *A Chapter of Accidents* Goronwy incorrectly dates his disappearance as 1952.) Before his flight, he phoned Rees at home. Rees was out; Margie took his incoherent message. He was about to do something peculiar, Burgess told her agitatedly, which only Goronwy would understand. In the next days, Goronwy concluded that Burgess had defected to the Soviet Union. More than twenty years later, he records in *A Chapter of Accidents* that it was at this point that he came to realize that Burgess had been telling him the truth when he had confessed to being a Communist agent. Throughout the war and after, Burgess had continued his service to the Comintern.

Even the most authoritative studies of British espionage are a confounding tangle of inconsistencies and of trails which are not pursued to their proposed ends. Although Goronwy regularly makes his appearance in these works, relative to the celebrity of such figures as Blunt or Burgess or Philby or Maclean he remains essentially an illusory figure. The historical literature leaves wide gaps in the narrative of his life, casts a shadow which is never fully defined. A shadow it nevertheless is. Goronwy himself of course complicated the public record of his career by his need to disguise his own role in Soviet espionage. He give us, for instance, two versions of the days following Burgess's flight from England, his story in *A Chapter of Accidents* and the story he told Andrew Boyle a few years later, nearing the end of his life, which Boyle recounted in his. volume, *The Climate of Treason.*

According to *A Chapter of Accidents,* when Rees realized that Burgess had defected to the Soviet Union he telephoned the information to an official of MI5, a mutual friend of his and Burgess. The official is unnamed. That same evening, Goronwy says, the official transmitted the message to someone more highly placed than himself in MI5. The next day Goronwy was visited at his home outside London by "another friend of Guy's" who came to urge him not to share with the British security services his conjectures about Burgess's flight. This friend, too, is unnamed and Goronwy goes on to tell us that he rejected his visitor's appeal and went to the headquarters of MI5 where he was interviewed by one of its officers, again unnamed. Not only did this officer confirm Goronwy's belief that Burgess had gone to the Soviet Union. He volunteered to Goronwy the further information that Burgess had been accompanied by Donald Maclean.

The story given by Goronwy to Boyle in 1977 has little in common with this account in Rees's volume five years earlier. In his story to Boyle, Goronwy again states that a mutual friend of his and Burgess came to plead with him not to reveal anything about Burgess to the security services. But now he names this visitor: it was Anthony Blunt. The remainder of his story to Boyle is both new and shocking. Convinced—he tells Boyle—that he must share what he knows with his government, after Burgess's flight he phoned David Footman, a friend in the offices of Intelligence. Footman had relayed the information to a higher official, Guy Liddell, who a few days later called Goronwy and arranged an interview with him in his office. But Liddell had then delayed their meeting and shifted it to lunch at his club. To this meeting he brought an unexpected third party, Anthony Blunt. "Blunt and Liddell," Boyle writes, "took up where Blunt had left off. They jointly urged Rees not to press with his speculation about Burgess," explaining to Rees that while they had evidence of espionage against Maclean, they had none against Burgess. They warned Rees that things would "go hard with him" if he persisted in his charges against Burgess. Goronwy nevertheless persisted and eventually Liddell was forced to put him in touch with another security official. This time the interview took place at Intelligence headquarters and without the presence of Blunt. Goronwy was now listened to but in "strained silence." He was treated, he recalled to Boyle, as if he were himself the traitor.

By Boyle's report, several days passed before Rees was

again summoned to MI5 for further questioning. When he was at last reinterviewed, he held back nothing—except, apparently, the fact of his own engagement in espionage. This pertinent information he seems to have withheld even from Boyle. From this fuller, more accurate account which he gave Boyle, we learn that, in his second meeting with Liddell, Goronwy revealed that Burgess had once identified Blunt as a fellow-conspirator.

As evidence of the way in which at this time the political winds were blowing in England through the halls of power, the story given us by Boyle is startling enough. But it was not only in official circles that Goronwy's attempt to disclose what he knew about the Cambridge spies brought him alone into disfavor. His belief that it was his duty to speak up against Communist infiltration ran counter to the temper of the period and violated that seemingly most sacred of Britain's moral imperatives, loyalty to one's friends.

Rees's revelations were no surprise to Andrew Boyle: he had long been on Blunt's trail. On November 15, 1979, largely as a result of the publication of Boyle's book, *The Fourth Man*—its title was only later changed to *The Climate of Treason*—Prime Minister Margaret Thatcher was forced to admit in Parliament that as far back as 1964, fifteen years previously, Sir Anthony Blunt had confessed his espionage to the British Security Services: he had been recruited by Soviet Intelligence while still a Cambridge don and throughout the war had regularly passed information to the Soviet Union. Nothing had been officially done in response to Blunt's confession, nor did the British government fall as a result of Thatcher's admission, or even totter. In proper British fashion, the scandal was absorbed. Sir Anthony was now relieved of his title but he never went to jail. As if in classic self-parody, a well-situated member of the British intellectual establishment is said to have remarked that Blunt's having been deprived of his accustomed place at the high tables of Cambridge was one of the worst catastrophes of the century.

Rosamond Lehmann is not without her share of responsibility for the bad light in which Rees is viewed by the British historians of espionage. In an interview with John Costello which Costello reports in his influential volume, *Mask of Treachery,* Lehmann described Goronwy as "a thumping liar." The interview in which she gave this characterization of Rees took place in the mid-Eighties. Rees had by this time been dead for several years and the British public was by now well aware of the existence of the Cambridge spies. We are moved to ask what precisely was the thumping lie of which Lehmann was accusing Rees. Relative to whom did she indict her old lover: a truthful Burgess? A truthful Philby or Maclean? A truthful Blunt? If she was suggesting to Costello that Goronwy was himself a Comintern agent, why did she not forthrightly come out with her charge? And in that way did his concealment of his activities as an agent differentiate Rees from the spies whom she failed to indict?

The fact is that throughout the Thirties Rosamond Lehmann was herself an ardent fellow-traveler, as who among the left-wing writers and intellectuals of her circle was not? When her husband, Wogan Phillips, came into his title and as Lord Milford took his seat in the House of Lords, he was an avowed Communist. A few days after Margaret Thatcher acknowledged Blunt's treason in Parliament, Blunt gave a lengthy interview in which, his moral confidence unshaken, he told the British press that, yes, in the mid-Thirties he had chosen "political conscience against loyalty to country." He could have been speaking for most of his intellectual generation. Throughout the Western democracies at this time, it was by its tolerance of Soviet Communism that political idealism defined itself and its opposition to the regressive forces of capitalism.

In 1956, Burgess and Maclean appeared on television in Moscow and Goronwy's conviction that Burgess had fled to the Soviet Union was unarguably confirmed. Burgess was Lehmann's friend, too, as was Blunt. Rosamond Lehmann might similarly have guessed what had been Burgess's destination when he disappeared from his own country. When Burgess emerged on Moscow television, a weeping Blunt all but con-

fessed to Lehmann that he was also a Soviet agent. It is doubt-
ful that she needed to have the political connection between
Blunt and Burgess or their connection with the Comintern
spelled out for her.

I met Rosamond Lehmann only once: on a visit to London in the early Seventies, Lionel and I were invited to dinner
with her at the home of a London doctor, Patrick Woodcock.
The only other guest was Christopher Isherwood. Dr. Woodcock was not a writer but he had many literary friends. I was
delighted to meet Isherwood. As a fiction critic many years
earlier, I had reviewed his novel *Prater Violet*. It was a small
book but it had towered over most of the novels which came to
my desk.

The literary reputation which Lehmann had earned with
Dusty Answer had steadily faded with the years and the celebrated beauty of her young womanhood had dramatically vanished—it was in fact difficult to imagine that it had ever existed.
I had been warned that she had gained an extraordinary
amount of weight but I could not have been prepared for her
altered appearance: at Dr. Woodcock's, she all but overflowed
the little sofa in his sitting room. So radical a change in appearance was not to be explained as simply the depredation of time.
For my sake, for the sake of all of us, it had to be understood as
a willed rejection by Lehmann of her previous self, perhaps in
circuitous fashion related to another of the assaults upon reality
which were reported of her. It was widely said that she supposed herself to be in communication with her dead daughter.

Just as Isherwood's *Prater Violet* had once saved me, if
only for the time it took to read it, from the dispiriting run of
novels which had to be dealt with by a weekly reviewer, now, at
least for the few moments that I was able to engage him apart
from the rest of the company, he rescued me from the contemplation of where time had carried Rosamond Lehmann since
the glory days of her young womanhood. We were at last forced
to rejoin the rest of the party and I cannot recall which of us it
was, she or I, who brought Goronwy's name into the conversation. I daresay it was I. "Goronwy!" Lehmann spat out venom-

ously. Her contempt was unmediated. I remember reading of Freud that when he was dying of cancer, he refused medication to ease his pain; he didn't want his mind dulled, and he was indignant to learn that his personal physician had been giving him a narcotic. *Bei welchen Recht?* By what right, he demanded, did someone administer to him a medication he had expressly forbidden? *Bei welchen Recht:* the three hard words had remained my address to all impermissible power, the cry of brave spirit overridden by hostile circumstance, and they echoed in my mind as I thought of the virtuous authority that Rosamond Lehmann took to herself in her condemnation of Rees.

To the end of his life, ill and dying, with Margie gone, Goronwy had only reason to depend upon. It had not always stood by him but he had stood by it. To depend upon reason is to leave oneself open to the unreason which fills the universe. The reliable Rosamund Lehmann could break off her chat with the dead in order to pass judgment upon the unreliable Goronwy.

In the fall of 1975, Goronwy made his first and only visit to New York. Our son, who had been living in London, had come home to be with his dying father. Leaving Lionel in his charge, I took Goronwy to lunch in the Oak Room of the Plaza Hotel, the nearest approach we then had in New York to the Connaught Grill in London. Goronwy would appreciate the similarity and the differences. He had an Englishman's lunch, a full-course dinner, and after lunch we rode up Fifth Avenue by bus. On our ride, I pointed out some of the passing sights of the city: the view across Central Park, the Children's Zoo, the Frick and Guggenheim Museums, the Metropolitan Museum of Art. As we crossed 110th Street to the West side, we had a glimpse of the Cathedral of St. John the Divine and, beyond it, Columbia University.

Goronwy visited alone with Lionel for a few minutes at our apartment and then I exchanged places with our son—he took over as Goronwy's guide for the afternoon. I never again saw or heard from Goronwy though he lived for another four years. On Lionel's death, Jenny Rees wrote me an affectionate letter. Goronwy's expression of condolence was his piece in *Encounter.*

From this memorial I learn that Goronwy spent the next morning after his visit with us at the United Nations. His arrival in New York had happened to coincide with a crisis in the city's financial history; its bonds were careening into worthlessness, and financial stability had had to be restored by a major injection of funds from the Teachers' Union. The improbable seemed to accompany Goronwy. The remainder of his column, following his tribute to Lionel, is devoted to an account of the debate and affirmative vote in the Third Committee in the General Assembly of the United Nations on the condemnation of Zionism as racism. He writes:

> It is difficult to convey the sense of mingled horror and incredulity with which I listened to the debate in the Third Committee. One knows of course that there are real and genuine grounds for conflict between the state of Israel and its Arab neighbors, and that this conflict provokes acute and bitter dissension, in which right is not entirely on Israel's side. And one would concede that the United Nations provides the only public forum in which such a conflict might become the subject of rational discussion, out of which, however improbably, some fruitful result might possibly arise. But what was shameful and disgraceful was that the discussion should be conducted, as it was in the Third Committee, in terms, not of a political conflict between states, but of a squalid and brutal anti-Semitism of a kind, one had thought, the world would no longer tolerate.

He continues:

> There were ghosts haunting the Third Committee that day: the ghosts of Hitler and Goebbels and Julius

Streicher, grinning with delight to hear, not only Israel, but Jews as such denounced in language which would have provoked hysterical applause at any Nuremberg rally and justify a special edition of *Der Stürmer*. And there were other ghosts also at the debate; the ghosts of the six million dead in Dachau and Sachsenhausen and other extermination camps, listening to the same voices which had cheered and jeered and abused them as they made their way to the gas chambers. For the fundamental thesis advanced by the supporters of the resolution, and approved by the majority of the Third Committee, was that to be a Jew, and to be proud of it, and to be determined to preserve the right to be a Jew, is to be an enemy of the human race.

Recently, I spent an evening with British friends who were visiting in New York. Because I had already begun this remembrance of Goronwy and he was much in my mind, I brought up his name. It was unwise of me. Fifteen years after his death, nothing had changed in the way the mention of him was met. These friends of mine had all been acquainted with the Reeses; one of them had known them far more intimately than I. They spoke of Goronwy dismissively, almost derisively. There was a considerably younger woman in the party. She had known Goronwy when she was growing up in London and she seemed to be made uncomfortable by the unkind tone in which they were speaking of him. In an aside to me she murmured, "He was always very nice to me." And she added, "He was the most attractive man I have ever met." I smiled at her use of these familiar words. I felt a quick flash of affection for her.

My English friends had no criticism of Margie Rees. They were agreed that Margie was a dear, a darling. And what she had had to put up with, married to that scoundrel! There was of course also no word of criticism of Burgess or Blunt or any other member of the Cambridge ring. I was unable to keep an edge of anger out of my voice as I brought the talk back to what, as I saw it, was a crucial omission. "And Burgess? Or Blunt?" I asked. "What about them? They weren't scoundrels, just our everyday garden-variety spies?" This was met by a short second of silence among the company, like an intake of breath, before our host smoothly turned to his neighbor and broached another topic of conversation. I and my notions of spies and spying, of honor and dishonor, of proper and improper loyalties, were not to be given a further hearing. Ever. For my uncongenial views and for the bad manners they bred in me, I was written out of the lives of these friends.

In his *Encounter* column, Goronwy linked his censure of the United Nations with his warm commemoration of Lionel. Celebrating him as an individual, Goronwy also spoke of him as an American and a Jew. "It was an essential part of the pleasure of his friendship," he wrote, "that he remained always and unmistakably an American." The point of his American identity has not often been made of Lionel and, making it here, Goronwy may well have been thinking of his own Welsh identity and the part it must surely have played in the shaping of his life. Rees the Oxonian, Rees the Londoner, Rees the man of the world had never forgotten—had perhaps never been let forget—his Welsh origin. To consult the documents surrounding his life, not least of them Elizabeth Bowen's *Death of the Heart,* is indeed to have the realization freshly imposed upon one of the extent to which the hostile judgment passed upon Goronwy after the Aberystwyth episode was due to his being outside the social fold—Bowen's novel makes it clear that even where he might seem to be warmly welcomed among the author's own kind, he was the object of their social condescension. England, as it was then viewed by its literary and intellectual establishment, belonged to those who by birth had their designated place in its ruling social order. And while Goronwy himself never raised the question of whether Burgess's treason would have been condoned as it was if Burgess had been the product of a grammar school rather than of Eton, or whether he, Goronwy, would have been condemned as he was for his

Aberystwyth disclosures if he had been an Etonian rather than the product of a Cardiff grammar school, his memoir clears the ground for just such speculation.

Well before Goronwy was a patriot of Britain, he was a patriot of Wales and it forever suited his temperament to cherish this complication. It is said of him that he was lacking in loyalty to his friend Guy Burgess, but it can never be said of him that he lacked in loyalty to his parents or to the circumstances of his birth, whatever the distance he traveled from the confining influences of the "Calvinistic Methodism" of his upbringing. It was as if, because he wasn't born to the society in which he found himself at Oxford and after Oxford and therefore didn't finally belong to it, he could suppose himself to be free of its dictate. He could violate its proprieties and transgress its borders. We may not know what led Burgess to his preference for the disreputable associations which he is said to have enjoyed on Bentinck Street, but Goronwy's readiness to join in this company is, I think, readily explained by his sense of himself as someone who by birth bore the ineradicable taint of the outsider.

I should like to suppose that Goronwy would have been pleased by Jenny's biography of him, but I am not certain of this. I am not sure that he would have appreciated it as it deserves. It was my impression of Goronwy that he was lacking in parental involvement and pride; the fact that Jenny fails to indicate this is testimony to the generous spirit of her book. In the first year that Lionel and I knew Goronwy and Margie, their twin sons attended the same school in London as our son. Now and then we would speak, as parents inevitably do, of the errors or deficiencies in the way our children were being dealt with. Goronwy contributed his customary good sense to these conversations but he spoke as from an emotional remove: his children were not in the forefront of his feeling or thought.

Jenny's volume is painstakingly thorough; it could scarcely be more objective and balanced. Clear-eyed, she is also deeply respecting of her father. Chapter by chapter, she traces his family background, his university career, his literary associations and professional undertakings. She situates his story in the public domain and, as much as possible, keeps herself out of it. Although she mentions Rees's womanizing, she regards it as outside the proper province of her investigation. Her Mr. Nobody is a public person, even a public issue.

I'm troubled by the title of Jenny's book, *Looking for Mr. Nobody;* I feel that it is misleading. It seems to me to suggest that Jenny is writing about someone who, in Henry James's happy phrase, fails to rise to the level of appearance. Actually, it refers to the fact that Goronwy felt of himself that he was without "character." He had no "I." At Oxford, well before the distractions of his friendship with Burgess, he read Hume's *Treatise of Human Nature* and found in its pages on personal identity the phrase which he would later use in self-description, "a bundle of sensations." Jenny recalls a rhyme which her father frequently repeated to his children:

> As I was going up the stair,
> I met a man who wasn't there.
> He wasn't there again today;
> I wish that man would go away.

While I do not entirely comprehend what Goronwy meant by his lack of identity, I take it that he was speaking of his lack of a discernible intention or direction in his psychological make-up rather than of a pathology of depersonalization or of the small space which he may have supposed that he filled in the universe.

The purpose of Jenny's book is clearly stated: she wishes to solve the mystery which always hung over her father's life. More specifically, she is determined to find out whether or not her father was ever a Soviet agent. In 1993, in their volume, *Deadly Illusions,* Costello and Tsarev had named him as a co-conspirator with the Cambridge spy ring. This had never been said in Costello's previous volumes but by the time Costello and Tsarev published their joint study, the Soviet Union had collapsed and Western scholars had new access to Russian files. Was this how Goronwy's role had come to light? Was this the Secret which her parents had for so long tried to conceal?

Jenny was not prepared to accept the accusation against her father without further proof than was offered in *Deadly Illusions*. If, at the time of the Aberystwyth scandal, Goronwy's critics suspected him of espionage, they had never made the accusation. To be sure, in an interview which Anthony Blunt had given shortly before his death in 1983, he had named Rees as a fellow-conspirator and this statement had been publicly reported. But it had made little public impression. It was the charge brought against Rees in *Deadly Illusions* that finally impelled Jenny to seek out the truth of her father's relation to the Cambridge spies.

In the end, her search led Jenny to Moscow and a meeting with Tsarev himself. She had already spoken to him from London by phone—for many years Tsarev had been stationed in London and he spoke fluent English. To her phoned inquiry about her father, he had replied courteously that yes, Rees had briefly been a Soviet agent. It had been his task to supply political hearsay—he was assigned to listen to conversations at dinner at All Souls, a frequent dining place for persons high in government service, and to pass on any information he picked up which might be of use to the Soviet Union. Her father had been recruited in 1938, Tsarev further told Jenny, but he had terminated his service the following year when he had broken with Communism in consequence of the Nazi-Soviet Pact, and after the Pact he had not again been heard from by Soviet Intelligence. All in all, the involvement had been modest and short-lived. There was no file for him in Moscow. What information existed was to be found only in the file of Guy Burgess. As Rees's daughter, Jenny was at liberty to see it.

A less urgent investigator than Jenny Rees would no doubt have been content to close the book with this exchange. Jenny, however, was unsatisfied; she was determined to learn exactly what Tsarev had meant in saying that Rees had been "recruited" in 1938. What did the word imply? Did it mean that her father had been a fully-fledged agent of the USSR?

In search of answers with which she could rest, Jenny decided to go to Russia for a direct interview with the Soviet historian. Tsarev's Moscow headquarters were in a building adjacent to the old Lubyanka prison. In his office Jenny came at once to the point of her visit. What did Tsarev have in mind when he used the word "recruited" of Rees's engagement in spying for the Soviet Union? Had her father been a fully-fledged agent?

"A fully-fledged agent, no," Tsarev replied in response to her insistence upon precision. But an agent he had nevertheless been and one who was wholly aware of the nature of the operation in which he cooperated. "They were recruited for the cause, the Communist cause," Tsarev spelled out the situation for Jenny. With pedagogic patience, he summed up Rees's role. "Rees could not be called an 'agent.' He was a 'source' and an 'operational contact'." He was motivated, said Tsarev, by "romanticism" and "ideological conviction."

And so Jenny's investigation had at last come to its end. She had discovered the truth of her father's relation to the Cambridge spies. Rees had been a Soviet agent, but he had not been a fully-fledged agent, not a spy in the sense in which his Cambridge associates were spies. He had had a code name but he had not been under immediate orders, expected to do as he was bid, whatever the assignment. In the language of spy scholarship, he had been "an agent of influence." In the contest for power between Communism and democracy, he had played his small part: he had made his minuscule contribution to the success of the other side by passing on such news as could be picked up at the dining tables of All Souls. This paltry involvement he had then spent the rest of his life trying to hide and redress, only to bring his world tumbling about his ears.

Rees hadn't been important enough to have his own file in Moscow, but he had been promising enough to have a place in Burgess's file and a code name, "Gross"—the name was apparently a crude amalgam of the "G" of Goronwy and his last name. Reporting to his Moscow contact, Burgess had boasted that he had "Tony"—Anthony Blunt—in Cambridge and "Gross" in Oxford as "talent spotters." But as Tsarev put it to Jenny, " 'Gross' had never realized himself in the role Burgess had singled out for him. We know he did not because this talent spotter [in Oxford] was somebody else." Even as a spy, Goronwy had failed to fulfill the expectations that the people of his acquaintance had for him!

Tsarev's summary to Jenny of Rees's performance as a spy gave me the answer to a question of my own. Throughout the war and even in his position of trust on the staff of Field Marshal Montgomery, Rees had maintained his intimacy with Burgess, visiting regularly at the Bentinck Street flat. As I re-read *A Chapter of Accidents,* this struck me as incautious in the extreme and, as I say, I also found it difficult to believe that as late as 1951 Goronwy was uncertain whether Burgess had really been a Communist agent and, if he had been, whether he was still engaged in this activity. Jenny's interview with Tsarev supplied a possible explanation, if not an excuse, for Rees's carelessness in having maintained his friendship with Burgess and even for his doubt of Burgess's continuing allegiance to the Soviet Union. Following the Pact, when Rees had himself broken with Communism, both Burgess and Blunt—Tsarev told Jenny—had similarly announced that they were no longer Communists. This was not the truth, but Goronwy had believed them or at least hoped that he could. Not until Burgess defected to the Soviet Union did Rees allow himself to realize the extent of his friend's deception.

In his own account of things, Rees reports that in his anxiety to wring the truth from Burgess—had he or had he not spied for the Soviet Union? Was he or was he not still a Comintern agent?—he had resorted to a dangerous lie: he had told Burgess that he had deposited with his lawyer a sealed letter in which he recorded Burgess's 1936 confession to him. This was a dangerous move. The threat would not have been lost on Burgess and could well have proposed a countermove. With his connections in Moscow, Burgess could at any time store away incriminating information about Rees. There is no evidence that Burgess did this. So far as we know, he never deliberately set out to implicate Rees in his espionage or otherwise do him harm. But the fact that clever Goronwy could have delivered himself into Burgess's hands in this fashion indicates how little he belonged in the hazardous company of fully-fledged agents.

"Romanticism" and "ideological conviction": the terms are Tsarev's but could we better describe the motives which, in the Thirties and Forties, moved not Goronwy alone but so many intellectuals in his country and ours to choose Soviet Communism in preference to the problem-ridden processes of democracy? Time passes and for those who were not yet born in the Thirties and Forties, it becomes daily less credible that a few decades ago Stalin's repressive regime could appeal as it did to the idealistic young and not only to the young but to their elders who, we could suppose, might have known better, reputable writers and artists, lawyers, doctors, university professors, clerics, so many of whom gave themselves so trustingly to the beguilements of the Soviet propaganda machine. When I think of this folly of a generation, it seems hardly fair that Goronwy, whose service to the Soviet Union was so brief in duration and whose assignment as a Comintern agent was all but ludicrous in its nature—to eavesdrop on his dinner table companions at All Souls!—should be singled out as he was for scorn.

We remind ourselves, however, that Goronwy was condemned by the British intellectual community not for his politics but for his betrayal of a friend and here the national lines, the division in habits of thought between the two countries, England and America, baldly announce themselves. Whittaker Chambers was thought to be a liar because he said that Communists had infiltrated our government. He claimed that he had been a friend of Alger Hiss; Hiss denied the relationship. If Hiss was his friend, as Chambers claimed in bringing his charge against him, Chambers was as guilty as Goronwy of betraying a friend. One never heard this accusation brought against him.

Yet it is not necessary that we share the British exaltation of friendship to recognize that Goronwy was indeed treacherous, peculiarly so, in condemning a friend for conduct in which he had himself engaged. A double standard of this sort is not permitted us. Brief and light-minded as Rees's service to the Soviet Union may have been, it had to be confessed to before Goronwy was free to denounce others as sternly as he did.

It is possible that he eventually came to this realization—conscience demanded it and this scamp and scoundrel, this rogue and roué was never rid of conscience; it was his guide and torment. Long before the hard judgment of others could reach him, Goronwy judged and convicted himself and to refuse to forgive oneself is of course to be forever damned. Goronwy's conscience never gave him the chance of freedom from condemnation. His guilt was at last the whole of his identity, his "character" and his "I."

Jean Baudrillard

The "Laying-Off" of Desire

In facial features, sex, illnesses and death, identity is perpetually changing. This is the body as destiny, which has to be exorcized at all costs—through the appropriation of the body as projection of self, the individual appropriation of desire, of one's appearance, one's image: cosmetic surgery on all fronts. If the body is no longer a site of otherness but of identification, then we have urgently to become reconciled with it, repair it, perfect it, turn it into an ideal object. Everyone treats their bodies the way men treat women in projective identification: they invest them as a fetish, making an autistic cult of them, subjecting them to a quasi-incestuous manipulation. And it is the body's resemblance to its model which becomes a source of eroticism and "white" seduction—in the sense that it effects a kind of white magic of identity, as opposed to the black magic of otherness.

This is how it is with body-building: you get into your body as you would into a suit of nerve and muscle. The body is not muscular, but muscled. It is the same with the brain and with social relations or exchanges: body-building, brainstorming, word-processing. Madonna is the ideal specimen of this, our muscled Immaculate Conception, our muscular angel who delivers us from the weaknesses of the body (pity the poor shade of Marilyn!).

The sheath of muscles is the equivalent of character armour. In the past, women merely wrapped themselves in their image and their finery—Freud speaks of those people who live with a kind of inner mirror, in a fleshly, happy self-reference. That narcissistic ideal is past and gone; body-building has wiped it out and replaced it with a gymnastic Ego-Ideal—cold, hard, stressed, artificial self-reference. The construction of a double, of a physical and mental identity shell. Thus, in "body simulation," where you can animate your body remotely at any moment, the phantasy of being present in more than one body becomes an operational reality. An extension of the human being. And not a metaphorical or poetic extension, as in Pessoa's heteronyms, but quite simply a technical one.

The contemporary individual is never without his clones—reincarnation of the old fatality of incest, of the infernal cycle of identity which, at least in the fable, still had an air of tragic destiny to it but which, for us, is now no longer anything but the code of the automatic disappearance of the individual. We can't exactly even speak of individuals any longer. Individuation was part of the golden age of a subject-object dynamics. Since he has become truly indivisible, and has thus achieved his perfect—that is to say, delirious, self-referential—form, we cannot speak of the individual any longer, but only of the Selfsame and the hypostasis of the Selfsame. As is illustrated by the absolute, intransitive difference which marks the final point of that self-reference: "my," "your," "his or her" difference. The pure and simple appropriation of difference. Previously, it was at least the other who was taken to be different. Metastases of identity: all the particles disperse into individual histories. To each his cocktail, his own life story, all equivalent in their simultaneously differential and insignificant character. Each one defended by such a scrambling system that his voice, speech and face will soon be unrecognizable to the others, except to those who have a personal decoder—including when making love: the body will materialize only for those who have the key to the decoder. Soon we shall all be decoding machines. Since every spontaneous relationship, every natural movement of desire, is laid off *[en chômage technique]*, then the technical ritual will have to substitute for this "technically" unemployed desire.

Madonna Deconnection: Madonna is "desperately" fighting in a world where there is no response—the world of sexual indifference. Hence the urgent need for hypersexual sex, the signs of which are exacerbated precisely because they are no longer addressed to anyone. This is why she is condemned successively and simultaneously to take on all the roles and all the versions of sex (rather than the perversions), because for her there is no longer any sexual otherness, something which brings sex into play beyond sexual difference, and not just by parodying it wildly, but always from within. She is, in fact, fighting against her own sex; she is fighting against her own body. For want of some other who would deliver her from herself, she is unrelentingly forced to provide her own sexual enticement, to build up for herself a panoply of accessories—in the event a sadistic panoply, from which she tries to wrench herself away. Harassment of the body by sex, harassment of sex by signs.

It is said that she lacks nothing (this might be said of women in general). There are, however, different ways of lacking nothing. She lacks nothing by virtue of the artefacts and technology with which she surrounds herself, in the manner of a woman producing and reproducing herself—herself and her desire—in a cycle or closed circuit. She lacks precisely that nothing (the form of the other?) which would undress her and deliver her of all this panoply. Madonna is desperately seeking a body able to generate illusion, a naked body costumed by its own appearance. She would like to be naked, but she never manages it. She is perpetually harnessed, if not by leather and metal, then by the obscene desire to be naked, by the artificial mannerism of exhibition. But this produces total inhibition and, for the spectator, radical frigidity. So, paradoxically, she ends up personifying the frenetic frigidity of our age.

She can play all the roles. But is this because she enjoys a solid identity, a fantastic power of identification, or because she has none at all? Surely because she has none. But the trick is to know—as she does—how to exploit this fantastic absence of identity.

We know people who, for want of being able to communicate, are victims of profuse otherness (as we speak of profuse sweating). They play all the roles at once, their own and the other person's; they both give and return, ask the questions and supply the answers. They embrace the other's presence so fully that they no longer know the limits of their own. The other is merely a transitional object. The secondary gain from the loss of the other is an ability to transform oneself into anyone at all—through role-playing, virtual and computer games, through that new spectrality Marc Guillaume speaks of, with the age of Virtual Reality still to come, when we shall don otherness like a data suit.

This whole movement of construction of an artificial double of the body and desire ends in the pornographic, the culmination of a henceforth desireless hyperbody, of a now indifferent and useless sexual function. But a function which works all the better in sex-processing, like text in word-processing, art in art-processing, war in war-processing, and so on. It is in this transparency, this charnel house of signs of the body disincarnate, that pornographic images move (it is, indeed, transparency itself that is pornographic, not the lascivious obscenity of the body): everything is presented to the gaze there with a kind of objective irony. Transgression, prohibitions, phantasies, censorship—everything is presented as phallic "quotation." It is the minimal illusion of sex: become cool, ironic and promotional, porn has definitely not gained anything in pagan innocence, but it has gained something in media insolence.

It is the pure form of sex which can no longer be said to be encumbered by the mystery of sexual difference, nor the figures of otherness attaching to it. The signs of masculine and feminine no longer function there as such (as they do in erotic art) but as something purely sexual, dispelling all ambiguity: sexual difference is suddenly realized in its objective, anatomical, technical form as a surgical mark. The pornographic is thus the model of a society where sexual difference and the difference between reality and the image both disappear at the same time, and all registers become eroticized as they fall into nondistinction and the confusion of genres. Thus, if it was possible for la Cicciolina to be elected a member of the Italian Parliament, this is because the political and the sexual, having become transpolitical and transsexual, meet in the same ironic indifference. This previously unthinkable achievement is the mark of the profound travestying of our culture. The state of prostitution is quite simply that of the total substitution of terms, sexes and categories one for another.

In reality there no longer is any identifiable pornography, because the essence of the pornographic has passed into things, into images, into all the techniques of the visual and the virtual—all of which, in a way, deliver us from that collective phantasmagoria. We are doubtless merely play-acting obscenity, play-acting sexuality, as other societies play-act ideology, as Italian society, for example (though it is not the only one), play-acts power. Thus, in advertising, it is merely the comedy of the bared female body that is being played out. Hence the error of feminist recriminations: if this perpetual striptease and sexual blackmail were real, that would be unacceptable. Not morally unacceptable, but unacceptable because we would be exposed to pure obscenity, that is to say, the naked truth, the mad pretension of things to express their truth (this is the nauseous secret of TV "reality shows"). Fortunately, we have not reached that point. The hyperreality of everything in our culture and the High Definition which underlines its obscenity are too glaring to be true. And so they protect us by their very excess. As for art, it is too superficial to be truly worthless. There must be some mystery to it. There must surely be some meaning to such a riot of sex and signs, but we can't see what it is. Perhaps this worthlessness, this meaninglessness, take on a sense when they are viewed from another world, from another angle, like objects in anamorphosis? In the unreality of porn, in the insignificance of images, in all the figures of simulation, there is an allegory running beneath the surface, an enigma lurking in it all like a negative image—who knows? If everything becomes too obvious to be true, then there's still a chance for illusion. What lurks behind this moronic world? Another form of intelligence or a definitive lobotomy?

The dictatorship of images is, at any rate, an ironic dictatorship. Take Jeff Koons and la Cicciolina, and their erotic, allegorical, infantile, incestuous machine—at Venice, they came together to mime their real coupling in front of the depiction of that coupling. Autoerotic confusion, new aphrodisiac mysticism, no more and no less carnal or provocative than the fluorescent or geometric erectility of Gilbert and George.

Obscenity may be sublime or grotesque, if it shatters the innocence of a natural world. But what can porn do in a world pornographied in advance? What can art do in a world simulated and travestied in advance? Except bring an added ironic value to appearances? Except tip a last paradoxical wink—of sex laughing at itself in its most exact and hence most monstrous form, laughing at its own disappearance beneath its most artificial form?

What solution is there? There is no answer to this collective syndrome of a whole culture, this fascination, this mad whirl of denial of otherness, of all strangeness, all negativity, this repudiation of evil and reconciliation around the selfsame and its multiple figures: incest, autism, twinship, cloning. We can only remember that seduction resides in the safeguarding of alienness, in non-reconciliation. One should not be reconciled with one's body, nor with oneself, one should not be reconciled with the other, one should not be reconciled with nature, one should not reconcile male and female, nor good and evil. Therein lies the secret of a strange attraction.

—Translated by Chris Turner

Daniel Harris

A Psychohistory
of the Homosexual Body

In 1899, pulp magazine mogul Bernarr Macfadden, the author of *The Superb Virility of Manhood: The Causes and Simple Home Methods of Curing the Weakness of Men,* published the first bodybuilding magazine to appear in America, *Physical Culture,* a publication that spawned literally hundreds of imitators in the decades to come, from *Muscles A Go-Go* to *Manorama.* For nearly fifty years, Macfadden advocated the revitalization of our country's masculinity, which he documented in photographs of naked athletes whose spectacular physiques he hoped would inspire the viewer to transform himself from an effete, potbellied slouch into a rippling, all-American he-man. As early as 1903, however, this eccentric entrepreneur, who later started his own cult, was alarmed to discover that an unwanted intruder had weaseled his way into the audience of *Physical Culture,* a type of reader who was not at all interested in trying out on his own body "the simple home methods of curing the weakness of men" but was perfectly content to feast his eyes on the effect of the cure on others. Disgusted by homosexuals' infiltration of his magazine, the mild-mannered founder of "Cosmotorianism," "the happiness religion," launched a lifelong vendetta against gay men and even went so far as to encourage fag-bashing as a means of eradicating "the shoals of painted, perfumed, kohl-eyed, lisping, mincing youths that at night swarm on Broadway . . . ogling every man that passes."[1]

Perhaps in response to the virulent homophobia of such ideologues as Macfadden, who turned *Physical Culture* into his own bully pulpit to champion the cause of the American male in his battle against effeminacy, gay men began to publish their own physique magazines as early as the 1940s and 1950s. At first, there was little to set these apart from their legitimate bodybuilding counterparts, but by the 1950s traces of camp began to emerge in such audacious periodicals as *Grecian Guild Studio* and *Physique Pictorial*. The editors made their proclivities particularly clear in homoerotic art by such illustrators as "Art Bob" or George Quaintance, whose sketches of half-naked telephone linemen sweltering in the sun or frolicsome college athletes clad only in jockstraps cavorting on dormitory beds "compare most favorably," one author opined, "with the magnificent art treasures handed down from antiquity."[2] *Physique Pictorial's* "Four Alarm Fire," for instance, depicted in explicitly sexual detail a room of scarcely clothed firemen scrambling to pull on skintight uniforms over their ample crotches and protruding rear ends, an image that the magazine's editor claimed would remind readers "of the tremendous debt of gratitude we owe these brave defenders of our homes. Let us do all we can to lessen their burden. Follow the fire safety rules."[3] Similarly, in "Mail Call," a cabin of bored sailors on a ship receive their mail wearing scanty undergarments even as they thumb through girlie magazines, an image that drama-

---

1. *Gay New York* (Basic Books, 1994), p. 179. Defending the photographs in *Physical Culture* from those who were more titillated than they were inspired, the publisher of such salacious trash as the New York scandal sheet *Graphic* (nicknamed by its Manhattan readers "Porno-Graphic") haughtily proclaimed that "there is nothing nasty, . . . vulgar, . . . [or] immodest in the nude" but that "the nastiness exists in the minds of those who view it, and those who possess such vulgar minds are the enemies of everything clean, wholesome, and elevating." *Gay New York*, p. 116.
2. *Physique Pictorial*, Spring 1955, p. 27.
3. *Physique Pictorial*, Summer 1955, p. 21.

tizes the "heartbreak of being forgotten" and the necessity of sending our boys overseas "good happy news of all the wonderful things happening all about you."[4]

Constantly harassed by the FBI and the U.S. Postal Service, the editors of gay physique magazines appeased government censors by striking exactly the right note of cloying virtuousness. Attempting to pass themselves off as members of a "persecuted cultural minority" victimized by a federal "crucifixion of the arts,"[5] gay editors indignantly filled their magazines with outraged self-justifications. They pretended to be sophisticated art lovers rather than lewd entrepreneurs who trafficked in dirty pictures of unsuspecting heterosexual teenagers, whom their photographers snatched off the football field and out of the boxing ring, often from right beneath the eyes of their adoring mothers. *Physique Pictorial,* in particular, always waxed poetic about its "mission" and self-righteously reassured its readers, as well as the government employees who steamed open its envelopes, that the admiration of "a fine healthy physique" is not a loathsome act of depravity but "a great compliment to our creator who planned for the utmost perfection in all of his universe."[6] "Just as infinite beauty surrounds us in flowers, music, [and] all of nature including . . . the intricate galaxcies [sic] of the heavens, so in the perfect human body do we find limitless variations of harmonious rythms [sic] expressing a magnificent beauty which makes the soul sing."[7]

It was not until the early 1960s that the editors of gay physique magazines began to acknowledge publicly the prurient function of their photographs. They also became increasingly frank about the sexual orientation, not only of themselves and their readers, but of most of their models, the surly (and occasionally felonious) heterosexual auto mechanics, janitors, service station attendants, steel mill workers, paratroopers, plumbers, and farm boys who were often openly contemptuous

4. *Physique Pictorial,* Summer 1955, p. 15.
5. *Physique Pictorial,* Summer 1995, p. 1.
6. *Physique Pictorial,* Winter 1954–55, p. 2.
7. Ibid.

of the gay photographers who took their pictures. "Dale left Los Angeles under most unusual circumstances," *Physique Pictorial*'s editor reported of one model in 1960, "after a home in which he had been visiting was burglarized. This of course does not amount to an accusation."[8] By 1964, the editor had become considerably less coy and begun printing a lineup of the mug shots of "Delinquent Models!" who had robbed and beaten their tricks, or in the case of naughty Ronnie Akers, had tossed a man's beloved poodle into his outdoor swimming pool, thus "causing it to catch a cold which eventually resulted in its death."[9] Years later, *Physique Pictorial* even published an issue that featured the naked photographs of past models who had murdered, not just poodles, but actual gay men, such as adorable Danny who "is now serving a 25 years to life prison term for the brutal slaughter of a Bel-Air millionaire" or cherubic Kyle who "strangled [a trick] to death with [an] electric skillet cord, wrapped his frail body in a blanket and dumped it along the side of the upper end of the Hollywood freeway."[10]

From 1960 until its demise in 1983, *Physique Pictorial* regaled its readers with vivid descriptions of the misbehavior of its models, whose burglaries and homicidal escapades served as a perverse method of vouching for the boys' heterosexual authenticity as blue-collar rough trade. The editors never stopped reminding their readers of the vast differences of sensibility, class, and physical appearance that separated them from the men on display, who were both disparaged and romanticized as irresistibly masculine lowlife, at the same time that the reader was implicitly portrayed as law-abiding and well behaved. Ultimately, however, these ironic captions celebrating the criminal activities of the magazine's straight trade were not entirely complimentary to the homosexual reader, for while he was praised for being a meek, defenseless gay man at the mercy of the underclasses, he was simultaneously denigrated as being

8. *Physique Pictorial*, January 1960, p. 10.
9. *Physique Pictorial*, July 1964, p. 29.
10. *Physique Pictorial*, November 1983, pp. 12–13.

unworthy of photographic representation. The vision of the gay body implicit in many physique magazines was that of a sexless sissy whose scrawny frame would have looked out of place amid the comely parade of swaggering straight homophobes that early gay magazines held up as the very standard of the "superb virility of manhood."

As recently as the 1970s, the entire physique phenomenon both reflected and reinforced a culture of profound physical inadequacy in which gay men were indoctrinated to believe that it was the straight man whose body merited being seen and worshipped, while their own had minimal erotic appeal. Although gay physique magazines did publish photographs of homosexuals, usually of aspiring actors or dancers (whom *Physique Pictorial* scoffed at as "sylvan creatures . . . that flit about on tippy toe"[11]), by far the majority of the images that appeared were, by the open admission of their editors, of straight men. Until the last twenty-five years, gay soft porn was thus fundamentally unreceptive to images of its own readership, thus creating inevitable feelings of self-contempt, such as a black audience would have felt if all of the pornography sold to it before the 1970s had featured photographs exclusively of white people. From the very beginnings of gay culture, homosexuals' images of their bodies have been haunted by a sense of weakness, futility, and unattractiveness, of sexual subordination to the heterosexual Übermensch. As a result, the gay body is psychologically unstable and vulnerable to an infinite variety of cosmetic manipulations and surgical rearrangements as we attempt to overcome the sense of physical inadequacy expressed with such demeaning candor in physique magazines. Our pent-up reservoir of self-contempt has resulted in the extraordinary malleability of the gay body, which has been subjected to the grueling ordeal of everything from rhinoplasties and hair implants to weight-lifting regimens and electrolysis, from tattoos and UVA tanning to tummy tucks and pedicures.

With the emergence of the first skin magazines in the

---

11. *Physique Pictorial*, May 1964, p. 3.

mid-1970s, the aesthetic of gay erotica changed dramatically. From the unkempt lower-class boys who strut through *Physique Pictorial's* pages in combat boots and motorcycle helmets, we arrive at the suave centerfolds of *Blueboy* and *Mandate,* where luscious yuppies, who are identifiably gay, lie around mountains of plush cushions photographed in a hypnotic soft focus. In the course of only a few years, the homosexual's desires seem to have leapt upscale from cement workers and street sweepers to collegiate jocks and budding bankers who, their eyes glazed [over] with lust, lounge around their bachelor pads after work in an enticing state of undress. For the first time in history, the manufacturers of commercial gay erotica seem to have responded to a desire on the part of gay men to see bodies that have the same highly groomed and fastidiously hygienic appearance as their own. Gone are the unwashed bodies of grease monkeys reeking of oily axle rods and leaking chassis, and in their place are the deodorized bodies of middle-class professionals who bathe regularly, douse themselves with expensive colognes, and style their hair with mousses and gels. The skin magazines of the disco era build an altar to what might be called the "bourgeois body" of the well-adjusted homosexual who, with the help of gay liberation, is slowly and painstakingly disengaging himself from the destructive spell of menacing straight boys and setting his sights on a more accessible group of his sexual peers.[12]

The bourgeois body of the modern homosexual was not, of course, the invention of gay liberation, but the political advances made during the 1960s and early 1970s did have a sig-

---

12. I use the word "bourgeois" advisedly and in a special figurative sense. I certainly do not mean to suggest that there were no lower-class homosexuals before Stonewall but simply that many homosexuals, regardless of their class, were acutely conscious of the maintenance of their bodies and often cultivated an extravagant style of dress and grooming modeled on the deportment of upper-middle-class men. Even lower-class homosexuals would have been susceptible to this hyperfastidiousness, which would have set them apart from men at the same economic level. Blue-collar straight men would not have shared with their homosexual counterparts this typically gay self-consciousness about their hairstyles, skin care, methods of bathing, body odors (often concealed beneath loud colognes and aftershaves), and even their clothing, which was frequently expensive, even beyond their means.

nificant impact on gay men's appearance. Regardless of their social class, homosexuals have probably always tended to be overgroomed in comparison with the general population, to wear loud aftershaves, to fuss unnecessarily with their hair, to manicure their nails, or to experiment with the famous "beauty secrets" popular among gay men during the 1950s, such as placing wet teabags on the skin beneath their eyes to reduce the swelling or massaging Preparation H into their crow's-feet to eliminate their wrinkles. But if the proverbial vanity and physical self-consciousness of gay men has a long and venerable history, the political activism of the Stonewall era contributed a new element of urgency to the effeminate appearance of the homosexual's body. The rise of the gay rights movement created a climate of permissiveness that allowed homosexuals to exaggerate their already finicky style of self-presentation.

Until the 1960s, fears of social disapproval, as well as the unavailability of skin-care products for men, held the bourgeois body carefully in check, thus driving many homosexuals into a kind of bootleg, beauty-supply underground where, out of desperation, they became self-medicating cosmeticians who filled rubber gloves with vaseline in order to soften their hands and tied strips of cloth beneath their chins to prevent snoring, which causes wrinkles around the mouth. Gay liberation and the growth of the male beauty aid industry, however, freed the bourgeois body from its closet, from its makeshift elixirs and home brews, and stimulated a self-pampering narcissism that culminated in that encyclopedia of overgrooming, *Looking Good* (1977). Extremely popular among gay men during the late 1970s, this male fashion and beauty guide represents the very summit of the gay obsession with hygiene that fundamentally altered the look of our bodies in the years following Stonewall. The book offered extremely detailed recommendations about a wide variety of do's and don'ts: that one should douse one's face with a minimum of thirty handfuls of water before applying moisturizer; that one should cut one's nails so that they conform to the curve of the fingertips, since "ovals or

points are *de trop*";[13] that one should blot—but never wipe!—
one's cheeks with a tissue when one's bronzer begins to trickle
down one's face from perspiration; and that during a pedicure,
one should separate one's toes with "cute little paper
pompons."[14] Gay men had suddenly found the courage they
needed to cross a crucial psychological threshold and coddle
themselves with everything from cucumber facials and "Retex-
turing Whole Egg Masques" to mascaras that "come in colors
for extra oomph" and eyeliners whose two basic shades, "champagne" and "mocha," "bring out the beauty of your eyes day
into evening." Politics have thus played a pivotal role in the
very appearance of the homosexual's body, permitting us to
powder, spray, and scent it in ways that would have been impossible in the decades before Stonewall. The growing social
acceptance of homosexuals' physical self-preoccupation gave us
the license to act on long-suppressed desires to get into our
mamas' makeup bags and smear our faces with bronzers, blush-
ers, and foundation bases, cosmetics that only the most marginal members of the gay community had the courage to use
before the 1960s. With gay liberation, the bodies of one major
sector of the gay population were radically feminized.

Not all of the models in the first issues of the skin magazines published in the 1970s were perfectly coiffed specimens
of the immaculate bourgeois body. Proletarians wearing construction hats, military fatigues, and police uniforms continued
to appear, but they differed in one crucial respect from the
lower-class boys represented in the physique magazines. The
men in the early issues of *Blueboy* and *Playguy* were not real
proles. They were *faux* proles, gay men dressed up to look like
proles, dramatic impersonations of hayseeds in overalls chewing
on straws, hillbillies with rifles and raccoon caps, and mechanics with neat streaks of axle grease daubed on their cheeks with
aesthetic precision. In this complicated class masquerade, in
which gay men assumed the tattered costumes, butch stances,

13. *Looking Good,* Charles Hix, Photos by Bruce Weber (Hawthorn Books, Inc.
1977), p. 182.
14. *Looking Good,* p. 187.

and threatening demeanors of the blue-collar models in *Physique Pictorial,* we catch the homosexual in the very act of formulating an entirely new look for his body, one modeled on the image, not of the aristocratic dandy, who provided the paradigm for the pre-Stonewall gay body, but on that of the working-class male.

With the rise of gay liberation, the sexless homosexual eunuch acquired enough self-esteem that he attempted to overthrow his sense of physical inadequacy to straight men. Beginning in the 1970s and then gathering momentum in the early 1980s, as AIDS inspired a whole new type of anguished health consciousness, we started furiously lifting weights in order to claim our rightful place in front of the camera rather than perpetually behind it where we were previously forced to sit passively on the sidelines and reverently admire our dangerous heroes. As early as the 1950s, one segment of the homosexual population had begun to abandon the colorful cravats and brown suede shoes borrowed from the stereotype of the upper-class aesthete and actively adopted various badges and costumes associated with working-class men: the olive drab of the soldier, the chaps of the cowboy, the dark shades and motorcycle jackets of the biker, the facial hair of the Marlboro man, and the tattoos of the sailor (including such stereotypic designs as panthers that claw their way up biceps and kitschy Catholic images of bleeding hearts, weeping Virgins, and gaunt Jesuses pierced with crowns of thorns). The emergence of the *faux* prole, more widely known as the "clone," was a vivid indication of how completely, after decades of studying the bodies of heterosexual rough trade, we had absorbed their physical aesthetic, which led us to initiate a process of self-refashioning that has continued well into the 1990s.

Gay liberation thus produced two entirely contradictory images of the gay body, dividing it in two, creating our own subcultural Dr. Jekylls and Mr. Hydes. On the one hand, the license afforded by the growing climate of tolerance and permissiveness ushered many gay men into a whole new era of self-pampering, the slaphappy spirit of which can be summed up in *Blueboy*'s words of hygienic wisdom, "when you cleanse you moisturize . . . *Never* one without the other!"[15] These radically feminized creatures guiltlessly transgressed sacred masculine taboos against narcissistic self-absorption by waxing tufts of hair off simian shoulder blades, twisting their facial features into grotesque expressions as part of a daily regimen of antiwrinkle, "faceometric" exercises, and even "matching the color of [their] eye shadow to [their] outfit or eye color," as *Genre*'s "Lipstick Shtick" column recently suggested.[16] On the other hand, gay liberation gave men the confidence they needed to wage war against precisely these effeminate stereotypes and to assert themselves in exaggeratedly masculine ways, cultivating an implausibly studied machismo. As a result, the feminized body of the dandy, brought to a peak of perfumed, permed, and blow-dried perfection by the new male beauty industry, collided head-on with attempts to masculinize the gay body. Rather than solving the self-image problems that had long plagued homosexuals, gay liberation ironically created an entirely new set of problems which divided a community that was once far more uniform in its physical appearance into two warring factions (each of which accused the other of being "unnatural," with the bourgeois homosexual dismissing the clone as fake, "mainstream," and "conformist," and the clone, in turn, dismissing the bourgeois homosexual as "synthetic," prissy, and affected).

The rugged, unkempt look of what might be called the "antibourgeois body" of the clone was resonant with disgust for the consumerized appearance of the beauty maven whose immaculate and inviolable temple the new urban cowboys proceeded to desecrate in highly symbolic ways, piercing their ears and nipples, tattooing their biceps, growing hair on their faces, and even going unwashed for days at a time to enhance their naturally fetid odors. Whereas homosexuals had traditionally modeled their bodies on the patrician ideal of the clean-shaven,

15. "Grooming Beyond the Haircut," *Blueboy,* December 1981, p. 58.
16. *Genre,* October 1994, p. 74.

upper-middle-class aesthete, many men now took an unprecedented step downscale and rejected this aristocratic appearance
for an even more spurious blue-collar look loosely based on
quixotic images of old-fashioned frontiersmen and hearty ple-
beians like marines and truckers.

As a device for improving the self-esteem of homosexuals,
the antibourgeois body was an extremely problematic invention, given that the gay man's newly acquired blue-collar physique stood in marked contrast to his bourgeois life and profession. The antibourgeois body was therefore conceived, like any
modern, easy-to-clean kitchen appliance, with the utmost consumer convenience in mind: its piercings and tattoos could be
easily concealed beneath the crisp white shirts, expensive silk
ties, and neatly tailored suit jackets of traditional business at-
tire. Because of this adaptability, the clone could pursue the
most conservative of professional careers without betraying to
the world the real man lurking beneath the mild-mannered
facade of the bank teller and the office clerk who, as soon as the
five o'clock whistle blew, metamorphosed into a marine, a cop,
or a cowboy in full working-class regalia. Even today, tattoo
artists and piercers still openly acknowledge—and even
praise—the duplicitousness of the antibourgeois body; they
comment without a trace of irony on the "satisfaction of knowing that one is different underneath one's business suit" and
marvel at their favorite customers who pull the wool over the
eyes of their straight colleagues, such as the man who "has over
200 piercings and if you saw him on the street you'd just think
he was somebody's grandfather. You'd never in a million years
guess!"[17] White collar by day, blue collar by night, the antibourgeois body is a reversible body, a toy that can be taken
out in the evening and put away again at the crack of dawn.
While the homosexual is anxious to escape the effeminate
stigma of his professional life, he is entirely unwilling to give up
its material advantages and therefore attempts to straddle two

---

17. *Modern Primitives (Re/search* No. 12: Re/search Publications, 1989), pp. 92,
154.

separate classes, to have the best of both worlds, to attain the sexual charisma of the prole and retain the creature comforts—the glass coffee tables, Japanese prints, and porcelain figurines—of the bourgeois gay man. The clone thus leads a dual existence, living a fractured life with a fractured identity.

Ironically, both the bourgeois body of the queen and the antibourgeois body of the clone were vulnerable to a new form of insecurity. In opening himself up to the products of the cosmetics industry, the homosexual added another destabilizing factor to his physical self-image. As companies began to market to gay men "papaya peels," mint cold creams, and eye makeup that promised to "enhance the excitement of your come-hither gaze," they employed exactly the same techniques that they traditionally have used to coerce women into buying their products. Through advertisements that evoke in macabre detail the disfiguring effects of neglect, manufacturers have always threatened the female consumer with a form of facial blackmail in which they present graphic descriptions of the warts, wrinkles, and blotches that will permanently scar her skin if she is foolhardy enough *not* to buy their products. Behind every cosmetic advertisement in *Vogue, Mademoiselle,* and *Glamor* is the implied face of a ghastly pariah whose ravaged features, afflicted with a nightmarish array of dermatological disorders, form a cautionary portrait of the woman who failed to heed the cosmetic industry's apocalyptic warnings. Skin-care companies do not coax and seduce, they preach and terrorize. In order to force people to purchase their panaceas, they exaggerate the extreme delicacy of the face, its precariousness, fragility, and brittleness, its urgent need of "intensive care," "therapies," "formulas," and "face systems," the rhetoric of triage for the mutilated accident victim, and imply that only the "biological moisturizing agents" created in "the Skincare Laboratories of L'Oréal" or Estée Lauder's "nonacnegenic" and "hydration"-promoting lotions can "salvage" or "rescue" it. When manufacturers discovered the gay market, they infected gay men with the same dread of the cratered visage of the rash and incautious shopper who flirted with disaster by using lotions that are "possibly dangerous to facial skin"[18] and scouring pads so abrasive that if "you scrub too hard . . . you'll bleed."[19] With the growth of the male beauty market throughout the 1960s and 1970s, this new source of anxiety begins to disrupt and complicate the homosexual's image of his body, which is now at the mercy, not only of the intimidatingly masculine physiques of homicidal rough trade, but the equally murderous cosmetic industry, which drives him to take ever more expensive precautions to stave off the encroachments of age.

In attempting to assuage our fears of disintegrating into the battered carcasses of worn-out old queens, we have succeeded in creating another problem altogether, the problem of what might be called homosexual artificiality. Many gay men are haunted by the conviction that, by anointing themselves with "hypoallergenic" lotions, "unique under-eye *crèmes*," and the skin-care products of such openly gay companies as Dorian Gray Ltd. (which during the 1970s sold "Jeunesse"), they have lost their naturalness and become ageless, artificial creatures with skin taut from too many face-lifts and pouting, bee-stung lips swollen with collagen injections. By succumbing to the extortion of the cosmetics industry and pickling ourselves in preservatives, we have become little more than virtuoso feats of self-taxidermy. Straight men, by contrast, maintain their "naturalness" and masculine authenticity by allowing themselves to disintegrate and refusing even to lift a hand to arrest the process of aging. Examples of this uncultivated masculinity can be found in *Physique Pictorial*, where the editors harp, not only on the violence of the models, but on the alarming rapidity with which they age, as well as the indifference they manifest toward maintaining their beautiful bodies, whose transience becomes a measure of their virility. In order to reassure the viewers of the heterosexual "genuineness" of the men on the page, the editors compose extemporaneous *carpe diem* poems about the models even as they brandish in their readers' faces their police dos-

---

18. *Looking Good,* p. 73.
19. *Looking Good,* p. 75.

siers: "since this photo was taken, David has become considerably heavier and lost his 'boyish charm' "[20] "Dust . . . once had a far better build, but like many others, neglected it when life came too easy for him";[21] "Gerald Sullivan had gotten a bit mature at the time we did these studies";[22] "when we last saw Forrest he had more tracks on his arms than NY's Grand Central train station and he was worthless for modelling at that time."[23] In contrast to the gay body, the straight man's body has an extremely short period of perfection, coming to fruition for a few brief years in his teens and early twenties and then quickly sliding into a state of irreversible decline in which he gains weight, loses muscle tone, and then, within months, spreads and sags into premature old age. The speed with which the heterosexual's body goes to seed testifies to his lack of vanity and self-preoccupation, the girlish narcissism that leads the homosexual to mummify himself in the quack cures of consumerism. In contrast to the careless blue-collar slob, gay men are timeless vampires, Dorian Grays who flaunt their perennial good looks even as their once youthful portraits, locked away in their attics, shrivel and turn to dust. Having become the slave of consumerism, which fed his fears of getting old, the gay man launches a restless, lifelong effort to rid himself of his guilty sense of fakeness, of artificiality, and to recover his "naturalness," which he restores through a series of elaborately costumed impersonations.

In the act of remaking themselves in the images of such mythical icons of American masculinity as gunslinging cowpokes and close-cropped leathernecks, homosexuals failed spectacularly to alleviate their nagging sense of inadequacy to straight men, whose unaffected sexual self-confidence continues to serve as the subcultural touchstone of manly authenticity. Rather than rejecting outright the notion that gay men are less "real" than straight men, the post-Stonewall subculture in-

---

20. *Physique Pictorial,* October 1964, p. 13.
21. *Physique Pictorial,* May 1979, p. 3.
22. *Physique Pictorial,* July 1972, p. 28.
23. *Physique Pictorial,* September 1982, p. 12.

ternalized this belief and embraced without reservation the standards of masculinity formulated by straight society, building around them the mystical ceremonies of a whole new folk religion. When we attempted to heal the pathology of the gay body by embarking on the costume dramas of the new machismo, we did not succeed in freeing ourselves from our belief in the heterosexual male's evolutionary superiority nor did we accept on its own terms our overdemonstrative style of talking and gesturing. In fact, we did precisely the opposite, and became our own worst enemies, harsh, homophobic critics of the campy demeanor of the typical queen. In the process, we intensified the instability of the gay body, which was in some sense less psychologically disturbed when we were content simply to drool over the physique photographs of straight men rather than to reshape ourselves according to their physical paradigm. After Stonewall, many gay men did not engage in liberating acts of self-acceptance, as we are often led to believe, but in emotionally demeaning acts of self-cancellation.

However butch, tattooed, pumped up, and pierced many homosexuals have become since the 1970s, the acts of desecration we perform on the bourgeois body, scrubbed with astringents and reeking of Chanel No. 5, are never entirely successful. Even the most subversive efforts to masculinize the body are often suffused with the aesthetic sensibility of the designer queen who fusses over his tattoos and worries over his nipple rings with the same distraught air of indecisiveness with which he might decorate his apartment, choosing the right color scheme and coordinating the pattern of the curtains with the carpets.

The process of selecting a tattoo, for instance, is often described in gay magazines, not as the drunken lark of sailors, who once chose naked ladies and grinning skulls from cheesy "flash" boards, but as a task as complex as that of an upholsterer who pores over fabric swatches:

> Pick where you want [it] to go on your body, and try to
> visualize it . . . Your idea should be large enough that

it can be perceived and understood from a few feet
away. It should be placed in a way that complements
your body, because when you move, so does the tattoo,
and that is one of the subtle beauties of the art . . . A
little bitty rose is kind of lost on a big arm . . . Think
of your body as a moveable canvas with 18–20 square
feet of surface area—approximately the same as one
side of a normal door. [And remember that the sun]
will fade out any delicate shading and promotes blurring. If you spend a lot of time in the sun, keep the
color scheme simpler and darker, and even consider
foregoing the tattoo work altogether, particularly if you
prefer a nice tan.[24]

The writer describes an act of self-vandalism, so popular among
the lower classes, in distinctly upper-class terms, as if the gay
man were trying on a designer suit or vacillating over a radical
haircut at a beauty parlor, rather than trying to impress schoolgirls, as proletarian boys did during the 1950s when they frequently tattooed their left biceps so they could display them
outside of their car windows as they cruised past the drive-in
diners and drugstore soda shops.

In an article entitled "Tattooed Tit Enhancement" in the
gay S/M magazine *Drummer,* the author advises his readers
that, before they engage in the common practice of enlarging
and darkening the aureole around the nipple through tattooing,
they collaborate with their lovers in sessions of "colorization
foreplay" in which they decorate their breasts with Magic
Markers and experiment with the "design, color, and size of the
aureole"; such sessions make "great Tit Scenes in themselves,"
we are told, "as the Tit Coach works out with the Tit Jock
savory visions of how big the aureole and how dark the ink of
the burgeoning nipples."[25]

As these examples reveal, the gay man's body has become

---

24. *Drummer,* #141, August 1990, p. 19.
25. *Drummer,* #143, October 1990, p. 20.

a living, breathing battlefield in which the queen and the clone grapple for supremacy. No matter how macho the gay man tries to be, his strut inevitably becomes a mince, his deep voice a husky Marlene Dietrich contralto. His tattoos and piercings are refracted through a deeply embedded and ineradicably bourgeois sensibility, which cannot be suppressed but pops up inappropriately right in the midst of the most manly rites of passage in which the real person emerges like a flower arranger or a window dresser who flounces around making tough aesthetic decisions, his brow furrowed, his pinkie stabbing the air.

Over the past two decades, the very rituals of body defacement that once served the subversive function of defiling the aesthete's prissiness have gradually been transformed into methods of body beautification, as can be seen in the utter change in the nature and purpose of tattooing and piercing in contemporary gay culture. Whereas the tattoo was once inspired by the male-bonding rituals of sailors, criminals, and gang members, who bequeathed it to their gay tricks as a symbol of their masculinity, it has now assumed a central role in the new unisex look of androgynous chic and as such has been completely voided of its previous manly associations with the blood brotherhood of felons and merchant marines. Moreover, whereas the cheap "flash" art of anchors, eagles, and "In Memory of Mother"'s originated among the lower classes, the custom-designed tattoos of the nineties fin de siècle "auteur" school originate in the highly individual sensibility of the cultural elite who plan their tattoos in consultation with professional illustrators as if they were one-of-a-kind art objects. Similarly, the clone's piercings, which once served a narrowly erotic function (specifically of heightening sensations in the nipple), have now become distinctly ornamental, appearing in nostrils, septums, eyebrows, navels, cheeks, and even tongues, which are punctured with a glittering array of studs, hoops, amulets, and brooches. Likewise, the bristling walrus mustaches, mutton-chop sideburns, and straggly beards popular during the 1970s and early 1980s have been converted in the

1990s into dapper goatees, which, far from indicating chest-thumping burliness, are meant to be neat and tidy, suggesting the natty style of a fastidious and carefully tweezered aesthete. Even homosexual's strenuous bodybuilding workouts, which we first used to butch ourselves up, have ultimately become a sign of the queen's obsessive interest in grooming and self-maintenance. By the early 1980s, when the new extremes of AIDS-inspired health consciousness drove homosexuals to immerse themselves in what has been called "gym culture," muscularity had become so synonymous in the minds of most people with gay narcissism that a well-toned physique was an almost certain giveaway of one's sexual orientation. In the course of only a few years, the masquerade of proletarian machismo that homosexuals adopted during the 1960s and 1970s has begun to collapse, and the sensibility of the aristocratic dandy has begun to reassert itself through all of the testosterone-induced fantasies in which it was buried for over a decade. The bourgeois gay body has gradually eaten through the husk of cartoonish virility in which it was imprisoned and begun to aestheticize even the most recalcitrantly macho things, which have been turned into dainty body illuminations, intricate embellishments, and exotic arabesques.

One part of the homosexual's anatomy in particular has become the subject of an almost allegorical struggle between the bourgeois and the antibourgeois body: the foreskin, a sacrosanct part of the penis that the *faux* prole has fetishized as a distinctive physical feature of lower-class American men, who are in fact circumcised less often than their middle-class counterparts. The impassioned manifestos against circumcision that homosexuals are constantly nailing to delivery-room doors are filled with intense indignation, especially those disseminated by U.S.A., the Uncircumcised Society of America, a sort of Save-the-Whales group for the prepuce whose members have actually written anthems in celebration of the foreskin. The following, for instance, is intended to be sung to the tune of "America the Beautiful":

O hood divine, O skin sublime
O foreskin dark or fair . . .
O wrinkled tip, O pouting lip,
Your beauty is all there.
Unveil, unveil man's tool of life
And cover it again . . .
The thrills are true, the pleasure too;
Why can't all men own you?[26]

The subject of hymns, poems, monthly magazines, and even a whole line of specialty pornography, the pouting lip is now an endangered species championed by hordes of gay supporters ready to take up arms in defense of the "natural beauty" of the "unadulterated cock." Magazines like *Uncut* comb medical literature for examples of atrocities perpetrated against foreskins, which over the centuries have fallen victim to such groups as Moslem warriors who, during the Middle Ages, "scalped" their European opponents on the battlefield, carrying away their foreskins in trophy bags or impaled on their spears. Similarly, anticircumcision propagandists commemorate World War II as the armageddon of the foreskin, the final showdown when savage physicians in the U.S. Army engaged in foreskin witch-hunts, flushing out innocent victims whose "wingflaps" one particularly insidious doctor in the South Pacific gleefully threatened to add "to my collection of pickled foreskins."[27] In anecdote after anecdote, the anticircumcision brigade invents for itself a history of oppression and harassment, a colorful martyrology that abounds in horror stories of uncircumcised schoolboys tormented in the locker room by their sadistic "clipped" peers, or hair breadth escapes by enlisted men who narrowly manage to evade the scalpel of the army surgeon, who mows down recruits in a vast holocaust of foreskins, decimating the American population.

For the homosexual who is striving to suppress the finicky

---

26. *Blueboy*, September 1984, p 78.
27. Bud Berkeley, "A History of the Foreskin," *Drummer*, Vol. 6, #54, 1982, p. 27.

bourgeois gay body, which abhors the smell of smegma as much as it adores the scents of the cosmetic counter, the wrinkled tip becomes, not only a symbol of proletarian "naturalness," but a badge of resistance against the puritanical forces of hygiene and regimentation that are attempting to reduce the gay man's body to something as odorless and antiseptic as a test tube. The proud owners of antibourgeois bodies nurse their own persecution complexes, savoring delusional fantasies that they are the victims of the sexually backward machinations of the medical establishment, as well as of mainstream gay men, who stalk them wherever they go, snipping the air with gleaming surgical scissors.

Many who have had the misfortune of being circumcised have gone so far as to act on these nostalgic longings for the pristine masculine body. They try out complex restoration techniques that involve stretching the skin of the penis with bizarre scope-like contraptions or using do-it-yourself kits that require tying the head together with loops of thread and then stuffing the pocket with items like cotton balls, marbles, and BB pellets.

In the heated debates that gay men wage over the foreskin, the ironies and contradictions of the antibourgeois body emerge with painful clarity, for while homosexuals often hold up naturalness as an antidote to the artificiality of the cosmeticized body, they are willing to undergo the most *un*natural cosmetic techniques to combat this artificiality. Moreover, they are blind to the contradiction of decrying circumcision as a criminal violation of the male body in its natural state while at the same time violating their own bodies by skewering their nipples, nostrils, navels, penises, and testicles with disfiguring piercings as invasive as any botched circumcision. The antibourgeois body is allegorized in profoundly inconsistent ways which demonstrate how artificial the whole enterprise of recovering one's lost, pristine masculinity really is.

The emergence of what the gay community calls "bear culture" provides yet another example of the civil war being waged in the physical aesthetic of our bodies between the young, hairless studs featured in porn films and the self-styled mountain men and redneck brutes who are trying to subvert the subculture's oppressively unrealistic standards of beauty. The bear phenomenon, which originated in the mid- to late 1980s, represents one of the most violent assaults that gay men have made to date against the overgroomed bodies of urban homosexuals, whom the editors at *Bear* magazine despise as perversions of masculine authenticity. Reviling "buffed baby boys,"[28] "hairless little flips," "18 year old bar bunnies," and "pretty cityboys with pretty preppy dreams dancing in their heads,"[29] bears hold up as the paradigm of real, "honest-to-God" men miners, loggers, lumberjacks, and Hell's Angels who rev up their "hawgs," guzzle moonshine, develop enormous beer guts, and wear grizzled Whitmanesque beards like Old Testament prophets.

A pornographic bear short story entitled "Mountain Grizzly" (by "Furr") revolves around the conflict between men who like the depilated buttholes and squeaky-clean bodies of blond surfers and those who prefer the ripe pits and mats of woolly chest hair of "rough, tough, big-bearded dudes carousing around a campfire, playing harmonica, fiddle . . . guitar, [and] passing the jugs of 'Pie.' "[30] After a ranger rescues a city slicker whose tent was washed out in a mountain storm, he apologizes to his guest for his raunchy smell, having lived alone in the wilds of the Rockies for such a long time. This confession inspires his guest to launch into a vitriolic lay sermon against gay overgrooming, during which he tells his host that "I think the perfumes and garbage most 'city folk' wear are a lot more objectionable than the way a person smells naturally."[31] To prove his point, he promptly jams his nose into the man's armpit and then dives for his crotch, rubbing his "stache" in the ranger's natural juices. These coy gestures of flirtation have their desired effect and his host, variously referred to in his guest's

---

28. *Drummer,* #140, June 1990, p. 26.
29. *Drummer,* #119, July 1988, p. 19.
30. Jack Fritscher, "How to Hunt Buckskin Leather Mountain Men and Live Among the Bears," *Drummer,* #119, July 1988, p. 22.
31. *Drummer,* #119, July 1988, p. 29.

ecstatic exclamations as "Daddy Bear," "Grizzly Bear," and "Daddy Grizzly," proceeds to sodomize "baby bear" up his "cubby-hole."[32]

Such attempts to aestheticize hairy, out-of-shape bodies are in part motivated by fatigue with the amount of energy required for the onerous maintenance of the bourgeois body, which can be kept at its deodorized peak of svelte perfection only through backbreaking regimens of diet and exercise. But the cult of burliness is also fueled by an unprecedented new spirit of acceptance of a physical phenomenon once dreaded in the gay community, the unspeakable taboo of aging. While the old queen was once the pathetic laughingstock of gay culture, a much-derided spinster who collected antiques and knitted tea cozies, in the age of the bear she has been taken out of her mothballs and recast as "Grizzly Daddy," a figure whose physical disintegration has been invested with the authority and virility of an aging patriarch. As the incarnation of older gay men's impatience with the tyranny of the youthful body, which is always sleek and hairless, the bear might be defined as a Dorian Gray who has destroyed his own portrait. The bear is a man who allows himself to age in public, refusing to reverse the ravages of time by burying them beneath Max Factor foundation bases, facelifts, Grecian Formula rinses, and hair replacement systems.

If the bear movement is inspired by perfectly reasonable frustrations over the prevalence in the gay community of a single prescriptive body type, its hirsute ideal of rugged masculinity is ultimately as contrived as the aesthetic of the designer queen. While bears pretend to oppose the "unnatural" look of urban gay men, nothing could be more unnatural, urban, and middle class than the pastoral fantasy of the smelly mountaineer in long johns, a costume drama that many homosexuals are now acting out as self-consciously as Marie Antoinette and her entourage dressed up as shepherds and shepherdesses. The bourgeois urban sensibility emerges all too clearly through the

---

32. *Drummer*, #119, July 1988, p. 30.

agrarian facade of these "shit-kicking . . . bearded guys in full leather buckskins, wearing fur animals on their heads . . . spending their . . . winters out trapping skins and fur [until], come the spring thaw, YEE-HAW!—these American bear-trappers come down from the high country."[33] The contradiction implicit in the bear aesthetic between the ghettoized mind-set of the urban homosexual and his bucolic fantasies, which hark back to the bygone era of the Hatfields and McCoys, becomes especially evident in the closing scene of "Mountain Grizzly." Here, Daddy Bear proposes to his "cub" that the next time he comes up to the mountains they erect a fist-fucking sling in a clearing, a strange urban nonsequitur imported straight out of the famous sex club the Mineshaft, and set up incongruously in the placid, Arcadian setting of the forest primeval. Just as the designer queen inevitably peeps out from beneath his blanket of blue-collar tattoos, so inside of every bear there lurks . . . a Goldilocks.

The entire bear phenomenon is unnatural in another respect as well. Although bears profess to venerate the paternal authority of older men, it is difficult to imagine a more infantile preoccupation. Regression is ironically one of the major aims of the new religion of maturity. The movement is tainted with the kitsch of "The Care Bears," as can be seen in the personal ads in *Bear* magazine, which are full of "furry little critter[s]," "papa bear[s]," "baby bear[s]," "teddy bear[s]," "honeybear[s]," "cuddly grizzlies," "older fur balls of quality," "cute little daddy's boy[s]," and "warm fuzz[ies] in [their] 30s" who want "to hibernate in [a] den" or engage in "den play," "denning," or even "den shopping." Images of pedophilia are central to bear sex scenes, which often revolve around the hairy bogeyman's invasion of the nursery, as well as the violation and misuse of soft, squeezable stuffed animals, of plush koalas and silky pandas who are seeking "brawny, uncut papa bear[s]" to "expand an already sick-minded cub's limits" or to engage in "fuzz therapy" with "gosh-darned really good [bears]" ("no morbidly

33. *Drummer*, #119, July 1988, p. 22.

obese bears, please"). While the bear movement projects hostility toward the perennially youthful bourgeois body, it, too, is based on a central fantasy of boyishness and vulnerability, on the infantilism of the decrepit. If you skin the bear, you find, not a toothless hillbilly with a shotgun and a still, but the typical age-obsessed queen with a subscription to *House Beautiful* and a Japanese tea garden. Just as the tattoo has become a brooch, so the bear's fur is really a mink stole. It is ultimately impossible to imprison the bourgeois body, to deprive it of its lotions, starve it of its *eaux de cologne* and depilatories, and stuff it in the hair shirt of apelike masculinity. Its effeminate refinement infuses everything it comes in contact with, reappearing in the course of time like an image that has been painted over, a pentimento that shines through the fading tattoos and the thinning hair, the Mardi Gras masks and Groucho Marx noses in which we have disguised it, hidden it away out of shame.

Bob Shacochis

Missing Children

One morning last April, groaning with self-reproach but not yet contrite, I woke up in an unfamiliar place, somewhere I had never slept before yet nevertheless under my own roof. I had done this maybe a half dozen times in the two decades my wife and I had been together—abandoned her, crying and curled into herself, in the bed we shared and exiled myself to a spare room or downstairs couch, tugging a stubborn blanket of fury over my head like a temporary shroud.

The image of bedtime estrangement—a potent domestic cliché—evokes fault even in the absence of fault, but the tension between us that had erupted the night before into a matched set of absurd accusations had nothing whatsoever to do with infidelity and everything to do with faith: faith that, despite the odds, we could survive as a couple even as we confronted the defeat not of romance but of the garden of our mutual flesh. For during the past eight years, while America cried crocodile tears over the apparent dissolution of its families, my wife and I had knocked our heads against emotional and physiological brick walls trying to manufacture a family of our own. We had tried our very best to heed Babe Ruth's stalwart advice—"Never let the fear of striking out get in your way"—but if baby making were baseball, our team was now playing its final season, and the last game was all but over.

Early on in our life together, my wife had decided to avoid pregnancy, which is not the same as the desire to remain childless, although that's how it had seemed to me at the time, back at the beginning of the 1980s, when I was in my early thirties and first raised the subject of children with the woman I lived with and loved. More than wanting the freedom to anchor herself in a career, she simply didn't wish to be pregnant, she told me, ever; pregnancy was synonymous with trauma, perhaps even self-destruction. And although I was alarmed by her rhetorical absolutism, I was also willing to tell myself that this was not her final word on procreation, that the subject could be deferred without disadvantage and then favorably resolved—that, like all things, it would be held accountable to its own season.

Still, my literary and biological clocks had apparently been set to the same mean time, synchronized to similar imperatives, and it made full sense to me that my first breaks as a writer, when I began faintly scratching the fact of my existence on the palisades of the external world, coincided with the wistful clarification of my desire for offspring—on one of many levels, the impulse to secure readers, to pitch a rock into the generational pool and contemplate the concentric rings that ripple through a self when one's blood-past has made a concerted effort to speak to the future. This was a gift I myself had not inherited (only the dimmest record of my peasant ancestors survived), and, for reasons of self-admiration, I envied my future progeny, whom I hoped I might one day engage, through my writing if nothing else, on terms so intimate that the existential distance between parent and child would compress to mere logistics, and never would I be mistaken for a stranger but recognized as a fellow traveler.

Although children arrive on earth adorned with metaphorical ribbons of immortality, a life with a child is, finally, only a life of days actually lived. Shakespeare's third sonnet, which warns "Die single, and thine image dies with thee," is quaint and sentimental, vulnerable to the vicious paradox of time and the technological eternities, illusory and fleeting, that proliferate across the surface of contemporary life. Beyond the increasingly bad moral premise of the biblical command to go forth and multiply, the rationales for having children felt rather metaphysically arbitrary to me, weighted with self-love and often preempted by accident, but there were lines in the sonnet that struck me with the force of crippling hunger, lines that made me imagine one day seeing the face of my wife in the face of my son or daughter—"Thou art thy mother's glass, and she in thee/Calls back the lovely April of her prime." If my words were meant to reproduce myself, my corporeal seed had a loftier, more lovesick goal: to reproduce my wife. And although I understood this was, in its most gentle form, the ideal scenario of love, and most represented my preference, it was, I had to concede, only one of many variations on the theme of parenthood.

For if love itself were a destiny, like geography or genetics, once a child washed ashore in your life, was it really so important where that child came from, did it matter how it arrived? The shape of her eyes, the color of his skin? Maybe, I told myself, yet maybe not. Which is to say, however much I wanted a child, I didn't feel bound to any specifics or obligated to motivations that reared inward, back to the barn of DNA. Nor did I believe that having children was what it meant to grow up, or that having children was an innately self-magnifying event for an adult rather than, as is sometimes the case, pathetically self-subverting. We weren't, to our knowledge, fundamentally lonely, needy, or incomplete people, my wife and I; we could discern no gap in our collective psyche that needed to be repaired by a child. Yet if procreation was not the zenith of an individual's existence, it was still an immense and astonishing opportunity. Why ignore a vital clause in the divine contract, not necessarily between men and women but between humanity and life? Why show up at the celebration empty-handed, with nothing to give back to that from which you have taken?

If, for the moment, my wife resisted the appeal of kids underfoot, fine, because as the years passed our life was whole without them. So when, at her prompting, we stopped using contraceptives, it seemed to me we had tacitly decided to wait and see what happened, and this rearrangement seemed a workable balance between what chance found and determination might deliver. I told myself that, regardless of what either of us intended, someday an alarm clock would ring, wake my wife from her reluctance, rouse me from my dreamy ambivalence, and we would consciously, conclusively, propel ourselves into the future and mate. And it did, in fact, happen . . . the way sadness happens, the way it takes up permanent residence in your life. One heartbreak and then another, and then that's it: something precious has receded, beyond reach, forever.

Sooner or later, I suspected, the focus would sharpen, and so it did on Christmas Eve, 1988, in a cabin in the Uinta Mountains of Utah. My wife and I found ourselves trapped in a blizzard with Tyrone, our aging Irish setter, our surrogate son. He was dying, and as I watched his labored breathing, I hated myself for removing him from the old-dog comforts of Florida to expose him to this terrible blast of cold. Finally my wife insisted we buck up, drink a bottle of wine, try to enjoy the meal I had cooked on this damaged but still sacrosanct occasion, and then afterward, the Christmas treat she had been anticipating all day: we'd repair to bed and listen to our friend Ron Carlson on National Public Radio, reading his beguiling short story "The H Street Sledding Record."

But as the moment approached, the radio's reception tore away into tatters of static, and my wife howled. It was Ron himself who had lent us the cabin; there was a copy of his collection, *The News of the World,* there. My wife announced she would read the story herself, out loud. Shivering on a couch across the room, she began. The story is about a young couple in Salt Lake City who each Christmas Eve go sledding with their daughter. It's a law, I think, not of life but of humanity, that you create your own myths, find things to believe in, things smaller than God but larger than a credit card, in order to inhabit a loving universe, and this fictional family's annual attempt at the H Street sledding record—the moment the daughter wedges herself between her mother and father atop the sled and they accelerate into the snowy darkness—becomes the defining rite of their union. My wife kept her composure until the last two paragraphs, when her voice began to waver: "Now the snow spirals around us softly. I put my arms around my family and lift my feet onto the steering bar."

I watched dismayed as my wife locked up in agony on the final lines, the book slipping from her hands. "I want my own daughter," she said, her voice barely audible. She lifted her head, her lower lip trembling, and looked at me. "I want my own daughter," she cried adamantly, as if suddenly understanding that she had been opposed in this desire and it was time to fight back against whatever it was within her fate that had designed this prohibition. "God! God *damnit,* where is my little girl?" I leapt up from the bed to rock her in my arms while she exhausted herself into sleep. She was thirty-five years old. I was thirty-seven. This was the Christmas when my wife and I realized there was indeed a missing person in our life together, and this was the moment we began the enormously difficult quest to track and rescue that person, that child, from the wilderness of our shared imagination.

That Christmas also marked the end of our biological innocence, our sense of ourselves as autonomous beings patterned by the mystery of creation rather than, after technology's sublime seduction, mere organic systems as readily manipulated as the electrical impulses inside a machine. And although this is a story that has counted and recounted its years, its blood cycles, begging an ending that never arrives, becoming a small, private tale of weariness and despair, but equally of tenacity and hope, it is also, and primarily, a travelogue about a journey we took into the kingdom of science and beyond. I couldn't tell you what this other place was called, the world beyond the envelope of empirical remedy, but its cities are named Dream and Myth, Angel and Supplication, and its central crossroads are named Anything You Want and Delusion.

A few weeks after we returned from Utah, we lost Tyrone, our alter ego: the purest, simplest, and most viscerally consistent reflection of our joy in togetherness. Tyrone had been with us since the early days of our relationship. We, a childless couple, were not and had never been two, always three. I didn't expect our lives would ever be the same. For weeks I sat mourning in a chair, stupefied by the awful, intolerable emptiness of the house, and yet I thought I didn't want another dog; maybe now was the time to seize complete freedom, take advantage of our lack of responsibility for another life, however much I savored the clarity and mechanisms of such responsibility. My wife coaxed me back to my senses. It was time, she finally said, to go on.

We got a new pup, very much like obtaining a new chamber for one's heart, and now implicit in my wife's domestic building code was a clause acknowledging that our relationship had been rezoned for kids. "You're sure?" I was compelled to ask. We had been together thirteen years, and after our first year, when she had told me she never wanted to be pregnant and told me why, I told myself to be patient and never pressed the issue. She is a remarkable woman, beautiful and strong, an intelligent and mature woman who, as a junior in high school in the late 1960s, was out of it enough to get unwittingly pregnant. This happened before *Roe* v. *Wade,* and her parents, as you might imagine, reacted in a manner that could not have been mistaken as sympathetic. In order to have a legal abortion she had to be declared mentally unfit by not one but two psychiatrists, and so her folks dragged her off to the shrinks, then dumped her alone at Columbia Hospital for Women in Washington, D.C. My dear girl. No one thought to tell her what was about to happen, that the fetus was too far advanced for traditional intervention and instead would require a saline-solution abortion, actually a method for inducing labor, and its result would not necessarily be immediate. The OB/GYN doctors pumped my wife, who was once this frightened girl, full of salt water, and then housed her away in a room for three days, waiting for her body to evict the child, which it did on the fourth day, her womb evacuating its voluminous contents onto the tile floor. She was sixteen years old and five months' pregnant and alone. I never knew this girl, but I knew and loved the woman she had become, and if what had happened to the girl was something that the woman could not overcome, I understood, however helpless I felt in that understanding.

Now I needed reaffirmation of her own certainty, her willingness to push off from shore into the unknown and its surprising challenges, especially now that she was enrolled in law school, and yeah, she answered, she was sure. For the next two years we did what, conventionally, you do: we threw away the condoms and fucked. Beyond the customary rewards of lovemaking, nothing happened, although there were subtle changes in our conjugal pattern, a density that clustered around significant days of the month. I developed a keener sense of my wife's bodily rhythms, the tempo between ovulation and menses, and now I awoke to the *peep* of her digital thermometer as she tracked the rise and fall in her temperature that would signal the ovaries' release of eggs into the fallopian tubes. Without urgency, we went about our lives, conscious of our agenda but not (yet) neurotically enthralled by the process. We had set up shop, we were open for business, we had a modest goal, one customer was all it would take to measure success in our enterprise, we were frustrated but not alarmed, yet in the back of our minds, increasing in frequency, was an unsettling echo: *Nothing's happening.*

For baby boomers approaching middle age, the narrative of baby making has been ironically reversed, and frolicsome screwing no longer can be relied upon. The goddess Technologia is not now the protector but the enhancer—the madam, the pimp—here in the brothel of reproductive science, with its endless promises of redemption.

We had been living in Florida only a few years; my wife needed a trustworthy gynecologist. Female friends recommended a specialist, the best in town—let's call him Dr. Cautious—and, after an examination, which revealed no obvious cause for her inability to get knocked up, my wife became his patient. I soon fell victim to the diagnostic chronology and became suspect number one, ordered to sample the male version of the small but memorable humiliations commonplace to women in the literal maintenance of their inner lives. What I mean is, I had to provide semen for analysis—ejaculate into a jar, a dubious, shabby pleasure. How absurd the moment: the cold glass cunt, the quick indifferent hand, the presentation to a technician of this pathetic colloid specimen.

Several days later, we received the results. On the face of it, the news was somewhat of a relief. The analysis suggested that I might be the bump in our reproductive road, a condition easily repaired: no hot baths, boxer shorts, and, to compensate for my smoking, large doses of vitamins B and C. After two weeks of this regimen, it was clear my semen was adequate, and we were instructed to have sexual intercourse, after which my wife had to throw on her clothes and rush to the gynecologist's office for an appalling postcoital examination meant to determine if her body, reacting to my sperm, was issuing the wrong chemical signals, treating the pearly troops like hostile invaders. But no, nothing was amiss, we were all friends here in the birth canal. Dr. Cautious was cautiously optimistic. My wife and I allowed ourselves a half dozen months of mindless normalcy, bed-wise, before we were forced again to admit the obvious, only this time the obvious echoed with unsuspected depth and darker meaning. As two halves of a projected whole, we were failing to come together, turned back from our greatest ambition as a couple. We were failing to connect, not with eternity but with the present, the here and now, and the danger in that was a sense of self-eradication.

While Dr. Cautious stoically advised patience, my wife, tentatively at first, tried to convince him that what she felt instinctively was true—that she was walking around with a rare disease, nonsymptomatic endometriosis—and although she won this battle, she lost the war. Who would not agree that one level of hell is exclusively reserved for the insurance companies, medicine's border guards, who cast a beastly eye upon all would-be immigrants. Finally Dr. Cautious acquiesced to exploratory surgery, but our health insurance company responded with Las Vegas rules: if surgery identified a problem, they'd pay; if surgery was inconclusive, the $10,000 cost would have to come somehow from our own empty pockets. Lacking hard evidence that anything was wrong, the gamble seemed foolhardy indeed, and it took a full year, another year of futility, to switch our policy to a more magnanimous HMO.

Exploratory laparoscopy confirmed my wife's worst suspicion: the most severe class of endometriosis had gummed up her reproductive tract, and fibroid tumors as well as scarring condemned her to permanent infertility without corrective surgery. Good news, sort of; the procedure had a high success rate, but the preparation for it was a hormonal nightmare: my wife was made to endure two months of chemically induced menopause designed to shrink the marble-size growths and thus facilitate their removal. The operation was, in fine postmodern fashion, videotaped, so that later my wife and I could review it at home, watch in macabre fascination her uterus being scorched by a laser. "Look," came Dr. Cautious's laconic voice-over, "there's your gall bladder."

Five months later, my wife was pronounced fit, and a month after that she waved in front of me a little plastic stick from a home pregnancy test. Pregnant. I cheered, of course, I felt a surge of joy, yet no true sensation of accomplishment, knowing full well we would have to hold our breath as we crossed the immeasurable distance between a blue line on a stick and the deliverance of a child. A month later my wife returned home euphoric after her first sonogram, waving the indecipherable image of our embryonic union—a fingernail-size fishbaby. I couldn't relate to the linear storm of squiggles, which seemed of secondary importance to the sea change in my wife's demeanor. She had never felt better, she claimed, she had never felt this good in all her life. I soon found her on the phone, talking excitedly with her friends, her sisters, her mother, and I told her perhaps she should wait until the end of the first trimester to spread the happy news, but she couldn't contain her jubilation, she wanted to share the hard-won moment with those who loved her, and if the unthinkable happened, then, she thought naively, she would share the pain of that moment too.

The following month, December, I was on assignment in northeastern India, waiting for the sun to rise over southwestern China and burst forth among the peaks of the Himalayan range that dominated the near horizon, a mammoth uplift of the earth's crust culminating in the five summits of the world's third-highest, and most sacred, mountain—Kangchenjunga. As I climbed out of my jeep, something amazing happened. A shooting star blazed down, burning *below* Kangchenjunga's 28,099-foot summit, streaking down perhaps another mile before it extinguished. I was dumbstruck for a moment, and then I blurted out to my companions, "That was about my child." In the days ahead I would recount the story of the shooting star, and my listeners would congratulate me on such a lucky omen. Within a few weeks I would receive their letters at home in Florida, prayers that all was well with the child, that my first-born would be a son, but by then I knew that the very hour I had seen the star flame across the face of Kangchenjunga, halfway around the earth, the fetus had died and my wife was in the midst of a miscarriage.

Twelve months of rueful insularity passed, the condolences of our friends and relatives met by my wife's self-imposed silence. Faith returned us to the bedroom and failure returned us to another Christmas, another cascade of tears. I was caught by surprise and sat down next to my suddenly bawling wife on the sofa. "Honey, what's wrong?" I asked, embracing her. "The baby died a year ago today," she wailed. I didn't quite understand and stupidly asked, "What baby?" The truth was, I had never permitted myself to imagine the child that had inhabited her womb for a scant three months, a most ephemeral bond between us, tissue-thin, and prematurely ruptured. I had stored away my acceptance until I saw her belly inflate, until the day she placed my hand on its roundness to feel the first kick. Of course I knew the fetus had existed, but other than the enigmatic experience on the mountaintop in India I had not connected with that existence, and for me this shadow-child remained shapeless, faceless, and nameless, forever lost in the cosmic mail, something that had profoundly inspired us but had come no closer to our lives than a falling star.

But for my wife it was different: she had acknowledged this baby's presence in her breasts, her toes, her skin; and when its thimble of life had spilled—not a miscarriage technically but a death that would have to be cleaned away in the hospital—she had known that too, before any doctor's confirmation.

There were cognitive and psychological issues I came to realize were not mine and never would be, given my gender and its biological limitations. In the ongoing rehearsals for parenthood I was conception's silent partner, a passive investor, spermatologically speaking, whereas my wife was the line producer, subject to the paralyzing responsibilities of opening night. Awash in melancholy, I watched the burden of doubt crease her face. She felt under siege by the possibility that her continuing infertility would defeat our relationship: Was she dispensable? Would I awake one morning as merciless as Henry VIII? Such questions seemed anachronistic and landed like punches on my heart, yet it was true that it became more and more difficult to conceal my dissatisfaction with the progress of the campaign. Dr. Cautious ordered more tests, but to me his stewardship seemed defined by infuriating hesitation. Let's find out where we're going and get there, I lobbied my wife. All problems ought to have solutions.

As the year went by I was often on the road, one of us parachuting in on the other the days she ovulated. The schedule grew tedious, but there was a certain harried romance to it all. In six months we made love in Florida, London, New York, Missouri, and twice in Washington, D.C. My wife had finished law school and landed herself a demanding job as a staff attorney in the Florida State Senate drafting First Amendment legislation, her area of expertise, but she made no secret of her loneliness, falling asleep twenty-five out of every thirty days sandwiched between our two new dogs but otherwise deserted, and my guilt whispered to me: *give her a child to keep her company.*

Instead of abandoning hope, we amended it, developing contingency plans. We began to speak about adoption matter-of-factly, with an explicit though not fully parsed understanding that we would stay the biological course, run with the trickle of our luck until the trickle ran dry. Adoption was and always had been our safety net, and we in fact considered it a second act, a sequel; once we got rolling we were going to fill up the house. Whenever I headed overseas, before she kissed me goodbye, my wife would say in a fanciful voice, "Bring me home a baby," and I knew she meant it. First, though, we were going to expend all biological options like a twelve-step recovery program: one day at a time.

That summer I went to Haiti to cover the U.S. military intervention, traveling between the island and Florida for the next eighteen months. Dr. Cautious injected dye into my wife's womb, discovering a blockage of scar tissue in one fallopian tube and clear sailing in the other. I was made to jerk off into more bottles, then more tests, more pale assurances. My wife was beginning to feel like a tawdry lab experiment, and I frankly was getting fed up, not with her but with Dr. Cautious.

One night I returned from Haiti and found my wife in bed, her face swollen from weeping. She didn't often cry, and never for sentimental reasons. It was her habit to put on a brave face, to cloak her tribulations behind false cheer. Once or twice a year her suffering would overflow the cup of its solitude, and this was one of those times. Someone close to us had died in an accident, another was terminally ill, and her sister, she had just learned, had breast cancer. "I've been lucky," she told me bitterly, the tears streaming down her face. "There's tragedy in every life, but I've been spared. My tragedy is to have no children. I waited too long for everything."

Never had I heard my wife venture so near to self-pity, either before or since. Our struggle wasn't making either of us strong, only resigned, our hearts slowed by sadness. Her words frightened me, and their wretched poignancy galvanized me into action. Our advance to the next level was long overdue, and I insisted on accompanying her to a consultation with Dr. Cautious. Was I pushing this beyond her capacity and desire? No, she said, this is what she wanted, too. But no matter how much a couple discusses such things, the right and the wrong of a decision are never easily determined or entirely resolved. At the gynecologist's office, I listened to him murmur the platitudes of his profession—"just keep trying, hope for the best"—and I felt my pulse rise in reaction to the complacency of this well-intentioned but uninvested man. "This is no good, and I want it to stop," I said. I was now forty-three years old, my wife was forty-two, and time was the luxury of other, younger couples. "What do you want to do?" he asked, and we left with a referral to the fertility clinic at the University of Florida.

On the morning of our appointment in the summer of 1995, we drove to the Park Avenue Women's Center in Gainesville, Florida, where we sat in a waiting room filled with madonnas and infants, inhaling the postnatal smells—diapers and talcum and milky vomit—of our imagined destiny. We were fetched to an interview room and introduced to Ginny, a compassionate nurse who would serve as our guardian and guide into the enchanted forest of in vitro fertilization. The questions were common sense, the literature lucid and comprehensive—ovulation induction, egg retrieval, fertilization, embryo transfer, egg donation, and cryopreservation of "surplus embryos." Ginny explained success rates: IVF—25.3 percent; egg donor IVF—43 percent. A roll of the dice, we were told, but also a "realistic option for many infertile couples who might otherwise never become pregnant." A doctor came in to scan our medical histories, cluck over our age, and close the deal. "I recommend

we proceed aggressively," he said, and despite my wife's appre-
hension, I seconded the motion. Ginny returned to discuss the
finances: in the next eight months, in $5,000 increments, we
would empty our savings account, take out a bank loan, and
borrow against my future earnings.

After we were both tested for AIDS, my wife underwent a
pelvic exam. I was directed to the bathroom, given old copies of
Playboy—erotic white noise—and told to masturbate. This fat-
uous, unwanted pleasure was my one sacrifice on the altar of
fertility, a free ride compared with where my wife now stood
poised, a seasoned veteran of repeated bodily invasions, on the
feudal threshold of new tortures. We reunited in an examination room, where Ginny began uncapping syringes and lining
up innocuous vials of saline solution. Once we started down this
path, I would be called upon to give my wife a monthlong
sequence of daily injections in the ass, with a needle the length
of my middle finger, and now Ginny was going to teach me how
to do it. She demonstrated how to mix the hormones, fill the
syringe, tap it free of air bubbles, jab it to the hilt into an
orange. There was a pamphlet Ginny showed me, with a line
drawing of a woman's backside, identifying the half-dollar-size
area on each buttock that could safely receive the needle without injuring the sciatic nerve.

"Okay," said Ginny, "let's have your wife lie down and
pull up her skirt." I felt a flush of vertigo. "You're kidding," I
protested, but of course she wasn't: this was my only opportunity to get it right with the proper supervision, and as I leaned
over my wife's butt with the gleaming needle, I told Ginny I
didn't want to do this. "Just plunge it straight in like a dart,"
Ginny coaxed, and so I did, horrified as I watched my wife
grimace, her hands contract, and her knuckles whiten, and as
soon as I removed the needle from her flesh I lay down atop
her, aggrieved, kissing her cheek and apologizing. Teamwork, I
thought, had never been so ruthless. Ginny had been a paragon
of empathy, though, and I thanked her. "You have the perfect
job," I said ignorantly, "bringing so much joy into people's
lives." She brightened for a moment, but then her eyes turned

doleful, her mouth grim. "Yes," she said, "but when it doesn't work it can be devastating."

We soon would be well educated in the exact nature and magnitude of that devastation. Mid-August I was back in Haiti, and my wife began self-injecting Lupron, a drug that produced hot flashes and insomnia, into her abdominal wall to suppress and then synchronize egg development in her ovaries. A few weeks later I was home in time to begin turning her backside into a pin-cushion, shooting doses of Pergonal and Metrodin, to begin stimulating egg development, into her buttocks morning and night. Neither of us was brave about the hateful needles, and the tension between us rose; under the stress of hurting her, I'd yell, she'd weep, and for a month the process itself made us adversaries. We both lived in dread of the injections. Frequent blood tests, which turned her arms black-and-blue, and ultrasound exams, in which she was painfully prodded by a wand inserted into her cervix, multiplied the hellishness of her torment.

Finally, when her ovarian follicles had achieved the optimal size, I shot her up with a hormone to trigger ovulation and we drove to Shands Hospital in Gainesville to be "harvested." For the second time in our lives, I impregnated my wife, although this time fertilization occurred in a petri dish, at the hands of Jack the white-coated embryologist, who, like a reincarnation of a nineteenth-century Fabergé artisan, further manipulated the cluster of cells in a new technique called "assisted hatching" and painstakingly abraded the shell of each embryo with an acid solution in order that it better adhere to the uterine lining. Two days later four embryos were placed inside a Teflon catheter and transferred into my wife's womb. We drove home. By the time she dragged herself to the clinic for a pregnancy test, the results were moot, because two days earlier, in a gush of tears and blood, whatever children who would ever unite our separate DNA structures, marry the essence of our flesh, and blend our natures into the next generation of us had vanished back into the unknowable starry night of nothingness. We were permitted two more attempts by the wizards of reproduction, both aborted early in the game when it was clear that my wife's body would not respond to the drugs.

It seems it's always meant to be December, and I am always meant to be away, when the news that fractures the foundation of our lives arrives. I called her from Haiti and listened quietly to her ragged, fatigue-ridden voice. Ginny had phoned that afternoon: my wife's ovarian reserve was depleted, her infertility was irreversible, she was biologically incapable of procreation and permanently exiled from the purest form of motherhood, though not from motherhood itself.

I came back home to watch my wife, shattered and bereft, decorate the Christmas tree, to rise early in the morning, day after day, to bake cookies for the holidays—*to bake and bake and bake and bake.* What was she going to say, what words would she use to describe her anguish, to tell me what was going on in her mind, to explain what happens to the heart when a woman's reproductive time runs the course of its season? And what more could I do than promise her, with a lover's force of conviction, that another Christmas would not pass without a child in the house?

Time in season, mine; time out of season, hers. How do you reconcile this severance, the split that occurs in a couple's imagination when what ends for the female continues on for the male? For a man, history's answer, unlike technology's, had been brutally simple: choose between the barren woman and your unborn children. But science had rolled the dilemma between its magician's fingers and come up with another option.

The April argument that sent me trudging to the guest room dispersed much, if not all, of the pressure that had built between us as we ventured further on the thin ice of possibility, loaded down with the weight of our decision to proceed with our fourth in vitro fertilization attempt. I had been afraid that my wife was balking at this, her final commitment in her role as immaculate guinea pig, afraid I had somehow coopted her into agreeing to try something she didn't want to do—accept the oocyte of another woman into her womb. It was the most delicate of issues, and I thought I had given my wife plenty of room to arrive at her own decision. Six months earlier she had said she would consider egg donorship only when it was clear that all other options had been foreclosed. If she said no, that would be okay; we would redirect our dwindling money, time, and energy toward adoption. What she said she expressed rather bluntly—"At least we'll know half of what we get, right?"—and whatever her doubts, she still wanted to seize this last chance to carry a child. But this would be it; for my wife the process had escalated toward the time when she would hand herself back to nature and be at peace, beyond reproach, beyond the secular optimism of machines and the artifice of miracles.

It was stress, not the strategy itself, that caused our freefall into that April night's hostility—a silly detail, the timing of a phone call to Ginny—but by the next day the conflict was forgotten, and the following month the last xeroxed calendar— OVULATION INDUCTION/ASSISTED HATCHING—taped to the refrigerator came down, a calendar similar to its three predecessors, each an anxious countdown through the spectrum of faith and the torment of science to the imagined felicities of maternity, and each climaxing with the death of hope. It was hope, more than anything else, that my wife most feared these days.

The next morning we were in Gainesville, in an operating room at the university's hospital. High-intensity lights, state-of-the-art computer-age electronics. Everyone was in green surgical scrubs except for my wife, who was draped in a flimsy institutional gown, prone on the table. Her feet were placed flat, and her legs were bent at the knees, a drape spread from one kneecap to the other, making an open-ended tent between her thighs. Her expression was upbeat, but in the far, courageous recesses of her eyes, under the surface of her resilient smile, I could see the look of someone persecuted over and over again with no possibility of escape.

The three faces of the stork—the doctor, Ginny the nurse coordinator, the embryologist—hovered over the table, gaily inspecting what my wife held in her hand: objects, icons, fertility fetishes—things she kept in a yogurt container. Her desperate cocktail of beliefs. There was a walnut-size clay sculpture of a Paleolithic Venus—the prototypical earth mother—sent by her ill sister in San Francisco. In a doll-size leather pouch, a saint's medal, perhaps the Virgin Mary with child, carried throughout World War II by the father of a friend who herself had two IVF daughters. In a spice bottle, several grams of holy dirt, said to produce miracles of healing, that my wife had scooped up from the floor of the mission chapel in Chimayo, New Mexico. On a chain around her neck she wore an evil eye I brought her from Turkey, her schoolgirl confirmation cross, a prelapsarian mosquito embedded in amber, and a small ring of happiness jade, a gift from a friend in China. Here on the frontier of neo-primitivism and the techno-voodoo of the new millennium, I couldn't resist a wisecrack. "Hey, she's even got a chicken's head from last night's sacrifice," I joked.

"You don't notice them pooh-poohing any of it," protested my wife.

"Why not?" said the embryologist. "You don't really think we have all the answers, do you? Who knows how all of this really happens?"

Collectively, we were all trying to ignore how bizarre this was—so weird it made me spin, the moments when I contemplated what we were doing. In my own hand I held a questionnaire filled out by the anonymous twenty-three-year-old woman with whom, two days previously, I had had test-tube sex. There was a cover page, a profile of the donor—short, "attractive," in Ginny's eyes, of German descent, a college graduate, a family history of heart problems—and on it, a statement of motivation that both intrigued and baffled me: "She wants to do something nice." Something *nice?* The language of altruism struck me as girlish and archaic. The night before I had dreamed about this young woman I will never meet; we sat in a room together and talked, although I couldn't remember what we said. At breakfast before coming to the hospital, I told my wife about the dream. "What did she look like, what color was her hair?" she asked (Ginny had told us the donor's hair was dark blonde). "Not really dark blonde," I said to my wife. "It had red undertones." Now, as I flipped through the questionnaire, my wife placed her finger on the page, pointing to a box stating the woman's hair color: strawberry blonde.

This is the part my wife prefers that I not write about— not the quirky, clutching mysticism but the enormously complicated choice of egg donorship, which neither of us had ever suspected would elicit such callous response from our closest friends. *Why would you want to do that?!* they challenged my wife on the telephone. Almost invariably these were women with their own children, women whose souls had never been lacerated by the psychic catastrophe of infertility, women who would never know the toll of our quest to have what for them was so easily given, women who would never blink at the mention of a sperm bank. Their swift, unthinking judgment brought out the devil in me: in my fantasies I took away their children, then proposed a deal—they could have them back, altered yet recognizable; their children would more or less look and act as they always had, yet they would no longer possess their maternal genes. It would be as though I had given them the opportunity to bear their own stepchildren in their wombs. That, or never see them again. What do you suppose they would choose?

The doctor pushed a button; above my wife's head, a television monitor descended from the ceiling, and there, on the screen, in translucent cabbage-green monochromatic simplicity, were the magnified kids, in truth no larger than the molecules of ink in the very tip of my pen, poised to write the word "gestation," the word "family." Three perfect human embryos in colloidal suspension: one five-cell cluster and two four-cell motes that, within the next few minutes, would be implanted into my wife. I studied the images with a mixture of awe and alienation. These were fairies, I suppose, angels dancing on the head of the embryologist's pin. More idea than substance, spirits videotaped on the cusp of potentiality, not quite of this world, clinging to the slightest speck of flesh in transition from nonexistence to being.

On the OR boom box, Jimmy Durante was singing "Make

Someone Happy." The doctor had his head between my wife's legs. The embryologist approached with a stainless-steel cylinder in his hands, something that resembled a cake-frosting applicator. The doctor fed the tube's catheter past my wife's cervix, the embryologist unscrewed a cap at the top of the cylinder, and gravity nudged the embryos home. "We don't want to see you coming back out of there," Jack told the fairies, "for nine more months."

A Saturday afternoon, ten days later, the beginning of Memorial Day weekend, last May 25. We were nervous wrecks, my wife and I. She had spent the morning sweeping the patio, then making mango sorbet and baking almond cookies for a dinner party we would host that night. A few moments earlier I had asked her how she was feeling and she said, "Weird," but there was no way to gauge the significance of this, and she went upstairs to lie down. In two more days—Monday—she would go to the hospital for a pregnancy test, if she could hold out that long. In the newspaper that morning I had read that on this day, sixty-one years ago, the great Babe Ruth hit the final home run of his career. That's something, I told myself, feeling a pang of encouragement.

Writers are perpetually giving birth to the vastly extended family of their characters. Sometimes, at night in the bathtub, I say their names, testing their appeal, the weight and music of the life-creating sounds: Kyra, Catherine, Jerusha, Jack, Sam—Sammy? Who are these people? I wonder to myself, trying to visualize their every detail. Sometimes they fall out of the cradle of my mind into a quasi-immortal existence on the page. The other night, though, I said their names and knew differently. Kyra, Catherine, Jerusha, Jack, Sam—Sammy? These are the children who will not come to me, to us, our ever wayward children.

Because it was a holiday, not business as usual at the chain of clinics and hospitals she depended on, my wife had meticulously prearranged the logistics of that Monday, Memorial Day, to avoid a breakdown in the lines of communication. After my wife's morning blood test, the clinic in our hometown would call in the results to the answering machine at the Park Avenue Women's Center in Gainesville; the on-call (but off-site) nurse who was substituting for Ginny would telephone the machine, listen to the recording, and then contact us with the news before noon. That's not how it went, however, because instead of phoning Gainesville as we had planned, the clinic that performed the blood test sent a fax to an empty office, and by noon, when we hadn't heard anything, my wife called the clinic, where the technician confirmed that the results had been "sent" to the women's center hours ago but refused to tell her anything else. She screamed in frustration and fear.

"Go run some errands," I said, shoving her out the door. "And by the time you get back they'll have called."

But no one called, and when she returned I watched my wife flip out, flinging the packages she carried into a window, knocking things off countertops, hitting back at me as I tried to subdue her, refusing any attempt at consolation, until finally her uncontainable hysteria imploded and she stumbled vacantly up the stairs to bed. I spent the remainder of that afternoon on the phone; finally I connected with an on-duty IVF doctor at Shands Hospital, and after he had phoned me back with the results of my wife's blood test I opened a bottle of wine, took a glass from the cupboard, climbed the stairs, and have never felt so dead as when I stood by our bedside and watched my wife face me and saw, *still*, the quick, upturned hope that was there, shining through the pain, as she turned to hear what I would say.

Sometimes I have to hold my wife harder than I ever dreamed or wanted, and repeat—as I have throughout the worst moments of the years behind us—a faith-borne cruelty, telling her yet again that this story has a happy ending.

Hubert Butler

Little K

In order to treat this subject objectively I had thought of calling them A, B, C, D and E. C, D and E would be my three grand-daughters, A and B their parents, but I find I cannot reach such heights of detachment and that I must call them by their true initials, J, D, C, S and K.

I do not see them very often, for they live in America. C is five years old and rather serious. She does not say very much, preferring to nod for "Yes" and shake her head for "No," but the whole time she is remembering and judging. I have an idea that when she grows up she will reject a great deal that most people accept. I feel very close to her and wish I could be beside her when the time comes for her to make decisions. S, who is still only two, is very different. She accepts everything and everybody and flings herself laughing and chattering into the arms of those she knows. C and S both remember K, my youngest granddaughter, of course, but there is always so much happening that they do not often ask about her. C liked to be photographed holding her but K went away when she was two months old and they will, I think, soon accept her absence as permanent. [So little happens to K that once at least I shall give her her real name, Katherine Synolda (1987).]

On my way to see K this morning, I walked through the park at Yonkers and tried unsuccessfully to find the Doric temple from which you are supposed to see the broad sweep of the Hudson River and the Palisades beyond. The park is laid out so as to make you forget that the largest city in the world stretches all around it. I walked down woodland paths, where wild copses of acacia and fir were choked and bent with their burdens of honeysuckle, and I came at last to a romantically ruined manor house with sagging roof and rotting window frames. The park is a place in which to relax, to tear yourself away from the complex and sophisticated problems of the city, where everything is pulled down before it has time to grow old, and plastic flowers outnumber real ones a hundredfold. So nature is allowed to half strangle the shrubberies and tear the manor house apart. But, in fact, you cannot walk very far without being reminded of the well-organized sorrows and joys of the city. At one end there is a Cardiac Centre and the jungle slides away from it deferentially towards the river; the rough paths compose themselves into gentle gradients suitable for wheeled chairs and cautiously shuffling heart cases. There is a smooth lawn with rectangular panels of salvia and petunia as neat and tended as temperature charts.

At the other, merrier end of the park, the derelict manor house, embedded in kalmia and rhododendron, has a notice on it: NO WEDDING PHOTOGRAPHS TO BE TAKEN HERE.

If you find relaxation here, it is by withdrawing and pretending; it is that fragile sort of peace which the gravely disturbed find in barbiturates.

East of the park and higher still above the Hudson is the long, low white house where K lives. I met D there and together we went to her room. She is with ten other babies and she has her name on her cot. She has a sweet baby mouth and chin and large blue eyes and above it a high domed forehead, which would have been lovely too were it not for the sharp ridge that runs down it from her skull. She has, I am told, agenesis of the corpus callosum. That is to say the central part of her brain has not developed and, therefore, the optic nerve too is defective. The whites of those beautiful eyes are tinged with blue and she is all but blind.

"But look," said a kind nurse, "she blinks when I wave my hand. I think she can focus a little too."

K did indeed blink, but it seemed to me that she just felt the draught of the nurse's hand.

D unclasped her hand, which was folded up like a bud, and showed me the palm.

"That's the simian line going straight across. You meet it in mongols. But it's not a sure test, as she isn't a mongol. I showed it to an obstetrician and he just held up *his* hand at me. He has the simian line too. All the other children here are mongols. Look at their lower eyelids! Look at the way their ears are set—very low!"

The nurse leant over and touched a small tin box attached to the cot and a tiny tinkle came from it.

"She loves her little musical box," she said.

There was a pause while we watched for a sign that K was loving it but none came. The nurse closed it by saying, "She never cries. She's so good." (Later D told me that, when K was born, she did not cry, like other babies, but was unnaturally quiet.)

"Will she ever be able to walk?" I asked.

"Oh, why not? Of course!" she replied encouragingly.

"And talk?"

"Oh, I expect so. But you must ask the doctor." She was embarrassed and broke off to greet a little boy who trotted into the room.

"Hello, Sammy! Back again?" and to us she said, "Sammy is the brightest of our little mongols."

I asked to see the older children and she took us into a sunny courtyard, where ten or twelve of them were playing. The swings were soaring up and down and a big ball was rolling about. A tall, almost handsome boy in a jersey with BEATLE printed on it rushed up to us jabbing his left shoulder and shouting something. It sounded like "Resident! Resident!" "No, we're not residents here," D said, "we're just here on a visit." "Resident! Whi How!" the boy bawled on, and we grasped that he was saying that he was the President of the United States. A girl of twenty with a broad blue band round her head, which was flopping from side to side, charged up to us. A swollen tongue stuck out of her mouth and she barked at us something we could not understand.

"Do they ever quarrel?" I asked the nurse.

"Oh, indeed they do!" She smiled at the innocence of my question. Then we went to the room of the totally unmanageable. "Don't you come!" I said to D but he insisted on going with me. These children cannot be given toys, because they destroy them. Some were incontinent and some had limbs that were frenetically askew. Television was on non-stop. ("They love their television," said the nurse.) Many of them had dreary commonplace delusions like the Beatle boy, taken from television or secondhand from the newspapers. One or two had some droll hallucination which two months ago I would have found touching and even entertaining.

As we went down the passage we passed the open door of a small room and in it I saw a charming-looking woman with greying hair. Her husband was with her and they were talking to a young defective. ("He gets fits," explained the nurse, "that's why he has the black eye.") As the mother saw us she turned to the boy with a gay and loving laugh. He looked unresponsively back and I knew that her animation was directed at us rather than at him. She was telling us that she was ready to do her part in trying to lift the great curtain of sadness that hung over us all.

When we reached the hall two merry little girls dashed past us, with their parents behind. "I know who you've come to see!" said the nurse, bending down to them. "Yes, Lucy! Lucy!" they shouted, and tore ahead. The nurse smiled at us as though to say, "You see, it's not all sadness. Children take it quite as a matter of course."

But I think it is all sadness, unnecessary sadness, from which the world has piously averted its eyes. The realities are concealed from us by a labyrinth of platitude as specious and unnatural as the honeysuckle jungle at Yonkers. There is not a child in that large establishment whose parents have not at one time thought what they dare not articulate: "I wish that my child would die!" And many, perhaps most, are still thinking it and secretly praying for it.

MME. VANDEPUT AND THE NINE CATHOLICS

As we drove home, D told me that one in ten of all the children in the United States is defective. I thought he must be exaggerating but when I got back I turned to the appendix of the book about the trial at Liège of Suzanne Vandeput, who killed her armless "thalidomide baby." The nine gently disapproving Catholic authors of this book, doctors and priests, give statistics of the mental defectives in France. They are about 7 percent of the population. How many of these, I thought, can be as well cared for as our little K, surrounded from babyhood with toys and paint boxes and swings, with practised smiles and laughter that is innocent or lovingly simulated?

The nine French Catholics are thinking of that too. Their book is learned, tender, imaginative. Not in one sentence do they denounce Suzanne; she was wrong, of course, they say, but they see her sin against a dark background of callousness, stupidity and smugness, and they recognize that science has transformed the human scene and totally changed the nature of our problems: "The new drugs," writes Father Roy, "can be as dangerous as they are salutary. The number of abnormal children is increasing; the doctors are opposing the process of natural selection by allowing beings to exist which are in no way human."

They are aware that the support that Suzanne Vandeput received from press and public in Liège and beyond was not only sentimental and unreflecting but scholarly as well. Father

Roy quotes, with bafflement and sadness rather than horror, two French doctors, Barrère and Lalou, who present a humanist point of view:

> Our age has effected so many transformations on man that the moral problems raised can no longer be answered by the ancient formulae. It is almost a new reality that we must learn to accept and mankind will need many years to construct a new humanism founded on the new man. Euthanasia seems to be one of the keystones of this future edifice.

The fact that this is quoted without horror shows that the nine writers are aware how unresponsive we have mostly become to the ecclesiastical anathemas of the past. With the advent of totalitarian and nuclear war the old Christian taboos on killing have fallen into such confusion that one moral argument has now to support itself with ten practical ones. Most of their arguments are therefore addressed to the humane and farsighted rather than to the devout.

(1) Only one writer, Father Roy, uses an argument that a sceptic or a Protestant might find offensive, for he links the euthanasia of the defective with divorce as a source of bad examples. Divorce, he says, is not only a disaster for the children of broken marriages but it also influences others to part, who without this way of escape might have "risen above their selfishness" and "attained to a richer marital understanding and love." But a non-Catholic could argue that divorce has brought as much relief as tension, as much joy as sadness, and that this is no argument at all.

(2) Father Beirnaert, S.J., predicts "personality disturbances" for the child whom Mme. Vandeput said she was going to bear in order to replace the armless child that she killed. It is right that we should reflect on such indirect psychological effects, but they are unpredictable. How can we judge their importance? One of the nine, Dr. Eck, speaks frankly of the marriages that were broken because of a defective birth, and the

jealousy that normal children, brothers and sisters, sometimes feel because of the special love which a good mother will sometimes give to her defective child. All these things may happen. But love and wisdom can sometimes solve these problems, sometimes must recognize that they are insoluble.

(3) Dr. de Paillerets asks how can one decide that one malformation will justify infanticide, while another will not? How can we decide who will be unhappy, who not? Healthy people may be miserable and severely handicapped people may be cheerful.

(4) He asks how can we be sure that cures will not be discovered for defects that now seem irremediable?

(5) He says, if doctors, even in exceptional cases, were to become the auxiliaries of death rather than of life, would they not certainly lose the confidence of their patients? "Without this confidence medicine cannot exist." And he says that, since the time of Hippocrates in the fifth century B.C., this "unconditional respect for human life" has been obligatory. He quotes the Hippocratic oath, which all doctors are still obliged to swear.

(6) The sixth argument is very odd:

Infanticide [he says] puts a curb on the enthusiasm of those who through their research contribute to the increase of our knowledge, and on the enthusiasm of those who, devoting themselves to the care of the unfortunate children, now find that we are equivalently disowning them and regarding their work as unnecessary. Medicine needs support from all of us if it is to keep its essential dynamism.

It is possible that one day some instrument will be invented which will register human sympathy, warmth of feeling. Surely, if it was attached to Dr. de Paillerets as he wrote this, it would register zero. How otherwise can he think of a parent's agony in connection with the progress of medicine and the nursing profession? It rouses instantly the suspicion that it may be in the interests of geriatrics and allied studies that men are sometimes forced by doctors to live on beyond their natural span.

(7) The seventh argument also betrays a curious professional egoism, disguised as modesty. Dr. de Paillerets dreads the possibility of some kind of medical commission entrusted with the task of selecting infants for death. "What a terrible temptation is this for us to accept such a right over the life and death of others."

But what parents would ever grant to doctors such a right? It is a right that only those who love the child and are close to it could claim and exercise. The doctors' function should be a minor one. It should be little more than that which, under pressure, the Catholic bishops of Nazi Germany permitted when they decreed that Catholic doctors and social workers could report to the authorities those afflicted with ills calling for sterilization, provided they did not at the same time order or authorize sterilization. The operation was performed in scorn rather than love, and permission was granted with casuistry, but it is not impossible to imagine that religious men and doctors could, without casuistry and without scorn, help a parent in a sad decision.

Most of these seven arguments deal with problems that we meet every day and that are solved rightly or wrongly according to our instincts and knowledge. There are stresses and strains in family life which we can palliate but seldom elude. A great sadness will produce other sadness whatever we do. It seems to me that when Dr. de Paillerets considers these practical arguments against infanticide he has already despaired of defending the only absolutely compelling argument, which is that all killing is a mortal sin. He may have reflected that public opinion, like war, sometimes has the power to modify the most uncompromising dogma and that there was an absolute and peremptory quality about the support which the people of Liège gave to Mme. Vandeput.

PALLIATIVES

In our time there has been so much ecclesiastically condoned and sanctified killing that few clerics would nowadays have the effrontery to bring up again, without diffidence or qualification, that dishonoured and bamboozled old commandment, THOU SHALT NOT KILL. Father Roy condems the doctor who simply repeats it and concerns himself not at all with the tragic situation of those who must cherish the helpless being which medical science has preserved for them. Left to herself nature would often have borne away the malformed child in a miscarriage or by some ordinary illness like measles to which, without inoculation, the often feeble defective child could have succumbed. The doctors feel a greater responsibility towards their profession than towards their patients. When a friend of mine with a defective child asked that it should not be inoculated he was told that he must not "tie the hands of the doctor."

The nine French priests and doctors are fully aware what a burden of responsibility they bear for what is happening. For the doctors save and prolong lives that are useless and unhappy and the priests mount guard over them with moral precepts. They urge upon their colleagues, in recompense, a devotion, a dedicated study, a depth of understanding, which is far beyond the reach of most men.

Dr. de Paillerets writes of the meagre, badly supported research which is being done on encephalopaths. In Paris it is often many years before the defective child can even be received into a specialized establishment. "It is our duty as doctors," he writes, "to expose this scandal. . . . The Liège trial has occurred but the real trial is yet to come and, if we do not act in this matter, our place will be in the first row of the accused."

And Father Roy, stressing the urgency, asks if we are prepared to postpone the laying down of new major roads till the specialized homes are provided. This question carries its own answer with it. No, we are not.

The nine Frenchmen also urge that the parents of the afflicted should form associations to discuss their common problems and share the burden. And Father Roy distinguishes between the "pity," a negative, egoistic thing which men are ready to show, and the "compassion" which is demanded of them and which forces them to share the sufferings of the afflicted and to act. He quotes Bernanos: "Modern man has a hard heart and tender guts." He weeps for the sufferings of others and winces at the thought of being involved in them.

Is there any likelihood that these generous ideals will ever be fulfilled? The next day, in search of enlightenment, I went uptown to see Dr. S, the obstetrician who had delivered K. He confirmed what I had suspected. There is no reality in these dreams of Father Roy. Dr. S is a kind and brilliant man but his talents have made him much sought after and there is no likelihood that he will ever desert his other patients in order to show more than perfunctory sympathy with the parents of defective children. Nor, as far as I know, has there been any "dedicated study," any researches into the origin of K's misfortune which might be helpful to others.

Then there is the question of parents' association. I learnt from one of the nurses in the home where K is that Dr. S himself has a mongol child there. Yet he never told J or D about him, though he, as a doctor, frequently handling our problems both in his home and in his profession, could have forwarded such an association more than anyone else. About this I do not feel I have any right to reproach him. We are all of us preternaturally sensitive about our defective children. For educated people they may represent a private anguish that is well nigh unshareable. This intense "privatization" of our problem (to use an American word) belongs to the Age of Scientific Organization, as does the increase in the number of abnormal children. The bourgeois, for the most part, live in small labour-saving flats and it is usually obvious, if not obligatory, that the defective child should go to an institution where he can receive "proper care." Though it may well be that the parents think of their child every hour of the day, they do not have to talk about him or constantly plan for him. Only rarely will talking help them. About this I understand Dr. S.

It was very different when I was a child. Our rector had a mongol daughter and the neighbours frequently took charge of her. (Father Roy would say that it was not half frequently enough.) She is looked after by her relations and I still see her sometimes, a woman of fifty. It is possible that our rare gestures of true "compassion" were largely neutralized by our chattering "pity." But even such small efforts as we made would now be difficult and unwanted. The compassion which Father Roy demands is not compatible with professionalism. Doctors, nurses and social workers must take their courses, earn salaries, go where they are told, and so must the clergy. Their lives are too full, too controlled for them to have any time for that total imaginative involvement which is compassion. There is no reality in these dreams of Father Roy. The revolution in men's behaviour which he desires cannot happen in a scientifically organized society. The position which he is trying to defend is based upon moral precepts which have lost their validity. The relief which he promised will never come.

I asked Dr. S what he thought of euthanasia and he said that Mme. Vandeput was wholly wrong. All life is better than all death. He was coming to believe that only in rare cases was even abortion justifiable.

"Are your objections religious?"

"If you mean am I a Catholic, the answer is no, but I believe in God."

He was surprised that I should know about his little boy and he told me that he had often longed for him to die but he no longer did so. He had wondered too whether he had been wrong in sending him to an institution.

I did not ask him why he had not told J that he was a fellow sufferer, as this might have comforted her a little. I now regret my shyness, as I believe his answer would have shown that our attitude towards the defective is now one of absolute negation. No trace remains of the old belief that they are in some way the special children of God.* They are just genetic mistakes which, since we cannot, like the Greeks, extinguish them, we must relegate to some place where they are no nuisance to society.

Dr. S's God is different from mine. Churchmen are now ready to admit into their ranks those who reject all historical certainties and see God and his son Christ as constructions of the mind by which the human imagination tries to express its revelation of the divine. This revelation varies from man to man. To me God is the assurance that the world of men is not purposeless or evil and that we can trust ourselves to it and that, when old laws lose their significance, new ones will slowly shape themselves to take their place. As for Christ, he is the assurance that a man can learn when and how to free himself from the power of the law, however strongly it may be reinforced with venerable traditions and popular approval. The show bread may have to be eaten, the sabbath profaned, the prostitute exalted. "GOD" is the promise that out of this disorder a better order will ultimately ensue.

NATURAL LAW AND THE GREEKS

My mention of the Greeks recalls to me that I have not answered one of the arguments (no. 5) used against Mme. Vandeput. It is medical rather than religious but seems to suggest, as the clergy do, that there is some sort of Natural Law at issue, which we neglect at our peril.

---

* A friend of mine claims that this is untrue and that here in Ireland the Steiner movement is represented in the village communities at Duffcarrig and Ballaghtobin and other places. I have visited Ballaghtobin, which is in Co. Kilkenny, and know how dedicated men and women have devoted themselves to improving the lives of the handicapped adults. They think of the mentally defective as fellow individual spirits who have slipped sideways on the evolutionary ladder, but who command innate respect, dignity and potential. Some of the villagers among whom they live accept this and conclude that mongols, to whom in particular the movement addresses itself, are in the world to teach their busy "sane" fellow travellers the true value of brotherhood, love, acceptance. Hence they view them as "special" and inherit the children-of-God outlook. I appreciate but do not share this sentiment. [1988]

Dr. de Paillerets quotes the Hippocratic oath which doctors have considered binding upon them since the fifth century B.C.

> I shall not give a homicidal drug to anyone, no matter who may ask me to do so, nor shall I initiate the suggestion that it be given.
> . . . The least exception to the unconditional respect for human life would place the doctor in a position which he could not accept. It would curb the enthusiasm which is the prerequisite of progress in medical knowledge. Furthermore, it would destroy the confidence of the patients, without which there can be no Medicine.

But surely the oath is greatly misinterpreted and the historical foundations of medicine strangely misunderstood. The Hippocratic oath mainly concerned the Greek habit of administering poison to those condemned to death. Hippocrates considered it beneath the dignity of a doctor to become a paid executioner. Moreover the world in which Hippocrates practised gave a limited authority to the doctor in the matter of life and death. His duty was to cure those who wished to be cured, but he did not interfere with ancient practices. In his day and for a century or two afterwards, in all the city-states except Thebes, deformed or sickly children were exposed. Aristotle, a great admirer and younger contemporary of Hippocrates, thought the custom should be made law, for he writes: "With respect to the exposing or bringing up of children, let it be a law that nothing imperfect or maimed should be brought up." Plato gives the same advice to the lawgivers in his ideal republic. Is there any evidence that Hippocrates opposed what was a universal custom?

The Greek father could decide whether a child was to live or die, for the infant did not become "a member of the family" till he was formally presented some days after birth. Infanticide was not eugenic, though Plato and Aristotle would have treated it as such, for the father had a right to eliminate even a healthy infant whom he did not wish to rear, and this was freely exercised in the case of girl infants whose dowry might present a problem. The unwanted infant was placed in a cradle or pot and put in the corner of the marketplace, in the temple or wrestling ground. It might be picked up and reared by a stranger, so sometimes some objects of value were wrapped up with it. But the father had the right later to claim it after it had been reared, so the infant was usually left to die.

Only at Sparta was the absolute right of the parent over his children disputed, for the state would sometimes weed out, for eugenic or military reasons, sickly infants whom the parents had spared.

All this is very shocking to Christians, if Christians have not forfeited their right to be shocked at such things by their connivance at Auschwitz and Hiroshima, but some great classical scholars have shown sympathy. Of Greek infanticide Zimmern writes:

> The Athenian had a traditional horror of violence and interfered, when he could, on behalf of the helpless. If he consented to exercise his immemorial right over his own offspring, he did so with regret for the sake of the city and his other children, because it was more merciful in the long run. We have no right to cast stones either at him or his fellows.

And Bernard Bosanquet writes in his *Companion to Plato's Republic:*

> The high mortality of young children today suggests that we are superior to the ancients more in theory than in practice. . . . Can any race safely arrest selection? It is quite conceivable that the actual infant mortality on the ancient system might be less than ours at present.

Plato and Aristotle both had the pragmatic, society-centered religion of most modern scientists. They did not see in the eugenic infanticide, which they preached, anything incompatible with orthodoxy. After a sentence or two about infanticide Aristotle returns to the subject of childbirth and urges that for the sake of exercise and the tranquillity of mind which is favourable to successful parturition, the pregnant woman should walk to the temple every day and offer prayers to the gods who preside over matrimony.

All this has a callous, calculating sound. In our society our leading thinkers are more humane and imaginative, but Greek society itself was less cruel and impersonal and we have discovered new forms of physical agony and lonely introverted misery of mind of which the Greeks were incapable. The gulf between Plato or Aristotle and daily life at Athens was large, but not so large as that between, say, D. H. Lawrence and daily life at Nottingham, or the Bloomsbury group and Bloomsbury (it would be easy to discover some more modern and apposite antithesis), and I do not feel perverse or paradoxical in suggesting that there has been a real deterioration.

What are the principal forces that have drawn us away from the Greeks? First there is "science," which, looking for conformity in men, tends to impose it. It classifies all living things by their shared characteristics. It pares down those distinctions upon which personality is built and which defy classification. It achieves its best results by treating men as statistical units rather than as individual persons. Such methods are damaging to that flexibility of conduct on which Greek ethics is based.

Secondly there is professionalism, which claims exclusively for itself spheres of authority, fields of investigation and experiment, which were once open to ordinary men, parents, neighbours, friends.

Thirdly there is universal democracy, which aspires to offer to the whole multiracial, heterogeneous world laws which all will accept. That means boiling down into a simple code of Dos and Don'ts a vast complex of interlocking moralities deriving from very varied traditions and customs.

The Greek moralist or lawgiver always had in mind the small community in which public opinion could sometimes enforce the law, sometimes replace it. So occasionally Aristotle, instead of saying, "Let there be a law that . . . ," says instead, "Let it be held in utter detestation that . . ."

Today public opinion, manipulated by pressmen and politicians, has become so ignoble a thing that we distrust it and put our faith instead in the law. Its chief defect, its inflexibility, becomes in our sad circumstances a merit.

Finally there is Christian theology, which has shaped the law, so that even those who reject its dogma are still bound by it. Bosanquet, for example, argues that our respect for human life has been deepened by religious doctrines, even discredited ones, such as that concerning the fate of unbaptized children in the world to come.

Modern churchmen are evasive about the future world, its penalties and prizes, and tend to judge our actions in accordance with their conformity to something they call "Natural Law." But it seems to me that Greek custom was closer to nature than we are and that it is not "natural" for a doctor to insist on prolonging, by drugs and inoculations, the life of a defective child against the wishes of its parents. Bosanquet is surely justified in writing of the "immemorial right which a parent has over his own offspring."

In regard to infanticide I ought to add that the Greek practice had been inherited from primitive times. It can be traced among such primitive peoples as the anthropologists have investigated and it is usually linked with religion or food. The Aruntas of Australia suckle their infant children for several years and a new child whom the mother thinks she will be unable to rear is killed at birth. It is thought that the child's spirit goes back whence it came and can be born again. Twins are thought to be unnatural and are immediately killed.

Among the Todas of South India twins are also regarded

with dismay and one of them is killed. Newborn female babies are sometimes laid in the mud for buffaloes to trample on. These practices are most prevalent among the priestly caste in the Nilgiri Hills where Western influence is weakest. Margaret Mead describes them as "the desperate expedients to which a simple people have to resort to fit their survival rate to their social structure. These practices are dying out but so are the Todas." She tells much the same story about the South Seas and the Far North, where the Eskimos practise female infanticide. And there is much in our own social history which is seldom remembered and is never written. An Irish friend of mine, herself the mother of a loved and cherished defective child, remembers as a girl being told how in her country neighbourhood a malformed infant was usually put at the end of the bed and left there unfed and untended till God, in his good time, should take it. I have never heard of this elsewhere or read of it but I believe it to be true.

No sensible person, of course, considers that primitive people can give us directives as to how to behave. We are not qualified to learn much from them or they from us. Yet there is a tendency to argue from the "natural law" which we are supposed to have inherited from the remote past. There is no such thing. The most that a traditionalist might claim is that in all times, lands, peoples, we can trace, however faintly, one constant passion, the distaste for cruelty, injustice, waste. It is sometimes a minority sentiment but, when held with tenacity, it invariably prevails.

Surely today any deeply concerned parent, grandparent, or friend would agree that we have to retreat from many strongly held convictions which we have inherited from the past, and that "desperate expedients" may have to be contemplated, if slowly and laboriously a new ethic and a new morality are to be built around our new convictions. How widely are these convictions shared? Am I just dreaming when I think that almost all those who have the same cause for sadness think as I do?

In *Le Dossier Confidentiel de l'Euthanasie,* Barrère and

Lalou endorse what I have said about the attitudes of Greeks and Romans with quotations from Epicurus and Seneca. To them a man was the master of his own body and had a right to leave it when it could no longer give shelter and sustenance to his faculties. It was not till St. Augustine that suicide and euthanasia became the crimes which Christians hold them to be today. And even in Christian times devout men could think differently. St. Thomas More in the Second Book of *Utopia* wrote that when an Utopian was dying in incurable anguish, the priests and the magistrates exhorted him.

> Either to dispatche himselfe out of that payneful lyffe as out of a prison or a racke of tormente or elles suffer himselfe wyllinglye to be rydde oute of it by other . . . But they cause none suche to dye agaynste his wyll . . . He that killeth himselfe before that the pryestes and the counsel have allowed the cause of his deathe, him an unworthy they caste unburied into some stinkinge marrish.

And Francis Bacon had similar ideas.

As for the present state of the law in various countries I must depend as others have done on R. Raymond Charles's *Peut On Admettre l'Euthanasie?* The laws of Spain, Holland, Hungary, Italy, Poland, Norway, Denmark, Brazil treat with leniency those who kill from pity with the consent of their victim. Peru and Uruguay go further, for they permit the judge to grant exemption from all penalty where no selfish motive can be discovered. In Europe the Penal Code of Czechoslovakia arrives more cautiously at the same conclusion.

In the United States and the U.S.S.R. the law has advanced and retreated. In 1906 the Ohio legislature passed the first reading of a law permitting a man who was dying painfully to summon a commission of four to judge his right to end his life. A few months later Iowa voted for a law of still greater latitude, for it embraced defective children and idiots. However, when Congress had to pronounce at Washington, its verdict was wholly hostile.

In the U.S.S.R. a law of 1922 which abolished the penalty for homicide whose motive was pity was repealed a few months later because of evidence that it was being abused.

Sometimes the law seems to nourish itself on its own vitals, developing without relation to what happens around it. In Nazi Germany in 1944, when the slaughter at Auschwitz was at its peak, a law was passed which prescribed the full legal penalties for those who from pity kill the incurable and the mentally deficient.

How then does it happen that in France and Britain, countries with long humanist traditions, no special exemption for those who kill from pity is embodied in the law? Is it perhaps that in these sophisticated countries there is an awareness that in human relationships there are zones in which a man may make his own terms with the Source of Law, whether he deems this to be God or the Natural Order, and that such a man needs no intermediary? Certainly in France, at least, euthanasia trials, despite the law, have usually ended with an acquittal or token punishment for those whose integrity is manifest.

CHRISTIANITY AND KILLING

Was there ever before so much mental confusion about the killing of men by men?

When does human life begin? There is the widest dispute. When does it end? Even that is not so clear as it once was. Granted that a man may kill in self-defence, is he also obliged to? And, if so, how many others is he obliged to defend by killing as well as himself? His family, his friends, his neighbours, his fellow citizens, his nation? And has he to kill on behalf of the friends of his friends and on behalf of the nations who are allies of his nation? And should he practise preventative killing? Should he in this way defend himself or his friends or his nation when they think they are threatened? Or might be threatened? And has he to kill people in order to bring about justice in the world, in the way that his elected representatives think best?

Wherever his duty may lie, what actually happens is always the same. The individual, till a man rushes at him with knife or gun, can kill nobody, not even himself. The state can force him to kill anybody, though his whole soul rebels against the killing, and the churches, because for their survival they have made their own pacts with the state, can give him no support in his rebellion. On the contrary they will support the state against him and often bring to bear all their supernatural sanctions against the individual, so it seems to him that he will be damned in the next world as well as in this if he does not kill those whom he neither fears nor dislikes.

Their clergy are kindly sensible men, anxious to preserve the venerable institutions which they serve and whose future is precarious. Therefore almost without exception they have interpreted the commandment THOU SHALT NOT KILL in the way that is most pleasing to secular authority. They have given their blessing to those that kill from fear and hatred, and they have condemned as sinners those who kill from love.

When I was thinking of this, *The New York Times* came in and I read of a seventeen-year-old boy in Detroit who had tried to kill himself with a stick of dynamite rather than go out to kill people of whom he knew nothing in Vietnam. In the adjoining paragraph I read how five hundred rabbis, American and Canadian, assembled in Toronto, had by a majority vote censured the Vietnam War and insinuated that its roots were largely commercial. Later on I read how other denominations had also debated the war, and, except for the Orthodox of America, had also by a majority censured it. In fact there can never again be a war whose "justice" is uncontested by religious men. It is a measure of their helplessness, their cowardice or their confusion of thought that they still continue to sanction war. They will still censure a bewildered boy for killing himself rather than become a killer. Should we censure them? I think not. They are caught, as we are, in a trap from which it is very hard to escape.

Yet the churches still consider themselves to be the unflinching champions of the rights of the individual and the family, of the sacredness of human life; there is an ostentatious straining at gnats by those who have swallowed camels.

Even the nine Catholic authors, though they write so modestly and perceptively, sometimes appear to picture themselves as representatives of an austere tribunal from whose unbending judgment the timid layman shrinks away. Father Beirnaert, S.J., for example, says that a merciful doctor will sometimes in disregard of Christian principles suppress a defective child "because he finds the morality of the Church too severe."

On the contrary, it is not its severity that is repugnant but its extreme flexibility. The churches make absolute judgments, but they qualify them for the powerful and only enforce them against the weak.

Father Roy, for example, says, "The affirmation of respect for human life must therefore be absolute and universal—that is, categorically binding all mankind—if we are not to founder in multiple disasters." This covers Mme. Vandeput but not Hitler, for conscience obliges Father Roy to add a footnote about the right to kill in war. He makes a distinction between "human life," which must be absolutely respected, and "biological life," which we can destroy in self-defence, or in "a just war." And he says that the Church, while tolerating killing in war, has "never given formal approval to it."

Surely this distinction between "human life" and "biological life" is a dishonest one? Does a man's life become biological rather than human when he puts on a uniform? The only true distinction is that between views that it is politic to hold or "tolerate" and those that are not. Father Roy's Church, a vast multiracial organization which is unpopular with many, cannot afford to assert unequivocally against everybody the sacredness of life, as it was asserted in the first two centuries of Christianity. In those days there was no conscription and all that the Christian expected from the state was to escape its attention.

The distortions and compromises which we accept as inevitable had not yet been forced upon him.

Can we still accept them? I think not. There has been a great change. Long after other historic events are forgotten the name Auschwitz will recall the most stupendous crime in history. And, linked to it enduringly is the greatest non-event, the Silence of Pius XII, more terrible now that his apologists have argued that prudence and Christian charity demanded it. For this argument shifts the guilt of impotence from one man to the whole of Christendom and justifies a billion meaner connivances.

The gospels say that a darkness fell upon the earth when Christ was crucified and when a new era began. Surely the Silence of Pius has the same symbolic quality. It was mysterious and ominous, like the silence of woods and fields that precedes a total eclipse of the sun. It must herald some great change, either the final collapse of Christianity or its rebirth in some new and unforeseen shape.

In fact, if there is a rebirth, I believe that the ancient law THOU SHALT NOT KILL will have to be interpreted with greater severity and not less. And, if it is to be qualified at all, those who kill from loving compassion will seem to us far more forgivable than those millions of conscripted killers whom the churches forgive and even exalt.

The problem of "unnatural death," that is to say death which is not due to accident or bodily decay, is a unitary one. The hastened death of the defective baby and the incurable adult to whom life is only useless pain is linked to the involuntary death of the criminal and the conscript soldier and allied to all other assaults which we make upon human life, to birth control, sterilization and abortion. We shall never be able to face the problem of the useless, the unwanted, the criminal, the hostile, the unendurable life with courage and understanding, so long as our laws compel the innocent to kill the innocent against his will. So long as the churches condone it, the taint of expediency must colour everything they say. Nothing can change till the leaders of the Church dare to say once more, "Those that take the sword shall perish by the sword."

This would be a lightning flash, dazzling and destructive, that would shake the world. Many venerable establishments would crumble, but the dark unvisited places which breed ugliness would be illuminated. All the things that we do or fail to do in the antechambers of life or at its exit would be seen in their proper perspective, birth control, sterilization, abortion, euthanasia. Our judgment, no longer clouded and crippled by the great betrayal, the stupendous fallacy, would be free to act. Our little K's life, a frosted bud that will never open and bear fruit, would be allowed to drop.

CHURCHES UNDER PRESSURE

The ideal does not become more remote when the real is closely examined. The man who intends to escape must know each stone of his prison walls as though he loved it.

The narrow territory on the verges of life and death, which is now almost all that remains of the once vast spiritual dominion of the churches, is constantly under dispute. Let us observe how its Christian defenders behave when they are under attack. If most of my information is about Catholics, that is because in recent years they have excelled others in self-scrutiny. Let us watch how they acted when the Nazis tried to interrupt the cycle of man's life at its generation, in its prime and in its decay. We shall see that in general the churches capitulated to the powerful and compensated themselves for their defeat by tyrannizing over the defenceless.

Maybe this is just a law of life. If you have to draw sound from an instrument whose principal chords are dumb, you must strike those that remain all the harder. As their power to enforce laws that are binding on peoples and governments declines, the churches enforce them with special vigour in those spheres where men are solitary and amenable to persuasion. In all that concerns childbirth and sex and marrying and the death of relations, we are so much alone as to be almost grateful for public interest and hence ready to be counselled, cajoled and coerced. The warrior defeated in the field finds consolation in being a tyrant at home.

In Germany, which sometimes calls itself "the Heartland of Europe," ideas which are current elsewhere are often acted out so boldly and dramatically that, like the details in an enlarged photograph, we can see universal human behaviour most clearly in a German context.

There were three stages in the attack on the sacredness of human life, and corresponding to them two great ecclesiastical and one partial triumph. The Nazi sterilization laws attacked the unborn; the euthanasia campaign was directed in the first place against life in its decay; genocide, which was an attack on life in all its stages, was little more than an extension of the "just war" which the Nazis claimed to be waging.

It was to the question of procreation that the Nazis attended first. In May 1933 Hitler laid before the German bishops the draft of a law providing for voluntary sterilization. The Catholic bishops rejected it as a violation of the encyclical *Casti Conubii*, 1930, but the concordat with Hitler was about to be signed and the day after the signing a law for forcible sterilization of the diseased was approved. Catholic resistance was strong but, National Socialism having been accepted, the encyclical had ultimately to be set aside. Finally even in Rome compromises were made, and in 1940 the Sacred Congregation ruled that Catholic nurses in state-run hospitals might under certain circumstances assist at sterilization operations. It was argued that, if a recalcitrant nurse were dismissed, she might be replaced by an anti-religious person who would withhold the sacraments from those in danger of death. And, though it remained sinful for a Catholic physician to apply for the sterilization of any patient, he was allowed to report to the authorities the names of those afflicted with ills calling for sterilization.

The relationship of Church and state followed this familiar pattern of quibble and counter-quibble; when the Church was forced to some shameful capitulation, it invariably tried to make good its losses by some tiny usurpation in the domestic sphere. And thus it was that the German hierarchy forbade the marriage of sterilized persons, since "by natural law the main purpose of marriage is procreation." However, in the first three years of the decree 170,000 people had been sterilized and the Catholics among them made a formidable body. So even the Church was forced to retreat and to withdraw its veto.

Then followed the euthanasia campaign and a Church-state war of great significance, for in it the Church proved its power and influence and demonstrated that it was unwilling to use them except when public opinion was favourable. On 1 September 1939 Hitler decreed that all those with incurable diseases should be killed and before the end of the year establishments for the shooting and premises for the gassing of victims were opened in Württemberg and Hesse. As soon as rumours of this reached the clergy there were furious protests and after the campaign had lasted two years and 70,000 patients had been killed, there was an abrupt change of policy. The principal credit for this must go to Bishop Galen of Münster, who delivered a famous sermon demanding that those who had done the killing should be prosecuted for murder. He warned them that human life was sacred except in the case of self-defence or a just war, and that invalids and seriously wounded soldiers would be next on the list. Some of the Nazi leaders wanted Galen hanged but they dared not do so, so great was his popularity in Münster and in all Westphalia. Instead, the campaign of euthanasia was called off.

This great Church triumph was significant in several ways. It showed that in our frailty we are strengthened by being able to appeal, beyond our conscience, to infallible dogma. In other words it is easier for us to say: "That is forbidden by the encyclical *Casti Conubii*, 1930," than to protest: "That revolts me to the bottom of my soul!" But the disadvantage is that if we wait for the august and infallible Voice to proclaim the truth and the Voice is silent, we are more helpless than those who have treated their consciences as primary and not secondary sources of enlightenment. For the testing time for Christians in Germany came not when the government began to kill their crippled and defective kinsmen. It came when the Nazis began to kill their innocent and helpless neighbours the Jews. When the Voice was silent and the priest and the Levite passed by, it was inevitable that the ordinary man should consider it no concern of his and that the cold and cruel heart should be sanctified.

At that time the ecclesiastical opposition to euthanasia, successful as it was, showed that the bishops knew about gas chambers before the Jews did. They knew that they were built for the elimination of the "unproductive" and that Jews were officially declared "unproductive" and that many clergy had endorsed this view. They knew that they had been deported to the east—the bishops were not mentally deficient—and they had heard rumours.

If the purpose of religion is to arouse our conscience and to sharpen our sensibilities to the perception of evil, the churches had failed disastrously. What they offered was not a stimulant but a drug. In the matter of euthanasia we must turn aside and listen to the voice of our own conscience.

There is abundant evidence that the bishops' minds had been befogged by the theory of the just war and the image that it had printed indelibly on their imaginations of the conscript soldier as a knight-errant and even, in the fight against Bolshevism, as a soldier of Christ. In a fog of crusading holiness Auschwitz was hard to distinguish from an air raid, one of those sad events which it is necessary to endure and to inflict if, in our imperfect world, justice is to prevail. In order to preserve morale one must not say too much about specific cruelties and injustices of the war—in fact, better say nothing at all. So that Guenter Lewy in his magnificent book *The Catholic Church and Nazi Germany* writes: "While thousands of anti-Nazis were beaten to pulp in the concentration camps, the Church talked of supporting the moral renewal brought about by the Hitler government." And Gordon Zahn, in *German Catholics and Hitler's Wars,* declares that after exhaustive research he could only find a record of four German Catholics who had openly refused military service. He attributes the "near unanimity of support" for the war from German Catholics to "the external pressure exerted by leading Church officials" and the spiritual influence that their words and examples were bound to have on their flock.

For years after the true character of the war had revealed itself the clergy went on proclaiming it a just war and denouncing those brave men who refused to serve. For example, when the Austrian peasant Jägestätter chose to be beheaded rather than to take part in what he deemed an unjust war, his bishop reprimanded him severely for his disloyalty. They were all of them deceiving themselves in the interests of ecclesiastical survival.

Years later the President of West Germany, Lübke, said in a memorial address, "No one who was not completely blinded or wholly naive could be completely free of the pressing awareness that this war was not a just a war."

That is to say that much innocent blood was shed, often by innocent men, because of the Church's failure to follow its own teaching. Lewy believes that had the leaders of German Catholicism opposed Hitler from the start, they would have made the home front so unreliable that he "might not have dared going to war and literally millions of lives would have been saved." But once a war has started it is not easy to see how the Church, with its intricate relationship with the government of every state, would be able to oppose it. When nations are engaged in combat it is already too late to ask where justice lies and to urge soldiers to desert.

I hope I have shown how vacillating the Christian approach to those problems has been. The encyclical about sterilization was only scrupulously observed so long as observance was not likely to injure the faithful seriously and damage the prestige and authority of the Church and alienate its disciples. The euthanasia of the innocent was only vigorously denounced when it concerned people of the same race as the denouncing ecclesiastics. The problem of the "just" or "unjust" war was never seriously considered. I believe that there is not a bishop in Germany or in all Europe and America who would now dare publicly to assert that Hitler's war was a just one. Yet when they were already in full possession of all the facts, thousands of bishops, and not only in Germany, asserted this.

PUBLIC AND PRIVATE KILLING

I see only one path through this moral chaos. The Church sometimes claims to be a higher court attending to those spiritual needs of mankind which governments, concerned for its material welfare, must ignore. If that is so, could she not insist that a man is the master of his own life and that he cannot be obliged to offer it or preserve it against his will? The community may try to educate him in the use of this right but cannot deprive him of it. If he should abuse it, no doubt we might suffer "multiple disasters," but not so many as we suffer through denying that that right exists.

In the matter of killing in self-defence, which the Church tolerates and often commands, this new code of ethics might work more justly and effectively than the old one. Science allied to bureaucracy concentrates power in the hands of the few; a genius in a laboratory conceives an idea and shares it with a governing minority. As a result great cities crumble, army corps collapse, empires capitulate. The only antidote to the captive genius and his captors is the free man's passionate conviction. He normally operates single-handed and is trusted by neither Chruch nor state. All the honours, all the blessings, go to the conscript armies. These armies are composed of a few men who identify themselves with the aims of the government and are prepared to kill for them, a few more who are convinced that it is their duty to suppress all private judgment and to kill as they are ordered, and finally vast hordes of ignorant or innocent or deeply reluctant conscripts. If there is often or ever a clear-cut antithesis of good and evil, the last place to look for it would be in the opposition of rival armies. This is an old story which we have come to accept as inevitable. What we should not accept, what is obscene and intolerable, is that the churches should bless this arrangement and continue to preach as Father Roy does that "respect for human life must be absolute and universal and that it must be categorically binding on all mankind."

Only a Quaker or one of the other pacifist sects can talk like that without the grossest hypocrisy.

Yet if the Quakers are wrong and we have to kill in defence of innocence and justice, how best can it be done? In scientific warfare the innocent and the just who are conscripted and forced to use modern weapons will be as indiscriminatingly murderous as their fellows and must be resisted with the same mechanical ruthlessness. There is only one way in which death can be dealt out selectively and that is by assassination, a form of private enterprise on which the Church has always frowned. Those who took part in the 20 July attack on Hitler are now recognized as great heroes who, had they succeeded, would have ended the war and preserved the unity of Germany. Yet at the time they received nothing but discouragement from even those of the Church leaders who had opposed the Nazis. Cardinal Faulhaber, for example, when questioned by the Gestapo after the plot had failed, is said to have expressed the most vigorous condemnation of the attempt and to have affirmed his loyalty to Hitler.

Yet it is obvious that assassination, when a man chooses his victim of his own free will and, risking his life, takes upon himself the complete responsibility for his acts, can have a nobility that must always be lacking in the mass slaughter of conscripts by conscripts. And after the event the successful assassin will certainly get the blessing of the Church. It has been said that Bishop Preising, who had been informed in advance of the 20 July plot, was to have replaced the pro-Nazi Orsenigo as Papal Nuncio to the government of assassins. Whether or not this is true it is certain that Archbishop Stepinac cordially welcomed the government of Pavelitch, whose members had been involved in the assassination of King Alexander. All the Croatian bishops extolled Pavelitch, who was himself received in audience by Pope Pius XII.

If the Church were to accept assassination as a form of resistance, which, however deplorable, was preferable to conscript warfare, it might be able to judge it by some subtler criterion than success. In that case it would surely condemn Pavelitch and Stepinac and praise Stauffenberg and Preising.

But could the Church ever show greater indulgence to the assassin than to the soldier? Not as she now is. Being herself a social organization, she is always disposed in a time of crisis to ingratiate herself with the great political aggregations to which she is affiliated. Though she often claims to be the defender of the individual conscience, she usually concedes that when mankind organizes itself into powerful national groupings, it can legitimately dodge the impact of those "absolute and universal laws" which are "categorically binding" on the individual. In the matter of killing, the churches will therefore line up with the worst of governments till it is defeated, rather than with the best of assassins before he succeeds.

I have written sympathetically of assassins without recalling any particular one of whom one could unreservedly approve. The German heroes of 20 July seem to have plotted to destroy Hitler principally because he was losing the war. Bonhoeffer, who excites interest and was executed for his complicity, does not seem to have been deeply implicated. Pavelitch was a bloodthirsty fanatic. Perhaps I have most sympathy for Princip and Chubrilovitch, the assassins of Sarajevo, who, as many think (not I), precipitated the First World War. Why are assassins mad or simple or discredited people, or else like Princip have a fatal illness? I think it is because public opinion is conditioned to abhor what they do and only the most desperate conviction and courage will induce a man to risk a healthy life for it. He knows that a conscript who mindlessly kills a hundred other equally harmless conscripts will be criticized by nobody, while a brave and resolute man who rids the world of a tyrant is staking his honour and his reputation as well as his life.

How trivial my problem seems compared to his, yet I have linked them together because law and religion have already done so. I too ask more than orthodoxy could ever concede. I am claiming much more than the right over my own life, which in the long run no one can permanently withhold from me. I believe that love can give us the right of life and death over those who are helpless and dependent on us. And that when circumstances are desperate we must snatch it, as did those parents who flung their children from the trains transporting them to Auschwitz. It is a right that can never be confirmed by any legislature, for the essence of law is impartiality and detachment, and those who are detached cannot judge the depth of love and the urgency of despair.

THE NORMALITY OF LOVE AND THE LAW

It is not healthy to live alone for long periods with dreams which you cannot realize, for it is certain that little K's parents can never claim their rights and it is improbable that I will. But you can obtain relief from a particular problem by generalizing it, observing its impact upon others and preparing for its solution by posterity. So I took the subway downtown to East 57th Street, New York, where the Euthanasia Society of America has its headquarters, and there I came to my senses. The secretary told me that there is no likelihood that in our lifetime euthanasia for defective children will be legalized. "You see," she said, "religion is very powerful in America. Even to work for legalization might be unwise. We have to approach our objective step by step, and the first step concerns the elderly and hopelessly diseased who wish to die." She showed me an article in *Harper's Magazine* of October 1960, "The Patient's Right to Die" by Joseph Fletcher, who has a chair in ethics and moral theology at Cambridge, Mass.

This article is very illuminating but confirms what the secretary said. It is the problem of the old who wish to die which occupies the mind of these reformers. He tells the familiar story well. He describes how we have altered the whole pattern of life and death; men live far longer than they used to do and die painfully and slowly as their faculties decay. "The classical deathbed scene with its loving partings and solemn last words is practically a thing of the past. In its stead is a sedated, comatose, betubed object manipulated and subconscious, if not sub-human."

The doctor who from worthy motives refuses to prolong this indecency must first be protected by the law; the next to be championed is the doctor who deliberately curtails it. The case of little K is something quite other; it cannot even be considered.

Evidently modern medicine has caused us to invert the thinking of the Greeks, for whom old people, whose lives were never artificially prolonged, presented no problem, since if they were not reasonably healthy they soon died. Not even Aristotle or Plato, who favoured the killing of defective children, required that old people should be helped into the tomb.

Reading Mr. Fletcher I have come to think that in fact the Greeks understood better than we do the nature of the affections. We stress the "sacredness of life" but a Greek would consider that life becomes sacred but is not born so. The reverence which we feel for the young is woven out of memories and hopes and gathers in complexity as they grow older. But where there are no memories and no hopes the Greeks would only see "biological life," to use a phrase of Father Roy in a way which he would greatly dislike.

"Biological life" is something that we spare and cherish from biological instinct, and instinct will perhaps only slowly develop into love. Where there are no hopes, we may come to feel resentment or even hatred towards the life which instinct bids us cherish.

There is indeed in general estimation nothing sacred about the instincts. We defer to them perhaps even less than we should do, inhibiting all those that are incompatible with social order. The sexual and philoprogenitive instincts, the instinct of self-preservation and many others, are subordinated to the needs of the state. Even the maternal instinct submits to control.

Joseph Fletcher talks of a new "morality of love," which he also calls "the morality of human freedom and dignity." He does not define it, but he seems to think that it is something that the law could be brought to tolerate. Could it? To me, this morality of love will always be apart from, and sometimes in conflict with, the law. For as the law extends its scope wider and wider over men of all creeds and races, it will concern itself less with the intimate relations of men and more with their public communications. Its goal will be to avoid social collisions. The only support that the morality of love could offer to a man in conflict with the law would be the assurance that he was doing right.

A pamphlet which I was given by the Euthanasia Society, combined with Fletcher's plans for a graduated reform of the law, made me wonder whether I even wanted the legislation of what he calls "the morality of love." Attached to the pamphlet is a specimen application form which the seeker after death would have to send to "the authorities" (in this case not GOD but some medical-legal committee). Can death safely be made something you apply for like a widow's pension, a traveller's visa, a set of false teeth, filling in details about your age, your illness, the degree of your pain? Is it some tenderness of guts that makes me squeamish? I should like to ask permission to die from those I love, for they alone can judge whether it is time for me to go. I would prefer that old laws should be generously applied than that new ones should be made. Otherwise in a bureaucracy one application form begets another. It might happen that when the Society had won its cause, the application form for dying would breed as its legitimate heir an application form for living. Even if this did not happen, the pressure on useless people to make them feel unwanted is intensifying. There used always to be room for an old grandfather by the chimney corner but now there is a waiting list for every bed in the hospital.

Father Roy was talking sense when he said that "this principle, the suppression of abnormal children, first announced as a right, is in danger of being insensibly transformed into a duty," and that "war is being prepared against the feeble and the abnormal."

This danger is a real one and if infanticide were left to the medical services it might become a branch of eugenics and under government control. This would be an outrage upon the "morality of love, of freedom and dignity." For what we have to assert is that a man has a right over his own life and a shared right, in certain cases, over the lives of those that are dear to him. We cannot define these rights, but love, which is not transitory, has duties and powers and will define them according as we acknowledge its authority. I believe that it would define them unmistakably for those that love little K.

Because of this, it might be better to take a life in defiance of the laws of the state and to be called a murderer than to arrange a legal death, if by so doing we allowed it to appear that the state had any right over the lives of the innocent. Though we might come to claim that even an adult belongs to those that love him, we could never admit that he belonged to such random collectivities as the state, the people, the nation, the race.

In another respect I feel myself in sympathy with the nine Catholic writers. Fletcher links artificial insemination with birth control, sterilization and abortion as "a medically discovered way of fulfilling and protecting human values and hopes in spite of nature's failures or foolishnesses."

Now artificial insemination seems to me to belong to a different category from these others. It is a prim suburban device for replenishing the nursery without the illicit pleasures of adultery or the illegal obligations of polygamy. It is anti-social and anti-historical, and an affront to those who believe in the ties of kinship and are ready to be bound by them. It undermines the solicitude that a man must feel for his offspring. The most carefree adulterer cannot free himself from concern for the child he has begotten, even though it may be hard for him to express it. A "donor" on the other hand releases his child into the unknown and will never think of him again.

And artificial insemination is only the first of the scientific marvels by which the family is liable to be transformed. It is now possible for a woman, through the transplantation of fertilized ova, to bear children unrelated to her own family as well as to her husband's.

Would Fletcher consider such devices as ways, like artificial insemination, of "protecting human values and hopes"? I think that they violate them and that though they may be legal, they should "be held in utter detestation."

How can artificial insemination be integrated into a "morality of love," since to love the real father of one's child instead of his assumed father would bring fresh complications to an already complicated situation? If Fletcher does not see how fraudulent and furtive such arrangements are, he has not understood the true nature of family love, how it develops out of ties of blood, out of shared memories and associations, responsibilities. He does not see what a huge part the sense of continuity plays in the love we bear for our children and their children. I think of my little K as carrying with her till she dies the rudiments of tastes, qualities, talents, features, prejudices which I and her father and mother have seen in those akin to us or observed in ourselves. Because of this sense of continuity she is called, like many others of my family, after an ancestress who lived centuries ago and of whom we know nothing but without whom we should none of us exist. Because of her affliction she will never be able to coordinate her inheritance or develop it. She is starting on a long and hopeless journey in more or less the same direction as we and ours are travelling and have travelled. She may be travelling it alone when we, who brought her into the world, are no longer there to shield and love her. Is this conviction that her destinies and ours are interwoven a necessary part of family love or something that can be detached from it and quite irrelevant? I can only say that it is not irrelevant for me and mine. And sometimes when I have been thinking up arguments for the legalization of infanticide, I pull myself up with the reflection: "What business is it of theirs anyway, the doctors, the police, the judge, the jury, the hangman?" Little K is ours, irrevocably ours, in virtue of our deep involvement and I abandon myself to a vision of the future that is more like a Chinese puzzle than a dream, for even as I construct it I see all its intricate improbabilities. Yet there is no other way, at present, in which "human values and hopes" can be protected.

ORDER AND CHAOS

There is very small chance that any widespread change of opinion about these things will occur during peaceful times. Not till
something desperate happens will parents of defective children
dare to articulate the knowledge which they have found in their
hearts, or look to others to endorse it. The average man is
unconcerned. Since death and decay await us all, he might take
a remote interest in euthanasia for the old and sick but he will
be more likely to dodge the law when his time comes than to
try to change it in advance. I cannot see that even for the
elderly or diseased who wish to die, there is any likelihood of a
change in the legal or religious position till the graver problem
of the conscript killer has been faced. A reconsideration of this
by Church or state might cause a revolution in the structure of
society, as Christianity did in its first centuries. In the rebuild-
ing of a new order, a man might recover the rights which he
once abdicated to the state.

Certainly the desire for a revolution, a rebirth, is there but
no one knows in which direction to look for it or how to prepare
for its coming.

The state seems to wish to renounce its right to kill or to
expose its citizens to be killed for causes they do not approve.
Capital punishment has gone and the rights of the conscientious objector are acknowledged though not widely acclaimed.

Can it go further without laying itself open to internal
decay and external assault?

In the Church, too, there are signs that under pressure of
science and public opinion some of its most sacred taboos are
being relaxed. If birth control is permitted, a very ancient and
fundamental belief about the human soul will have been abandoned. At the other end of life, science has pushed back the
frontiers so far that most people can outlive their faculties. This
means that the preservation of life, which was once a sacred
duty, no longer appears so.

Therefore Pius XII has said that, when life is ebbing

hopelessly, doctors need not try to reanimate their patient but "may permit him, already virtually dead, to pass on in peace." And Dr. Lang, the Archbishop of Canterbury, wrote that "cases arise in which some means of shortening life may be justified." There are clergymen on the committees of euthanasia societies.

Yet in these directions Church and state, with their survival at stake, must move so slowly and cautiously that frequently their leaders have to appear as the enemies of the causes in which they believe. A great prelate may find it impossible to exhibit in public the rebellious wisdom and gentleness of his nature. Whatever his private views might be, he could not give public comfort to the conscript who felt no hate and refused to kill, or to the men and women who killed because they wished to spare suffering to those they loved. That is the price he pays to the people for the platform from which he is permitted to address his message *urbi et orbi* or to his nation.

The pyramidal structure of a great state or a great Church imposes prudence. By his exalted position at the apex a prince of religion is exposed to pressure which obscurer men can dodge, and, as with a general who capitulates, his surrender forces submission on men still capable of resistance. Pius XII, for well-known reasons, lagged very far behind the most enlightened of his bishops in his defence of the innocent. The bishops on their part, crippled by the weight of bonds and bargains by which their relations with the state were regulated, passed on to their priests the responsibility of protesting. The priests passed it on to the laymen. And, equally fearful of damaging the Church, the laymen passed it on to those outside the Church. Was there in all Germany a Christian who resisted Hitler as promptly, unreservedly, heroically, as the non-Christian Ossietzky? But the clerics were justified in their prudence. The pyramid still stands, a massive monument to the advantages of discretion.

But even now its security would be endangered by any serious squabble with the state. So it is unlikely that leading churchmen will ever support aggressively the rights of conscience or question unbecomingly the justice of any war in which their government is engaged. Until something happens to interrupt the easy tenor of events, this prudence is obligatory. For if the government were to grant to each citizen the right to decide who his enemy was and whether he should be killed (a right which many savages enjoy), not only would armies be in danger of disintegration but so would states and churches. There would be chaos of a kind.

But what kind? We have been conditioned to think that even war is better than chaos or disorder. Though we do not, like many great Victorians, actually value war (Ruskin said it was "the foundation of all the arts, all the high virtues and faculties of man"), many see it as the mother of invention, of better aircraft and nuclear discovery. And a huge number of respectable people find in it great enjoyment and liberation of spirit. In contrast few social opportunities and interesting assignations are to be offered by the disorder that results when some conflict of principle, normally inhibited, flares up into violent civil discord. And everybody condemns it. Yet the free human spirit is less enslaved by the worst kinds of social disorder than by the best kind of war. The most dreadful crimes of the century have been committed by orderly people subordinating themselves to the commonweal. When the Czechs unburied the corpses of the thousands who had been massacred at Theresienstadt, they were able to give each victim an individual tombstone, for a number had been attached to his or her big toe which corresponded to a name and an address in a carefully kept register. It was not brutal people who did this, but hundreds of selfless and dedicated morticians and stenographers. The massacres which were conducted chaotically, as in the Balkan countries, were not nearly so comprehensive. The killers often tired or felt queasy or amorous or compassionate or accepted bribes. Nature was able to assert itself. And nature is not evil till we make it so.

In fact fruitful ideas are often nourished by what the Organization Man calls disorder. They grow like ferns in the interstices of crumbling walls. You cannot say, as some do, that the ferns are pulling down the wall, for unless it was already collapsing the ferns would not have a foothold there.

Today, in the huge discrepancies between official belief and private behaviour, almost any revolutionary idea could comfortably take root and slowly dislodge a stone or two from the established certainties. Half of Europe is officially dedicated to the belief, which shows no sign of being fulfilled, that the state will one day "wither away," its mission accomplished. Would it matter if the other half also came to think of states and governments as provisional, as methods of collective administration concerned with the problems that arise when men meet each other impersonally in large numbers, with traffic, that is to say, rather than with ethic? Such a view might be more congenial to us than it is to the Russians who preach it. Things would move slowly but by degrees problems of morality and ethic, of punishment and penance, might be released, finger by finger, from the palsied and uncertain grasp of the Church and the state, and settled quietly by men who knew each other.

Maybe the right to kill is the last that the state will relinquish, but the pattern of society is changing rapidly. Consider Charles Whitman, the psychopath, who killed his mother and his wife and then climbed to the top of a tower in the University of Texas and killed or injured forty passersby before he was himself killed by the police. Friends, relations, neighbours, all knew what he was like and might have foreseen and forestalled what happened. Do we not need dreams, ideas and plans that will strengthen the authority of those who are fond of us, or at least interested in us, and weaken the power of the remote, indifferent people who are normally appointed to judge us?

This is fantasy, of course. But the world of Auschwitz was a fantastic one, built upon evil dreams, which no one except the dreamers thought could be realized. The ordinary familiar methods failed to disperse them. We might do better with what is extraordinary and unheard of.

THE SMALL COMMUNITY

So it appears that for me and mine the situation is hopeless for many years to come. Legalism becomes increasingly more powerful than love, and religion sanctions it. The secret ways of ending life are carefully guarded by the specialist. Only a doctor can defy the law and terminate an unwanted life without being detected. Frequently, of course, he will refrain from "respirating" a malformed infant. But in this he cannot be said to be animated by love but by certain scientific classifications.

Even in that kindly book about the Liège trial, the nine religious writers print an appendix in which the retarded are divided into four grades according to their IQ percentages. Little K belongs, I believe, because she has only two-thirds of a brain, to the lowest group of the four, and Hitler's doctors would have given her a high priority for the gas chamber. But by these physiological groupings we distort the problem and make it likely that a categorical "No" will one day lead to a categorical "Yes." Science has, in fact, by reducing the significance of the individual human life, disintegrated love and impaired the rights which a man has over his own life and his child's. Almost everybody today would agree that the doctor, the judge, the clergyman and the geneticist should have greater authority over the life and death of a baby than those who begot him and bore him.

The nine French authors, dreaming of fresh fields opening up for the compassionate heart, the dedicated volunteer, have exiled themselves from reality, as I do when I speculate how I can end little K's life, which can bring only suffering to her parents and to herself. Measuring our convictions, we may be ready to believe that present reality will change more easily than they will. In the meantime I see that I cannot follow my conscience without causing complications for everybody and in particular for those I wish to help, and so I put all my proudest hopes into reverse. Because I cannot take life I become anti-life, and I pray that little K will have a sort of vegetable apathy and that she will never be so conscious of her inadequacies as to suffer for them.

But how can one wish that anyone one loves should be as stupid and helpless as possible? That is a sin of course far worse than the act which I accept as right but cannot perform, yet I am driven to it by a society which refuses to recognize the rights of love.

Moreover, I am forced to admit that till the whole structure of society changes, there are excellent reasons for this refusal. In an acquisitive society, where property is accumulated and inherited and men advertise themselves by their offspring, where labour has to be mobile and families move from place to place, it would be very easy for prudence to pass itself off as love, and for respectable people to engage in a covert war against all physical and mental non-conformity. It would be very difficult to establish that kind of community in which the fraud would be detected and "held in utter detestation." In an open society love is easy to simulate. One cannot trust it, and even when one can, one could not allow our social institutions to be shaped by such a trust. As democracy widens its scope and we reach towards a universal government with uniform laws, it is less and less safe to judge a man's acts by the purity of his motives. We have to be impartial, which means impersonal. In a mass society news of our actions reaches far beyond the small circle which they directly affect, so we must be punished not for what we do but also for things that are done by those unknown people who imitate us. That is to say that if we do what we know to be right, it may be something that society is forced to condemn.

Will this always be so? Can there ever be a society in which the rights of love are recognized and even the law bends before them? If so, it will necessarily be a small society. It will differ I think from the kind of society in which Aristotle preached and Hippocrates practised, because Aristotle thought it was a matter of law, not of love, that defective children should be killed. One may suspect that such laws, where they were enforced, were very loosely administered. The city-state

grew up as an aggregate of many families and was itself a vastly
inflated family, and its laws must have been flexible enough.
Despite Aristotle, natural affection probably played a larger
part in their application than eugenics. It was not the state but
the parents themselves who exposed their infants on the
mountainsides. All the same, good citizenship and not love was
the criterion by which behavior was judged, and if Aristotle had
his way the state would have usurped the rights of the parents
and made the exposure of defective children the concern of the
city not of the family.

But even if we wished to, we could not re-create the city-
states. Where else can we look? In our loose and inchoate society are there any traces of a submerged or nascent community
in which the rule of love is observed and to whose collective
judgment we could refer? There are many; but they crystallize
round some specific problem and evaporate as soon as it is
solved. And of course there are our families, more permanent
in their mutual dependence but seldom acting as a unit. If they
had the confidence and assumed the authority, it seems to me
that my family and D's could judge more wisely about what
concerns them intimately than any government could. And, if
we considered, too, the judgment of those friends to whom we
are bound as closely as by ties of blood, we should have a
community as capable of deciding its own affairs as, say, Meg-
ara or Sicyon ever claimed to be.

In such a community the weight of the decision would
bear most heavily on those that love most, but concern would
travel outward from the centre, the focus of agony, to the periphery, and authority to endorse or dissent would be propor-
tionate to love. If such a community were to coalesce out of
chaos, I would trust it to decide wisely about little K or to form
a loving background for such a decision.

But it has not coalesced and there is as yet no sign that it
will. And, even if it did coalesce, how could it ever acquire legal
status? This question can be illuminated by another question.
How would it be possible to withhold legal status from the
offspring of scientific marriages, the children of sperm-filled

capsules and transplanted ovaries? The answer to these questions is that the law in both cases is helpless. These matters are outside the law, and men and women must decide for themselves.

Before there is any change we shall have to live through this period of remote and impersonal control and, in the meantime, for the sake of future freedom, a greater burden than ever before will fall upon the man who refuses to conform. Politically, socially, domestically, the individual may have to make in solitude great and tragic decisions and carry them through in the teeth of a hostile and mechanical officialdom. Ossietzky and Stauffenberg, Sinyavsky, Daniel and Djilas are well-known names, but they owe their deserved celebrity, at least in part, to the publicity services of their country's enemies. In other spheres thousands of men and women will have to fling themselves fruitlessly against the barriers before they collapse. Their names will be known only to a very few, and by the time they are due to be honoured they will be forgotten.

Joseph Fletcher says that we are at the end of the theological era and that those who do not believe in personal survival after death do not fear it as much as those that do. Certainly this is true of me. As it approaches, I seldom look forward but often backward, thinking of the things I have never done, the faculties that are likely to decay before they have been used.

When I do look forward, I see a faint line becoming fainter as I draw closer to it. Beyond it I will live for a certain period in the thoughts of those I love or have influenced. This measured immortality belongs to almost everybody, but for little K the dividing line is dim and blurred. The emptiness beyond can scarcely be more empty than that through which she is passing now. Maybe in ten or twenty years, as little K, climbing very slowly, has reached the highest rung she will ever reach, she will meet me there descending much more rapidly. If that were so, she would be the companion that I would choose above all others to travel back with me into nothingness.

Hilton Als

My Pin-Up

By now, the word "Negress" has come to mean many things. The Negress is perceived less as a mind than as an emotional being. In the popular imagination, she lives one or several cliché-ridden narratives. One narrative: she is colored, female, and a single mother, reduced by circumstances to tireless depression and public "aid" and working off the books in one low-paying job after another in an attempt to support her children—children whom, according to tax-paying, law-abiding public consensus, she should not have had. Like my mother.

Another narrative: she can be defined as a romantic wedded to despair, since she has little time or inclination to analyze how she is regarded by America's social welfare system, which sees her as a statistic, part of the world's rapacious silent majority. Like my mother.

Another narrative: she gives birth to children who grow up to be lawless; she becomes involved with men who leave her for other women; she is subject to illness and depression. Her depression is so numbing that she rarely lets news of the outside world (television, radio, newspapers) enter her sphere of consciousness, and much of her time is spent shielding herself and her children against the news of emotional disaster she sees day after day in the adult faces that surround the faces of her children, who, in turn, look to her to make sense of it all. Like my mother.

What the Negress has always been: a symbol of America's now forgotten strain of Puritanical selflessness. The Negress is a perennial source of "news" and "copy" in the newspapers and magazines she does not read, because she is a formidable char-acter in the internal drama with which most Americans sur-round the issue of self-abnegation. If the Negress is repre-sented in the media, it is as a good neighbor who is staunch in her defense of the idea that being a good neighbor makes a difference in this common world. And this: she is a good neigh-bor uncritical of her faith, even as her intellect searches through the Byzantine language of the Bible for a truth other than her own. Her ability to meld language with belief without becoming sarcastic (sarcasm defines our sense of contemporary speech) is one reason the Negress is both abhorred and adored. Take, for instance, this story, reported in the *New York Post:*

> The Trinidad woman who lost her legs in a subway purse-snatching is not looking for revenge—but she hopes her mugger will become "a better person" in prison. . . . Samella Thompson, 56, fell onto the tracks in the Van Wyck Boulevard Station in Jamaica, Queens. . . . She was trying to jump onto the plat-form from an F train as she chased a homeless man who had grabbed her sister's purse. . . . The feisty mother of five's attitude is "you have to take life as it comes." Thompson wished [her attacker] would know God.

The Negress serves as a reminder to our sentimental na-tion that its countrymen are shaped by a nonverbal confusion about and, ultimately, abhorrence of the good-neighbor princi-ple, which they absorb through the language-based tenets of

Judaism and Christianity. And since most Americans are suspicious of language and spend a great deal of time and energy on Entertainment and Relaxation in an attempt to avoid its net result (Reflection), this absorption leads to a deep emotional confusion about the "good."

To women who are not Negresses—some are white—the Negress, whether she calls herself that or not, is a specter of dignity—selfless to a fault. But eventually, she troubles her noncolored female admirer, since the latter feels compelled to compare herself and finds herself both privileged and lacking. This inversion or competitiveness among women vis-à-vis their "oppressed" stance says something about why friendships between women are rare, and especially so between noncolored women and Negresses.

The Negress's will to survive is enhanced by her need to survive for her children. But being the source of such strength is sometimes too much for the Negress. Sometimes she contrives to marry something other than herself or her children in order to escape it, that something being a black male. When maleness manages to brush up against the Negress, it is usually violent, so its presence is felt. But it eventually absents itself from the Negress because her intellectual and physical focus on surviving leaves no room for maleness's self-centeredness.

Man Seized in Rape of 3-Year-Old in Public

A Manhattan man raped his 3-year-old niece about 25 feet from the Franklin D. Roosevelt Drive at the start of the rush hour Friday evening. . . . The suspect, Leroy Saunders, 29, was caught a few blocks away after assaulting the girl under a tree on a grassy knoll. . . . Mr. Saunders, with his pants down to his ankles, assaulted the girl, who was naked below the waist. . . . The girl's mother, who is Mr. Saunders's sister, said, "You just don't expect that from kin." But she declined to talk further about the case. "I just want to go to my

apartment to rest," she said. . . . Neighbors said the
mother, whose surname differs from her brother's, had
six children.
                —*The New York Times,* July 17, 1991.

The fact that Leroy Saunders's sister, mother of six, three
of whom were in foster homes, had to "rest" after her daughter's attack on a grassy knoll and perhaps consider the facts
later was not unusual given what I assumed when I read her
story: that she was a Negress. What was, or perhaps was not,
unusual, given that there was no photograph accompanying
Man Seized in Rape of 3-Year-Old, was that immediately upon
reading it, I attached black faces to this narrative of "kin" gone
awry, a grassy knoll, pants down around the ankles, and a
mother's need for rest after an atrocity committed against her
child.

That Leroy Saunders's sister has a surname different from
her brother's is not among the pertinent facts that make up the
Negress in her. The fact that she did not expect such behavior
from "kin" is. This word—"kin"—is a regional colloquialism
peculiar to the South; it evokes a narrative. One can imagine
Leroy Saunders's sister as an inbred Negress, saddled with bad
men and children swollen with need and the welfare system.
No husband or father is reported as being attached to her "different" name or to her children. But the use of the word "kin"
implicates her in Saunders's crime: in a common world, her
actions are crimes too. Her use of the word "kin" not only
indicates her commonness to her readers, but also her forbear-
ance, her unwillingness to give her brother up, regardless of the
facts.

The story of the Negress is not difficult to understand if
you listen. My sisters spoke the same language of kin, one saying of another: "She is so nasty. Having one baby after another,
and none of them by the same father. Like a dog." I assumed
that Leroy Saunders's sister was another Negress living in strict
avoidance of the facts, just as I assumed his niece was another
Negress left in a world where her future actions would proba-

bly illustrate Leroy Saunders's turn of mind against her. What
the *Times* made clear was how Leroy Saunders's sister and
niece would not be a story were it not for him. Generally the
Negress wears the rouge of a peculiar emotional verbosity that
is not, in fact, verbal.

I grew up with the youngest of my four older sisters, who
was eleven years my senior, during the '70s, a period characterized by a breakdown in the traditional social order, at least as
we had known it. The '70s were a synthetic version of the more
galvanizing active radicalism of the '60s. As a leftover time, the
'70s suited us, perfectly, since we considered ourselves leftover
people, Negresses like our mother. Being younger and, in some
respects, less intelligent than our mother, we were conscious of
wanting to develop our own social stance, even as we affected
her stance of disinterest, because we admired her. I think we
misread our mother's exhausted concern as lack of concern; she
never didn't care.

Unlike our mother, we affected an interest in people who,
because they had the same skin color as our own, presumed we
were interested in the race and its struggle. We were not interested in the race and its struggle. We were not interested in
strident abstractions, being so emotionally abstract ourselves.
We were West Indians living in New York; we were smug in our
sense of displacement; we took freely from both cultures in
order to be interesting. The furor and energy that our black
American contemporaries focused on dreams and hopes we
found ridiculous. Their ideology was totalitarianism made simple: economic independence from "the man" and an entirely
black-run government. We were especially distanced by the
movement's xenophobia: members of the Black Power movement referred to West Indians, and their ambitious progeny, as
black Jews.

My sister discovered Black Power around the same time
she discovered her need for a father; as a concept, the movement lent itself to the idea of "serious" black men who were
"committed." She was drawn to Black Power because of its

distinctly American male cast of mind. As a girl of West Indian descent, she considered American black men exotic, charming in their narcissism, and in their generally ahistorical stance.

It would not be excessive for me to say that my sister and I probably also considered American blacks disgusting on some level, even though we didn't admit this to ourselves, given our melodramatic silence. We weren't attracted to much that we didn't find repugnant. We couldn't be in love with something we could not control. Disdain is controllable, no matter how feigned; love is not. And we believed we would feel less overwhelmed and more distanced from our difference vis-à-vis American blacks if we were disdainful of them—a romantic view. Our romantic view of American blacks included feeling "bad" for them because they weren't us. We wanted to save them from themselves. We were very big on rescuing people, having had a mother like ours.

Although we did not know it then, my sister and I used our cursory involvement in the Black Power movement—sit-ins in Harlem, many, many poetry readings in the Bronx, and demonstrations everywhere—to catapult ourselves past our mother's nonverbal emotional verbosity, her increasing disinterest in the world at large. The outings I looked forward to most were not those that involved picketing, or canvassing votes for now forgotten community "leaders," but listening to the women who sometimes took the stand at rallies and spoke, the women who wrote and published books and recited their words in public, unlike my sister who hid or burned her diary and buried her language in the creases of her careless lovers' necks.

The women we heard read—Sonia Sanchez or Nikki Giovanni—were addressed as "Sister." They wore brightly colored dashikis, head wraps, and robes. Their poetic skills were limited. Their work was strident, empty, and invigorating. It valorized the black male. The black male those poetesses and my sister imagined did not exist—which is one reason they had to imagine him. Those women embraced the ideology spouted during the revolution that was always about to happen because they wanted to maintain the fantasy that the revolution was the assertion of a black masculinity that was about to be. That masculinity would serve my sister's purpose: it would be forceful enough to dismantle Negressity and its aura of depression.

That many of the male members of the black revolutionary movement were irresponsible and childlike was beside the point. That they were in search of the same authority figure whom most of them had never known in their matriarchal households—Dad—as their female comrades was also beside the point. What made the women different from the men in the movement was the will they applied to *creating* Dad for themselves.

The poetesses my sister and I listened to commanded the respect of their male "comrades" because they reinvented them as officers of war. As those women poets spoke, in their conspiratorial, self-congratulatory, syncopated voices, another tone broke in, a tone which expressed their need for Daddy to shut them up. It became clear to me that their language was not the product of reflection or the desire to reflect; if they thought before they spoke, they'd be forced to realize that what they were screaming about was their need to be silenced. Instead, they identified their need to be oppressed by their idea of a black male as an "emergent black tradition," its foundation being the abstractions of Black Motherhood and Black Pride.

The movement's most popular poet, Nikki Giovanni, wrote in a poem titled "Seduction," which was published in 1970:

one day
you gonna walk in this house
and i'm gonna have on a long African
gown
you'll sit down and say "The Black . . ."
and i'm gonna take one arm out
then you—not noticing me at all—will say "What
about this brother . . ."
and i'm going to be slipping it over my head
and you'll rapp on about "The revolution . . ."

while i rest your hand against my stomach
you'll go on—as you always do—saying
"I just can't dig . . ."
while i'm moving your hand up and down
and i'll be taking your dashiki off . . .
then you'll notice
your state of undress
and knowing you you'll just say
"Nikki,
isn't this counterrevolutionary . . . ?"

And Sonia Sanchez wrote in "Black Magic" in 1978:

magic
   my man
is you
   turning
my body into
a thousand
smiles.
   black
magic is your
touch
   making
me breathe.

The images these poetesses offered in verse—a simple, uncomplicated, thuggish sexuality projected onto their construction of the black male—were perfectly legitimate but dumb, easily co-opted by the pornographic imagination that continues to produce such magazines as *Black Tail, Sugah,* and *Ebony Heat.* During the revolution, the Negress replaced her starched cap of servitude with a brightly colored turban made of knit cloth, but she did not reinvent her internal structure.

When the Negress is seen in books, such as Toni Morrison's *Beloved* or Terry McMillan's *Waiting to Exhale,* that are

marketed according to their "anger" quotient, or in films, such
as Charles Burnett's *To Sleep With Anger,* that are remarkable
for their willful construction of the "benign" Negress, or in
theater pieces, such as *Having Our Say,* that avoid reference to
class issues among Negresses, she is shown as less than herself,
but is still more than our current cultural climate can handle.
Angry or silent, she carries a tray loaded with forgiveness, bitterness, rancor, defensiveness, and slatternliness. She had rejected language. In most of the books about her, the authors do
not question what the Negress is, because they cannot face her.
The Negress in their books is shut off from ideas or speech of
her own, like a mad, woolly relative. Like the Negress in Toni
Cade Bambara's *Gorilla, My Love:*

> It does no good to write autobiographical fiction cause
> the minute the book hits the stand here comes your
> mama screamin how could you and sighin death where
> is thy sting and she snatches you up out your bed to
> grill you about what was going down back there in
> Brooklyn when she was working three jobs and trying
> to improve the quality of your life and come to find
> . . . that you were messin around with that nasty boy
> up the block and breaks into sobs. . .

Or the Negress in Toni Morrison's *Sula:*

> Hannah rubbed no edges, made no demands, made
> the man feel as though he were complete and wonder-
> ful just as he was—he didn't need fixing. . . .

What would the Negress be if she were stripped of her
role? Would she be just another banal woman undone by domestic despair, fortified by her class aspirations and fantasies
about being fulfilled through marriage? It is difficult to imagine
the Negress being anything other than what she has come to
symbolize in contemporary literature: authorial conceit and ambition. The writers who present the Negress are intent on

building an empirical universe in which the only voices heard are their own, and since the Negress does not speak, but *moves* through their fiction as either an adventurer or a victim, her existence depends entirely upon the fictional system they build for her. They create the Negress in order to kill her, because she represents the matriarchal society they are at pains to forget, even as they cling to her because of her ability to milk sympathy from the audience—or provide it.

The Negress in literature is a construct who does not exist independently of her creator's need to fulfill his or her audience's expectations of "black" writing. She signifies "oppression" and, by extension, blackness. They make the Negress bigger than she is in order to mythologize her. As a myth, she does not have to be complex or subtle. She is larger than life, like Pilate in Toni Morrison's *Song of Solomon*. She is uglier than life, like Celie in Alice Walker's *The Color Purple*. And she appears to superb theatrical effect from time to time, especially when her presence represents someone else's failure of expression, as in the late British playwright John Osborne's *The Entertainer*:

> Archie: Did I ever tell you the most moving thing that I ever heard? It was when I was in Canada—I managed to slip over the border sometimes to some people I knew, and one night I heard some negress singing in a bar. *Now you're going to smile at this,* you're going to smile your educated English head off, because I suppose you've never sat lonely and half slewed in some bar among strangers a thousand miles from anything you think you understand. But if ever I saw any hope or strength in the human race, it was in the face of that old fat negress getting up to sing about Jesus or something like that. She was poor and lonely and oppressed like nobody you've ever known. Or me, for that matter. I never even liked that kind of music, but to see that old black whore singing her heart out to the whole world, you knew somehow in your heart that it didn't

matter how much you kick people, the real people, how much you despise them, if they can stand up and make a pure, just natural noise like that, there's nothing wrong with them, only with everybody else. . . . There's nobody who can feel like that. I wish to God I could, I wish to God I could feel like that old black bitch with her fat cheeks, and sing.

When describing the Negress, writers describe themselves away from her, as they rush headlong into the void of patriarchy. In their books, the Negress is replete with tears. She smiles. Her chest heaves. Her body is that of a servant not begging for respite. She burns brightly in the imagination, like a dull witch.

In order to understand her, I have written my life in the margins of hers. Is this love? How did I love my mother? After a certain point, I rarely expressed it physically for fear her touch would be so hideous and lonely. How do I love her still? In my imagination.

William T. Vollmann

The Prophet of the Road

YUKON TERRITORY, CANADA (1983)

Pity the poor biologist who had to prove (I never found why) that caribou in the Canadian Barrenlands lose a pint of blood a week to the mosquitoes. Of course caribou have more blood to spare than we; perhaps it is not as bad as it sounds, to pay a pint a week for the privilege of living. I remember summer days in Alaska when I could hardly see the backs of my hands because they were so thick with mosquitoes. And a bush pilot told me how he once overflew a man on a hilltop who seemed to be signalling him with long black streamers; these too were mosquitoes in their thousands, using the man for a windbreak while they attacked him, rising and falling in eerie concordance with his frantic arms, veiling his face with whining hungry blackness. It is usually difficult to apprehend the concept of an ocean by analogy with a single drop of water, but in the case of these unpleasant creatures, one will fall upon you with sufficient vampirish alacrity to represent the whole swarm, unlike a dewdrop which lies so docile in the palm as to seem altogether alien to reeftides and shipwrecks. The dewdrop is at rest anywhere. The mosquito seems fulfilled only when installed upon your skin, its six knees drawn tightly up above its wings, the forelegs stretched partly out like a basking dog's, antennae alertly cocked, head down, proboscis stabbed into you to drink a little more of your life. Even in this state of fulfillment the creature appears tense. It is ready to withdraw from the wound at any time (although as it swells up with blood it becomes less able to do so quickly); it gains, in short, a furtive and half-disengaged orgasm, which is all that natural law permits when a pygmy rapes a giant. The spectrum of feeling between lust and fear and satiation in mosquitoes must be very narrow. When they crouch restlessly on leaves or ceilings they do not seem so different from when they are feeding. This family Culicidae is a family of machines. Delicately tooled with bands and scales, equipped with near-infallible sensors to locate their victims, they've been adjusted by their maker to the behavior best suited to carry out their mission in a given place. In the tropics they are silently multitudinous. Knowing that if one doesn't get you another one will, they launch themselves directly, though by all means taking advantage of leaf-shade and darkness. Temperate latitudes do not hold so very many of them. As a result, they are cunning and wary there. On a black sticky night, a single mosquito in a room may succeed in biting you half a dozen times. When you finally turn on the light to search for it, you cannot find it. Farther north, and again they have less need for these subtleties. Kill one or ten, it makes no matter. A hundred more will come. Proof that the manufacturer is not concerned about the potential loss of a few automata is given by the noise they so often emit, which not only alerts the victim, but also annoys, as anyone who's endured the quavering whining of a mosquito lodged inside the ear would agree. This provocation, combined with the itching, would require a Brahmin's self-control not to avenge. Anyhow, kill them, shoo them away, or let them bite, it makes very little difference. They will win out. I remember how grateful I was when the days were cold enough to keep them sluggish; and even when they swarmed everything was so beautiful with flowers and red sphagnum moss that they didn't matter until I began to get tired; parting the river-brambles and river-trees I forded braids of rivers without minding the mosquitoes on my face; and then I climbed the tussock-hills to where the tundra was very thin, like the greening on a pool table, and had a nice view of rivers and snowdrifts, always the sound of a river to remind me that mosquito-songs were not all there was, and sometimes a bird sang, too. If I was lucky there might be a breeze to scatter the mosquitoes; and I could eat my lunch very quickly. But I'd often stop early on those days, not having been able to rest enough. (Doubtless if I'd been born there they would have affected me less.) Pitching my tent was unpleasant, because the time it took was more than sufficient for my guests to thicken about me and I could not fight them all off since that required constant use of both hands and I must use at least one to work. If I slapped a tickle on my cheek, I'd kill a dozen bloated mosquitoes, my palm wetted with my blood. I did have repellent, but it didn't stay on long, because the thick clothes which the mosquitoes compelled me to wear made me sweat. So by evening, when I was exhausted, I'd squeeze a few more drops of that bitterly toxic elixir onto my skin before shaking the tentpoles out of their stuffsack, but I'd always miss a few places: maybe my ankles that time (secure, I'd thought, behind the armor of my pants-cuff), or the inviting slice of flesh at the back of my neck, just behind my collar. I'd scarcely have one pole assembled before being seized by that maddening itching, which I was already tensed to expect, and as I forgot everything but slapping the pole would fall apart again, and I'd have to laugh, since swearing wouldn't have helped. At least I did have thick clothes on and could get the tent up in due time, then crawl inside and zip the door shut behind me, kill the twenty or thirty mosquitoes who'd ventured in (they were not good at hiding), rub some cold canteen-water over my burning lumps, scratch my swollen face and hands, and relax upon the top of my sleeping bag, listening to mosquitoes pelt against the fly of the tent like rain. The next day, more mosquitoes. Four miles up Inukpasugruk Creek was a waterfall climb. Surges of water made me uneasy. I didn't know whether it was runoff from rain over the ridge, or whether a glacier-finger waited for me. The mosquitoes weren't too bad. They only bit my eyelids, earlobes, cheeks, knees, buttocks, wrists, hands and ankles a few times. The worst thing, as I said, was that singing whine. It was not enough that they bit; they must also make that noise, louder as they got closer, always teasing, uneven so that I could never get used to it; and one note became a chord as more of them came singing around until I could think of nothing but where they would land next. I'd sweep the air and my arms would meet mosquitoes; I'd make a sudden fist anywhere and mosquitoes would be caught inside. — Of course it was a failure on my part to be so disturbed by them. There's a scene in Tolstoy (in "The Cossacks," I think) when mosquito-bites suddenly become glowing love-bites and the sportsman strides happily through the forest of his own self-reliance. — And what about the Inuit, who'd lived with mosquitoes for perhaps twenty centuries without repellent? An old lady from Pond Inlet once told me that she could remember living in a sod house. The mosquitoes had been very bad, but her family fanned themselves with feathers. They'd done that every summer for all their lives until the whalers came to stay.

And now I did not have to think about the mosquitoes too much, either because I was in my tent again looking at the bloodstains on the ceiling where I'd squashed the ones that had followed me in and bitten me and gotten away for a minute or two before I caught up with them, and I could see the shadows of so many others on the outside of the nylon, smelling the blood inside me but unable to get at me, waiting for me to go out, and then after I ran back inside scratching my new bites and killing the assault guard, the others would land on the fly again, waiting now for the sunny night to end so that I'd expose my flesh to another day; but meanwhile I was inside and they could not torture me; I did not have to slap the backs of my thighs every minute on general principles, or sweep my sleeve across my face to kill mosquito-crowds; and it was astounding how quickly I forgot them. They were all around me and had not forgotten about me, but I'd shut them out and they meant nothing. I cannot remember what I thought about. Most likely

I did not have to think about anything, because I'd gained asylum into an embassy of the easy world that I was used to, enjoying it flapping round me in the sunlight like a boat, all blue and orange, with the shadow of the blowing fly bobbing up and down.

When I hitchhiked from San Francisco to Fairbanks, mosquitoes surrounded me with the hymning hum of a graduation—not right away, of course; not until I got to Canada. As soon as I was safely in a vehicle they could not affect me anymore and I rode the familiar thrill of speed and distance, lolling in the back of the truck, with a beautiful husky kissing my hands and cheeks, and we slowed to let a moose get out of the road and at once I heard them again. — A mosquito bit me. — I was on the Al-Can Highway now. I forgot the night I'd given up, not yet even in Oregon, and stayed at a motel, my face redburned and filthy, my eyes aching; and it had felt sinful to spend the sixteen dollars on the room but it was raining hard as it had been all day, so no one would pick me up. In hitchhiking as in so many other departments, the surest way not to get something is to need it. The more the world dirtied me, the less likely someone would be to take me in. — But the next morning was sunny and I had showered and shaved, which was why a van picked me up within half an hour and took me into Oregon, and as I rode so happily believing that I now progressed, I didn't even consider that the inside of the van was not so different from the inside of the motel; I was protected again. When I remember that summer, which now lies so far behind me, I must own myself still protected, in a fluctuating kind of way, and so a question hovers and bites me unencouraged: Which is worse, to be too often protected, and thereby forget the sufferings of others, or to suffer them oneself? There is, perhaps, a middle course: to be out in the world enough to be toughened, but to have a shelter sufficient to stave off callousness and wretchedness. Of course it might also be said that there is something depressing and even debasing about moderation—how telling that one symptom for *average* is *mean!*

On the long stretch of road between Fort St. John and

Fort Nelson, where the mosquitoes were thickest, we came to where the Indian woman was dancing. It was almost dusk, round about maybe nine or ten-o'-clock. The country was full of rainbows, haze and yellow flowers. Every hour or so we had to stop to clean the windshield because so many mosquitoes had squished against it, playing connect-the-dots with the outlines of all things. We pulled over and went to work with ammonia and paper towels. They found us as soon as we got out. The driver's head was a big black sphere of mosquitoes. There were dozens of them in the space between my glasses and my eyes. When we got back into the camper, mosquitoes spilled in through the open windows. We jittered along at fifty miles an hour over the dirt road until the breeze of our passage had sucked them out. By then the windshield was already turning whitish-brown again from squashed mosquitoes. The driver did not want to stop again just yet, but I noticed that he was straining his eyes to see through the dead bugs, and I was just about to say that I didn't mind cleaning the windshield by myself this time (I was, after all, getting a free ride), when far ahead on that empty road (we hadn't met another vehicle for two hours) we saw her capering as if she were so happy, and then we began to get closer to her and saw the frantic despair in her leapings and writhings like some half-crushed thing's that could not die. Not long ago I thoughtlessly poured out a few drops of dilute solvent upon waste ground, and an earthworm erupted, stretched toward me accusingly, stiffened and died. But the convulsions of this woman went on and on. Just as her dance of supposed happiness had seemed to me entirely self-complete like masturbation, so this dance of torture struck me as long-gone mad, sealing her off from other human beings, as if she were some alcoholic mumbler who sheds incomprehensible tears. It was not unti we were almost past that I understood behind our hermetic windows that she was screaming for help. I cannot tell you how terrifying her cries were in that wild place. The driver hesitated. He was a good soul, but he already had one hitchhiker. Did he have to save the world? Besides, she might be crazy or dangerous. Her yellings were fading and she was becoming trivial in the rearview mirror when he slowed to think about it, and it was only then that we both understood what we had seen, because protected brains work slowly: mosquitoes darkened her face like a cluster of blackberries, and her legs were black and bloody where the red shorts ended. The driver stopped. Mosquitoes began to pelt against the windows.

We had to help her get in. She embraced us with all her remaining strength, weeping like a little child. Her fearfully swollen face burned to my touch. She'd been bitten so much around the eyes that she could barely see. Her long black hair was smeared with blood and dead mosquitoes. Her cheeks had puffed up like tennis balls. She had bitten her lip very deeply, and blood ran down from it to her chin where a single mosquito still feasted. I crushed it.

That afternoon, no doubt, she'd been prettier, with sharp cheekbones that caught the light, a smooth dark oval face, dark lips still glistening and whole, black eyes whose mercurial glitter illuminated the world yet a little longer, shiny black hair waved slantwise across her forehead. That was why the man in Fort Nelson had decided to support her trade. Reservation bait, he thought. She got in his truck, and there were some other men, too; they used her services liberally. But unlike slow mosquitoes, who pay the bill, if only with their lives, the men had their taste of flesh with impunity. The weren't entirely vile. They didn't beat her. They only left her to the mosquitoes. They let her put her clothes back on before they threw her out—

She'd tried to dig a hole in the gravelly earth, a grave to hide in, but she hadn't gone an inch before her fingers started bleeding and the mosquitoes had crawled inside her ears so that she couldn't think anymore, and she started running down the empty road; she ran until she had to stop, and then the mosquitoes descended like dark snow onto her eyelids. Two cars had passed her. She'd craved to kill herself, but the mosquitoes would not even give her sufficient peace to do that. I'll never forget how I felt when she squeezed me in her desperate arms—I'll never forget her dance.

That was the most horrible thing that I have ever seen. For awhile I thought about it every day. I know I thought about it when at the end of that summer I was hitchhiking home and had gotten as far as Oregon, where I slept entented in a tree-screened dimple on a field by a white house, hoping that no one in the white house would see and hurt me, and the next morning I ducked under the fence and was back on the shoulder of the freeway and it was already a very hot morning, so I was drinking from my canteen (which I'd filled at a gas station in Portland) when another hitchhiker came thumping down the road toward me. He was like a prophet from the old times. He wore a long robe and carried a great wooden staff which he slammed down at every step. He was not so old, and yet his beard was long and gray (possibly from dust), and his gray hair fell to his shoulders and his eyes were wild like a bull's. His face was caked with dust. He licked his lips as he came near me, and his eyes were on me unwaveringly, so I offered him water as he came closer and closer, continuing to stare into my eyes, and then he shook his head sternly and walked on. I did not live up to his ideals. There was another hitcher I'd met in Washington State who'd been crazy and called himself the Angel Michael and whispered to me that he didn't know anymore whether he was a boy or a girl and I believed him because he was so angelic: angels are undoubtedly hermaphrodites. In the same way, I believed in the prophet wholly. I could not but admire him for rejecting me. He went on and on down the freeway shoulder, with barbed wire at his right shoulder and cars at his left, growing smaller (though I could still distinctly hear the tapping of his stick) and I wondered what he would have done or said if it had been he and only he who came across the woman whom the mosquitoes were eating. I could almost see him there on the Al-Can, toiling on, mile after mile, his face black-veiled like that minister in Hawthorne's tale, black-veiled with mosquitoes; he'd walk on and stab the gravel with his staff and never deign to brush away a single mosquito; he'd glare terribly through eyes swollen almost shut by mosquito bites and go on, mile after mile, week after week; and maybe someday he'd come upon that woman shrieking in her crazed torment. Would he have stopped then; would the mosquitoes leave her for him in a single flicker of his divinity, after which he'd pass on in silence, followed by unimaginable clouds of humming blackness? Would she fall to her knees then and thank God and regain herself? — Or would he never have stopped at all, marching contemptuously on, ignoring her need as he ignored my gift, and dwindled just the same along that highway's inhuman straightness?

Aldo Buzzi

Travels to Djakarta, Gorgonzola, Crescenzago, London, Milan (1963–83)

I

Years ago I found myself in Indonesia, in Djakarta, which was once called Batavia, sitting at a table in a restaurant in the heart of the Chinese quarter of Glodok—near Kota, to anyone who knows this city, immense in extent, where the long streets change their names every two or three blocks, causing the visitor to go mad. I was reflecting on the menu, undecided between serpent soup, roast monkey, or a simple stuffed dog with hot pepper.

A young woman sitting at the next table with some other people was showing off her beautiful feet, at once thin and soft, brown on top and pink underneath, on which no shoe had left the slightest mark. In Indonesia feet are considered the most fascinating part of the female body, and everyone knows what small female feet mean to the Japanese; it is also known that in Vienna, around 1910, the tram stops were always crowded with groups of gentlemen waiting to admire the small feet of pretty women poking out from under their skirts for an instant as they boarded the car.

I myself have always had a weakness for women's feet, and I hate people who tell jokes in which feet are associated with the odor of certain cheeses, like Appenzeller, Camembert, Gorgonzola. For these same people, armpits can smell only of goats, and the . . .

"It," a sommelier would say, "has an intoxicating bouquet of roses and Parma violets. . . ." I would add that "it," because of its form—rounder than any solid of revolution or any circle traced by a compass—and because of its inscrutable mixture of the human and the divine, can be considered one of the most convincing proofs of the existence of God, certainly more convincing than the ontological argument of Saint Anselm.

And yet how long has the misunderstanding of the two kinds of love, the sacred and the profane, lasted, a misunderstanding that has confused the minds of countless poor devils and she-devils? I remember an old lady who boasted of having never shown herself naked to her husband. Asked how she had conceived her numerous children, she answered that she had a nightgown with a little flap in the front, usually fastened by a mother-of-pearl button, through which . . .

Thus she lived (with a husband worthy of her in every way) and died, convinced that she had followed the road of virtue that leads directly to paradise, which, if it is inhabited by similar angels, is nothing but the inferno—rather, the worst inferno, because it is not that of the lustful, the gluttonous, the prodigal, the miserly, the wrathful, the slothful, the heretic, the unbeliever, the violent, the fraudulent, or the betrayer but the most horrible of all: the inferno of the idiot.

A friend, after reading these last lines (the nightgown with the flap), told me that a similar story, though without the mother-of-pearl button, is found in a book of Carlo Dossi's. This seems yet another confirmation of the fact that by now everything has been written and the writer of today can add of his own at most a mother-of-pearl button; and often he does not add even that. . . .

From Milan the train travels silently toward Gorgonzola through a green plain divided geometrically by canals full of clear water, with granite locks. Rows of enormous poplars with dancing leaves (*Populus tremula*) lead to villas and farmhouses of splendid design, all destined to be covered in a few years with cement. And then the day will come when there will be a lack of good arable land, and all that cement will have to be removed, at enormous expense, in order that the earth underneath may be found again: in order to eat, to survive. As the train passes, large herds of cows with clean, fragrant coats look straight into my eyes without ceasing to chew their cud, as is their habit. Probably they are thinking the same thing. To Liszt, who had come to visit him, the old Rossini said he had composed some rather tasty little piano pieces, and had titled them "Fresh Butter," "Lentils," "Peas," "Macaroni" . . .

The interior monologue was born on a train. Joyce, rather than inventing it, perhaps used it excessively. It seems to me that Joyce took a route opposite to that of a normal writer: he began with a classic *(Dubliners),* continued with writings that became more and more complicated *(Portrait of the Artist, Ulysses),* and ended with a novel *(Finnegans Wake)* that is untranslatable and practically unreadable. Even if it's true that defects are an integral part of perfection, I would like to try eliminating part of *Ulysses*—pages that are more or less incomprehensible, plays on words, on style, on punctuation, things still taken up, unfortunately, by the last Joyceans—and see what happens.

One of the first stations is Crescenzago, home of the delicious cheese called crescenza. In Crescenzago there was a little restaurant with a beautiful young waitress. . . . So, even if you discard a few pages . . . Many of Joyce's admirers might have had the same thought, but . . . To hell with serpents, monkeys, and dogs. I decided to order the same dish they served her, and when they brought her some spring rolls, I—instead of writing the order on the appropriate pad, which is on every table—simply pointed out the dish to the waiter. Of course, to point I used my thumb and not my index finger—to point with the index finger is considered a serious offense there—and I used my right hand because the left is considered dirty, being used for post-defecatory ablutions: toilet paper is unknown in the toilets there. I thought once of the embarrassing situations in which a beautiful left-handed girl might find herself; but surely I was mistaken, because tradition is always stronger than anything.

Meanwhile, various tour buses had stopped in front of the restaurant, and a crowd of hot tourists had invaded the place. An infinity of feet—deformed by shoes and by calluses of every sort, and by twisted nails painted in lively colors to attract attention to their deformity (feet that irresistibly evoked the most vulgar jokes)—and dozens of buttocks that could testify only to the existence of the devil noisily found seats at the tables. The proprietor, one of the seven million Chinese with the family name Chang, turned up the volume on the speakers in honor of the guests. In addition to the eternal "The Orient Is Red," the most recent successful songs were being transmitted from Peking: "Recover the Losses Caused by the Four" and "Govern the State Centering the Work on the Class Struggle."

At the tourist office in Gorgonzola I take a leaflet with a plan for the tour of the city: photographic safari in the public park, which is inhabited by dwarf goats, hens, cockerels, pigeons, pheasants, swans, guinea pigs, ponies, donkeys. Then a stop at the ancient bakery on the Martesana canal and consumption on the spot of a fresh, ring-shaped loaf of French bread. After the ancient bakery, a visit to the terra-cotta kitchenware workshops, with shopping; a visit to a cheese factory (as in London one might visit a brewery), with, at the end, a taste of Gorgonzola accompanied by a little glass of sweet wine, offered by the firm as an aperitif. Finally comes lunch at the ancient inn where Renzo, the humble hero of Manzoni's great novel *The Betrothed,* fleeing Milan, stopped for dinner, and where the seat he occupied (nearest the entrance, "the place for the bashful," says Manzoni) is marked by a plaque on the wall—just like the place reserved for Curnonsky in so many restaurants in Paris and the rest of France, where the celebrated prince of gastronomes could sit and eat, free, whatever he wanted.

After lunch, to complete the tour, there remain two monuments to photograph: the chapel in the middle of the Piazza della Chiesa dedicated to Saints Sebastian and Rocco, which was erected by Saint Carlo Borromeo during the plague of 1577; and, behind the church, the beautiful ancient bell tower, at the top of which Bishop Ottone Visconti hid, after losing the battle of Gorgonzola (1278), and thus saved his life.

It is true that Curnonsky could sit and eat whatever he wanted free, but it must be said that in his last years, just when these plaques became so widespread, he was constrained to live on milk alone.

Normally Curnonsky would have a good meal at midday, and at night, for dinner, a hard-boiled egg. His name was Maurice Edmond Sailland, and by his friends he was called Cur, or Curne. From his youth he had had literary ambitions, while his father wanted to start him in trade. Why, the young Maurice asked himself, should I not write? Why not? *Cur non* (in Latin)? This was the modest origin of his curious pen name, completed with a Russian ending, in homage to the fashion of those days, which originated with the czar's visit to Paris. After working as a ghostwriter for Willy, Colette's first husband, he turned finally to gastronomy, with what success everyone knows. He died at eighty-three, when he fell off a balcony; and perhaps, flying down toward the pavement of the courtyard, he was thinking, for the last time: Why not?

Gorgonzola, I am told, was invented by chance in the last century by Signor Vergani, yet in the Piazza della Chiesa there is no monument representing him in the act of making the fortunate mistake in his work. This unintentional birth has nothing embarrassing about it; rather, it unites Gorgonzola with other classic delights of gastronomy, such as (to give a single example) chicken Marengo, which was improvised, with the means at hand on the battlefield, by Napoleon's Swiss chef: a chicken destined (perhaps) to live longer than the memory of the battle itself, and—destiny is strange—created for a man who, in addition to the many faults of which Madame de Staël accuses him, had the unpardonable one of considering time spent at the table time lost.

Gorgonzola has established (it seems) a twinship with Stilton, the English city that gives its name to the cheese with blue mold which is quite similar to Gorgonzola and is served with a piece of crusty bread and a glass of port. Today the production of Stilton is threatened by an enormous coal bed that has been discovered just beneath the land where the cheese is produced. The land of Gorgonzola doesn't have coal beds, but in any case they would not be a threat, because Gorgonzola—and here is the most startling information—is now made not in Gorgonzola yet in Novara, in Piedmont.

Other modifications to the tour of the city:

The terra-cotta workshops: they don't exist any longer.

The Manzonian inn: where it was there is today a furniture store.

The chapel of San Carlo: it stood until the end of the eighteenth century; then nothing more is known of it.

The bell tower: it was demolished a century and a half ago, when the new church was built.

What is Gorgonzola today, without Gorgonzola, without the ancient bell tower, without the Manzonian inn, without the chapel of San Carlo Borromeo, without the terra-cotta workshops, without a monument to Signor Vergani?

Is it nothing? Is it just a place like so many others, a place where everything there was to see has been destroyed or taken away?

Maybe so. And yet, I think—on the train returning to Milan, and assailed again by the temptation to interior monologue—it is nevertheless worth the trouble to go to Gorgonzola, even if only for the animals in the park, for passing through Crescenzago, for the lack of tourists, for the taste, on the still and silent banks of the Martesana, of the fresh French ring bread, which comes out of the oven at eleven, as I recall. . . . Men and women could be divided into two categories: those who can wear a watch on their wrist, and those who cannot, because the watch hangs crooked, with the back of the face hitting the bone. . . . Yes, it's worthwhile to go to Gorgonzola if only to pass through Crescenzago.

The beautiful waitress of Crescenzago had the whitest skin, lightly rosy on her cheeks, whose fragrance was the sum of all the natural perfumes emanating from a lovely female body—among them, besides the already mentioned scent of roses and Parma violets, the scent of vanilla cake, of the bosom (except for the bosom of Joan of Aragon, the queen of Castile, which smelled of ripe peaches), the Paradise perfume of the mouth, and so on.

Perhaps someone may wish to know something more. How she looked: blonde or brunette, the eyes the mouth; tall, medium, short, plump; hands, feet . . . But physical descriptions, good for passports, are useless in a narrative work. Better, then, to point to some particular more indirect: she had a childish smile without being childish, her flesh was firm and yet soft, she appeared tall or short according to the moment, her feet were equal to her hands. The sight of this enchanting girl, while with one knee next to her cheek she was attending to the toenails of one foot, was, as the Michelin guide says, worth not only a detour but a journey of its own.

I I

Joan of Aragon was very beautiful. Her bosom, as I just said, had the fragrance of ripe peaches, a quality that even today has never been attributed to any other woman. The king, Philip the Fair, at first was stunned by that fragrance. Then, probably, he got used to it. Joan was desperately in love with him and extremely jealous; upset by his betrayals, she developed a morbid melancholy that soon became madness. Philip had her shut up in the castle of Tordesillas, where she remained a prisoner for many years. When Philip the Fair finally died, Joan for a long time did not want to be separated from his coffin. Her subjects called her Juana la Loca—Joan the Mad. Thus she became one of that group of historical personages— among them her husband, Philip the Fair, Pépin the Short,

Henry the Fowler, John Lackland (brother of Richard the Lion-hearted)—whose nicknames canceled out all other aspects of their personalities.

The kings of Aragon were rich in nicknames. Besides the usual ones dictated by the adulatory rhetoric of the courtiers— the Catholic, the Magnanimous, the Just, the Great, the Conqueror—I find Henry the Sickly, Peter the Ceremonious, Alfonso the Kind, and Alfonso the Chaste. Among them Joan would have felt ill at ease, embarrassed by rather than proud of her perfume, which today, with fruit that ripens in the refrigerator, would seem even more intoxicating. A portrait of her in the Louvre is attributed to Raphael; it seems, however, that he did not actually see her, since, he says, he sent an assistant to Naples to paint her face from life. But the idea of the portrait was his. Her bosom, as far as one can tell from the little that is visible above the bodice's embroidered edges, fastened with a jewel, seems more compact and abundant than that of La Fornarina, which, fortunately, is visible. Philip the Fair, like Dr. Bovary, perhaps failed to comprehend: he found himself before *"une femme en toilette fine, charmante et sentant frais, à ne savoir même d' où venait cette odeur, ou si ce n'était pas sa peau qui parfumait sa chemise."*

Anyone who, visiting the Louvre, finds himself before the portrait is struck by Joan's gaze, which fixes him intensely (as in Naples she must have fixed her gaze on the painter's eyes), as if she wished to confide something to him, perhaps the secret of her fragrance.

Another portrait of Joan, by an unknown painter, is in the Royal Academy of Arts in London, Here, too, she is beautiful, with a dreamy look that immediately draws one in, her bosom enclosed in a rigid corset that seems to guard the perfume.

While I stood there looking, fascinated, and with the sensation that the mystery was finally going to be cleared up, the guard, of whom until that moment I had taken no notice, broke the enchanted silence, saying: "Closing time, ladies and gentlemen."

Going out of the Royal Academy into Piccadilly, I walked

along Duke Street and turned immediately into Jermyn Street, heading toward the shop of the famous perfumer Floris. I wanted to ask if there exists, or ever had existed, a perfume of ripe peaches. But then I let it go.

The vein of madness that runs in the Spanish branch of the Hapsburgs goes back to Joan of Aragon; and perhaps it is also in those who look at her too intensely.

I return for a moment to what I was saying about the beautiful girl of Crescenzago—that is, to the best way of describing a person. The meticulous enumeration of physical characteristics, used so much in bad novels, serves no purpose. Every new characteristic, rather than blending with the preceding ones and little by little completing the portrait, cancels them, so to speak, and increases the fog that forms between the page and the reader. On the other hand: when Gide says of Claudel, "As a young man he had the look of a nail; now he seems a pestle," Claudel is immediately present, vivid, even though we do not know if he is tall or short, or what color his eyes are.

Lautréamont describes the beauty of the Grand Duke of Virginia thus: "Handsome as a dissertation on the curve that a dog describes running toward its master."

Lautréamont died very young, on November 24, 1870, in Paris, while the city was besieged by the Prussian army. Like nearly all the rest of the population, he must have suffered severe hunger—which is difficult to believe, since one instinctively thinks of Paris as an immense agglomeration of good restaurants. "It's no longer horsemeat that we're eating," Victor Hugo wrote in his diary; he was among the besieged, but certainly in better conditions than Lautréamont. "Perhaps dogmeat? Perhaps mouse?"

Paris had seen worse, and anyway the gastronomic talent of the Parisians did not fail even in the most atrocious circumstances. In 1617 the Maréchal d'Ancre, much hated by the people, was assassinated. The day after the assassination, his body was exhumed and cut in pieces by a savage crowd, which the day before had not been able to vent its hatred thoroughly. One of these "posthumous executioners" tore the heart out of the Maréchal's chest, intending to devour it in front of everyone. But before he brought it to his mouth he had it cooked *à point* over a charcoal fire, and sprinkled it with aromatic vinegar.

Not many years later, in the time of the Sun King, the *souper à sonnette* was invented—the "bell dinner," during which the ladies sat at the table dressed only in powder, perfume, and jewels. On the backs of their chairs hung loose robes, to put on whenever the servants, summoned by the bell, entered to perform their duties. No servant of the time has left a memoir that might enable us to understand what thoughts passed through his mind while he was serving, for example, *côtelettes de mouton en papillotes*—a creation of the Marquise de Maintenon, who, according to someone, had made these dinners fashionable. Perhaps the most aphrodisiac effect was reserved precisely for the servants; and perhaps in the silvery sound of the bell one can discern the first signs of the future revolution.

Seen close up, the Sun King was less radiant than one would think. He had two teeth when he was born, but when he was a little over twenty he had to have all his teeth extracted by the court surgeon, because of an illness. There are various accounts of this matter: some say all, some many, some one. (His father, Louis XIII, on the other hand, had forty-eight teeth instead of the usual thirty-two.) In any case, the operation was not a success; the King lost a piece of his palate, and during meals bits of food often came out of his nose, which etiquette did not permit his fellow diners to notice. The King, for his part, would have liked to eat alone, but not even he could escape the etiquette that prescribed his presence at table.

It is for this reason that when I sit in my place at the Trattoria del Nonno (not marked by any plaque or sign on the wall) and open the red plastic folder and scan the typewritten menu passing over all its usual errors and see so many dishes

crossed off because they have run out among them just the one
I was intending to have and at the same time feel a draft of cold
air entering from the street together with a customer nicknamed Concorde because of the shape of his nose who goes
and sits at the "family table" where the barber is holding forth
. . . it is for this reason, as I was saying, that to recover my
serenity it is enough to think for a moment of a banquet at the
Court of the Sun King in the royal palace of Versailles.

Having finished the soup I ask for a glass of white wine.
Then, since the wine and the soup were excellent, some meatballs.

"How many?"

"One."

It would be difficult in another place to order this way—
to invent a meal as one is eating, according to one's appetite,
even inverting the traditional order of the courses. Victor Hugo
recounts that the actor Frédérick Lemaître would gladly have
fish as the last course: "If he has turbot, he wants it served after
the custard."

Having finished the meatball, I order two more of them,
on which I sprinkle a generous knifepoint of gray pepper.

Here gastronomes will curl their lips. For them the word
"pepper" must always be preceded by "freshly ground." But we
must admit that there also exists pepper ground some time ago:
it rules over innumerable tables in more modest establishments
that lack pepper mills—they would be "freshly stolen"—and
has a particular taste, different from that of freshly ground
black or white pepper (doubtless very good), a taste, however,
that I like, and I believe I am not the only one who likes it.

Having finished the meatballs, I order another glass of
fresh white wine, which invites meditation. The beneficial effect of wine on the drinker has never been described so well as
by Zeno of Citium, according to what Galen wrote in "The
Faculties of the Soul Follow the Temperament of the Body,"
which is reported with great elegance by Guiseppe Averani in
one of his most erudite lessons: "Zeno, as the founder of the
austere and rigid Stoic doctrine, a man by profession harsh and

rough and bitter, used to compare himself to *lupini:* just as *lupini,* when they are soaked, soften and sweeten, so he, drinking and plunging into the glasses, his native harshness and bitterness laid aside."

Zeno of Citium should not be confused with Zeno of Elea, a disciple of Parmenides, considered by Aristotle the inventor of logic ("cruel Zeno," Valéry calls him), and remembered above all as the inventor of the celebrated race between Achilles and the tortoise (one of his four paradoxical proofs against motion), in which, as everyone knows, swift-footed Achilles cannot succeed in catching the slow tortoise, who has departed with a small advantage.

—Translated by Ann Goldstein

Thomas Larson

Freshman Comp, 1967

That I was a severely bookish eighteen-year-old must have been fairly evident to my dormitory roommates at the University of Missouri my freshman semester. The night before classes began, they tried to pry me away from my desk for a keg party, to which I responded, "I can't go. I need to finish studying the introductions to my textbooks." I believed those small Roman-numerated pages would offer insight into the learning models that awaited me. In fact, so intent was I to begin my education that after saying goodbye to Mom and Dad a few days earlier I rushed out to purchase my course books and then, parked at my desk, nearly memorized the glossaries of each text. I wanted more than a head start; I wanted to achieve, as my dad suggested, the notice of those who mattered, the professors with whom I was soon to be engaged, and I hoped, enthralled. If called on in class, my responses would prove just how formidably prepared I was.

The following morning (classes began on a Thursday that semester), I woke at dawn, got dressed, gulped coffee, then walked from my men's dorm, Atchison House, Donnelly Hall, through the three high-rise women's dorms, onto Maryland Avenue, and there beheld people streaming out everywhere on their way to class—women in groups of three, plain or tweed jumpers with bow ties, men in pairs or solo, with Weejuns, dress shirts and V-neck sweaters. I wore my faded blond corduroy jacket which I'd bought at the Salvation Army for fifty cents. By the time I strode past Crowder Hall, home of the ROTC (anti-Vietnam protests would erupt there the next year), the concrete sidewalk below my feet felt like destiny, as it must have for hundreds of others, stopping at traffic lights, ducking in a market, winding around trees and manicured lawns, hurrying by dawdlers. Maryland Avenue dead-ended at the Red Campus, the older, pre–Civil War red brick buildings with their turrets and manorial splendor. I rushed by the six bare columns, remnants of a facade whose structure had burned down long ago and which stood with lonely detachment in a vast green quadrangle. My first class, Principles of Geology, was in a 350-seat lecture hall that, surprise, was jam-packed with people when I arrived.

I found a seat in the aisle, heard the litany of class requirements, took notes furiously about plates and faults and the ages of rock and sediment, recalling the yellow and tan layers of limestone that I saw exposed in freeway cuts driving to Columbia from St. Louis. The professor seemed more interested in enunciating the terms of geological origins than he was in making sure we got his information. He told us to hold our questions for lab; the teaching assistants would answer us there. By the end of fifty minutes, I was tired of his stilted diction and slow delivery. But one hour a day of this and one hour of Spanish, which met at noon, was nothing. When I went outside and watched hordes of students disperse on new paths, I was elated again. As I walked, I forgot the tedium of lecture and marveled at the harmony of college life. Apparently there was no turmoil here between black and white, liberal and conservative, no vice or crime or poverty that I could see. True, the students were one class and the faculty another. But I already noticed older men with book-laden arms and contented gazes, lingering with people half their age, in some cases strolling from one building to another, engaged in animated, extemporaneous talk.

Next morning, a Friday, I went to Introduction to Philosophy and felt, intellectually at least, like a child. It seemed every first course was Intro To or Principles Of or Basic Concepts In, the point being, I supposed, that we had not only to forget everything we knew but we probably, according to the university, really never knew anything to begin with. Deflated, I journeyed beyond the Student Union to the White Campus, the newer buildings made of blond Missouri limestone. There I entered Composition English 1 at one o'clock. My teacher, Mr. Marquard, a grand name for a writer, which I assumed he was, kept us ten minutes, saying we needed to buy the text, take it home over the weekend and, after reading any section at random, write a page or two in response. Anything. Use your brains. Half the class had no idea what he meant; but I did. When he excused us, I slid by the questioning herd to whom he exhorted, "Be creative, explore, invent."

Our textbook, *Writing with a Purpose* by James M. McCrimmon, included an excerpt under "Prose Style" that illustrated the common loose or cumulative sentence which dominated written English. It was taken from Walter Pater's book *The Renaissance,* a chapter on Sandro Botticelli. Pater was describing the world-famous painting *The Birth of Venus.*

> An emblematical figure of the wind blows hard across the grey water, moving forward the dainty-lipped shell on which she [Venus] sails, the sea "showing his teeth" as it moves in thin lines of foam, and sucking in, one by one, the falling roses, each severe in outline, plucked off short at the stalk, but embrowned a little, as Botticelli's flowers always are.

McCrimmon pointed to the subject and verb, then wrote of the lack of any patterning element in the sentence, the way it runs along sensually describing the vision of Venus rising from the wave, the way the sentence seems to reflect a mind in the process of thinking. This was contrasted with a periodic sentence from the same chapter.

> [Botticelli's] interest is neither in the untempered goodness of Angelico's saints, nor the untempered evil of Orcagna's *Inferno;* but with men and women, in their mixed and uncertain condition, always attractive, clothed sometimes by passion with a character of loveliness and energy, but saddened perpetually by the shadow upon them of the great things from which they shrink.

Next McCrimmon emphasized the balanced construction of "neither . . . nor" and the dividing semicolon that set up statement and contrast, the way carefully weighted phrases and clauses, unlike the cumulative sentence, reflect a mind that has already ordered its thinking. Notice, too, that the point of the periodic sentence is saved for the very end.

Yes: There were two ways to write sentences and those two ways were infinitely varied by the author's decision whether to convey to his or her reader ideas in the state of their formulation or ideas in their already formulated state. Pater preferred the loose to the periodic, the thinking-it-through to the well-thought-out, suggesting that for him the cumulative mode represented the action of *his* mind. Style made meaning translucent, and such clarity was what a writer was after. Style, in fact, preceded meaning, so McCrimmon seemed to say. Yes: The rhetoric of the masters had hooked me. I could barely wait to prefer my own sentences.

Wanting to write was my dream even before I went to college, though I couldn't know then what being a writer entailed. I had read writers' autobiographical statements about their own lives, for one, John Steinbeck, who believed an author needed to work at dozens of odd jobs until his thirties when he might, so Steinbeck said, have something worth saying. But I had only worked construction in the summers. I was a total novice, all freshman. I had written poems, a few stories, many letters, several high school analytical essays, one against capital punishment, which my teacher praised excessively. My sensibility for literature had been shaped, though, from incessant reading. One habit of mine, much of my senior year, was to wake at 6 A.M. and read before school. I stole the habit from a bookstore owner I knew who, beginning at first light, so she said, read a book a day. I often read the summers away; I loved American novels, dawdling over Carson McCullers' smoky prose or John Updike's animistic descriptions. Reading enchanted me into reflection while it also taught me the pleasures of immersion and quietude. Thus it was easy to be stirred by reading aloud Pater's lusty rhythmical language, the spell of classical rhetoric to and from my lips, igniting that flame of the brotherhood of the pen, a swoon and clutch as religiously enlightening as any medieval monk felt at prayer in his cloister. Chock full of sentence lore, I walked out of the commons and into the evening, the night air cool as clean linen, hung as though for lovers, and before beginning my two pages for Marquard, I headed once more to look at *The Birth of Venus.* Where? Art books in the library.

At the center of the college, between Jesse Hall, the massive administrative estate of the Red Campus, and the Memorial Student Union, the student-faculty landmark of the White Campus, was Ellis Library, a temple of horsehide-gray granite. Inside I followed the blue-veined marble steps up to the fourth floor, my feet slipping a little on their icy surfaces. The smell of oak banisters rubbed with oil mixed with the musty odor of a million tomes; those scents, released every day when a patron opened the leaves of a book, floated throughout the high-ceilinged reading rooms. In spring, blossoming magnolias on the lawn that circled the library would add, from the cranked-open high-arched windows, yet another syrupy smell to the august atmosphere.

I found a book with color plates of Botticelli's paintings and, as I had in my puny, single-level high school library, stared again at the garlanded goddess of beauty, of whose countenance Pater wrote, "The sorrow in her face was at the thought of the whole long day of love yet to come." There was the androgynous "emblematical figure" blowing the birth wind, the "dainty-lipped shell" on which Venus rode, the "falling roses" that adorned her arrival. And there too was Venus herself, demure and sensual, virginally desirous and yet withholding her fullest attention from us, the viewer. She was shrinking from us, too. She was old and young and, in her morning newness, as yet unloved. She seemed willing herself a number of contradictory commands: to be chaste, to remain the silent object of divine beauty, to welcome sexual union, knowing that every dawn she would reappear, borne again by an amorous wind.

Leaving the sanctuary of the library was not possible in my swooning condition, so, lying on the floor in the stacks, I wrote my two pages. I described the floating figures, their camaraderie, their undefiled sensuality, aping Pater's cumulative energy as much as I could. (Marquard's comment on my paper a week later was VERY NICE JOB!) But, though I was happily lost in my aloneness, staring at Botticelli's figures made me yearn for their kind: exotic, impassioned libertines: arty types; poets and painters and actors—those capable of *frisson*. I suddenly realized there had to be such artistic, aesthetic presences in Columbia, Missouri, in the flesh, with whom I might commune.

Such presences were not to be found on my dorm floor. I felt only narrow curiosity for the guys down the hall like Richie Mullins from Patchogue, Long Island, who wanted everyone to get laid so he was fixing us up with female pen pals from his hometown whom we'd visit come spring break, or Mike Kelpe from Alton, Illinois, a foreign-language whiz kid who seemed to have come to Mizzou merely to drill us on our Spanish verbs. College for them was like summer camp, a stopover, a nine-month bash where Budweiser, megawatt stereos and evening-long brag sessions ruled: When do we organize the first panty raid? How many girls did *you* lay in high school? (The truth was, I hadn't laid any, though I fantasized about it regularly.) In

Atchison House, an intellectual, cultured seriousness was non-existent; worse, none of them, not even my roommate, read literature.

It took a week or two but finally I found the aesthetic crowd. On Friday afternoons they packed the three front-windowed booths at the Heidelberg Bar and Restaurant on Ninth Street. There, upperclassmen toasted the sober traditions of English literature while graduate students and sophomores made wild caricature of their bearded professors' stammers and locutions. A few of us brave freshmen looked on, anteing up quarters for another pitcher of beer.

In these booths my other education—about jealousy and desire—also began where I witnessed the well-defined circles of literary intimacy formed between the students and teachers who regularly drank at the Heidelberg. I was on the periphery with other freshmen and sophomores, sitting a booth-wall away from the graduate students, who occupied the booth with the lesser student-poets, who, in turn, were next to the largest booth with the teacher-poets and the better student-poets, at whose center sat, usually withdrawn or else quietly readying to speak, the renowned Tom McAfee. The Alabama-born and -raised McAfee, who besides William Peden, a short story writer and critic, and Donald Drummond, a classicist poet, was the most famous of the published writers at the university. A professor of literature and creative writing, McAfee taught classes full of adoring students, especially once they had read his first book, *Poems and Stories,* which one reviewer called "brutally ironic."

Getting closer to McAfee was the general desire of most in this all-male clique. (At the time, females were not allowed in these literary groupings because women, so the men decreed, must remain the ardent objects of men's poetry. I'm certain women writers then simply stayed away from us, uninterested in our gender elitism or, worse, our pawing them for inspiration.) In any case, the literary procurement process, as I deciphered it, was strange indeed. The farther you were from

McAfee, the more you were supposed to say, under the misguided or correct notion that he might hear you and approve and somehow invite you to his table where you said much less than before because, well, McAfee himself didn't say much and so you, too, to be like him, kept your mouth shut, learned from his example, were happy to be there. McAfee's palace guard, I observed, existed in a tumble of postures, but after long hours of drink their bodies collectively sank like corks floating in oil. If they kept up with McAfee's consumption through last call, they could accompany him to his home, a room on the ninth floor of the Tiger Hotel where the rarefied talk often went on till dawn. So they said. The intrigue grew for me in proportion to what McAfee & Co. discussed, which was no doubt quite spare, yet which I imagined was sentient and sacred.

One afternoon McAfee read in the Student Union auditorium. He was by nature a consumptively nervous man, and the reading seemed to intensify his apprehensions about being close to people. He mumbled his poems with such severe understatement that I thought he was ashamed of his work. His short poems were wry, detached, maudlin. And they were disturbing in their intimate turbulence. Poems like "Much of My Anguish":

> Much of my anguish has been
> Purposeless but pure:
> I never sin
> In a high-brow Catholic way
> But to the chords of a Methodist preacher's pure
> Squealing shout at the devil.
>
> My guilt flares up at every natural evil
> I suffer: a girl's bad breath,
> A spastic hand, any kind of death.
> Electric shock or insulin
> Might deaden my guilt, but who is there to pray
> For all the silly people lately
> In pain—whom I drink for and whom I hate.

Reading such verse on my own, I heard the poet's intelligence sing. Hearing McAfee read the lines in public was an excruciatingly sour show of his self-consciousness. Did he actually feel his poems were too personal to bear live exposure? Did his writing exist only on the page and not in the voice?

Afterward, I was befriended by a writer for the campus newspaper, the *Maneater*, and suddenly, with five other young Turks, I was in tow on the next leg of the journey. The plan was for us to accompany Jerry Dethrow, one of McAfee's favorites, to Dethrow's house, where he would change his clothes and check on his girlfriend. Then we'd drink to McAfee's triumph back at the Heidelberg.

Jerrell Dethrow was a case. First of all, that name: Dethrow! Besides the obvious it rung a bell out of the Wild West, a name off a tombstone, some gunslinger or Indian scout. Tall and wiry, from Columbia's own Boone County, he drawled like a feed store clerk, cussed with verve and often quipped aphoristically, a line either witless or remarkable. About McAfee he once said, "That fucker can write some heartbreaking poems." About academics, "Who wants to read all that faerie queen crap from England." About something everyday, "Which of you dumbshits wants to go fishin' Sunday?" Statements or questions, never any dialogue to speak of. As I observed him in those first weeks of my apprenticeship, I determined that the poetry in Dethrow came from his sensitivity, a ponderous bit of bobcat animosity which, when riled, he enjoyed inflicting on anyone close by. Astonishingly, though, that animal was attached to a self-examining modesty, the proverbial storm-centered stillness. The combination of spitfire and self-possession radiated a dangerousness which I envied: That's the way the poet was meant to be.

Dethrow's place was a large white clapboard house, a cat-clawed couch on the front porch, a rusted washing machine in the side yard. He lived there with his waitress girlfriend, who, he said, had been gone now for two nights. When we entered, he told us to dig out beers from the refrigerator while he took fresh clothes into the bathroom for a shower. We sat around the living room on more ratty couches, a cheap stereo like mine in the corner, empty beer bottles and ashtrays every two feet. A cheerless sight, his bed caught my eye through a wide-open door. A bare mattress beneath a torturously crumpled sheet, itself beneath severely flattened pillows. The bed spoke of lover's squalls, and I imagined the girlfriend had stomped out.

Wearing a clean work shirt, Dethrow sat down on a flimsy coffee table, elbows on knees.

"When's she comin' home?" someone suddenly asked, seeming much too intimate. I noticed the speaker had on a faded corduroy jacket just like mine, only green.

"Why?" Dethrow said, peeved.

"Why what?"

"Why do *you* want to know?"

"No, man, I don't want to know," the green-jacketed young man said quickly. "Forget it. It's none of my business."

"No," Dethrow said, "it's not." He scoffed, and those deep-set mystically flinty eyes of his stared at me with such severity that I quickly looked away.

Riding in the car to the Heidelberg, everyone guzzling, the conversation was all Dethrow's. He talked to us about how much he loved Robert Creeley, that remarkably laconic poet, and then he made a grand pronouncement, which sounded to me like the epigram of the poet's race. He said, "You know, boys, the poet's duty," and he took a steep swig of Budweiser, "is to say what he has to say and get off the fucking page."

That bowled me over, such a commonplace line, sprung more out of Harry S. Truman than Gerard Manley Hopkins. In the backseat quiet, I attributed such deftness of tongue to Mc-Afee's influence: The elder poet's flair for words had rubbed off on Dethrow, which meant, given the opportunity, it might rub off on me. In the meantime, I pledged myself to silence, like the green-coated freshman sitting beside me, whom I ignored although I felt his tortured embarrassment. He hung around us at future gatherings but he was only a sentinel, one of those owlish British butlers who hears all and says nothing. He spoke not, not out of deference to the muse, as I defined it; he spoke not, because he'd plunged from self-awareness into self-loathing.

Marquard's class was held in the Economics building of the White Campus, interlocking spired structures, built of crane-carried blocks of coarse-faced, quake-proof Missouri limestone. Far less imperious than the Red Campus, the White had its quadrangle over which I loved to walk from the open west end, toward the fifty-foot clock-and-bell tower of the Memorial Student Union, its lacy spires piercing the sky, pulling my sight higher, lifting me out of myself. Marquard's classroom felt a touch holy, too, with age and wear. Dark wooden desks, their seats worn honey-brown, covered the sagging floorboards, where in long crenellated rows black nail heads had popped up unevenly. A raised lectern creaked when Marquard ascended it. In the rear a bank of six oak-trimmed latticed windows bore the slant light of fall upon Our Professor.

Marquard, a friendly, portly man, with a white gospel singer's wavy hairdo and a tuba player's double chin, lacked the faraway, thin look of the poets I admired at the Heidelberg. His coat and tie and yellow dress shirt, his jowly laugh, his robust bookishness were decidedly unliterary, more intimate than distancing, more salubrious than consumptive. At 1 P.M. he entered promptly, carrying some bemused oddity in his head, as if literature and the art of composition—essay writing—were oddities which bemused one, as if he had pondered all day some grammatical construct, like the nominative predicate, into lasting bemusement. I liked that about him. He was preoccupied with ideas; he came into class ready to talk at his students, extending to us the exegesis of a Petrarchan sonnet he'd tackled with his colleagues at lunch or the plot development of a Thomas Hardy novel he was readying for lecture in his class on the English novel. In my mind I could hear Hardy write the sentence of Marquard's daily reality: "And into the class strode the grandiloquent master, determined to assail the young minds with the hammering ping-pong of a literary paradox." Once class began, Marquard focused on essays, pointing out a trove of stylistic features we student-writers must employ in our work. Each week, as he taught us the rhetorical stamps of illustration, compare/contrast, description and narration (ordered and enhanced by the McCrimmon text), we stepped to Marquard's beat: Learn the rudiments of the essay mode one week then receive the paper assignment on Friday, discuss more readings on Monday and Wednesday and then turn in our essays on Friday when Marquard would preview the next two weeks' rhetorical flourish we were to attempt along with model essays to again read and imitate. He held to this formation like Stonewall Jackson at Bull Run. His plan was simple: Read the masters in order to compose essays as they did. It seemed our slightest obsequiousness to that aim would please him immensely.

Marquard treated essays no differently from great literature, the equivalent of Tolstoy or Shakespeare. "Read these gems over and over again," he said, "and like poetry they'll reward you with new insights every time." The masters we studied included George Orwell, Samuel Johnson, William Hazlitt and, for me, the most facile of the elegant Brits, E. M. Forster. The grudging, contradictory truths of "Two Cheers for Democracy" or "My Wood" inclined me to the same pleasurable contemplation as I assumed it did Marquard. These eloquent grand daddies were followed by the occasional essayists, who stumbled upon the form in the margins of their novels or poetry or other art. Agnes de Mille, Katherine Anne Porter, Randall Jarrell, D. H. Lawrence. The essay, Marquard said, was the most rhetorically knotty yet democratically accessible form of composition, and any half-reflective temperament was easily attracted to its warehouse of changing opinion, unpopular idea, ghastly experience. People, not just famous authors, essayed an idea or a feeling to find out what their hearts were so desperate to say. "Even you students can write one," Marquard would tell us, "once you learn what an essay is."

Most impressive, Marquard embodied in himself the integrity which E. M. Forster or Henry David Thoreau demanded of themselves in their own work. One day he told us a story about an essay he was writing, which so happened to be about football and freshman English. All through the sixties, the Missouri Tigers were winners, perennially bowl-bound because the team was coached by Dan Devine. Devine was a tyrannical yet brilliant coach who, like Bear Bryant at Alabama, never opened a car door or paid for a meal, so eager were his boosters to support him. Just keep winning, Coach. Devine and his staff, so said Marquard, regularly called him and his colleagues, the lowly assistant professors, to check up on their players' progress in English, the most difficult of a jock's courses. Was Nagerski getting it? Did Herkimer have a prayer? One recent semester, Marquard was teaching one of Devine's players, a beer-gut tackle, a great first-year prospect, who was bobbing between C-minus and D-plus by the time of the final. Devine himself called Marquard and asked about the kid's chances. If the tackle didn't pass, so said Devine, and the boy had to retake English, that would put his scholarship in jeopardy, not to mention the team's trip to the Cotton Bowl. Marquard then quoted Devine with an odious and ridiculing tone. "And, what's more, Mr. Marquard, there'll be hell to pay with the alumni." Marquard replied, "The boy gets the grade he earns. Nothing more, nothing less, *Coach.*"

Some slouch in the front row muttered: "What happened? Ja flunk 'im?"

"You bet, Mr. Winston, ah flunked 'im."

On the respect meter, Marquard pinned the needles. What could be more revolutionary than taking on the powers that be right there in the institution's belly? Marquard was a radical, despite his suit and tie. But not everyone in the class agreed with me. There were plenty of cold-war patriots, young Republicans, agriculture majors forced into freshman English against their will. I sensed their disapproval. Though they didn't speak up, their dissent felt like humidity: Give the boy a second chance, for Christ's sake. What do you expect from a halfback?

"Some of you may think I was too harsh," Marquard continued, apparently used to filling in such freshman lacunae. "You think we shouldn't expect a lot from a football player, that he needs some extra attention, some help along the way, especially if we are winning football games. That'd be nice if it were true. But the more often we win, the more ethical we've got to be."

Another incredible statement! Marquard had given us his own experience imbued with an unforced, mercurial meaning, an example, I thought, on which to pattern our own essays. Life, *our lives,* if we dared to look, had such subjects which could easily shape our prose. And didn't he say that he was writing about the coach and the student himself? He'd said it in passing, as if to deemphasize his accomplishment. But clearly he practiced what he preached. Later, at the Student Union, I fell to contemplating my starry future over a paper-cup Coke and paper-boat fries. Marquard's effusiveness in the classroom had me convinced that truthfully written words meant bravery, honor, principle. It was his individual engagement and daring that I loved; that and the pontificating, the swagger, the teacherly rightness.

So, after Marquard's rousing tutelage, back to the Heidelberg I went. And there was McAfee, calmly desolate and inert, yet ringed by all those student bodies, some talking, most waiting. I sat down to drink with several TAs, one of whom chaired a discussion section of the large English Literature survey course. His name was Todd; he was preppie and cocky. Others were praising Norman Mailer and William Styron, brilliant contemporary novelists. How good, how expansive, how vigorous were their books. Todd said that he hated to inform them, though, but it was his belief that the novel as we know it was dead. "Not only is it dead," he said, "but it died with Mr. Joyce and *Ulysses,* and any picturesque bit of narrative since then is a derivative sham."

A couple others laughed at him. I looked to McAfee, whose reflection I could see in the window. He was staring at the rain.

"I don't mean to say anyone can't write a novel," said Todd. "I mean to say the novel as a form, like God, is dead. *The* novel, not *your* novel. The *novel.*"

What was the difference? I thought. Suddenly, I was speaking. "You mean all those novels I read during high school are dead?"

"Dead as a doornail," said Todd.

"But how do you know that? It's just your opinion." Others were watching me: I was speaking.

Todd scoffed. "Look, no one will ever write novels better than those of Joyce or Faulkner. As literature, their work is the pinnacle. Pinnacles aren't the end of literary production of a given form. But they are the end of the form's development. That's for sure."

"That's absurd," I said.

"Okay, a million more novels will be written"—he was being sarcastic or charitable—"and you and I will read them. Maybe even write a few. But the evolution of literature has its own story to tell. And evolution doesn't care what we do. I think it's time writers found not just something new to say, but some new—or old—way of saying it."

Even though I had spoken, I couldn't argue this point. I didn't have the words, and I knew it. I wanted the missing Jerry Dethrow, out chasing his girlfriend we had heard, to rescue me, to say, "You're full of shit, whatever your name is, and that's all there is to it." I wanted to yell at McAfee that the bastard couldn't just broadcast his opinion like that and not pay for it. I swallowed my beer, got up from the table and sighed dramatically at him. Outside, once I crossed the street, I caught McAfee in the window—a pale, oversensitive, meditative man, waiting for God's blessing. I wanted something from him: acknowledgment that I existed, a word or two of passion as Marquard supplied, something to shake my soul into creation. While McAfee was waiting for God's blessing, I was waiting for his.

Clumping home, I got woozy thinking about Marquard's style and that of McAfee. Marquard's enthusiasm for writing didn't square with McAfee's moodiness, his dark silence; no discussion of the genius's artistry was allowed. (Perhaps that's what made them geniuses!) All this was even more confounding because McAfee, the poet and short story writer, was published in literary journals and thin-spined books, evidence of his greatness. It came to me then that no one clung to Marquard even though he was engaged with his colleagues and his students. And yet everyone clung to the loner McAfee.

In mid-October a poetry reading was held in the auditorium wing of Ellis Library. I wanted not to go alone but my roommate had joined the poli-sci club, which met on Friday evenings, of all nights, and no one else from the dorm ever mentioned poetry. So I went by myself. I sat midway back, with a clear view of the podium and of McAfee, who arrived at the last minute in his trench coat and tweed British motoring cap. I hoped Marquard would show, in part to see me there, in part for me to see that he, too, supported local literature. (When the reading began Marquard had not arrived.) Also attending and sitting in lookalike pairs were the graduate TAs with their button-down shirts and blazers. Audience members sat so far apart, though, it appeared we all had the chicken pox.

The readers were three—a black man named DePock, a rugged-looking poet with a pointy red goatee and bushy red eyebrows named R. P. Dickey, and Jerry Dethrow. A dizzily drunk DePock went first. Though his subject was the lost generations of black men who suffered racial prejudice, the poetry itself was vulgar bombast and malicious hostility. He screamed in freakish tones how his brothers' ropes would one day noose the necks of "your" shiny white daughters, once their white-devil boyfriends had been done in the ass by African king studs. God, it was awful. It wasn't poetry; it was hatred. As he finished each piece, no one in the all-white audience responded. We were embarrassed or felt guilty, I couldn't decide which. Exhausting himself in about twelve minutes, DePock left the stage. The applause was underwhelming.

Then came Dethrow. He began reading his short poems, which mixed equal parts sarcasm, intolerance and self-deprecation with sculpted two-beat lines and a rich assonance. We clapped heartily after each one. Each poem was right on target.

Each poem was full of intensity. Each poem was soon over. As Dethrow read his little treasures, DePock, who was laid out in the second row with his feet up on the chair backs, started to cackle at him.

DePock's razzing got louder and louder until Dethrow struck the podium with his fist and declared, "Prosy poets from the projects ought to be shot." DePock yelled, "Hah!" And Dethrow let him have it, a poem which (made up on the spot, I believe) mimicked DePock vindictively.

> Honky policeman,
> Prowling the streets,
> Baton in hand
> Beating my people
> Into the gutter—
> Soon, we'll avenge the sins
> Of the white man,
> And this Ethiopian prince
> Will be proud
> To piss in your face.

Dethrow glared at his nemesis. "And you call that poetry, DePock, you piece of shit!"

DePock stood up and yelled, "You're lunch meat, faggot" and someone in front of him elbowed his face, sending him down instantly. He scrambled up, his glasses falling off. DePock picked the glasses up but couldn't get them on because suddenly R. P. Dickey grabbed him from behind in a full nelson, dragged him up the row and then up the aisle. Under the faint red glow of the EXIT sign, Dickey kicked the long handlebar of the door and it burst open. He grasped DePock's collar and the seat of his pants and threw him outside, bellowing like Zeus, "Get thee to the wind!"

Back inside Dethrow read a few more spare poems to an animated and appreciative crowd which, when he finished, whooped it up like hockey fans.

Next came our savior, Mr. Dickey. He read from his own

two skinny volumes which he pressed flat against the podium each time he found a poem he liked. He said, "Here's a good one," as though they were flowers for the picking. His poems were highly dramatic expressions of praise and loathing. He loathed commercial enterprise, country clubs, politicians; he praised horses, velvet, walking over mountains, and words themselves. He finished with a beautifully structured, long poem which repeated the commandment, "I insist." The phrase followed those things that Dickey insisted we abide—the ultrafine iron ore dust that blankets the steel mills on Chicago's south side; the patina green of a sunken naval destroyer in Pearl Harbor; a boy racing Popsicle sticks in a rain-swollen gutter; a year of peace and vegetable gardening in Vietnam (that image drew raucous applause). After a dozen such lines, Dickey built a quicker series of contrasts between concrete and prairie, melancholy and dreams, earthworm and oak, things which we all needed to swallow full into our "green beings," and then from the inner breast pocket of his coat he pulled a gun—a real gun!—aimed it above his head and fired. The audience jumped. "I insist," he growled the poem-spectacle to an end.

We leapt to our feet, cheered his gall, his brilliance, plus the fact that he shot the ceiling and not one of us. It was a blank; no ceiling dusted down from above. What a poet! What a poetry crime!

Afterward, I stood outside the auditorium's entrance, waiting for someone to lead us back to the Heidelberg for beers and celebration, when Dethrow walked up. I was just about to compliment him on a great reading when he said, "Hey, you want to come up to McAfee's with us?" I looked around. Behind me were a couple sophomores who'd been drinking with us earlier. We were just milling about, hoping to be asked. I guess he meant all of us.

I looked back at Dethrow. "Sure," I said.

"Okay, let's beat it."

Our small pack headed up Ninth Avenue, by the Heidelberg, by the Agora House, Columbia's best bohemian café, by

the Lutheran church in whose basement antiwar protests were
being planned, by several darkened head shops. One street
over to Tenth and the Tiger Hotel, up the elevator to the lime-
green carpeted hallway leading to Tom McAfee's penthouse
apartment. Inside, McAfee's pad looked like a hospital suite
with veneered furniture, stainless-steel carts and slippers up-
ended in the corner. There was a smell of whiskey and medicine. A dozen men or more were already drinking, R. P.
Dickey, the crew from the bar, the graduate TAs. I searched;
there was no Marquard.

I helped myself to a Budweiser and joined the large gag-
gle of men in the living room, who were imitating DePock's
bumbling poetry—verse as drunk as he was—and celebrating
Dickey's wonderful line: Get thee to the wind. "Wasn't that
from Shakespeare?" someone asked. "It is now," another
yelled. Someone else got Dickey to trumpet those words once
more, his deep brogue resonating throughout the tiny apartment.

I was standing beside Dickey and said, "Right now, with a
good breeze, I'll bet DePock must be high over Kansas," and
Dickey slapped me hard on the back and yelled, "Yeah, that
motherfucker's in orbit."

It was wonderful. Maybe I was duping myself big-time,
but I was delighted to have finally made it to McAfee's apartment where the circles of literary achievement so rigidly enforced in the Heidelberg no longer applied. I felt suddenly
equal to the others, all of us ringing the great poet's home like
ape-men returned from the hunt.

Just then a record began playing and a sudden silence fell.
An orchestra of strings announced a familiar ballad, "Stormy
Weather," and Jo Stafford began crooning the lyrics. Jo Stafford, the great female torch singer from the forties and fifties,
was the same singer of sentimental tunes McAfee spent hundreds of quarters on in the Heidelberg's jukebox.

Across the room, standing by the phonograph, McAfee
was singing along. Sort of. He looked as though he'd been
swimming too long in a heavily chlorinated pool; he began

swaying as if to fall, and then abruptly he did fall, onto the couch. While Jo Stafford sang, McAfee was almost spasmodic, his arms blustering the air, his index finger a conductor's baton, his head lolling from side to side. I guessed he was laced. Beside him on the couch was a young man from Chicago, who had joined us once or twice in the bar. An upperclassman I believe, maybe three years older than me, he had a head of exceptionally thick coal-black hair, curls and tousles cascading over his ears and onto his collar, then onto his shoulders. He was one of the first lavish long-hairs of the sixties I recall, a type we would later associate with pouty-mouthed rock stars. But in 1967 he was unique, an unsullied archetype of how the new man might be or, at least, look. In the bar, his coiffure drew stares from men and women; he also possessed an overwrought delicacy which added to his mystery.

Just as I noticed him, McAfee abruptly focused on the young man, too. McAfee seemed startled, as though he had missed seeing an ancient Chinese vase which had sat on the table next to him for years and suddenly there it was, where it always was, its bold reds and soft grays as alive as dawn. The poet said, "Do you mind, son, if I pat your head?" There was a father's tenderness in McAfee's stress on that word, son.

I sat down next to the pair and pretended to admire a landscape painting on the wall, a work no doubt from one of the poet's students. I heard the young man laugh at McAfee's request.

"You want to pat my head?" he said.

"Yes I would. But I must first ask permission."

"You may," he said, closing his eyes.

McAfee placed his right hand, its nails unclipped and yellowed from smoking, on the young man's head and started patting, much as one pats the upstanding virtue of a child. He patted and patted and the young man looked (in the corner of my eye) at once silly and self-conscious. The pat, then, seemed to give way to more earnest desire, less an up and down movement and more a crosswise palming motion, gauging the shape of the head, navigating its globe. The young man leaned forward as McAfee tunneled his fingers down inside the hair, the nails disappearing in the thick of it. McAfee's hand next began probing, digging in to scratch, knead, absorb the scalp. His possessiveness gave way to playful exploration: He flattened his palm and fingered tufts of hair between his wedging digits, pulling the hair up through his stained fingers and letting it fall back gracefully. Each of McAfee's movements was entrancing, whether he was wreathing a patch of curls around his index finger and then slowly withdrawing it or stroking the willowy bang over the young man's forehead or running thumb and forefinger along the scraggly hairs of his nape or burrowing into the cavity of each ear and pinching each lobe. In response, the young man craned his head to expose as many sides and angles as he could. He was such a willing partner.

Finally, McAfee returned his hand to patting, until the young man sat up and began to stretch. McAfee then put his own hand on his lap and sighed gently. The two men seemed spent. The young man thanked the poet, who glanced at him, shy, taciturn. Playing the flip side of the Jo Stafford record, McAfee sat down beside the young man again, a tad closer.

At once, the roar of talk and drinking, which I had blocked out, returned. I got up and looked around. No one was watching them; no one, apparently, thought this unusual. I walked into the kitchen and put my beer on a counter between two men arguing about Keats. I went into the bathroom, turned on the light, sat on the toilet, then turned the light off. I wanted to huddle in the darkness and contemplate who had ravished whom, whether the young man was the muse and McAfee was touching him for inspiration, or McAfee was the muse himself, bestowing upon his charge the gift of rapture.

Later that night, I wandered through the campus, the word YES bonging in my head like the bell in the Student Union tower. YES . . . YES . . . YES. This was what writers did. They sought such experiences in order to later write about them, and by writing about it myself, I would move a breath or two closer to becoming one of them. The whole spectacle, in the library auditorium and at McAfee's apartment, suddenly reeled through me as though I had filmed it, rolling like Otto Preminger on a short train track with a motion picture cameraman, simultaneously watching and constituting the action into existence. I saw it all, without seams, as an essay for Marquard.

I spent a week of afternoons and evenings perfecting the essay, chronicling the roughhoused ousting of DePock, the inspired readings of Dethrow and Dickey, my feeling welcomed at McAfee's apartment and McAfee's seduction of the handsome young man's head. I knew it was an unusual essay in its personal point of view, naming names and places right before my very nose. It was unusual, too, in its episodic unraveling. As I wrote it, events, feelings, characters, places kept unwinding themselves from inside me like string whirls away from multiple skeins and onto a textile loom, emerging on the other side as fabric. I wondered: Was it even an essay, with so much piecemeal shape and story design? I didn't know what to call McAfee's adventure with the young man's head; I didn't know if the essay had meaning; I didn't know what Marquard would make of it. I sensed, though, that he would admire my creativity and like a fellow traveler refer me for revision ideas to Emerson or Hazlitt, incandescent tutors for life.

I typed at it all weekend in my dorm room; another football game and keg party kept the rowdies away. On Monday I gave Marquard the original copy while I kept the carbon. He was surprised. "I don't often receive an essay this early in the week," he said. "You want me to read it?"

"Yeah," I said impatiently. I didn't write it for any other reason, I thought.

"What would you like me to do with your essay? Read it or grade it?"

I wanted him to evaluate it but instead I answered, "Please just read it and maybe we can discuss it," and he agreed to see me at 9 A.M. Thursday.

Marquard's office was in Arts and Sciences, a grotesquely plain three-story building, all steel rectangles and windows, which had none of the White Campus's shapely lines or roughened sandstone, no gargoyles perched on little shelves above arched entranceways. He and the English Department were on the third floor, down a hallway bordered by more doors each displaying the names of a dozen instructors typed on a 3 × 5 card. I was early. I waited at Marquard's door until he came out. When he did, he shook my hand and let me go in first.

He apologized, clearing the other chair of manila folders, his scarf and gloves. It wasn't his office alone, he said—gray metal desk, stacks of green and brown cloth library books, sheaves of essays and exams—he had to share it with other instructors. When they moved into this building last year, the department, he said, was already larger than the space allotted. There was some privacy. In this large wing of maybe twenty bull pens, each cubby had plastic corrugated dividers attached on top of its metal walls. A soft buzz from other teachers talking to students charged the air.

I glanced at the blotter-covered desk: There was my essay. Marquard's elbow rested upon it and when he moved his arm, I saw neither marks on words nor comments in the margin. He began paging through it, and I saw that he still had written nothing down. It must have enchanted him enough not even to consider a red-penned note. For a moment, we held quiet. He waited, I waited, and then suddenly I began swelling with dread: Under the merciless fluorescent light of the English Department offices, he would start accusing me of rhetorical blunders.

Finally, he said, "I assume this is all true."

I nodded quickly.

"I want to be careful about how I put this, Mr. Larson," he said, lighting a cigarette. An ashtray of half-finished, broken-butt Pall Malls sat before him. Flecks of cigarette ash stippled the blotter. "There is so much here that needs . . . unpacking."

My spine jellied but I stared at him.

"You probably don't understand where I'm coming from, do you?" he said more to himself than me.

"What is it that's wrong?" I asked.

"So McAfee likes to rub the heads of his young men, eh?"

"I think he's a student in his poetry class, the advanced one."

"Did you ask anyone who the fellow is, if he were, in fact, a student of Tom's?" The use of McAfee's first name brought an oppressive familiarity with it that made me think all teachers conspired against us, the freshmen, in particular.

I said no, I didn't ask who the fellow was.

"What do you think McAfee would say if he read this?"

I said I didn't think it was for McAfee to read.

"If not him, then who?"

"You," I said. "I was trying to show you the truth of what I had witnessed. Can't I write about such things?" I said, more like a sullen boy than a brave eighteen-year-old.

"You want the simplest answer I can give?" Marquard seemed testy, as if I had insulted him. "You can, and you can't. You cannot just write about the world as it is and expect a, that anyone will want to read it and b, that those you write about will agree to be so easily, so obviously identified. Why did you use their real names?"

I wanted to reply that the names in Virginia Woolf's essays were real. But I didn't know that for a fact. "Their real names are their real names," I said dumbly.

"If this were to be published, McAfee's career could be ruined."

I hadn't considered publication let alone ruin.

"Why don't you make this fiction?" Marquard asked.

"It didn't occur to me," I said, "that this *was* fiction. It was real. It was too perfectly real as it was. I mean, isn't fiction something that's made up, and an essay based on what the writer knows?"

"Yes, that's true—"

"You told us that in class—"

"I told you in class that essays have the truth of ideas and fiction has the truth of having lived those ideas, yes. I know." He was thoughtful, sucked hard on the soggy cigarette end. Other teachers leading in students kept walking by us. I caught the eye of one instructor who looked embarrassed for Marquard having to explain all this to me. He went on. "Fiction may be based on fact, but you must protect people, living people, by changing their names, disguising some of their characteristics, exaggerating their flaws or their virtues. Isn't that what you want to do?"

I wanted to say no, that wasn't what I wanted to do. But under the gun I wasn't clear what I was after. My intention may have been to capture the poetry reading's fine madness and contrast it with McAfee's laconic sensibility, but Marquard was saying I had done something else, implied something far more dicey. I had portrayed a sort of homoerotic encounter which, in my telling, had escaped me (I had only the vaguest notion that such attractions existed and they would never occur in public). While Marquard saw my portrait of McAfee as provocation, I saw it as a mere rape of the lock, more artistic stimulation than sexual gratification. I believed McAfee's artist-self initiated such experiences to beget their word-equivalents, and that was it, an idea far superior to sex. And yet, according to Marquard, sex in fact was the thing McAfee was after. Grasping this in the moment, I felt a duty to Marquard's view of reconstituting the world, not exactly into fiction, but at least away from actuality. I was struggling, however, to understand what exactly the dilemma was with writing down what I had witnessed.

"I'm confused," Marquard said, squinting at me intently, cocking his head. "These poets and their beatnik subculture, their desperation, their removal from the world you and I live in, their sanctimoniousness, their theatrics, their existentialism, all of this hardly interests me. But you—you find it fascinating, don't you? They've really hooked you, haven't they?"

"It beats the basement floor of Atchison House."

He laughed. "What about poetry? Do you write poetry?"

"When the mood strikes," I replied. "But poetry's another matter. Can't we talk about the essay you're writing, about the football player you failed?" Marquard recoiled as though I had asked him about his weight. "How have you protected the individuals involved? Have you used their names?"

"I have protected them," he said, "by not mentioning them. My essay concerns pedagogy and principle. It deals with how we do those students who play football a great disservice by passing them when they haven't learned the material. College, like life, is hard enough to have to fake your way through it as a football hero."

"So what's the difference?" I asked. "Whether we mention what actually happened, or we stand back and look at it socially. Aren't we trying to communicate the same thing?"

"The difference is, the essay concerns neither what happened nor what it suggests socially. Ultimately, it focuses upon you, the writer, and how whatever has occurred has affected *you*. The author and the author's ego are always the essay's true subject."

I felt Marquard pushing me into the ring, where I might box with this new opponent, my supposed self-importance.

"Look," he continued, "I won't pull down what you've written. But neither will I prop it up. I encourage you to keep at it. But the essay needs time. Not the time in which the writer lives or the time where the event still resonates in the writer's mind. But time, time passing, in many ways, a long time passing before the meaning can gel and the author can see its effect upon himself. In some ways, it's like the time which you haven't had yet. The poets and the poetry of this season will pass and mostly be forgotten. But you will remember them, even the minor ones. And what you remember will become much truer than what you experienced only one . . . week . . . ago." These words he thrust at me, he also pulled back once they stuck. "This," and he pointed to my essay, "belongs in your daybook, under your pillow, in your diary, in a letter to your true love, whoever she may be. What it says right now is too much of what it can't say. Someday that part of what it can't say will begin to speak through you and then it will be written and read as the truth."

We were both very quiet for a moment. He stubbed out a cigarette and lit another. Then he said he had other duties, and so handed me my essay and walked me to the door. I wondered whether his words, as mystical and personal as they felt, were the equivalent to McAfee's hand on the young man's head. Then, barely aware of the stairwell steps beneath my feet, suddenly I *was* that other young man, touched by my own master, an honor I thought only poets could bestow.

The following Monday, Marquard lectured his twenty-five freshmen on George Orwell's "A Hanging." His jacket off, tie loosened, shirtsleeves rolled, he used every bit of his body and voice to address us, gesturing wildly with his hands, stamping his feet, pointing at us fiercely, his animal assertion like a butterfly struggling out of its chrysalis. He paced and palmed the spine of the McCrimmon text like a bible, often exclaiming certainty to himself as he read Orwell's vividly precise sentences, sometimes rereading so the author's conundrums would resonate in our ears. "Listen to the language," he said. "Hear the man's mind in his sentences! Notice how the 'I' here is everyone, the ears and eyes of everyone, the sensitive and confused government-official narrator, the frightened victim himself, the blind European, Eurasian and Burmese bureaucrats present at the scene, the superintendent as well as the underling. And that little dog, that pathetic yelping reminder of injustice, a symbol of the whole bleeding subjugation of modern English history getting ready to fall off its mighty Trojan horse." We students dared not stare at the textbook. We beheld Marquard's eloquence, offered him trembling homage and fearful praise.

And then he asked, in another inspired cumulative sentence, whether we actually thought that the hanging Orwell describes so masterfully, so pitifully, had actually occurred in the way we had read it, that one morning among many similar mornings Orwell was present at just this particular hanging, which culminated with the Eurasian boy telling a joke about condemned men just before the jailers awkwardly go off chatting and laughing, relieved as hell to eat their breakfast?

"*Do* you believe," Marquard pressed us, "that in order for Orwell to have written this essay, the incident he reports, in the eight minutes he says it took to hang this man, do you believe it had to have happened exactly the way he reports it?"

No one in the class spoke; we were too frightened to believe anything.

"Are you greater fools than even I thought possible?"

Still no one spoke. I felt the silence rise from the paralyzing belief that it *was* possible to be greater fools than we already were.

"Well, what do you have to say for yourselves?" he demanded. "Come on!"

If anyone in that class had a voice to speak with, it was me.

So I raised my hand.

And I spoke, saying in essence what Marquard had said to me, yet with my own words. I talked of the writer's duty to the truth, to say what had happened as well as to respect the privacy of those who might be unfairly judged in the telling.

The class erupted then into discussion; ideas and responses took wing. If Orwell was using too much imagination in his tale, was he lying? No, he was writing fiction. But he calls it an essay. What happens, though, if all this did occur, but Orwell just rearranged the time and place for dramatic effect? If he did rearrange things, does that mean he is less trustworthy? When you re-create and do not tell your reader, you may lose your integrity. But your re-creation may serve a higher purpose, which is to make a point about integrity or, in this instance, the lack of it. And on and on we went until many of the usually mute students *said* what they thought, yes, no, maybe, I'm not sure. Marquard prodded us to go deeper, to argue, to cleave and clarify the paradoxes. At one point, he said that he wasn't sure whether there were clear answers to our questions. But that didn't matter. He said, "Your minds may never again have the passion they have at this moment, in this classroom."

When the hour was over and I left the intellectual embrace of several students who stayed on to talk further, I walked out into the clouded November light, stepped onto the long middle path of the White Campus, noticed other solitary fig-

ures lost in their bedeviling thoughts, plying their way to another class or home, perhaps darting into the library—and then
abruptly I stopped and beheld the overcast sky. I saw the poets
and professors and students, the whole college, inside a glass
ornament, and a great god was holding it up and watching us,
his eye the light, his breathing the rhythm of sentences my
mind kept creating. But as curious as this vision was, its allure
could not sustain me. Nor could my textbooks, the library or
the elegant old buildings I had grown to love fulfill that need in
me to know myself. These beings of sky and school formed the
portal to a journey I had only just begun. And on this course
Marquard got me going: That evening, following his great class
on Orwell's "A Hanging," I returned to my dorm room and
examined once more my essay, "A Night Out with the Poets,"
as I had come to call it. I hoped one day to redo the piece, yet I
didn't know to what degree I could trust to memory what I was
unable to trust in the first draft. So I chanced it. I tore up both
copies of the essay and pitched them, sensing rightly that revis-
ing my work would be no different from the revision memory
would make of my life.

Richard Howard

The Ghettoization of Poetry

For the first time, PEN has been able to present an award for *Poetry in Translation,* that intricate enterprise which is on certain occasions, as in Scripture, notably successful, and which is on most occasions, as in the words of Robert Frost (who said that poetry is what is lost in translation), in dispute.

By fiat, PEN has this year settled that dispute and declared the value of Mr. Davenport's enterprise, as I believe it will annually declare the value of analogous enterprises in verse translation. But just as PEN gives evidence of the resources to settle such disputes, it also has the power to appoint someone, usually a smiling public man, as the poet Yeats specified, someone perceived as harmless, say a former President of PEN—to speculate a little on even larger, even more acridly disputed questions—that is what we mean by a Keynote Speech. I am such a person, and I shall take advantage of my appointment, by Anne Hollander, since I believe that this year is as good, or as bad, an occasion to extend my inquiry beyond the much belabored territory of poetry in translation, in order to loiter a bit over the Situation of Poetry—poetry in general, all poetry, written and being written—in American Culture at the present time. I have been prompted to do so by my own qualifications on the one hand—that is, I am a reader of poetry, an editor of poetry, a teacher of poetry, and to some extent a producer of poetry; and on the other hand by an extraordinary development in our popular culture: I am referring to the establishment (by President Clinton, no less, prompted by God knows what councilors in this as in so many other domestic crises)—the establishment, I say, of National Poetry Month, beginning with the April just past, and apparently recurring with every April to come. I was never before so certain why April was declared by a poet to be the cruellest month; now I know.

So far, the symptoms of this particular National Month have been confined to certain bookstore windows, to certain television interviews and talk-show panels, to certain personal appearances, and chiefly—in a manifestation I find particularly noisome—to certain ragged bits of verse posted in the venues of mass transportation and mischievously entitled Poetry in Motion. But I perceive the institution of Poetry in Motion preceded the institution of National Poetry Month by a considerable interval, and I am further convinced that it is a far less drastic, less deleterious development (though doubtless a concomitant symptom) than the National Month itself, which I have no hesitation in calling the worst thing to have happened to poetry since the advent of the camera and the internal combustion engine, two inventions which the poet Wystan Auden once declared to be the bane of our modernity.

In between National Secretaries Month, during which (for the month, mind you, those in a position to have, as it were, secretaries are adjured, on a national scale, to be good to them, and National Take Our Daughters to Work Month (I am, of course, exaggerating: it is only a week during which this curious form of parental exposure is to occur), we have now wedged National Poetry Month. At last we have succeeded in wreaking upon poetry what the worst excesses of Progressive Education and the Palmer Method were helpless to effect: we have ghettoized a millennial human expression previously conceived as a pervasive and even prevalent part of conscious life, we have limited it to a temporal interval when it need not trouble us for another eleven months, and we have finally avowed its insignificance in the clearest fashion we possess: we have declared poetry to be a National and a Monthly commodity.

It is—Poetry is—already a problematic, if not a despised art among us. Despised because popular. More people are writing what they believe to be poetry, as any editor of a national magazine that publishes poetry can tell you, than ever before—many more are writing than are reading poetry, as you have so often heard. This situation is not a paradox, it is a necessary consequence of our cultural structure. The creative writing divisions and the poetry workshops are functioning at a Stakhanovite level, if level is the word I want, for we write what we wish to dispose of. We read only what we value and enjoy. So wretched, and so absurd, has the position of poetry writing become in our polity—unread though occasionally exhibited, despised though invariably ritualized, as at certain inaugurations—that not only are we determined to put the poor thing out of its agony, but we have made it a patriotic duty to do so.

We have not yet gone all the way, and though grave, the situation has not yet passed beyond the possibilities of a sort of recovery. I am here not only in my costume of Cassandra, or of Jeremiah, but with my prophetic robes of dawn about me too. You can discern them if you attend: I am here to offer, while there is still time enough and world, a modest proposal which may yet restore that art which was once the glory and the consolation of our race to something like its ulterior status. My proposal is simply this: to make poetry, once again, a secret.

For we have failed in our modern—our post-camera, post-internal-combustion engine—effort to make poetry known; we have merely made it public. I come among you to demand, if we are to save poetry, which means if we are to savor it, that we restore poetry to that status of seclusion and even secrecy which characterizes only our authentic pleasures and identifies only our intimately valued actions.

Two anecdotes will press home my point.

Gertrude Stein, visiting the United States for the first

time in thirty years (you will recall her observation: I am an American and Paris is my hometown), was invited to lunch at Metro-Goldwyn-Mayer, after her visits to Harvard and the White House on a lecture tour that passed through Cleveland (an occasion I perfectly remember, Miss Stein being the first woman I had ever seen who, according to the photographs in the newspapers, looked so much like a man, though not so much as the abundantly moustached Miss Toklas: I demanded to be taken to the lecture, but my mother denied this demand, the consequences of that denial being, I believe, dire to any future gender explorations of my own). When Miss Stein reached Hollywood, she was interrogated closely by Sam Goldwyn himself as to her remarkable success with the public, especially remarkable in view of the difficulty of her texts. How, Miss Stein, do you manage to get so much publicity? asked the head of the studio, his question not entirely disinterested. "The secret of public attention, Mr. Mayer," replied Gertrude Stein, "is small audiences."

And more recently, the late Joseph Brodsky, when he was Poet Laureate of the United States, had the wisdom and the daring to propose placing a six-poet anthology (I think the six were Dickinson and Whitman and Frost, Stevens and Williams and could it have been Marianne Moore? no, probably the sixth was Robert Lowell) in every hotel bedroom in the country, actually *re*placing the Gideon Bible with this oddly assorted volume and letting those whose desperate hours drive them to the printed page pasture here without any indication that one month is a better time to examine the triumphs of national expression than some other month. As in the case of Scripture, that triumph of poetry in translation, Brodsky's idea was that poetry would become a secret, a private, an intimate resource. After all, we have known for some time why Scripture is the world's best seller: it is because this book has a secret. Because on every page, in every line, it hints at something which it does not reveal, but which tempts us, arrests us, fascinates us all the more. And since I shall here be concerned with Scripture no further, what is to prevent me from betraying this secret? It is the same secret that Gertrude Stein revealed to Sam Gold-wyn—the secret that Scripture is addressed not to everyone but to each one, not to the public but to the individual. As that perverse Scripturalist André Gide put it, *le monde sera sauvé par quelques-uns* (the world will be saved by certain ones).

Brodsky was mistaken, of course, in assuming that poetry would flourish if it was easier to find—he ought to have known better from the situation of his own poetry and from that of other proscribed poets in his own country during all those Stalinist decades. Poetry will flourish—in terminal capitalism as in terminating communism—only when it is *harder* to find, when it is perceived as a valuable and virtually disallowed production that must be sought by need and by desire. We must eroticize the situation of poetry where we have only sanitized it; we must remember that poetry is, in the ultimate sense, a secretion from within, not a suntan lotion for external use only.

It has been, perhaps, an honest mistake these last fifty years, the commodification of poetry—it has given employment to many poets within our academies, and to the makers of fine face-creams everywhere—while it has managed to distract us from our heritage, to discourage us from reading the poetry of the past. But in its excruciation as National Poetry Month, the mistake is revealed for the malevolent destruction it indubitably is. Like the world itself, poetry will be saved by certain ones—by those who seek it out in secret, as they seek out whatever they love and enjoy. I salute you, therefore, on the brink of an enthralling and mysterious search, one in which no month, and even no week, is to be set aside for the public recognition of poetry. As those great exemplars of intimate enjoyment, those inspiring masters of the forbidden fulfillments of what our enemies call self-abuse Walt Whitman and Marcel Proust have shown us, poetry is to be ours every minute of every night and day, all the year round, insubordinately, insatiably, *in secret*.

Lynne Sharon Schwartz

Ruined by Reading

Rarely does the daily paper move me to reexamine my life. But a recent *New York Times* piece quoted a Chinese scholar whose "belief in Buddhism . . . has curbed his appetite for books." Mr. Cha says, "To read more is a handicap. It is better to keep your own mind free and to not let the thinking of others interfere with your own free thinking." I clipped his statement and placed it on the bedside table, next to a pile of books I was reading or planned to read or thought I ought to read. The clipping is about two square inches and almost weightless, the pile of books some nine inches high, weighing a few pounds. Yet they face each other in perfect balance. I am the scale on which they rest.

  Lying in the shadow of the books, I brood on my reading habit. What is it all about? What am I doing it for? And the classic addict's question, What is it doing for me? Mr. Cha's serenity and independence of mind are enviable. I would like to be equally independent, but I'm not sure my mind could be free without reading, or that the action books have on it is properly termed "interference." I suspect the interaction of the mind and the book is something more complex. I can see it encompassing an intimate history and geography: the evolution of character, the shifting map of personal taste. And what about the uses of language itself, as well as the perennial lure of narrative? But perhaps casting the issue in such large terms only shows how enslaved I am. Buddhism aside, there is no Readers Anonymous, so far, to help curb this appetite.

Luckily I am not prey to every kind of reading, for there are many kinds, as there are many kinds of love, not all of them intoxicating. There is pure and specific curiosity: how would an Israeli Arab regard growing up in an inhospitable state, or who was Albertine, really, or what is it like to be brilliantly gifted and in love and desperately ill at twenty-three years old? Then we don't read directly for the "high," though we may find it, in Anton Shammas's *Arabesques* or Keats's letters, but to satisfy the mind. Or less specific curiosity: What is anthropology, I used to wonder—the enterprise itself, not the exotic data, since ordinary urban life provides enough exotic data. How do you approach the study of "man" or "culture"? How do you tilt your head, what angle of vision? I read enough to find out how the discipline works, which is by accumulation and accretion, making a mosaic. You gather and place enough pieces, then step back and look. I saw the pattern most luminously in Ruth Benedict's brilliant study, *Patterns of Culture,* which still sits stalwartly on my shelf in its thirty-five-cent Penguin paperback edition, the pages going brown but not yet flaking, still viable, still credible. Even from the old-fashioned précis under each chapter heading I sensed that here I would find what I wanted: "Man moulded by custom, not instinct"; "All standards of behavior relative"; "Peoples who never heard of war"; "Death, the paramount affront." Irresistible. I read, there and elsewhere, and when the design was clear to me, I stopped.

We may read for facts alone: the eye skims along, alert for key words, and when they appear, like red lights on a highway, it slides deftly to a halt. That kind of reading propelled me out of graduate school. However useful, it does not feel like true reading but more like shopping, riffling through racks for the precise shade of blue. I would have made a poor and ludicrous scholar, like a diva singing ditties in TV commercials, or a pastry chef condemned to macrobiotic menus.

My addiction is to works of the imagination, and even if I became a Buddhist, I think I couldn't renounce them cold turkey. Not after a lifetime, the better part of which was spent reading. Was it actually the better part, though? Did I choose or was I chosen, shepherded into it like those children caught out early on with a talent for the violin or ballet, baseball or gymnastics, and tethered forever to bows and barres, bats and mats? We didn't know any alternatives; there was no chance to find them out. Reading, of all these, does not win huge sums of money or applause, or give joy and solace to others. What it does offer is a delectable exercise for the mind, and Mr. Cha, the Buddhist scholar, might well find it an indulgence. Like the bodies of dancers or athletes, the minds of readers are genuinely happy and self-possessed only when cavorting around, doing their stretches and leaps and jumps to the tune of words.

Despite all this mental pirouetting, or maybe because of it, I don't remember much of what I've read. My lifelong capacity for forgetting distresses me. I glance at a book on the shelf that I once read with avid interest—Dorothy Gallagher's *All the Right Enemies*, about the 1943 murder of the Italian anarchist Carlo Tresca—and while I struggle for the details, all I recall is the excitement of the reading. I couldn't give a cogent account of its dense intrigue or social history, yet I have some inchoate sense of the texture and dynamics of the subject.

At least I remember there was a murder at stake, something I can't always claim. When my younger daughter made disparaging remarks about *Billy Budd* I rushed to Melville's defense with a speech on the conflict between the rule of law applied generically and the merits of individual cases. Billy Budd struck a superior officer, I reminded her; according to the letter of the law, he must hang. And yet, and yet, we cannot quite swallow it . . . I ended in a glow of ambivalence. "It wasn't that he struck him," she murmured. "He killed him." I had totally forgotten, which was appalling. And yet, I consoled myself, I had remembered the conflict, and the dark malice of

Claggart, and Billy's faltering speech, and the terrible earnestness of Captain Vere, and the wry world-weariness of the old Dansker—modes of being swirling and contending like gases in the primeval void, to coalesce into a particular universe, a configuration of events. Wasn't that enough? Not quite. What happens is important too. What do I have, then, after years of indulgence? A feel, a texture, an aura: the fragrance of Shakespeare, the crisp breeze of Tolstoy, the carnal stench of the great Euripides. Are they worth the investment of a life? Would my mind be more free without them?

In truth I have made some tentative steps toward freedom. Over the last ten years or so, I have managed not to finish certain books. With barely a twinge of conscience, I hurl down what bores me or doesn't give what I crave: ecstasy, transcendence, a thrill of mysterious connection. For, more than anything else, readers are thrill-seekers, though I don't read thrillers, not the kind sold under that label, anyway. They don't thrill; only language thrills.

I had put aside books before, naturally, but with guilt, sneaking them back to the shelves in the dark. It seemed a rudeness of the worst sort. A voice was attempting to speak to me and I refused to listen. A spiritual rudeness. Since childhood I had thought of reading as holy, and like all sacraments, it had acquired a stiff halo of duty. My cavalier throwing over a book midway may arise from the same general desacralization as does the notable increase in divorce, marriage also being a sacrament and, once entered upon, a duty. Every day joy and duty pull farther apart, like Siamese twins undergoing an excruciating but salutary operation: they were never meant to share a skin; they may look alike but their souls are different.

So, like recidivist marryers, I take up the new book in good faith, planning to accompany it, for better or for worse, till the last page us do part, but . . . it stops being fun. Other, more intriguing, books send out pheromones. There are after all so many delectable books in the world. Why linger with one that doesn't offer new delights, take me somewhere I've never been? I feel detached from the book on my lap much as the disaffected husband or wife feels detached from the body alongside and asks, why am I here, in this state of withness? In a marriage, one hopes it may be a transient feeling—there may be extenuating circumstances, although these lately do not seem to possess great force—but in the case of a book, why not be abandoned, and abandon?

This is a far cry from my idealism at age twenty, when I longed to read everything, simply because it was written, like adventurers who climb Mount Everest because it is there. Other sensationalists must sample everything edible or try every feasible sexual posture, however slimy or arduous, respectively. Thus do they assure themselves they have truly lived. No experience has passed them by, as if exhaustiveness were the measure of the good life.

Gradually I lost, or shed, the Mount Everest syndrome. Bookshelves still tease and tantalize, but like a woman with a divining rod, I know now where the water will be, I do not have to scrape earth and dig holes seeking, only there where the rod begins to tremble.

The unfinished or unread books languish on my shelves, some bought because friends said I must read them (but it was they who had to read them), or because the reviews throbbed with largesse of spirit (but it was the reviewer I loved, just as Priscilla loved John Alden or Roxane, Cyrano. I should have bought the reviewer's book). Others were just too gorgeously packaged to resist. Book jackets nowadays have become an art form, and browsing through a bookstore is a feast for the eyes. In some cases the jacket turns out to be the best thing about the book. I am not one to snub beauty, wherever it turns up. Yet I have come to distrust book jackets calculated to prick desire like a Bloomingdale's window, as if you could wear what you read. The great French novels used to come in plain shiny yellow jackets, and the drab Modern Library uniforms hid the most lavish loot.

Once in a while I take my castoffs down and turn their pages for exercise, stroke them a bit. They have the slightly dusty, forlorn patina of people seldom held or loved, while their neighbors stand upright with self-esteem, for having been known, partaken of intimacies. I am regretful, but my heart is hardened.

I can face myself, abandoning even the most sanctified or stylish books, but there is forever the world to face, world without end. I envision a scenario: a group of writers sits around talking of the formative books, the great themes, let's say man grappling with nature, with death. Perhaps they are women writers, musing on men's compulsion to view everything in terms of struggle and mastery. One turns to me, saying, Well, for instance, *Moby Dick?*

I cannot lie about reading. A remnant of holiness still clings. It would be tantamount to a devout Catholic's claiming falsely to be in a state of grace. So I blush, confess I never finished it, and though they remain courteous, repressed shock and disapproval permeate the room (or could it be the women find me daring, the Emma Goldman of reading?).

I puzzled for years over how a friend, frantically busy at a publishing job, where manuscripts are thrust at you daily for overnight perusal, had read every book ever mentioned. Colossal erudition, I thought in my innocence, and speedy too. Till it struck me, as it might a child suddenly seeing through Santa Claus: it can't be. She lies. I wasn't filled with indignation, didn't even banish her from the ranks of the trustworthy. Simply: aha, so that's what's done, a helpful currency of social exchange like the white lie, and equally easy. You read reviews and jacket copy, and listen carefully. If you are reasonably *au courant*, who knows, you may even come up with critical judgments no less plausible or even valid than had you read the book. What has been lost, after all? Only the actual experience, the long slow being with the book, feeling the shape of the words, their roll and tumble in the ear.

Still, lying about reading feels too risky, as risky as saying you have seen God or drunk the milk of Paradise when you haven't—the kind of lie that might dilute the milk of Paradise should it ever be offered you.

Nor can I throw a book away. I have given many away and ripped a few in half, but as with warring nations, destruction shows regard: the enemy is a power to reckon with. Throwing a book out shows contempt for an effort of the spirit. Not that I haven't tried. Among some tossed-out books of my daughters which I rescued, to shelter until a foster home could be arranged, was one too awful to live. I returned it to the trash, resisting the urge to say a few parting words. All day long the thought of its mingling with chicken bones and olive pits nagged at me. Half a dozen times I removed it and replaced it, like an executioner with scruples about capital punishment. Finally I put it on a high shelf where I wouldn't have to see it. Life imprisonment. Someday my children, going through my effects, will say, "Why did she keep this wretched thing? She hated it." "Oh, you know what she was like. It was a book, after all."

To tell the truth, I had begun to think about reading before coming upon Mr. Cha. It was the spring of 1986, an uneasy time for me but a magnificent season for the New York Mets. As often happens with a new love or addiction, I didn't know I cared until it was too late. I had never followed baseball and felt safe from television, one of the devil's ploys to buy our souls. But alas we are never safe; in the midst of life we are in death, and so forth. My family watched the Mets. At first I would drift through the living room and glance, with faint contempt, at the screen. Gradually I would stand there for longer and longer spells, until I came to know the players by name and disposition and personal idiosyncrasies: how they spit and how they chewed, how they reacted to a failed at-bat—with impassivity or miming the ritual "darn-it" gestures—how their uniforms fit and which folds they tugged in moments of stress. The game itself I already knew in rudimentary form, having played punch ball on the summer evening streets of Brooklyn as the light fell behind the brick houses and the pink Spaldeen grew dimmer with each hopeful arc through the twilit air. All that remained was for the finer points to be explained to me. I was surprised and touched by the element of sacrifice, as in the sacrifice fly (the adjective evoking *esprit de corps* and a tenuous religiosity) and the bunt, a silly-looking play, several grown men converging to creep after a slowly and imperturbably rolling ball. I was impressed by the intricate comparative philosophy of relief pitching, and shocked by the logistics of stealing bases. This sounded illicit yet everyone took it for granted, like white-collar crime, with the most expert thieves held in high esteem like savvy Wall Street players. Then one evening—the turning point—I sat down, committing my body to the chair, my eyes to the screen, my soul to the national Oversoul.

I pretended an anthropological detachment. My quest was for the subtleties and symbolism—the tension of the 3–2 call, the heartbreak of men left stranded on base, the managers' farseeing calculations recalling the projections of chess players (if he does this, I'll do that), the baffling streaks and slumps, and above all the mystifying signs. For at critical junctures, advisors sprinkled on the field or in the dugout would pat their chests and thighs and affect physical tics in a cabalistic language. Soon it was clear I wasn't as detached as I pretended. The fortunes of the Mets, as well as the fluctuations of each individual Met, had come to matter. It was partly proximity, the *sine qua non* of most love, and partly aesthetics. When giraffe-like Darryl Strawberry lazily unfurled an arm to allow a fly ball to nestle in his glove, I felt the elation I used to feel watching André Eglevsky of the New York City Ballet leap and stay aloft so long it seemed he had forgotten what he owed to gravity. Not unlike the elation I got from books.

I never watched an entire game, though. I hadn't the patience. I would enter late, around the fourth or fifth inning, when the atmosphere was already set—not that it couldn't change in an instant, that was part of the charm. I was like those drinkers who assure themselves they can stop any time they choose. I could start any time I chose. I was not compelled to scoot to my chair at the opening notes of the *Star-Spangled Banner* like a pitiful little iron filing within range of the magnet.

Night after astounding night became a season of protracted ecstasy. It was not just the winning but the beauty of the plays and the flowering of each distinct personality: modest Mookie Wilson's radiant amiability and knack of doing the right thing at the right moment, boyish Gary Carter's packaged public-relations grin, Howard Johnson's baffling lack of personality, absorbent like a potent black hole at the center of the team, Roger McDowell's inanity, Bob Ojeda's strong-jawed strength and the departures and returns of his mustache, Keith Hernandez's smoldering and handsome anger at the world, Len Dykstra's rooted insecurities packed together to form a dense and lethal weapon, Dwight Gooden's young inscrutability, reflecting the enigma of the team—arrogant or just ardent? All became crystallized.

Amidst the glory was an unease, a tingling of an inner layer of skin. I grudged the hours. I felt forced to watch against my will. Yet what was the trouble? Watching baseball is harmless, unless compulsion itself be considered blameworthy—but I am not that stern a moralist.

The games were depriving me of something. There it was. The instant I identified the uneasy feeling as "missing," all came clear. Reading. Reading was the stable backdrop against which my life was played. It was what I used to do through long evenings. Never mornings—even to one so self-indulgent, it seems slightly sinful to wake up and immediately sit down with a book—and afternoons only now and then. In daylight I would pay what I owed the world. Reading was the reward, a solitary, obscure, nocturnal reward. It was what I got everything else (living) out of the way in order to do. Now the lack was taking its toll. I was having withdrawal symptoms.

I tried to give up baseball. I cut back, backslid, struggled the well-documented struggle. And then, abruptly, my efforts were needless. The burden fell from my shoulders as Zen masters say the load of snow falls from the bent bamboo branch at the moment of greatest tension, effortlessly. The Mets won the World Series and overnight, baseball was no more.

Had my struggle taken place eight years later, the much

decried baseball strike would have snatched my burden from me in a more cruelly abrupt, un-Zen-like way. How many people suffered through nearly two years of baseball's defection, bitter and bereft, seeking other pastimes that would yield the same forgetfulness, the same sense of wandering companionably with like-minded dreamers through a green and grassy myth? They watched movies and game shows, they took up aerobics, they switched their allegiance to basketball or hockey (some may even have turned to reading). But, they reported, none of these felt quite the same.

I was never a true devotee, just on a brief vacation, or aberration. I doubt that I would have suffered much, but I shall never know. Anyway, by then the team I loved, the names and the personalities—or personas—attached to them were gone. The Mets, as far as I was concerned, were no longer the Mets. Over and over I have been puzzled by the ruthless trading of players and the players' own promiscuity. How can you still root for a team, I've asked true fans, when the members change every year? Over and over I've been told it's the team that grips a fan's affections, not its individual components. But the team is an abstraction, a uniform, a logo, a pair of colors. The players are what matter, just as you cannot substitute paraphrased chapters for *Pride and Prejudice*, say, or *The Golden Bowl*, telling the same story in different words, and call it the same book.

In any case, my swift and troubling affair with baseball ended painlessly. The dramatic victory of the Series over, I returned to reading, to my life. Or was it to a retreat from life, the void at the center, from which, the Zen masters also say, all being springs?

How are we to spend our lives, anyway? That is the real question. We read to seek the answer, and the search itself— the task of a lifetime—becomes the answer. Which brings Mr. Cha back to mind. He knows what to do with his life. He treasures his free mind, or that part of it that Shunryu Suzuki, in *Zen Mind, Beginner's Mind*, calls "big mind," as opposed to the small mind concerned with particular daily events:

The mind which is always on your side is not just your mind, it is universal mind, always the same, not different from another's mind. It is Zen mind. It is big, big mind. This mind is whatever you see. Your true mind is always with whatever you see. Although you do not know your own mind, it is there—at the very moment you see something, it is there. . . . True mind is watching mind. You cannot say, "This is my self, my small mind, or my limited mind, and that is big mind." That is limiting yourself, restricting your true mind, objectifying your mind. Bodhidharma said, "In order to see a fish you must watch the water." Actually when you see water you see the true fish.

But some of us must see the fish in order to see the water. The water may be too transparent to grasp without varieties of fish to show its texture.

A poet friend of mine, after heart surgery, was advised by a nurse to take up meditation to reduce stress. "You must empty your mind," she said. "I've spent my life filling it," he replied. "How can you expect me to empty it?" The argument is verbal. In Buddhist paradoxes, empty can mean full and full, empty, in relation to mind and universe. Either way, though, I keep worrying about those fish, flickering beautiful things of this world. A pity if they were to become only means to an end, to a serene mind.

In *The Ambassadors*, mild, restrained Strether is sent to Paris to extricate a young man from his passion, and instead falls prey to the same passion. In a whirlwind of exhilaration he exhorts everyone around him to live. "To live, to live!" Very heady. Though not so, apparently, to Henry Mills Alden of Harper's Publishers, who rejected Henry James's manuscript when it was first presented: "The scenario is interesting," he wrote in his report,

but it does not promise a popular novel. The tissues of it are too subtly fine for general appreciation. It is subjective, fold within fold of a complex mental web, in which the reader is lost if his much-wearied attention falters. A good proportion of the characters are American, but the scene is chiefly in Paris. The story (in its mere plot) centres about an American youth in Paris, who has been captivated by a charming French woman (separated from her husband) and the critical situations are developed in connection with the efforts of his friends and relatives to rescue him. The moral in the end is that he is better off in this captivity than in the conditions to which his friends would restore him. I do not advise acceptance. We ought to do better.

Luckily for us, the fine-tissued novel did eventually gain the sanction of print and hard covers, between which "To live!" becomes the awakened Strether's motto, the Jamesian equivalent of a bumper sticker. Was I living, I wondered when I first read it, or simply reading? Were books the world, or at least a world? How could I "live" when there was so much to be read that ten lives could not be enough? And what is it, anyway, this "living"? Have I ever done it? If it is merely James's euphemism for knowing passion, well, I pass. Reading is not a disabling affliction. I have done what people do, my life makes a reasonable showing. Can I go back to my books now? For if "living" means indulging the cravings, why then . . .

There was life before reading. Not until the sixteenth century were manuscripts even available, except to monks and royalty. What could it have been like? There was life before language too—grunts and grimaces, tears and laughter (yet how much laughter, without language?), shrieks and groans and commiseration; all of that is easy to imagine. But to have language and no books? What to do after the corn is ground and the water hauled and the butter churned? Keep your mind free, as Mr. Cha suggests? Without stories to free the mind, emptiness might be true emptiness, like Freud's proverbial cigar. Well, there were storytellers, the old woman sitting at the fireside entrancing the family, or the troubadour chanting verses near the fountain in the piazza while women walked from the village oven with warm breads on boards balanced on their shoulders. But that is a social experience. With books there are no fellow listeners, no fleshly storyteller, none of the exertions of fellowship.

Historians contrast the unity and coherence of the Middle Ages with modern social fragmentation: among the hundreds of causes for the change might be numbered the privatization of stories—from a communal activity, listeners bound together by words that gathered them in and made their dreams audible—to a solitary voice whispering in your ear.

Today, in an odd quirk of history, public readings once again are enjoying a heyday, if not in the town square then in the corner bookstore or library or art gallery, the café or the park. Everyone, it seems, is writing something, prose or poetry, and everyone wants to read it aloud. We wring our hands collectively—and with good reason—over the impending death of the book at the hands of electronics, over widespread illiteracy and semiliteracy, and yet plenty of people will come to hear others read. How this can be seems a paradox, but no doubt history could show even more wildly polarized trends flourishing side by side.

Still, today's audiences are not seeking quite the same thing as their ancient counterparts. The troubadours, the golden-tongued grandmothers and village schoolmasters were prized for the wonder of their stories. They were the only source of stories. Now listeners come, I suspect, not so much to hear as to see the storyteller, in a spirit of celebrating celebrity itself. A curious cultishness has come to surround the writer—I think of how Dickens and Wilde crossed the ocean and strode down the gangplank to the roar of cheering crowds—as if the stories and the writer were one and the same.

But you cannot see or touch a voice. That is what makes it mysterious and subtle and endlessly alluring. And without the voices of my youth, my ghostly familiars, how could I have become myself?

Leonard Michaels

Pulp Fiction

In the movie *Pulp Fiction* there is a huge amount of talk which is intended not so much to advance the plot or deepen character, but to imitate the way people talk in life. Much of the lifelike talk in the movie could have been replaced by different talk. It would also be an imitation of life, and would be just as entertaining, rather like talk shows on television, where it matters little what is said from one show to the next. Talk, sheer talk, is entertainment. People get killed for their talk on talk shows, but this too is like life, certainly in America where talk is regularly interrupted by murderous violence in schools, streets, homes, and workplaces. *Pulp Fiction* has murderous violence as well as talk. It is a profoundly American movie, but what makes the movie interesting is its form, not simply the talk and violence. In the movie's form these elements, talk and violence, are dialectically related, as if one entails the other, very like partners in sexual intercourse who are excited by mutual reflection, or each by the other's passion. In the movie, a killer likes to talk passionately to his victims before shooting them. Thus, talk is foreplay, and shooting is orgasmic, a way of "getting off."

Colloquially, "to off" somebody is to kill. The same meaning attaches to the expression "to waste." The movie is much concerned with killing and with human waste, mainly anal. The major sex in the movie is anal intercourse, and it is accompanied by horrific violence. But the deluge of talk, including a long passage on diarrhea, makes talk something more than a metaphor for human waste. It is literally to be understood as an excretory production. Above all, it is an element of entertainment—an empty or emptying pleasure.

While talking in the movie, a character is accidentally shot in the face. The moment is frightening, but what concerns the other two characters present is the messy consequence of the accidental shooting. They are splattered with blood and must go directly to a toilet to clean themselves. While they are cleaning themselves, one makes a joke about menstrual blood, yet another excretory production. The character who was shot in the face, or wasted, had been in the toilet moments earlier. His fate in the movie, toilet-to-wasted, is also the fate of his killer. Exactly upon leaving a toilet his killer is wasted.

Because of the form—excretory-talk-violence—it is appropriate that the movie doesn't, finally, end. It only returns to the beginning. Thus, events in the movie lead, finally, to nothing final, and this is also true of the production of human waste. The movie leaves us, or we leave the movie, with an experience of excretory-talk-violence, or the experience of a form without closure, a form that is, in essence, forever open. It never ends, and thereby it assures us that human experience is as inconsequential as the character who is shot in the face. It is empty, innocent of meaning, or as emptying as any television talk show where people sometimes entertain us by disburdening themselves of heavy and evil matters, though mostly they just fart around.

To emphasize this formal implication of the movie, a suitcase loaded with mysterious contents—for which people were killed—is opened in the "final" moments. But we are not shown what it contains. Like the whole movie, then, it contains nothing but trivializing experience, and all the killing is part of an anti-climactic joke, meaningless, inconsequential, empty.

Despite the talk and killing, the movie must remain infinitely open to assure us that nothing really or finally happened. If anything really and finally happened, it would undermine the essential entertainment value of sheer talk and the movie would displease us. We would be confronted with meaning, obliged to think or feel the unpleasant weight of conscience. Thinking is a product of conscience, and definitive of human being.

Contemporary with the movie, an act of murderous violence led to a trial and four hundred days of talk. The jury finished deliberating in four hours, which seemed so quick that the verdict didn't feel like an end but an abrupt stop, or a trivialization of the talk, and the violence that led to the talk. A juror was seen raising his clenched fist—metaphorically, an act of violence—in a salute to the defendant, the murderer who was officially "Not guilty." Like *Pulp Fiction*, the trial suggests many things, but mainly that entertainment is endemic, perhaps crucial, to bourgeois society, and that nothing is more entertaining than our legal system. In fact, judges and lawyers actually do think of themselves as stars—literally entertainers—but regardless of what they think, that is exactly what they are, and if it weren't so terribly entertaining, the movie, the trial, and the state of the American soul might sicken us with worry.

James Allen McPherson

Umbilicus

In the late fall of that first year, when I was growing secure in my solitude, a friend, an Englishman, came to this house and offered what he believed was an act of compassion: "Now look here," he told me, "you are becoming a recluse. Why don't you go out once in a while? At least go out into your own backyard and see how delightful the fall is. I'm told that way north of here, along the Minnesota border, it is even more beautiful. Why don't you at least take a drive up there before winter comes?" His was a call back to the more complex rituals of life. After some serious reflection, I accepted it as such. I had always wanted to see the northeastern part of the state, the sources of the Mississippi. And so, on a Saturday morning, a golden and blue fall day, I pulled away from the security of this house. I drove northeasterly on county roads. I drove very slowly and very carefully from one rural town to the next. I saw the light brown beauty of harvested fields, when soybeans and corn and wheat had given up their energy to entropy, to the enigma of renewal, for the risk of winter and the promise of the spring. I saw that life, my own life, too, *all life,* lay under the promise of an agreement with something outside, and far, far beyond, the little roles we play on the surface of things. I am saying that the slow drive along the backroads reawakened my spirits. I began to reconsider the essential importance of risk to the enterprise of life. I mustered sufficient courage to stop several times along the road, once for lunch, and again for gasoline and oil. I drove as far north as I thought was necessary, and then I turned around and drove back toward home. But in the late afternoon, on the far side of Cedar Rapids, the engine of my car began to smoke and burn. By the time I had parked on the narrow road bank, the engine was on fire. It was here that the old sickness began to reclaim its place in my emotions. I began to feel that the burning engine was God's punishment for my abandoning the simple rituals that had become my life. I felt that, because I had left the refuge of my house, I had *earned* this fate. I abandoned the car. I steeled myself to walk back home, or at least to walk as far as the outskirts of Cedar Rapids, many miles down that county road, as a form of self-punishment. I focused my mind on my house, my bed, my table, and I began walking toward these three things, and *only* these three things.

But several miles along that road, approaching dusk, a truck with two men in it stopped just ahead of me. The two men, both white, sat in the truck and waited for me to approach it. "We saw your car smoking back there, brother," the man in the passenger seat said to me. "Can we give you a ride?" The two of them seemed to be laborers, or at least farmers. The gun rack stretched across the rear window took my memories back to the terror of that long road I had traveled to this place. There was the truck, the gun rack, the white faces, the road. But they did not have the oily Southern accent. I accepted their offer, and the passenger moved over and allowed me to take his seat. Now the three of us were squeezed together on the high seat. They gave me a beer, from the remains of a case of beer on the floor, and we drove toward Cedar Rapids. "A lot of our friends don't like the colored," the driver, who seemed the older of the two, announced to me. "But, hell, me and my brother here, we got colored neighbors. We go over to their houses sometimes for parties. They ain't exactly like us, but we like them all the same." We toasted with our beer and talked of the need for more brotherhood in the world, and of the house parties given by their black neighbors in Cedar Rapids. But at the first service station we reached, just on the outskirts of Cedar Rapids, we were informed that no tow truck was available. The attendant advised us to continue on into Cedar Rapids, toward a station where a tow truck could be available.

Now the older of the two men, in the proximity of safety and social gradation seeming to look more and more "poor white," used this opportunity to offer a radical plan. "Now look," he told me. "I already told you that we *like* the colored. We go over to their house parties in Cedar. You know that some colored are our neighbors. Now here's what I'm gonna do. There's a rope on the back of this truck. We can drive on back and tie that rope to the front bumper of your car. Then we'll just tow her on in to Cedar. You can pay us what you were gonna pay the tow truck, plus we'll do it for less money."

The cool fall evening was closing in. I hesitated, but the desperation of the situation caused me to risk some trust. I accepted their offer. With the bargain struck, with the night closing around us, we drove back to the dead car. We drank more beer in celebration of brotherhood, and we even made some jokes. At the car, after the ropes had been tied to link my own wreck to the back end of their truck, the connection, the *umbilicus*, was tightened until my car could be raised so that only its back wheels were grounded. The two brothers cautioned me to take my former place behind the wheel and manage my car as best I could while they drove the truck. I was handed another beer, for toasting our newly struck brotherhood, while we steered in unison toward the distant lights of Cedar Rapids. And so we started out, slowly and jerkily at first, but then with more and more speed.

Legend has it that all the "I" states are flat. This is not so. There are reasons why the Mississippi River begins in Minnesota, and why its tributaries contribute every drop of water in its meandering and then rapid flow down to the Gulf of Mexico. There are hills in this landscape, and hillocks and dales and rills. The expression *from here to there,* with its promise of fixed purpose, is found in the engineering of straight roadways. But, in contradiction to this illusion of purposeful will, nature itself still has something else to say. Nature will not cede an inch, without struggle, to *any* expression of fixed purpose. Something mysterious in nature, or in the restless growing edge of life itself, imposes a counterintention on all illusion of control. The Great River overflows its banks, flows and ebbs, crests and slackens, rushes and lingers, dies, and then is mighty and waterful again, according to its *own* instincts. So also the straightest of roads are forced to acknowledge the rhythms of the lands that lap under them. Such rhythms are gentle under the four wheels of a tractioned car. But under only two wheels, these same rhythms are foreboding. They speak waywardly of the tenuous nature of life. And in the fall, after harvest time, the uniform brownness of the field, or perhaps it is the withdrawal of the subtle shades of green, keeps one close to the recognition that *death* is the very next season *after* life. You must also add to this the horror of the peculiar angle of a windshield looking *up* into the dark, evening sky, closing down on the emptiness all around the roadbed, and over the top of a truck ahead that you cannot really see. And add also the swaying of the elevated car, first leftward, toward possibly oncoming traffic you cannot see, then rightward, toward sharp and narrow embankments, black-dirted and brown-coated and deathly deep. Imagine also the unsteady stretching of the ropes, the *umbilicus,* connecting the two vehicles. It stretches close to breaking when the truck moves uphill; it relaxes, and the weight of the towed car pushes forward freely and crazily, when the towing truck goes down a dale. Such a haphazardly improvised *umbilical cord* cares nothing for *verbal* affirmations of brotherhood. It encourages very bad manners. It permits the front of the towed car to bump the back of the towing truck, and when the towed car brakes—because its driver tries to steady it when it bumps the rear of the truck ahead, and releases the brake when the rope becomes too tight—both car and towing truck begin to sway dangerously. And add more to it. Add to it the fading illusion of rescue, and the more sharply focused recognition that these are two *white men,* blood brothers, both drunk on beer, who are pulling off the rescue. Add also to it the fact that you have had two beers yourself, and that there is a third beer, open but untouched, on the seat beside you. An additional inducement for fear is that, while these two white men say that they like the colored, and while the three of you have raised two toasts to *abstract* brotherhood, the world you live in, especially now, does not perceive things in this same idealized light.

Now, in the entire history of this country there has developed absolutely no substantial body of evidence to support either the authenticity, the genuineness, or the practicality of such a web of self-extension, such an *umbilicus,* extending from either extreme of this great psychological divide. There has been no *real* trust between black and white, especially in such life-risking circumstances. With each sway of the car, within every pull and slack of the rope, the improvised *umbilical* cord—up dale and down dale, inching and then swaying toward the evening lights of Cedar Rapids, the old life lessons came back. *There has never been a life-affirming umbilicus between black and white.* And if this is true, then something else must follow. If the rope should break and the car should crash, no one will really care or even attempt to understand just how this failed and sloppily improvised community of purpose had first come into existence. On the evening news, if even there, it will be dismissed as just another roadkill. *I will never be able to reclaim my bed, my table, or the simple, little, self-protective rituals—sleeping and eating and reading and being reclusive— that I had created to protect what remained of my life.*

I braked my car and both vehicles, my car and their truck, went off the road.

But the rope, the *umbilicus, held,* while both the car and truck swerved into the ditch at the edge of the roadside.

The two vehicles, the three of us, went into the ditch together. There was no moon over the brown harvested fields that evening. There was no magnetic field, no spiritual center. There was only the spilled can of beer, and its acrid scent mingled with the smell of burning oil, inside my car. Death was announcing itself all around.

I had no trust left in me.

But the three of us were unhurt. The two brothers, after inspecting their truck, dismissed the incident as no more than a joke played on the three of us by the rhythm of the road. "Now we told you we like the colored," the older brother announced. "See, the rope is still tight. We can just push our truck out of the ditch and then hook you up again to it. We'll still drive you on in to Cedar."

I paid the brothers much more than I had promised them, and I began walking down the road toward the lights of Cedar Rapids, toward my bed, my window looking out on my backyard, my table, and toward the simple rituals I had worked out for my life. These things still resided on the far side of Cedar Rapids. I walked away from the urgings of my brothers that we could very easily rescue both truck and car from the ditch, that we had only a few more miles to go before hitting Cedar, that they had always been good neighbors to the colored who lived next door. I kept walking away from them. In my own reduced frame of reference, my two rescuers, my brothers, had become two drunk white men, who, through uncaring, had put my life at risk. I walked away, while behind me they pleaded for the unimportance of money and for the practicality of their plan.

I left it to them to cut the rope, the *umbilicus,* connecting my dead car to their truck.

Richard Rodriguez

True West

Growing up in Sacramento, any imagination I had of the West (a landscape suggested by studio backlots in Burbank, which was south) lay east of the Sierras. The Sierras appeared on the eastern horizon, sheer and dreadful portals from which the Donner party would never descend. In summer, the mountains were obscured by Zeusy yellow clouds; sometimes storms of lightning—Olympian ruminations never communicated to the valley floor.

Except in the writings of John Muir. In 1869, Muir spent a summer in the Sierras. He had arrived at California by ship to grasp the implications of the coastline. America, he saw, comes to an end here.

In the 1950s, California was filling with westering Americans who were confident they had arrived. My parents were from Mexico. My father described California, always, as *"el norte."* My father's description had latitude, allowed for more America. To have grown up with a father who spoke of California as the North, a Chicago-accented neighbor who spoke of California as the West, to have grown up thinking of the West as lying east of here, is already to have noticed that "West" is imaginary.

American myth has traditionally been written east to west, describing an elect people's manifest destiny accruing from Constitution Hall to St. Jo' to the Brown Palace to the Golden Gate. A classics professor in Oregon rebuts my assertion that California is not the West. His family moved from Queens to Anaheim in the Fifties. They moved WEST. Simple. The way the East Coast has always imagined its point of view settled the nation.

In Warner Brothers' cartoons, the sun went down with a ker-plop and a hiss into an ocean that had to be the Pacific. Because I assumed I knew where the day ended, the more interesting question was "Where does the West begin?" I grew up with my back to the sea. From high school I had been mindful of Fenimore Cooper's description of a lighted window on the frontier. Nowhere else in American literature does a candle burn so brightly. That small calix of flame was a beacon of the East—all the fame of it. Where the light from that candle was extinguished by darkness, there the West began.

A couple of years ago, at a restaurant in the old train station in Pittsburgh (as coal cars rumbled past our table), my host divulged an unexpected meridian: "Pittsburgh is the gateway to the West." The same in St. Louis, the same in Kansas City. In Texas: Dallas is where the East begins; Fort Worth is where the West begins.

I was trained East. Louis L'Amour and Zane Grey wrote "westerns." Westerns sold for twenty-five cents to old men with wires running from their ears down to the batteries in their shirt pockets; men who would otherwise spend their evenings staring at the linoleum.

Josiah Royce, Nick Carraway, Damon Runyon—for those of us who had grown up in the West, New York was finishing school. Eating clubs at Princeton, authority, memory—all the un-American themes.

I remember thinking nothing could be more glamorous

than to be the *New Yorker* correspondent who would hold any hinterland—be it Paris, Rome, or Sacramento—up to the amused monocle of Eustace Tilley. The entire literature of the West was made up of such correspondents: Harte, Muir, Twain. Coldest winter I ever spent was one summer in Saaaan Francisco HAW HAW HAW.

I was trained East, an inveterate reader of "easterns"— Wharton, James, Kazin, Baldwin, Mailer. I noticed that the highest easterns—Wharton, James—were written as though they were westerns (westerns traditionally began with an innocent arriving from the East). Isabel Archer of Albany, New York, journeys to Europe, where she achieves inexperience amidst the etiolated foliage, the thicker light, the charged conversations.

Go east, young woman! I think we are just now beginning to discern the anti-narrative—an American detective story told from west to east, against manifest destiny, against the Protestant point of view, against New York, old ivy, the Civil War, the assurances of New England divines.

A florid, balding gymnopaede bellows to me from an adjacent Stair-Master in San Francisco that he is abandoning California. "Too—" he raises fur-epauleted shoulders to portray constriction. He is moving out West—that is the expression he uses—to a house thirty minutes from downtown Boise where there are still trees and sky.

The Boston Brahmin who sought an aperture as her life constricted to ice cubes and cable television didn't consider California when she thought of retiring in the West. Of her last trip to California she remembers only despair within a gold-veined mirror. She settled on Santa Fe, with its ancient, reassuring patina, recently applied with little sponges. She wears blue jeans, nods to "Howdy"; she goes to the opera, sometimes to Mass.

The apparent flattery the East Coast pays California is that the future begins here. Hula hoops, Proposition 13, college sit-ins, LSD, Malibu Buddhism, skateboards, beach boys, silicon chips. California, the laboratory. New York, the patent office. The price Californians pay for such flattery is that we agree to be seen as people lacking in experience, judgment, and temper. It seems not to have occurred to the East that because the West has had the knowledge of the coastline, the westerner is the elder, the less innocent party in the conversation. It is no coincidence that the most elegant literature cloudless Los Angeles has produced in this century is celebrated worldwide as *noir*.

Californians have been trying to tell eastern America that the country is, after all, finite. Only within the last few years—a full century after the closing of the frontier—have we gotten a bite on the cliché: *Tonight Peter Jennings asks, Is the Golden State tarnished?*

A few years ago, after an earthquake in Los Angeles, a television producer from the Canadian Broadcasting Corporation asked me for an interview on the future of California. The Canadian producer decided we would have our televised conversation at Venice Beach, the place tourists come on Sundays to experience comic extremity by the sea. I would sit in an Adirondacks chair, the blue Pacific over my shoulder. And, by and by, there I was on Venice Beach, wired for sound and my hair blowing east. I had become a correspondent. But this was Tuesday, a gray afternoon, the fog pouring in on a gale. Black teenagers wearing Raiders jackets stomped over cables that were lying about, kids so accustomed to TV crews they didn't pause to gander. An old guy wanted five bucks to stay out of the shot. A trio of German tourists, two men and a woman, and they all looked like Beethoven, stopped at each of the hundred and one T-shirt and counterfeit stands that lined the beach. The tarot readers set up their card tables and sat with their backs to the gray ocean, limp-haired priestesses of that huge, turgid brain. Panning the scene for something golden, we did eventually find one happy face. At the concrete muscle-beach exhibition booth, we came upon a sunburned old salt with sagging breasts, eager to pose for the camera in his red nylon bikini, winking insanely with every revolution and flex.

I I

Several seasons ago Ralph Lauren produced fashion lay-
outs of high-WASP nostalgia that were also confused parables
of Original Sin. Bored, beautiful children pose upon the blue
lawns of Long Island together with their scented, shriven parents. All are washed in the Blood of the Lamb. Their parents
have rewon Eden for the sake of the children. The knowing
children, however, have obviously found a disused apple under
the hedge and have swallowed it.

Mr. Lauren's more recent work attempts a less complicated innocence; he has had himself photographed astride a
horse. The *mise en scène* is the American West. According to *W*
magazine, in real life (as we say, allowing for variance), whenever Mr. Lauren wants to escape the mythology business he
repairs to his Double RL Ranch, a 14,000-acre spread outside
Telluride, Colorado. On a meadow within that reserve, he has
constructed a Plains Indian teepee inside which he has placed
genuine Navajo rugs and club chairs from London—"There's
stuff inside there an Indian never dreamed of," as one tickled
ranch hand remarked.

I do not intend to mock Mr. Lauren's Trianon *sauvage*. It
may represent an authentic instinct for survival, like the family-
built nuclear shelters of the 1950s. Leaving all that alone, I
should confess I have not made my own peace with wilderness,
never liking to be more than two miles from restaurants and
theaters. From an air-conditioned car, I often regret suburban
sprawl. Mine is an aesthetic regret. But as a westerner, I approve the human domination of Nature.

I have been to Telluride only once—for the film festival.
But I have often enough visited chic little towns that nestle in
the mountain states of the West. At a weekend wedding in
Idaho most recently, the guests had flown in from Los Angeles
and London. On the Saturday morning, nearly everyone rode
into the foothills on horseback.

I trudged one mile, perhaps two, in the direction of loneliness. A noise stopped me. A crackle or something; a pine cone dropping; a blue jay. I discovered an anxiety the white pioneers could have known in these same woods a century ago. Whose woods these are? Injuns'? Well, I am an Indian, and my shoes were getting scuffed. Snow White and the Seven Militiamen? And then an idea, more unsettling: the forest was empty. I turned and quickly walked back to the lodge, where Ella Fitzgerald's voice flitted through speakers in the eaves of the lobby.

Mr. Lauren, quoted in *W*, speaks in oracular puffs from beneath designer blankets: "I'm just borrowing the land."(. . .)"You can never really own it."(. . .)"It's only yours for a short time."(. . .)The *W* article notes the Double RL Ranch is circumscribed by fifteen miles of white fence.

In nineteenth-century daguerreotypes of the American West, the land is the dropped rind from a transcendently fresh sky. Time is evident; centuries have bleached the landscape. There is no evidence of history except the presence of the camera. The camera is debris; the pristine image "taken" is contamination. The camera can look only backward. Our backward glance is pure and naively fond. To see the future we must look through Ray-Ban darkly.

The Puritan theology of America predisposed pioneers to receive the land as "virgin." The happy providence of God had provided them a new Eden. The gift must have inspired exhilaration as well as terror. Evidence of exhilaration remains. Settlers dammed the waters, leveled mountains, broke their backs to build our regret.

Some neighbor's house in Sacramento, a summer evening. I have come to collect for the newspaper. "Come on in, honey," the wife said through the screen door. "Hold a sec. I've got goop on my hands." I watched as she finished rubbing liniment into her husband's shoulder. She noticed my fascination (though she interpreted it incorrectly), said, "Labors of Hercules," which even as a child I could interpret as meaning she was comically rearming her husband for battle with Nature. Nature meant labor. All he'd been doing was working on the lawn.

An acquaintance in his eighties had pits of cancer dug out of the side of his nose. My friend lamented his disfiguring fate in the present—"I use sunscreen; never go out without a hat." The young doctor's prognosis harkened to a pristine West: "This damage was done a long time ago, when you were a little boy and stayed too long in the sun."

I believe those weathered westerners who tell me over the roar of their air conditioners that the wilderness is no friend. They seem to me to have at least as true a knowledge of the West as the Sierra Club church. A friend, an ex-New Yorker, now a Californian, tells me she was saved from a full-scale panic attack while driving at night through a remote stretch of New Mexico by the sudden appearance of writing in the sky: BEST WESTERN.

Something in the heart of the westerner must glory in the clamor of hammering, the squealing of saws, the rattle of marbles in aerosol cans. Something in the heart of the westerner must yearn for lost wilderness, once wilderness has been routed. That in us which is both most and least human—I mean the soul—cannot live at ease with oblivious nature, nor do we live easily with what we have made. We hate both the world without us and the world we create. So we mythologize. Ralph Lauren has built roads on his ranch, sunk ponds, cleared pastures. "My goal is to keep and preserve the West."

Ralph Lauren's teepee of "commercially farmed buffalo hides" was painted by "a local mountain man" with figures representing Mr. and Mrs. Lauren and their three children.

Such is the rate of change in the West, you end up sounding like some hoary ancient if you recollect the fragrance of almond orchards where the mystic computer chip clicks; if you remember cattle where almond trees now bloom. I meet such middle-aged ancients. The man in Albuquerque has seen his hometown completely changed in forty-two years, even the sky. "They" have altered everything. They, presumably, are his own parents.

Once the shopping center is up and the meadows are

paved over and the fries are under the heat lamp, we park in a slot, take our bearings, and proceed to the Cineplex to watch Pocahontas's hair commune with the Great Conditioner. We feel ourselves very sympathetic with the Indian, a sympathy we extend only to the dead Indian. Necrophilia thrives throughout America, especially in the West, certainly as one approaches the Mexican border, or Borders Books. The *New York Times* best-seller list abounds with pale-face channelers of Cro-Magnon metaphysic—the medium in Sedona, Shirley MacLaine's agented alter ego in Beverly Hills, the *brujo* in the novel of Cormac McCarthy.

That part of me I will always name western first thrilled at the West in VistaVision at the Alhambra Theater in Sacramento, in those last years before the Alhambra was torn down for a Safeway. In the KOOL summer dark, I took the cowboy's side. The odds have shifted. All over the West today Indians have opened casinos where the white man might test the odds.

The dead Indian, Weeping Conscience, has become the patron saint of an environmental movement largely made up of the descendants of the pioneers. More curiously, the dead Indian has come to represent pristine Nature in an argument made by some environmentalists against "overpopulation" (the fact that so many live Indians in Latin America are having so many babies and are moving north).

Another summer day, late in the 1960s, I was driving a delivery truck to a construction site at the edge of suburban Sacramento. Making a sharp turn right, I saw a gray snake keeling upon the watery concrete. I make no apology for the snake. It is no literary device I conjure to make a theological point. It was really there in my path on that hot summer afternoon for the same reason that Wyoming sunsets resemble bad paintings.

I hadn't time enough to swerve or to stop. Bump. Bump. Front wheels; rear wheels. Looking into the rearview mirror, I saw the snake writhing, an intaglio of pain. I drove on.

Eventually I found the lot where I made my delivery. After a few minutes, I returned to my truck, retraced my way out of the maze. Only then did I remember the snake and look for it where I had slain it.

Several construction workers were standing alongside a sandwich truck, drinking sodas. One man, a dark Mexican, shirtless, had draped the snake I killed over his shoulders—an idea that had not yet occurred to Ralph Lauren, who at this time was just beginning to be preoccupied with WASP nostalgia.

I I I

On the afternoon of my fiftieth birthday, I have come to Point Reyes, a promontory from which one can see for miles along the coast of California, north and south. The ocean, seen from this height, is tarpaulin.

Just below the lighthouse warning signs have been posted by the National Park Service. There are photos of nineteenth-century shipwrecks. Cautions to swimmers. Undertow. Sharks. Beware, beware . . .

I descend to the water. Appropriate for an aging man to turn up his collar, roll his cuffs, and play at the edge. The ocean, as it should be, is young—unraveling and then snatching back its grays and pinks, celadons, and the occasional bonny blue. The relentless flirtation of it loses charm. One begins to imagine pagodas and lanterns, gardens of spices that lie beyond.

Adam and Eve were driven by the Angel of the Fiery Sword to a land east of Eden, there to assume the burden of time, which is work and death. All photosynthetic beings on earth live in thrall to the movement of the sun, from east to west. Most babies are born in the early morning; most old people die at sunset, at least in novels of large theme. We know our chariot sun is only one of many such hissing baubles juggled about, according to immutable laws. So much for immutable laws.

So much for mutability, for that matter. I have just had my face peeled. I go to the gym daily. I run. I swallow fistfuls of vitamin pills. I resort to scruffing lotions and toners. Anywhere else in the world I could pass for what-would-you-say. In California I look fifty.

Besides. The older I become, the farther I feel myself from death. It is the young who are dying. I remain unreconciled to the logic of an alleged nature. I am unnatural. As a boy I read Richard Henry Dana's *Two Years Before the Mast.* What I remember was the furious storm as the ship tossed about the Horn, all Nature pitched against us. My Dana was not the Dana whom D. H. Lawrence mocked for returning to Boston, to Harvard, to a clerk's position, a clerk's hearth, a clerk's fizzing kettle. My Dana was a white-throated, red-lipped romantic who sailed away.

Around the rock where I am sitting now, seabirds gather to rotate their silly heads; zoom unblinking lenses toward my fists, patient for manna. It is the last day of July, the feast of St. Ignatius. The wind is picking up and the waves come pounding in from the gray towers of Asia.

Imagine how California must have appeared to the first Europeans—the Spaniards, the English, the Russians—who saw the writing of the continent in reverse, from the perspective of Asia, adjusting the view of California through a glass, silent and as predatory as these birds.

By the time he returned to the East Coast, Dana was about the same age I was when I moved to Los Angeles. I was determined to throw off all clerkishness. Twenty-five years ago in L.A., one could sense anxiety over some coming "change" of history. Rereading Dana, I am struck by the obvious. Dana saw California as an extension of Latin America. Santa Barbara, Monterey, San Francisco—these were Mexican ports of call. Dana would not be surprised, I think, to find Los Angeles today a Third World capital teeming with Aztecs and Mayans. He would not be surprised to see that California has become what it already was in the 1830s.

From its American occupation, Los Angeles took its reflection from the sea rather than the desert; imagined itself a Riviera. Knowledge of the desert would have been akin to a confession of Original Sin—land connection to Mexico was a connection to a culture of death. In the 1960s, overcrowded Los Angeles attempted to preserve its optimism as Orange County. Ten years later, Orange County was running out of Protestant lawns for sale. Only desert remained—Riverside and San Bernardino counties.

More than aridity, California fears fecundity. Perhaps as early as the 1950s film *Invasion of the Body Snatchers*, nightmare images of pregnant pods and displacing aliens converge. Fecundity is death. (To manufacture life is to proliferate death.) Who's going to pay for fecundity? The question reminds us of scarcity, for we live at the edge of the sea. What is scarce is water. Metaphors Californians now summon to describe their fear of the South are, appropriately, fluid. Waves of people. Tides of immigrants. Floods of illegals. Sand, the primordial image of barrenness, uncivilization, becomes an image of unchecked fertility.

William tells me—he's a movie guy—in a smoke-free, vegan cantina (high-ho, Silicon), that cowboy movies will shortly make a comeback—"big time." The busboy, an Indian, approaches our table balancing two possible futures: "Regular or decaf?"

In the 1970s, decorators in Beverly Hills urged their clients toward realism: an aesthetic cooperation with the desert. Floorboards can be bleached, windows uncovered. The difference of L.A. is winter light. No chintz, no wrought-iron chaise, no snuggery. Sand, creams, taupes, apricots. Californians welcomed cactus into their houses even as Mexicans were pushing their dusty heads under the cyclone fence. The desert decor became a way, I suppose, of transforming the troubling future into something Californians might be able to live with.

It occurs to me that the admission of Alaska and Hawaii into the union further undermined the myth of the West by destroying the symmetry of the map. What happens to the notion of sovereignty when you have states outside the border? Heretofore, the United States was a literal description.

Watch. In tonight's weather report, the United States of

America is letter-box formatted to exclude Canada and Mexico. America is conceived by Americans longitudinally, excluding North and South. There is no weather in Guadalajara. There is no weather today in Montreal. Alaska is an isle of Lapanto hovering above the continent. Hawaii is a sidebar, somewhere to the left of the Arizona desert. Both states seem to be held in reserve—Alaska for the future, Hawaii for a blue Christmas.

One Sunday in December 1941, Hawaii became the point on the map most Americans would thereafter remember as our vulnerability to Asia. After the war, Hawaii became our boast: the Pacific is ours. But the reverse would also become true. We had waded out too far, we had been lured into complicated Asian waters.

We have always resisted the Asian prospect. Coolie labor built much of the American West in the nineteenth century. Nevertheless, the Asian was persecuted by California for coming at the continent from the fishy side. Celestials, we called them, had a devilish language of crossed sticks and broken banjo strings. The custody they exercised over their eyes implied they had discovered evil here but were keeping the knowledge to themselves. Inscrutable, we said at the time. Now we say Asians work inhumanly hard.

"Asians work too hard," says a friend of mine who has been towing a boat behind him for years. Asians are America's fastest-growing minority. Hispanics will soon be California's majority. Everyone knows Mexicans are fat mañanamen (even Karl Marx thought it better that the United States took California, because Americans would make more of it). But now it's Hawaiian-shirt time for America's Can-do-know-how-thumbs-up-Charlie-jig-jig of World War II fame. José Manuel Santo de Dios takes over the maintenance of the California landscape. When he's not washing dishes. Or flipping hotcakes. And Mae Wah Wong exemplifies work habits we used to approve as northern European. José What's-His-Name is up at dawn and drives a hundred miles to work. Mae's hundred and seven grandchildren have taken all the slots at Berkeley, the Athens of the West. Western canon go boom-boom.

Shots not heard in Hawaii. I think Karl Marx was not thinking of Keanu Reeves, but it was Marx, scribbling away through the winter of the British Museum, who believed the California Gold Rush was a more significant event than the discovery of the Americas by Columbus. After the Gold Rush, the Pacific would replace the Atlantic as the economic theater of the world. San Francisco is only now becoming the first mainland Honolulu, a breeding ground for Asian-Caucasian mixtures, with the additional complexity of Africa and Latin America. California's is one of the richest economies in the world. Marx would be interested.

The United States never had a true North until now. The American Civil War divided the nation; impressed upon the Union the distinctiveness of the regional South. But the North was never more than a political idea and a recipe for clam chowder. Economics prompted diplomats to sign the North American Free Trade Agreement. For the United States, NAFTA represents a revolutionary recalibration to north and south.

Mexico and Canada, so different from each other, are similarly north/south countries—neither has a myth of the West. In Canada, the North represents continuity, the unchanging character of the nation. Canadians, in autumn, still speak of the approaching North, relishing in that phrase the renewal of isolation. Whereas the Canadian South is little distinct from the United States. Mexico is the same in reverse: in Mexico, the great stone civilizations weighed upon the South. The North was a province of nomads and revolutionaries and, later, American confluence.

Coming upon the continent from the Atlantic, English Protestants imagined the land as prehistoric; themselves cast onto Eden. The Indian they named Savage rather than Innocent. The Atlantic myth of wilderness worked so powerfully on the first American imagination that future generations retained an assumption of innocence—a remarkably resilient psychic cherry. Every generation of Americans since has had to reenact the loss of its innocence. Vietnam was the loss of our innocence. Gettysburg was the loss of our innocence. Oklahoma City was the loss of our innocence. Ingrid Bergman's out-of-wedlock baby. Watergate. World War II. Other countries take cynicism with mothers' milk. America has preferred the child's game of "discovering" evil—Europe's or Asia's or her own or grandfather's. (Every generation of Americans likes to imagine that the generation preceding lived in the 1950s and that its own decade, the 1960s, is post-lapsarian.)

The east-west dialectic in American history was the story of man's license to dominate Nature. Railroad tracks binding the continent are vestigial stitches of the smoke-belching Judeo-Christian engine, Primacy o' Man. Having achieved the Pacific Coast, settlers could turn to regret the loss of Nature. (Though eastern America once named itself New Eden—New England, New York, New Canaan, New Bedford, new everything—in the California gazetteer there is nothing new.)

Twice a year, along the Pacific coast, people gather to watch the great migration of whales, north to south, south to north. The route of the whale has great allure for postmodern Californians because it is prehistoric, therefore antihistorical. The Pacific totem pole might be an emblem for a New Age, marking the primacy of Nature over man—a new animistic north-south dialectic that follows a biological, solstitial, rather than an historical imperative.

The old east-west dialectic moved between city and country, the settled and the unsettled. The plaid-suited city slicker disembarked at the western terminus of the nineteenth century to find himself an innocent amidst the etiolated foliage, the brighter light, the conversations in Spanish. Today's children of the suburbs hitch between tundra and desert, Idaho and Baja, cold and hot—versions of wilderness beyond which unpolluted Nature lies or oblivion or God.

The liturgy of the Mass still gathers a people "from age to age . . . so that from east to west a perfect offering may be made." But the future of Christianity attaches to a new, ecliptic north-south axis. Africa embraces the Catholicism disused by secular Europe; U.S. Protestantism has cajoled the penitential

Latin American centuries to tambourines. Or consider America's cowboy religion: Mormons followed prophecy from east to west, away from persecution, into the desert. By 2012, the Mormon majority will be Spanish-speaking. Meanwhile, Native-American animism (Father Whale, Mother Panda) thrives among the great-grandchildren of American pioneers. The sole orthodoxy permitted in our public schools is the separation of paper from plastic.

In something like the way the East Coast invented the West, California today is inventing a rectified North. From the perspective of California, Oregon is a northern state and Seattle is a northern city. Vancouver becomes a part of the continuum without regard to international borders. Several states now seem to cluster under the white belly of Alaska: Washington, Idaho, northern sections of Utah and Colorado, Wyoming, Oregon, and Montana, famous for secessionists.

I believe the journey to Alaska is a death wish, insofar as it is a wish to escape civilization rather than extend it. In the late 1950s (at the same time that California became the most populous state), Alaska became the horizon—an albino hope, a gray-rolled cumulus, a glacial obsession—like Melville's great whale. Alaska absorbed all the nouns that lay bleaching along the Oregon Trail. Solitude. Vacancy. Wilderness. Alaska became the destination for the footloose and the loner and the seeker of silence. Americans decided Alaska would be governed as a pagan reserve—Nature sacrosanct.

Wisdom and a necessary humility inform the environmental movement, but there is an arrogant self-hatred too: the idea that we can create landscapes vacant of human will when, in fact, protection is human intrusion. The ultimate domestication of Nature is the modern ability to say of Nature: Rage on here, but not elsewhere.

Seattle rises as the capital of the new North, as Los Angeles is abandoned to the Third World. Seattle is proudest of its internationalism—Boeing, Microsoft. But for many Californians, Seattle offers a refuge from cosmopolitanism. Those who abandon L.A. for Seattle abandon civilization for civility, perhaps for one of those sanitary, bright book-cafés where fed-up white people can sit alone, savoring the black bitter draughts of the South: Mexico, Colombia, Sumatra.

From the perspective of Mexico City, Los Angeles is a pale, comic city. From the perspective of Seattle, paint-peeling Los Angeles is the tragic antipode of the coast. L.A. assumes most of California, large portions of Texas, Nevada, the bottom halves of Utah and Colorado, all of New Mexico, Arizona, and stray Dade County, Florida.

I live within the precinct of Los Angeles, I suppose. Although it's true I drink bottled water, I am connected to the South, to desert, to death. True as well that as a citizen of this coast, I feel my future more closely aligned to British Columbia than to Massachusetts. I have become accustomed to the odd orientation within a nexus that occurs at the end of any epic historical route or at the beginning. The most important highway in California is Interstate 5, the northern route, connecting desire and fear. The skinhead crosses into Oregon to get away from the Guatemalan who is heading for California. America begins overhead: that jet is coming in from Asia. America comes to an end here.

See how the metaphor of the West dissolves into foam at my feet.

Pascal Bruckner

The Edge of Babel

In his autobiography, *Conclusive Evidence,* Vladimir Nabokov recounts that when he was at Cambridge from 1919 to 1922, after the Bolshevik Revolution, he was surprised to unexpectedly come upon "a Russian work, a second-hand copy of *Dahl's Interpretative Dictionary of the Living Russian Language.* I bought it and resolved to read at least ten pages per day, jotting down such colorful words and expressions as might especially please me, and I kept this up for a considerable time. My fear of losing or corrupting, through alien influence, the only thing I had salvaged from Russia—her language—became positively morbid."

Today, such concern for his lost country, his small linguistic heritage, would earn Nabokov charges of "regressive identification" or "fastidious timidity" as our age, more than any other, values multiplicity and openness as extremely progressive traits. In fact, rumor has it that a titanic battle is being waged by two camps as allergic to each other as capitalism and communism are. On the one side is the nationalist and xenophobic camp, clinging to its heritage like Molière's Harpagon to his treasure chest; on the other, the cosmopolitan camp, starving for otherness, curious about everything, anxious to exchange constricting nationalism for a roomier garment. The former, barricaded within their Frenchness (or Germanness) are depicted as resentful, doddering, and provincial. The latter are said to exude the aura of open spaces, youth, and hope. On the one side, the ugly contractions of fear and stinginess; on the other, the beauty of friendship and audacity. These alternatives surely exist, but must we accept them in such a narrow, simplistic version? Are we really condemned either to remain imprisoned in our birthplaces or to immerse ourselves in the many-hued multitude of cultures? Must we respond to this commandment that appears to be an inescapable obligation?

Cosmopolitanism constitutes *a priori* an eminently desirable value for no other reason than the attacks it has suffered from Fascists and Stalinists. Cosmopolitanism was once the privilege of European aristocracy and the bourgeoisie's children, then the curse of minorities routed by the war, exterminated through persecution and the Holocaust. Now, according to its adherents, cosmopolitanism is becoming our common condition. A new man is being born: no longer the isolated man of former times, cloistered upon his patch of earth, he is both bound and mobile, the sum of all preceding wisdom, an individual without borders, as adaptable to many-tentacled megalopolises as to interplanetary travel, and thus armed against any regression to chauvinism. This multinational citizen, ideally above the fray and able to integrate a wide spectrum of perspectives, would eliminate the recourse to arms with his universal understanding. This proposition does not lack grandeur and recalls the most elevated principles of the eighteenth century. Humanity is but one family, temporarily divided by ignorance and absurd prejudices. If all are properly instructed, peace will reign. Furthermore, this all conforms to the preamble of the convention which created UNESCO on November 16, 1945. "Wars are created in man's spirit. It is in man's spirit that the defenses of peace must be forged."

Here we see the reconciliation of two formerly hostile families: the "third-worlder" left and the anti-authoritarian left.

In the name of anti-colonialism, the "third-worlders" deny the West the right to elevate itself as the dominant culture. They recall the West to modesty, reminding it that its achievements are relative, and they force it to open itself up to those worlds it so unjustly oppressed. In the name of Europe and the end of East-West divisions, and in the name of the ecological solidarity that transcends all the continents, the anti-totalitarian left pleads for the dismantling of all barriers and for uniting all nations in a vast conglomerate. "In Europe today," writes Edgar Morin, for example, "the processes of dissociation and disintegration have joined in a race with those of association and integration." The attitude Morin adopts, again, is not a new one. It recalls the moralizing pacifism of certain Romantics. "Nation! A pompous word for saying barbarity," Lamartine had written as early as 1841. "Egoism and hatred have only one fatherland; fraternity has none . . . Every man is bred in the climate of his own intelligence; I am a citizen of any soul that thinks." All secession is, therefore, *a priori* negative because it disrupts the chain of events that is to bind all countries and prevent any risk of conflict. Furthermore, our century, unlike the preceding one, has experienced the horror of nationalism to the point of nausea. In short, after having been free because of nations, now we must be free in spite of them. "Be my brother, or I will kill you," said Rivarol in a variation on a formula in the spirit of the Terror. You must all be brothers, or you will be disqualified, proclaims the new doctrine of cosmopolitanism. Only those peoples anxious to join in a greater union would be worthy of humanity. The others, anxious to assert their uniqueness, to cut themselves off, would merit only the label of savages, of tribes. The future takes on the aspect of a terrible ultimatum: "Association or barbarity!" declares Morin. This very reasoning has enabled us to remain insensitive for so long to the suffering of the Croats and Bosnians in the Yugoslavian crisis. Of course, they were victims of aggression, but fundamentally, they were guilty of wanting to secede from the federation. (The Bosnians had the advantage of belonging to a multinational state.) By banishing them from the human race, we no longer had to feel compassion for their misery. We grouped the victims together with the henchmen.

One would like to applaud enthusiastically that common altruism that intends to overcome Eurocentric as well as local stereotypes and superstition through benevolence and instruction. Whatever sympathy or agreement it may inspire in us, it nonetheless seems problematic in more than one way, especially when it betrays, alters, or disfigures the original spirit of cosmopolitanism. First, taking up again an illusion appropriate to illumination, two realms are always confused in this kind of reflection: the ethical and the aesthetic. In the arts, where borrowing, plagiarism, and combinations form the source of creative richness, desirable syntheses occur that are impossible to translate into daily life. We cannot profit from another civilization's customs and habits without renouncing our own to a greater or lesser extent, unless we consider being cosmopolitan simply to mean eating couscous, tacos, fried rice, wearing Chinese silk, listening to Oriental music, or dying one's hair with henna. Yet certainly no single book, painting, or musical work carries in itself a particular moral imperative. The belief, for example, that the "spirit of the novel," in other words, "the playful subversion of dogma and orthodoxy," act as a critical conscience, unmooring us from our identifying impulses, depends on a very generous but unverifiable perspective. Even if the novel, as Milan Kundera well understood, is the democratic genre par excellence, one that presumes tolerance and conflicting points of view, there is no obligatory passage from the work to daily life. I can forget my prejudices while reading and enter the universe of a Chinese or South American author. I may feel myself on an equal footing with another era or other customs. Yet that will not alter my degree of open-mindedness once I abandon that literary space. Skeptical, ironic while reading, temporarily liberated from thousands of ties to my community, I become once again sectarian, partial, recaptured as soon as I return to my century and confront my peers. Works of art in themselves are profoundly amoral and are thus unable to eradicate humanity's barbaric foundation. In our naiveté, we believe that talent, intelligence, and sensitivity are inseparable from higher values, that they nourish and elevate us. But there is no link between genius, liberty, and justice. Obscurantist epochs have given rise to sublime works; tolerant epochs have proven arid. Even abject masterpieces (Sade, Céline) are nonetheless important inquiries into the human spirit.

Or, to express it more brutally still: we do not like the peoples of the Middle East simply because we read the Koran or "A Thousand and One Nights," just as reading Pushkin or Gogol has not brought us any closer to the Russians. We do not care for immigrants because we dance to Algerian raï music, any more than the young who dance to music with an African beat are freed from racist views concerning these same Africans when they meet in the street or must live with them. In addition, what we appreciate in Garcia Marquez or Tanizaki is not Colombia or Japan, but the particularities of a fate or a village able to elevate itself to the universal. What is a great novel? A bellringer's quarrel, an intimate adventure that grips the entire world. Worse still: the war in the former Yugoslavia has been prepared and is sustained by writers, novelists—Dobrica Cosic, the principal architect of Serbian nationalism, Milorad Pavic, Vuk Draskovic (who has since courageously joined the opposition)—and especially poets of whom the most famous, Radovan Karadjic, is a notorious war criminal. In present day Serbia, murderers versify, hatred is borne upon the wings of epic poetry, literature is put directly in the service of ethnic cleansing. We must abandon the idea that the cultural world with its successes and beauties can serve as a criterion or guide for the statesman or the moralist. Neither the most moving collection of poetry nor the sweetest music can offer any ethical truism, any gauge of just or unjust behavior. For a long time now, the true, the beautiful, and the good have parted ways.

There are things more serious still. We can ask if this indiscriminate eulogy of multiplicity does not conflate *cosmopolitanism* with *universalism*. Because of the "intertwining of all peoples in the web of the world market" (Karl Marx) because of the internationalization of merchandise and the media—which potentially brings all people into contact at all points on the globe—universalism is certainly the *vade mecum* of the new planetary world. It forms that universal sub-culture intended to replace all others, that mish-mash based on fast food, uniformity of clothing, television series, and muzak that claims to place all men under the same yoke, whether in Los Angeles, Caracas, Bombay, or Lagos! In this sense, Disneyworld and its miniature reconstructions of all the eras, mythologies, and cultures—albeit faded and toothless—is the epitome of universalism: a staging at once ridiculous and fantastic of universal brotherhood, of sweet human harmony. And even if world music is merely a pirating and recycling of all the rhythms of the planet geared towards consumption, it is in the midst of the theme park that Africa, Asia, Europe, the Wild West, the twentieth century and the future can coexist amicably under the banner of the new pidgin English, an impoverished language, a jargon for illiterate humanity. Yet universalism is nothing if not cosmopolitan. It can engulf, classify, and digest everything, because it destroys cultures by disemboweling and dismembering them, only to reconstitute them, embalmed like mummies in their tombs, destroying both their singularity and their complexity. It is a vacuum that swallows rituals, folklore, and legends as if Hollywood or Disney were the culmination of all the histories on this planet. Several years ago, Ted Turner, the head of CNN, decided to eliminate the word "foreign" completely, substituting "international" instead. He had one economic and strategic goal: to prevent CNN from appearing too American and make it appear a reflection the world would see in its own mirror. But this choice is also symptomatic: like Chaplin's dictator, playing with the globe like a child with his ball, each spectator is invited to consider the world a single village in which all residents are as familiar to him as the neighbors in his apartment building. And yet, this denial of differences between peoples and continents is universalism's pitfall, a fear of totality, whereas cosmopolitanism is a thirst for plurality.

When Juan Goytisolo writes, "A culture is most alive when its openness towards and hunger for otherness is greatest," he is probably equating all civilizations because they are fundamentally all the same to him. Contrary to our belief that we are crossing boundaries and bringing hostile countries together in vast syntheses, we are actually just falling into an abyss as long as there is no pain of apprenticeship, no sense of estrangement. Proximity eliminates the other by creating the illusion that we have access to it. "Speed destroys color. When the gyroscope spins rapidly, everything turns gray," wrote Paul Morand in 1937.

Is not tourism universalism's saddest image, even if inevitable: the spectacle of those glutinous mobs milling around the Louvre, Versailles, the Acropolis, the pyramids, the Prado, all alike in their differences, a polyglot series of crowds, sharing the same polished boredom with works of art? We can certainly always dream of unifying humanity from the bottom up, confiscating possessions, erasing myths and fables, if that is the price of peace. In the name of harmony and security, we can wish to eradicate the aristocracy (and the danger) of great civilizations, pushing all men into the common mold of disenchantment, impoverishing but taming man, rendering him uniform at all latitudes of the globe. Yet this reduction to the lowest common denominator is not even certain. Traditions and beliefs that have been crushed or denied can resurface even more impetuously when they have been lost and reconstructed artificially as incoherent monsters and hybrids. (Several countries of Eastern Europe, forced into amnesia and atheism by a half-century of Communism, are a tragic example of this.) Furthermore, we know that Fascism, like Integrationism, in no way represents a mad love of traditions and sacred texts endangered by modernity, but represents instead their ideological falsification and, in a certain sense, their destruction. Hegel had already highlighted the Enlightment platitude of the critical spirit that rejects faith, religion, and superstition but ends by lamenting "the loss of its spiritual world." Modern universalism denies cultural differences in the name of the impoverished universal of entertainment and consumption. That is why it fails to reconcile men. The friendship it postulates is as tepid as it is superficial.

Bringing McDonald's to Moscow or Teheran will never make ardent democrats of the Russians or the Iranians. Diversions alone will never eliminate Babel. There is always a dark side to Mickey Mouse's smile. [. . .]

True cosmopolitanism, in contrast to the stew of Babel, is rooted in the depths of several layers of memory, in numerous particularities. It does not indulge in flying over all the world's summits, its seas, and its elevations. It does not collect traits here and there. It becomes incarnate. Liberating oneself from one's roots, separating oneself from all one is near to join the foreign, does not mean floating freely like an atom, but means claiming additional possessions. It means counterbalancing the land of one's birth with additional homelands. That is why cosmopolitanism involves suffering. It is a trial that superior beings choose, finding joy and strength in overcoming habitual limits that seem absolutes common to all mortals. Consider Elias Canetti, a Sephardic Jew born in Bulgaria into a family which addressed its children in Spanish, who learned German, his parents' language, under his mother's harsh discipline. In teaching him, she found no hurdle too high and no humiliation too great, to her young son's initial despair and subsequent enchantment. "There was no question of abandoning other languages at the time. My mother believed that culture was the literatures of all the languages she knew. But German became the language of our love—and how exclusive it was!" Consider Nabokov and his account of the pain he experienced after 1940 when he adopted English as the language of his writing. "By changing my language, I did not renounce the language of Avvakum, Pushkin, and Tolstoy . . . in other words, I did not abandon a common language, but a vital and individual idiom. I had long been used to expressing myself as I wished and was not satisfied with the clichés of my adopted tongue. Thus the monstrous difficulties of this reincarnation and the horror of having to part with a living, docile being, initially plunged me into a state I need not describe. I will simply state that no writer of any stature experienced it before I did." As a more recent example, the Hungarian writer, Agota Kristof, living in

Switzerland and writing in French, constantly mentions the very great difficulty she has in using that language. In short, one is not born cosmopolitan, but becomes so in an act of unlimited devotion and respect and by taking on an endless debt to a foreign reality. The elation of playing in several keys, on several keyboards requires the incorporation of another world's structure, a modest and thankless apprenticeship to a foreign culture with its formidable opaqueness. Knowledge ennobles only to the degree that the measures taken to acquire it were excessive. If all normal education is an act of violence on a child, destroying his innocence and all gentle comforts in order to establish him in the realm of the word, then a cosmopolitan education is destruction to the nth degree, a very dearly paid access to a superior liberty. Moving from one civilization to another is a mutation, a metamorphosis that requires work and suffering and has nothing to do with a jet's painless connecting of all points on the planet. That is why those without homelands constitute the nobility and antennae of the spirit; men of crossroads, straddling borders, they possess an acuity normal men lack. They perceive things that common men cannot see. As outsiders they possess greater insight and are more unsettled. They reveal the essential, disrupt certitudes, and disclose the secrets of closed societies. They have had the courage to leave behind the comfort of a single family, of a single place in search of beauty in other parts of the world. They are condemned to remain exceptions (but necessary exceptions: the disappearance of Jewish communities in Central and Eastern Europe, aside from Hungary, is a spiritual catastrophe without precedent). What is Vienna without Jews? A swollen head atop a tiny body, a museum-city without substance, a mausoleum lacking both spirit and taste. It is impossible, unthinkable to turn cosmopolitanism into a right similar to health or housing by democratizing it. Even if there are a thousand forms, a thousand degrees, a thousand nuances, it will always remain the exclusive realm of a small number.

Transplanting oneself to a foreign culture always entails discomfort because each people possesses its particular individuality, even if only through a language which is not immediately translatable into another, and because dark regions that cannot be illuminated exist between countries. (Consider simply the divisions between Catholic Europe and Protestant Europe.) Exoticism as well as racism will persist even into the most ideal future as they cannot be eliminated without destroying what creates them: the strangeness of the other. If each culture is an absolute unto itself, all cultures are not complementary but supplementary. They surpass and cover up each other like jungle vines. The universe is hostile because I do not know it all and allergies are born of diversity. War, incomprehension, suspicion are not first and foremost the fruits of man's wickedness, but come from witnessing the many expressions of being that cause fear and panic. Relations with the foreign are an indissoluble mix of attraction and repulsion. If uprootedness and the loss of domestic security were not a painful asceticism, migration would simply be a matter of traveling throughout the universe as blood circulates in our veins. In short, there will always be others: the division of races, languages, and beliefs will always prevent the fulfilling of the dream of perfect communication and understanding within humanity. Whatever my digestive capacity or the size of my heart, I will never overcome the distance to one who draws near, one who is neither as near nor as far as one might believe. Therefore, except for God or Sirius, there is no global perspective that can encompass all others, a superior position from which all essences of the North and the South, the East and the West, can be apprehended. We must abandon the Renaissance's cherished dream of universal man and settle for the more modest ideal of accomplished man, always partially realized, always unfinished.

In contrast to this planet-wide tourism that embraces everything but adopts nothing, cosmopolitanism presumes, as its first condition, a knowledge of one's own national culture. To approach others implies, then, the possession of a homeland and a memory that must be cultivated (even if they are made relative). I can only offer hospitality to a stranger if I have a certain ground to which I can welcome him. Those who claim to come from nowhere, dispensing with customs and legacies, are often content merely to reproduce their worst aspects and are but pawns. In order to liberate oneself from the past, one must first study it and enter into a discriminating relationship of acceptance and rejection. Yesterday, one's heritage was straightforward and self-evident; today it is at best a changing and equivocal injunction for which we must fumble in the dark. We cannot choose our roots, but, once we have assimilated them, we do choose to accept or reject these roots and to abandon some in order to adopt others. We use them as a ground from which we can launch ourselves elsewhere. What is individualism itself but *the traditional rejection of tradition*, and thus a history, a depth to plumb?

In general we understand cosmopolitanism in the extended, spatial sense of the term. Why not also consider it in a temporal sense as a conversation with the great dead, creating with them that ideal, mobile society that is the republic of the spirit? If it is true that we are never at home in the past and that previous centuries are foreign continents, it is important that we resuscitate our dead "who are perhaps still living," (Dostoevsky) in order to replenish ourselves through contact with them and to irrigate the mausoleum of culture with new blood. In this sense, reading, studying, and meditating upon the classics is a source of truth and authenticity in understanding other traditions. To paraphrase Malebranche, the relentless interrogation of the past is the piety of the moderns, because the past is no longer self-evident. Dialogue with the past liberates us from its weight and from the tyranny of the present, offering us beautiful escapes into spaces in which we can breathe freely.

The obligation to persevere as oneself is as important as the obligation to openness. One is thus most susceptible to a cosmopolitanism that is embedded in one particular land and one particular language to serve as spring-boards towards others. Without a mother-tongue, a familiar landscape, or a tradition that "intertwines all that is transient" (Hegel) and that ties one to others, one can easily embrace any religion or custom in order to free oneself from all others, simply because no single one is essential (reducing oneself to a chameleon). A critical attachment to one's own nation must be celebrated, but it must not lack either an ability to examine or to love. One without the other would relegate us to exclusive preference or to useless blame. "If a Christian told me he wanted to convert to Hinduism because of his enthusiasm for the *Bhagavad Gita*, I would respond, 'The Bible has as much to offer as the Gita. But you have not really tried to discover it. Make this effort and be fully Christian.'" (Gandhi) Fitting oneself in the mould of another world, seeing oneself with the eyes of others, can also prove a detour in the return to the self. How many men, like Massignon, have been reconverted to Europe and the Christian faith after passing through Islamic lands? How many intermediaries between East and West have paid with a lifetime of work for immersing themselves into a foreign culture to the point of becoming sons of a double culture with all the accompanying risks and marvels? Ignorance of one's own history is the best way to remain ignorant of other histories. (In our time of amnesia and illiteracy, possessing even one cultural tradition seems an immense achievement to the majority.) How could a Frenchman, a German, an Englishman even begin to understand the currents within Islam or the metaphysical constructs of Asia if they are not familiar with their own religious heritage, whether or not they believe?

There is no need to be ashamed of one's rootedness, which is a means of liberation as well as a singularity, and a return to one's roots need not imply timidity, but could instead arise from reflection or a search for greater depth. Every border is not obsolete if it ensures the preservation of a people's integrity and cultural or linguistic treasures. Contrary to the widespread cliché, it was not a religious veneration of borders, but their very mutability that was the true tragedy for many populations, especially those of Eastern Europe, overrun and redrawn with each war and invasion. The great appeal of borders, once they are recognized and maintained, is that they can be crossed. Playing on their margins is more exciting than doing away with them altogether. Only conquerors dream of erasing borders, especially those of other countries! Against every Nabokov who chooses to write in English and in Russian, why not oppose a Roland Barthes who refused to learn any foreign language for fear that it would contaminate his work as a writer? Every life of the spirit is also cultivated upon the deliberate neglect of other spiritual possibilities. He who wishes to try everything, to raise himself up to universal heights, and chooses nothing so as not to sacrifice anything, condemns himself to distraction and ultimately to sterility. We must then reevaluate the difficulties, the blinders, the dissimulations, the many tricks with which a culture protects itself from a consuming indiscretion. Is not Europe's particular beauty a result of the way it has carved out on such small ground so many varied ways of life, all of them fragile and unique? Must we pronounce them outmoded and obsolete in the name of the universal? Must we disdain *a priori* the small legacies and solidarities and ridicule customs and local habits?

Aside from a few rare exceptions, traditional cultures were closed. There were no fissures or interstices through which doubt could penetrate. The outside always evoked a sense of menace, heresy, or evil. Each society was convinced that it embodied human excellence and rejected others as barbaric or animalistic. Such self-sufficiency is no longer possible. Humanity's sheer variety prevents us from living in the land of our birth as if it had been revealed the promised land once and for all. We have lost our national innocence and none of our traditions can claim to embody the unique and exclusive truth. Identity is always mobile and impure in a universe that is itself divided between several centers and not even the greatest power is complete or perfect. There is, to be sure, the silliness of small countries caught up in the "misery of their territorial disputes," (Istvan Bibo), their petty linguistic quarrels, their chauvinism, and their megalomania. It is also true that the abjectness of a particular ethnical nationalism, like that which rules today in Algeria and Serbia, need no longer be proven and that separatist viruses which crumble nations into micro-states are eminently problematic. It is possible that the nation-state is a transient reality and that post-national identities will compose humanity's face in the future.

At the moment, and especially for those of us in the West who operate in the gap between states that have lost their prerogatives and a political Europe that has not yet been realized, we still exercise our collective liberty through nations and consider ourselves their citizens. That is, we feel we share in their power. Nations are both indispensable and insurmountable because they not only transmit memory, favoring passions and fervor, but they also form the ideal framework in which a collective can influence its fate. We are never citizens of the world, but always of a particular nation that protects our rights and proscribes our obligations. There is nothing more ridiculous than the idea of a "terrestrial citizenship." (Compared to Martians, Moon-men, or the unlikely inhabitant of other galaxies?) It is on this very principle that Hannah Arendt had pushed for the existence of the State of Israel—a state in which all Jews could escape the status of refugees or exiles and finally enjoy the citizen's privilege of "the right to have rights." Such is the nation: that singular group through which one gains access to the universal, a contract between individuals within the context of a general spirit, itself inherited from common traditions. Suddenly diluting the nation in a greater environment will not lead to globalism, but will encourage local, regional, and tribal regression. (This gives rise to the dialectic between the satellite and the bell-tower that regulates our contact with the outside world, as the thirst for access to a global dimension is inseparable from the fear of disappearing into the immense.) And when nations decide to unite, as did the European Community, it is as sovereigns that they decide to resign all or part of their sovereignty. Until we find other forms of federal or confederate government, the best we can hope for in this realm—and this is the miracle of Franco-Germanic reconciliation since 1945—are laws regulating the peaceful co-existence of states. We cannot expect different peoples to love or to meld passionately with one another. We cannot demand that communities actively participate in their own dissolution. Europeans, exhausted by their divisions and secular resentments, no longer detest one another, but they do not love one another either.

In the former Soviet Union, learning the Russian language was compulsory for all children, whether Polish, Czech, Armenian, or Turkistanian. This law was not considered an enriching one, but a violation of liberty. We must thus distinguish the *optional cosmopolitanism* of free countries from the *forced cosmopolitanism* of countries subjugated to an empire or a federation. Can we not agree that in certain cases, the separation of peoples through disputes is preferable to their forced unity and that an internationalism founded upon fictional friendship can give rise to the worst tension (thus accentuating the balkanization it was meant to prevent)? No matter how well-intentioned, the slogan, "association or barbarity" remains idealistic in principle and schematic in implementation. Beware of unions' fetishism for union's sake which has been the alibi of all invaders starving for new territory. Union is superior to division only in so far as its benefits outweigh the disadvantages of isolation. Nonetheless, alliance presupposes a democratic and overwhelming agreement of the parties in question, an equilibrium of force, prudent integration, and above all, the possibility of divorce, as in any adult marriage. A forced nuptial is worse than celibacy: numerous solitudes are better than imprisoned peoples. Europe does not lack the ability to "associate," but the spiritual strength and the will to tear the countries of Central and Eastern Europe away from their ethnical tropisms (reflex reactions), their vengeful ruminations, and especially from the enviousness of their Russian older brother. Why have Slovenia, Croatia, Bosnia, and Macedonia abandoned "Serboslavia"? Not in order to turn inward, but to enter the Community, to breathe at last the air of larger spaces. And what did Europe do? It slammed the door in their faces in utter disdain for populations without strategic or economic interests. Idolatry of the many, of unification, of multinationalism is the screen behind which a less glorious reality is hidden. At the moment, Western Europe is nothing but an exclusive club of the wealthy, anxious to maintain order rather than achieve justice and who, in confirmation of the newly freed peoples' greatest fears, wish to return them to the bosom of Moscow or Serbia, replunging them into servitude, wanting them only to behave.

Preferable to the double dogmatism of openness and exclusion is a degree of porousness. Because the state of the world prevents any one society from permanently isolating itself, porousness would establish the proper balance between closemindedness and curiosity which engenders creative shocks and fascinating dissonances. The only way to avoid the double trap of chauvinistic pestilence and dissolution is perhaps through a kind of *paradoxical patriotism*—a patriotism that asks us not to renounce our country for the sake of our devotion to Europe, a patriotism that requires each of us both to cherish the best of the past and to consider the most interesting foreign achievements. It would be, finally, a patriotism of well-tempered modesty that could recognize the relative importance of each country without succumbing to humiliation or devaluation.

Instead of opposing a virginal and innocent Europe to ancient countries laden with crimes, we must consider them in a relation of tension, of unified opposition. Cosmopolitanism must counteract a narrow national sentiment without suppressing what the latter embodies in terms of indispensable local genius and values. Cosmopolitanism must be an antidote to the complacency of familiarity. Furthermore, the only good patriotism is a civilized one, that is, both accepted and limited. The only good cosmopolitanism is a grounded one that avoids dilettantism and the ease of eclecticism. Let us forgo extreme alternatives and facile reconciliations. Let us combine tradition with modernity, duration with transience, the nomadic life with sedentariness. Experiencing the marvel of several educations cannot occur without conflict, suffering, and painful choices. It is essential to argue for a fluid belonging, an uncertain identity. Identity is a tendency, not an immutable essence; too strenuous an attempt to define it, simply turns it into an obstacle that impedes with any desire to change. Identity is not an enclosure but a point of departure that enables the invention of a sequel to the past. In short, it is never fully formed like a ripe fruit that one need only pass from one generation to the next. It must be continuously constructed and reconstructed. There is no death of a nation, no death of collective memory. Unless it is to be the tomb of its own grandeur, a culture must also know how to liberate itself from its past, to break with, and even at times profane, its own customs. In order to renew itself a culture must hide within itself a composite heritage and be a battleground for a plurality of traditions to clash and to interact without destroying themselves. There is no loyalty to the self that does not include betrayal, no inconsistency that is not ultimately a superior degree of loyalty. (Similarly a language never belongs to simply one people. It can always be influenced by outer forces that will enrich as well as alter it.)

No matter how fluid or extroverted, our societies will always need the "great cosmopolitan souls" (Rousseau) of those migratory men who open up possibilities of conversation and even love between cultures, who reject egoism, and encourage exchange. Yet the *cosmopolitan spirit,* degraded into ideology appears merely as a diluted and vulgar *ersatz.* Desire alone does not effect cultural transformations. One needs determination, courage, and perhaps even the touch of madness all great mediators possess. In order to remain faithful to their memory, we must refuse to put forward makeshift goods. Let us not ape these great figures. Let us content ourselves with being democratic. In these times of resurging barbarity, that alone is not so bad.

—Translated from the French by Tess Lewis

Andrei Codrescu

Intelligent Electronics

I have gone through the hell of trying to figure out my tenth computer in fifteen years and I am just as baffled and irritated as I'd been that fateful day in 1979 when a KayPro4 landed on my desk in Baltimore and screwed up my life forever.

Most of us—techno-idiots who are swept away by superior sales techniques—find ourselves kind of weary, worn out by the losing battle against ever-newer technology. Each new machine humiliates us with identical problems. In the end, we become a little ashamed of confessing our frustrations because it seems that we should have learned something from the last disaster. The stark truth, however, is that no one ever learns anything: he only pretends that he knows something so he won't look the fool. Fools are encouraged by computer PR to think that they know a lot more than they do through the means of so-called "user-friendly" technologies. There is no such thing: "user-friendly" simply means that our ignorance is now shielded from itself by a screen of faux simplicity that makes it even more difficult to admit our ignorance. Implicitly, both the Macintosh and the Windows programs ask only one question: How can you be so stupid when it's so easy?

Sure. Only I started backwards. From the seeming difficulty of a language called CPM on my KayPro—which looked like a military bunker machine able to take a direct hit from a ten-ton bomb—to the cute faces on my Mac, stretches the vast bridge of fifteen years. For me, these fifteen years represent a certain regression from a poet without any worry or money to the present-day processor of words for articles, radio commentaries, and fiction, and still no money. When I was a young poet in San Francisco in the early seventies, all I needed to practice my profession was a pencil and a bar napkin and the presence in the vicinity of beautiful girls for inspiration. Back then, the streets were full of people who actually lived on them. People used to go to coffeehouses, hang out on their stoops and porches, and gather in large groups to throw Molotov cocktails at the National Guard. I used to write divinely inspired poetry with my pencil on my napkin. I would then read this napkin to a beautiful girl and if she liked it, I would be so inspired I would write another poem on the spot, and if she took me home with her, I would usually write two. Sometimes, I was so poor that I didn't even have a pencil and I used to drink in places where they didn't give you a napkin. On those occasions, my only writing tools might consist of a razor blade and my wrist. With these poetry tools I would then write on the wall— until either a beautiful girl rescued me or the management called an ambulance. That's why I had gotten on to this art in the first place: it was cheap. I didn't need paints and brushes like the painters, or fiddles like the fiddle players, or rich patrons like the sculptors and architects.

Alas. Heaven didn't last long. Enter my first typewriter, a gun blue Smith-Corona 220, ready to fire. Sure enough, I started writing prose: stories, novels, essays. I could only write poetry when I ran out the back door to my bars and cafés. It wasn't easy either: the Smith-Corona was the first of my machines endowed with the ability to hear me leave the house. Often, when I came back late, or left it unattended for a couple of days, the machine would take its revenge on me by smudging or locking or popping a spring.

The KayPro4 marked yet another stage of my enslavement: I have now forgotten just how many months of pain it took finally to produce a printed text through the bowels of it. This "forgetting," by the way, is the computer industry's most precious marketing tool. It is similar to the way women forget the pain of childbirth and go right ahead and have another child. Likewise, we forget the pain of our latest computer: we go right on and get another one. Anyway, the KayPro greatly increased my productivity and severely limited my freedom. Now, this was a paradox because in order to create I needed freedom, but in order to get freedom I had to be away from this machine. It therefore followed that the increased production I obtained from my computer was at the expense of creativity. So I started writing even less poetry.

Don't fear. I will not take you painfully, though it would give me great pleasure, through each and every one of the machines that over the years rapidly turned me into its slave. Suffice it to say that my art became a lot less portable, and even though I have a Mac Notebook now, I find myself bound by habit to the desktop. Once you turn this thing on it starts to blink like a vampire, demanding its quota of words.

Americans have been conquered by the computer. I say conquered to mean what until recently was being called a revolution, the computer revolution. In my opinion it's no longer a revolution: the "compurevolutionists" have won and there is a New Order in effect. We live in ECC, Era of the Computer Chip, and this technology calls the shots now.

In the previous age, the Early Post-Humanist Age, the issues were about liberation from oppression, freedom from work, spiritual development, the defense of nature, and art. This EPHA (Early Post-Humanist Age) wasn't very long ago, doubtlessly most of us remember it. Some of us may even believe that we are still in it. Dealing with intelligent electronics does not preclude having a social conscience, it could be argued. Maybe not. But let's see.

The first use of computers for the purpose of social betterment was in the ideologically neutral area of *networking*. It would seem that the increased ability to communicate and to link people of like minds would be a great benefit to people working for post-humanist causes. All the people who want to save the whales could get to know each other and they could link up with the defenders of the wolves and so on. But the actual benefits of networking are not in areas of social activism: they are in fund-raising and marketing. People who might have found solace in the disinterested company of fellow altruists find themselves *targeted* instead. The most vulnerable targets are precisely people who don't cover their asses all the time. The best targets for sales and partisan political rhetoric are people whose minds are still open: but instead of opening them to the common good, the savvy networkers open them to the fangs of the commercial vampire. The proof of this is the tremendous rise of shopping channels, soon to come to your beloved Net, and the Republican sales pitches that translated so well in recent elections.

I know the counterargument: there are efforts to keep the big Net commercial-free but that's like saying, "The Visigoths are still five miles from Rome." And, of course, there are more ways to skin a cat than deafening it with a jingle. From what I've seen, most of the stuff out there is either sex or ads or both. And it's all lies in any case. But let's take the case of a friend of mine in New York who started a special talk salon for high IQs in the hope that world problems would get some armchair brainstorms. Guess what? The high IQs, after some high-minded protocol dust, got right down to business: sex and money. If they had been meeting face to face, I doubt that they had would been this crass. Face to face one tries to find one's better nature. If only because one has some vestigial respect, or fear, of the other's soul. In the anonymity of the electronic exchange one finds the crassest thing first. The soul doesn't shine through. Intelligence does, yes, but intelligence without soul is like a fiddle without strings.

Okay, I'm no prude, and I'm not blind to the practical advantages of information in medicine and other industries. It's the creativity angle I'm working. To be creative, a person needs freedom. I've said that before, but let me ask you: is freedom increased or lessened by the use of a computer? I would say lessened if not entirely eliminated. First, you are bound to the keyboard. Second, you must respond to the time-consuming demands of (mostly) useless information. Third, you do not have the luxury of being able to reflect for long periods of time because, most likely, the clock is ticking. Fourth, you are connected willy-nilly to a community of users with whom you have nothing in common but the frustrations of the equipment. Time is a limited commodity, which has become ever more limited since the Industrial Revolution. With the latest computer technology, human time disappears completely: machine time takes over.

Okay, you might say, but this "time," this "freedom" that you say we used to have—it was time for what? Freedom to do what? Here we come to the crux of the problem. The question of information.

ECC (Era of the Computer Chip) is also called, sometimes, the Age of Information. It's not a bad name: it describes succinctly exactly what it is that we produce and consume now. An observer in, let's say, the sixteenth century, would be astonished to see the quantities of sheer information consumed by an average American in an average town on an average day. Our sixteenth-century observer would, at first, faint from the sheer excitement and delight at the volume of knowledge, and then would try to grab as much of it as possible. He or she would, however, be able to grab no more than about five minutes worth from our media before short-circuiting and vanishing in a puff of smoke. Why would a sixteenth-century observer short-circuit? Because a sixteenth-century observer, unlike a twentieth-century consumer, would try to make sense of the information by connecting it. A sixteenth-century human was probably the last being on the planet capable of knowing everything—and not just *knowing*, but having a connected picture of the universe in his or her head.

To be sure, this was a sixteenth-century European, and the *everything* he or she knew was only what had been written and translated in Europe. Still, that was a lot, considering that knowing so much involved making a great many connections in order to make sense of the information. After the Renaissance, the illusion of such knowing vanished: libraries became the repositories of all that humanity knew. It no longer became necessary to know everything: little by little people began to specialize in small areas, trusting that they could find what they needed by looking it up. Instead of a coherent picture of the world that each individual might, by reflection, form for oneself, we entered an age of fragmentation. In this age, no individual had more than a few pieces of the puzzle and they lay disconnected, waiting for this individual to connect them with information from the library. Information increased and libraries grew and grew until there was a problem of storage. Happily, computers showed up.

Now the problem of storage seems to have been solved, leaving only—only!—the problem of meaning. This, of course, is not such a great problem: very intelligent computers, very fast ones, could supply information almost as quickly as one's own memory used to when one had a memory. Fast computers are, in effect, a still-clumsy global nervous system that will get less and less clumsy.

So, what's the problem? The problem is that the storage space now far exceeds the amount of information we have to store in it. Everything we know can now be stored in a corner of the vast electronic storage bin. The storage space now begins to demand information from us at a faster and faster rate: in order to fill its insatiable and theoretically infinite maw we must now produce faster and faster and more and more. Very soon, like that Renaissance person, we will blow up and go up in smoke, not because we have too much in us to deal with, but because we don't have another thing to give to the machine that's sucked us dry.

When the Renaissance persons put what they knew in books and put these in libraries, they didn't have to hurry. They emptied themselves of the information that held their world together slowly because there was only so much room. We now have to empty ourselves fast of information that literally goes through us. We have no time to reflect on it, we have no time to construct a picture of the world for ourselves. We are simply extensions of the intelligent electronics demanding to be fed.

When I hear "virtual world" or "cyberspace" I think of archeology. I *already* think of this world space as an archeological site, our equivalent of the Roman temple. At this point in time, and maybe for another decade, the temple of virtuality is awake with the swoosh of information it sucks to feed itself. In a decade or so the info will be exhausted. There will be nothing to suck and the whoosh will die down. Already, all the inert info we've busy-stashed like squirrels in books, tapes, and now CD-ROM, has whooshed down the cyber-gullet. The cyber-temple walls are so vast that all our records take only a pinprick's worth of room. So, what happens when the info's been all stored and all the things you can do to move it up and down and sideways have taken their thimble's worth of space? Well, then, what happens is that the temple itself, deprived of its food, will start to eat at its own walls until they collapse on top of everyone in it—and everyone *is* or will be shortly within—and that will be the end of our particular world and culture. Thus, archeology. They'll dig up cyberspace like Apuleium and they'll say: They worshipped their gods in here and when they ran out of sacrifices their gods killed them.

The meaning of virtuality is the information used in constructing it. Virtuality only has meaning as long as it's under construction. Nobody can actually inhabit it: it has no smell. Or, as my friend Larry says: "You can't pass a joint through the Internet!" Once virtuality has been built out of all the information we have, it becomes meaningless. And we are empty, emptied by what we have given virtuality. This is the case of any temple: it has meaning only as long as it has belief. When belief is exhausted it collapses. Information in our age is a dangerous belief: we worship information. We believe in storing it and, in so doing, we are drafted to serve the architecture of the store. The original purpose of information was to mobilize the interior of the mind for deeper understanding. In order to be useful in that way it had to stay within. By giving it up to the computer, we have not only precluded our evolution but have ensured our obsolescence.

Okay, so I'm no Marshall McLuhan, who thought that the global village was just hunky-dory. But I'm no practicing Luddite, either. I'm writing this on my latest tormentor, a Packard-Bell 486, courtesy of my mother, who always had a knack for interrupting whatever I was doing. This particular interruption took a week. Mothers are probably in collusion with intelligent electronics—to keep everybody in where they can keep an eye on them. But mother is too big a subject, let me go back to the questions of freedom and time, "down time" as it is now called.

Yes, freedom, and time, and the question of what does a "coherent picture of the world" mean. Freedom is that referent-free space at the coffeehouse when you scribble on your napkin with the vague perfume of that potential girl in your unfocused nostrils. In that state, time is infinite. Not machine time, not clock time, not set-up time: infinity. (And that's not a car, please!) In this space of infinity-freedom you dream. You float, you dream, you have no boundaries, you are within a potential and generative state of mind. This is the mulch ground of the uncreated, the space prior to inarticulation, a place where articulation is, in fact, suspect. You are . . . in New Orleans.

You look out the frame of the streetcar window and let the live oaks and the big houses with their columns of piquant stories flash by without focusing on any of them. You go to Cafe Brazil and inhale deeply the aroma of espresso and young dancers at work. You go to the Faulkner Bookstore and say hi to his ghost. You hand over some money to the tap dancers on Decatur Street. Get immersed in street music. And this is no interactive program: things smell, resonate, and brace.

Under conditions of freedom and leisure, an individual might construct a picture of the world from the few bits of information still charged by the senses. It won't be the Renaissance cat's erudite, prescientific vision, but it won't be the overnetworked grudge's sense of eternal emergency, either.

Kai Maristed

Nicotine, An Autobiography

Of all the large and small extinctions scheduled for the coming millennium, one will be mourned mainly in secret. For some, no loss is more personal and poignant than that of the international, cosmopolitan solidarity of smokers. Day by day its poets and heroes, acolytes and fellow travelers are surrendering ground to a drab two-class society: the despised hardcore *addicts,* and the increasingly righteous majority of *nons.*

Recently, the R. J. Reynolds company launched a "no-secondhand-smoke" cigarette, aimed at fostering the two classes' continued, if uneasy, coexistence. In fact (according to the hoarse whispers of a retired chemist of this butt fiend's acquaintance), a nicotine-free cigarette was perfected years ago in a Winston-Salem laboratory (the chemist hoards a personal stash), but the project was squashed from the top: formula patented six ways to midnight and locked away. Never test-marketed. Whose bright idea was it to sterilize the golden goose?

Drift upstream to first memories and recognize this thing in all its transubstantiations as a kind of third parent. Mama smoked, Papa smoked, bless the child who inhales her own. The dove-gray striations hang in midair over playpen or crib, shiver at the transit of shadow-bodies. Smoke trickles from adult tongues and nostrils along with the stimulating fantastical flow of words. Older, you rise at dawn and, in an otherwise cold and empty living room, find your parents' spoor: butts pyramided in ashtrays, your mother's lipstick smooched onto her brand. Traces of the absent ones. Their half-collapsed unfinished packs prove they can't have gone far. Once, utterly absorbed, you dissect a cigarette: sample the dissolving paper and bitter-copper tobacco, peel gill by gill through the complex fibrous filter. Where does the mystery live? Years later, sobbing in adolescent desolation, you are offered a cigarette by mother or father. Sudden silence. You light up—wordless confession here—in the glow of their wistful, wondering approval. *She's nearly grown-up. Look, she's so much like us.* The point is: whatever may divide or change your mortal parents, smoking will remain their unity, your holy ghost.

In any case, you took that first drag young, so long ago that now it's difficult to recall a time when you functioned from one morning to the next with calm coordination without nicotine. That aspect of childhood seems mythical. What can it mean to "quit," when you are in significant part nicotine, just as you are made of water? But maybe in the beginning you did not light up with overt adult approval. Maybe rebellion was the goal—as you split a pack with a girlfriend, hiding out in the woods or an empty lot. To acknowledge this initiation verbally would be uncool, so instead (squinting, furiously shaking the match as it singes your thumb) you discuss rock music, or eyeliner, or French kissing. The hit creeps up inside: dizziness at first, head-sickness. You lean back against the graffiti-blasted wall. Swallow the nausea. Smile to show how you enjoy it. You *do* enjoy it; after all, you're a teenager. You are biologically and psychologically primed for contradictions: the embrace of revulsion, the seduction of risk. So this is your first time? It will be a long affair.

Today, only one of every four adult Americans remains hooked on tobacco. Impressive decline in one generation—following the surgeon general's tirades in the late sixties—but recently the quit rate has pretty much leveled off. Now, one of us in four still huddles against the rain, or winter wind, clothes spoiling, tears in the eyes, numb frozen-sausage fingers pinching a butt. Out here, whoever we are, we don't like one another. This is not anything to have in common. Our minds flee elsewhere—back indoors to our work, or to the party, the play, or lovers' crisis continuing without us—because we don't like the selves out here. Sucking the butt. Calculating how long the fix will last. Or not last. We are one in four, the shelterless lumpen proletariat. Pollsters record that eighty percent of us *want* to quit but fail. Visitors to any hospital may notice a cordon of nurses, orderlies, and doctors, all ferociously smoking, loitering a prescribed twenty-five-foot distance from the main door.

Inhaled, dissolved in the bloodstream, nicotine strikes within eight seconds.

> Nicotine, the chief alkaloid in tobacco products, binds stereoselectively to acetylcholine receptors at the autonomic ganglia, in the adrenal medulla, at neuromuscular junctions, and in the brain. Two types of central nervous system effects are . . . a stimulating effect, exerted mainly in the cortex via the locus ceruleus [which] produces increased alertness and cognitive performance. A "reward" effect via the "pleasure system" in the brain is exerted in the limbic system. At low doses the stimulant effects predominate while at high doses reward effects predominate. Intermittent intravenous administration of nicotine activates neurohormonal pathways, releasing acetylcholine, norepinephrine, dopamine, serotonin, vasopressin, beta-endorphin, growth hormone, and ACTH.

Capisce? Hard-core porn is much easier to lay hands on than serious information on nicotine, though any number of "inspirational" articles and pamphlets offer tips and tricks for controlling the "urge to light up." Do heroin users hope to get clean by sipping water, taking walks, phoning a buddy? But ex-junkies say smoking is harder to give up than dope.

The physiological information above was cribbed from an insert in the patch kit (prescription only, $25), a microscopic text addressed to medical doctors. (The box also contains a how-to in large print for the lay user.) To the butt fiend, this grim sketch of the "pleasure system" foreshadows even more ominous implications. So nicotine transforms to—or replaces—acetylcholine? Consider: as you have smoked with hardly a break since early adolescence, won't your body have lost all ability to make the natural chemical? A form of atrophy? Is the loss reversible? If so, after how long? Meanwhile, what happens in the brain without acetylcholine: raw nerves rasping like metal on metal, without the emollients of serotonin, dopamine, and the rest? Slippage of concentration? Mental seize-up? Or is all this just an excuse, are you exaggerating, paranoid, inventing agonies to come?

Another snip: the *New York Times* (August 31, 1994) reports that "some people's genes may predispose them to both smoking and depression." Psychiatrists suggest these unfortunates choose between nicotine or Prozac. This is a choice? For some doomed quitters, even Prozac brings no relief, and "smoking may be the lesser of two evils, since life is not worth living under the constant drain of depression." There is active suicide, and there is passive suicide, and sometimes fear feels like nothing more than hyperactive depression.

So why not switch to gum or the patch? No stain, no smell, no sticky carcinogenic compounds. The drug pure and simple, in a sanitary, socially sanctioned delivery form. It would be like going on methadone. Why not?

OVERDOSAGE: The oral minimum acute lethal dose in human adults is 40 to 60 mg (less than 1 mg per kilo). . . . Symptoms of poisoning include pallor, cold sweat, nausea, vomiting, abdominal pain, disturbed hearing and vision, peripheral paralysis.

It's not just the tar, stupid. Or the two-hundred-odd additives. It's a unique compound, $C_{10}H_{14}N_2$, this central soothing and stimulating miracle molecule, nicotine.

According to Lauren Bacall (who, despite Bogie's fatal cancer, went on smoking), the stagey business with cigarettes is thoroughly and boldly erotic, a semiotic of seduction in real life as on the screen. Wordless intimacy, often between strangers: widened eyes reflecting the shared flame, fingertips brushing. The hazy expulsion of pleasure, through relaxed, parted lips.

You hate propaganda. You despise the self-appointed smoke militia, with its Frankenstein's-lung horror posters and public humiliation tactics. To quintuple the cigarette tax showed majority rule in action (since three out of four voters won't pay), but none of the windfall goes to redeem the sinners from their vice. Meanwhile, strangers stop you on the street to say you are killing your children. Presumably these are the same vigilant citizens who want to jail pregnant women for drinking alcohol. These days, puffing in public feels daring again: a political act.

Even in pregnancy, you never exactly quit—although morning sickness imposed limits. Later—while smoking—you anxiously observed each baby for telltale stuntedness. As for your own mother, she smoked on with gusto and abandon until the tracheotomy in her cancerous throat forced a sudden no-backsliding policy. Watching her waste away, you did not dream of quitting. On the contrary. It was a stressful time, and without snatched respites of inflating your lungs with a cloud—then rising on its wave of nicotine—you'd have lost your grip completely. Hey, baby: you and Lauren Bacall.

Two or three packs a day. But no cough, no symptoms, heaven knows weight's no problem, and you're healthier than most your age. The smoke curling from under your study door is a family joke. Work hard: the price per pack keeps ratcheting up. At least you don't squander money on frills.

At a party someone asks: Why can't we use tobacco the way the Indians did? Once a month or so the tribe gathered, old and young, men and women, they passed the pipe, got buzzed, had some visions—then they could leave it alone. Why can't we?

Ah, the mouthwatering cigarettes of Europe. The aromas of steeped espresso and black tobacco tangle in sidewalk cafés. Schoolgirls with round creamy faces chain-smoke cigarettes, as do drop-dead elegant old women. Here's freedom. Here's to the republic of enlightened pleasure. (You wake up in your hotel room in the dark before dawn, clammy from the recurrent inexplicable nightmare of dying by your own hand. Switch on the lamp, fumble for a Gitane filter, with fingers stained ocher yellow.)

One year later, in Boston, a receptionist collects our checks. Sixty dollars times twenty-five "clients": no shabby wage for two hours of wonder-curing. Sultry summer afternoon. Climate of last-ditch hope and boisterous confession: we trump each other's stories, laughing in the relief of self-abasement. The famous healer enters. He is short with a trim beard and has preserved his furry Russian accent. We strain to identify words. While pacing inside our circle, talking, talking, he insists he is not a hypnotist. Stare at any man long enough and you will either fall in love or in hate. He pounces on the miracle—for one whole hour no one here has smoked. As the finale, we each receive a moment of personal concentration. He splays pale manicured hands over my head and sighs, "You have beautiful body. Must take care for it, please." Please.

Outside I feel uplifted—or already woozy from withdrawal. This determination to not-smoke is like biting down on a coin while undergoing an unpleasant medical procedure. Determination lasts all the way to the middle of the next morning. When it collapses, the first almost-virginal, mind-bending, releasing drag tastes alien, like a swig of lifesaving water from a dirty, rusted pipe.

Your youngest child would rather sing and dance than plug into Nintendo. But this winter he's tortured by a series of colds and coughs. Bruise-brown smudges appear under his eyes. One day, audible in his breath is a faint fogged whistle in each inhalation, like wind soughing at the end of a long cave.

Does he notice this sound himself? Oh, he says, it's nothing special. For a long time now, he can't breathe in all the way.

Not-smoking hurts. You picture your brain as remodeled by Oz: all cotton wool and flashing needles. After an hour, two at most, an intense constriction radiates from your chest—the heart—outward through shoulders and arms and down through the lobes of lungs. Paradoxically, not-smoking unleashes this sense of acute suffocation.

What is not true: that chewing on pencils, jellybeans, or any placebo can dull the edge of this claustrophobic tension; nor can fingering worry beads, or knitting, or sipping all-day liquids. So it's not oral satisfaction, or toys to fiddle with, that you crave. The truth is: as your nicotine titer drops, the neural network is being frayed and flayed apart. Nerves scream for the chemical they need to reconnect.

Also not true: that you are excessively irritable or uncontrolled. On the contrary, every not-smoking moment is a monument to extreme self-control. (In your worst dream, you notice an already half-smoked cigarette wedged between your fingers.) You may even be more tolerant of others than before. An inner catastrophe puts minor disturbances in perspective.

As after any devastating breakup, along with weeping jags, guilt spasms, resurgent desire, sleeplessness, apathy, incredulity, and the rest, comes virulent hatred. My nose is morbidly sensitive. I won't enter rooms that hold a recollection of smoke. To see someone light up gives me a queasy rush, like watching a surgeon's incision. I hate the tobacco companies and how their genius for exploitation exemplifies the sanctioned cannibalism of our species. As a girl, I used to see myself mirrored in the magazine ads for Parliaments and Winstons—prophetically prettier, adept at tennis or sailing, bookended by adoring males. With each cigarette I consumed, the infinite distance between myself and that image felt halved.

Times change. The market strategists' targets for the year 2000 in the United States are small kids. Poor city kids: the Little Friends of Joe Camel. But will there be enough budding butt fiends to save Joe? Not to worry. The serious money will come from smoke in distant places. Ad campaigns in Asia and Africa already depict female smokers as educated, affluent progressives, making a successful raid on the traditional bag of male privilege. There's truth to this, of course. And imagine: out there swarm billions of potential new customers. Girls discarding the veil, entering the factory, savoring that heady, hard-earned first drag. It's exciting. There's still a killing to be made in tobacco stocks.

What seemed unutterably necessary is gone. What was always knotted so tightly into minutes and hours has been stripped out. The days lurch along without punctuation. How to end a meal? Complete a phrase? Launch into a phone call? Blunt boredom, stifle hunger, anesthetize the heart against an insult or a break?

Who on earth are you now, anyway?

Paradoxically, this pervasive dizziness, this goofy light-headedness is a lot like those powerful first smokes. The short-term memory is shot to hell, though. Names mean nothing, calls go unreturned, plans are jettisoned, deadlines blown. Times seems both compressed and elongated, squeezed like a gummi-worm. But someone still wakes, sleeps, cries, and laughs, too. Apparently some kind of you is continuing without the old central assumption, deep-sigh rhythm of inspiration. Just how flimsy are the rest of the assumptions that make up "you"?

Would you suffer for any principle? What are your other addictions? Are you an alcoholic, salt or caffeine abuser, raving egotist, love junkie? Do you love those whom you say you love? Aren't the attributes you claim—"shy," "ambitious," "loyal," for example—merely chance conventions? You are in fact bold, complacent, and faithless.

Is there anyone who could know you?

We hear you're quitting. We understand that you are not yourself.

No, but facing a choice between suicide and loss of marbles, it seems better to go crazy. At least you can still change your mind.

You must be proud of yourself! they say.

A. Alvarez, from his recent book *Night:*

Loewi prepared two frogs, stimulated the vagus nerve of one, causing its heartbeat to slow down, then transferred the blood from the first frog's heart to the second's; when that slowed too, Loewi had his answer: nerves . . . transmitted their signals chemically. Later it was shown that the chemical in question, Loewi's *vagustoff,* was acetylcholine, the neurotransmitter that triggers dreams.

You sleep as if clubbed, but for only a few hours at a time. Instead of dreams you have waking hyperreal hallucinations. Daily, you weep. This is all chemical, don't forget. No sense looking for a "cause" for your constant anxiety, although certain randomly fired images—of a snowy street in Berlin, for example, of a stray cat purring over milk, of a sick friend outlined by the light of a window—can twist the anxiety to a new pitch. All of these images show something that no longer exists. They are about loss.

As in a fairy tale, rewards for the done deed materialize out of nowhere. Amazing—for once in life, promises are kept. Revisit that mirror: now that Cinderella has quit playing with ashes, her eyes are clear, her teeth pearlier, her cheeks rosy from a fresh supply of hemoglobin. Open the medicine cabinet, toss out aspirin, tablets and syrups against nausea and heartburn. You haven't needed any of this in weeks.

The newly laid-on five pounds of flesh make it easier to sit on hard chairs as well as to stay outdoors in winter. Even in freezing weather there's a reassuring sting of circulation in fingers and toes. Improved circulation brings other awarenesses and awakenings. From butt fiend to sex fiend—is that the happy ending?

You sprint across parking lots, dash two-steps-at-a-time up stairs. Often one of these exuberant bursts releases a second level of power and stamina. You might as well be flying. Physical energy demands outlet—you scrub the smoke-yellowed windows and walls, vacuum exuberantly. Cinderella, who used to suffer embarrassment over so many things—her dull gray skin, russet fingers, the smell of the house to visitors—now shudders at the whiff from a smoker's smile. That stench of decay. *Get away, Death-Breath!* Now, rooms which used to hold pots of ashes offer bowls of dried perfumed flowers instead. You can take a walking tour of good smells. Hey, Cinderella, high on all these changes—admit that your house has never before been nearly so nice and clean.

From *The Oxford Medical Companion:*

> ACETYLCHOLINE (ACh) is the body's most important neurotransmitter, i.e. a chemical substance liberated at nerve endings which transmits impulses to muscle and other nerve cells.

There is more, and cross-references, but nothing really new, nothing that explains. I feel like a gumshoe, hunting clues. Remember: tobacco is not categorized as a drug. But the *Companion* notes that lack of acetylcholine is a direct cause of myasthenia gravis. Also: the popular paralytic curare (featured in numerous fictions) works by inhibiting reception of acetylcholine. Such bits and hints color a ubiquitous, on-and-off quest reminiscent of Kafka's K., or Pynchon's V. Here in the library this cramped print, the silence, the x, y, z coordinates of thousands of books, all demand concentration. I have no concentration, only this flickering nausea. What is acetylcholine?

Incredible. So you've actually done it, friends say.
Nothing's "done" yet. The friends tend to lower their voices on the subject of smoking, as if afraid of starting off the avalanche of my backslide. Understandable. Statistically, women who have smoked since trainer-bra days don't stand

much chance. I know a sports pro who cold turkeyed for five months, then, laughing like a lunatic at her defeat, caved in. I know a quadruple bypass survivor who mail orders gourmet cigars. There's a drugstore clerk here, smokeless ten years, who bitches about her unabated craving with every pack she sells.

I'm lonely. I've joined a health club, pay to jog on a tread-mill, and don't even smile at the joke. Evenings I don't pretend to work. I'm hotly envious of the stars in TV movies—how they can smoke in the role, with the grand gesture. At the apex of terror or joy, the stars raise half-closed eyes to heaven and suck in the miasma, as if re-inhaling their own souls. Suddenly I remember what it was like to have heart's balm literally at one's fingertips.

It's been five months. I don't miss the taste or ritual, but who can tell me whether I'll ever find a way back to myself—to simply being instead of changing. Back to being me. Able to work as I used to, to concentrate, to grapple with a concept. Here, this is the hardest temptation: missing nicotine as soul food, to fill the void where I used to be.

I go looking for the past and by luck rediscover a friend who disappeared more than ten years ago. When we were young and outrageous, we danced together in disco contests, dated two brothers, praised each other, shared favorite clothes and shelter. I'm glad to have found her again.

These days she lives in a penthouse, an uncurtained fishbowl in the clouds. Her parents have passed away. She beat alcoholism by throwing her whiskey in the river two years ago. She was a good architect but no longer needs to work. There's no furniture. My friend sits on the floor, which is a sea bottom of possessions—books, pottery, unhung paintings, shoes, un-washed dishes—all dusty, filmed with ash or oil. With her strong hands and sure movements (she once apprenticed to a carpenter), she is rolling a homemade cigarette. Giving a side-ways grin, she holds up fingers briefly to show that they no longer tremble. Her fingers are yellow, her teeth are brown. It's hard for me to look at her etched frown and wrinkle-puckered lips. Carefully, she pokes a few crumbs of hashish, recently legalized where she lives, into the tobacco threads.

"Don't lecture, okay?"

"I know it's useless. I won't."

"The dope," she says, "I think I could give up. I've done it before. But nicotine is something else."

Two days later, she drives me to the station. Smoking a fat one down to the last gram. Flicking that scrap away, down into the track, so we can hug good-bye. We're both crying. Her tears slide through my hair. Her low voice resonates in my own head. "The only thing that might give me the strength for it," she says, "is if you ask me to quit because you love me."

"Please. I love you!"

Then I climb on the train and find a window to watch her walk away.

At home sometimes, in an apprehensive reflex, I still hold my breath and listen. But the frightening sounds are gone. My little boy's chest is clear, he doesn't gasp or cough, no matter how recklessly he sings.

Robert Heilman

Overstory: Zero

THE MAIN THING

The main thing is to have a big breakfast. It's not an easy thing to do at 4 A.M., but it is essential because lunch won't come for another seven or eight hours, and there are four or more hours of grueling work to do before you can sit down and open up your lunch box.

The kids on the crew, eighteen-year-olds fresh out of high school, sleep in an extra half hour and don't eat until the morning store stop on the way out to the unit. They wolf down a Perky Pie, a candy bar, and a can of soda in the crummy, good for a one-hour caffeine and sugar rush. They go through the brush like a gut-shot cat for a while and then drag ass for the rest of the morning.

But if you're a grizzled old-timer in your mid-twenties, you know how to pace yourself for the long haul. You're exhausted, of course, and your calves, hips, arms, and lower back are stiff and sore. But you're used to that.

You're always tired and hurting. The only time you feel normal is when you're on the slopes, when the stiffness and fatigue are melted off by the work. It gets worse every morning until by Saturday it takes hours to feel comfortable on a day off.

Sunday morning you wake up at four o'clock, wide awake and ready to stomp through downtown Tokyo, breathing fire and scattering tanks with your tail.

Your stomach is queasy but you force the good food into it anyway—a big stack of pancakes with peanut butter and syrup, four eggs, bacon, and a pint of coffee. There is a point when your belly refuses to take any more. Saliva floods your mouth and you force back the retching, put the forkful of food down on the plate, and light another cigarette.

It's dark outside and it's raining, of course. They aren't called the Cascades for nothing. It's December and the solstice sun won't rise until eight, three hours and a hundred miles from home, somewhere along a logging road upriver.

Raincoat and rain pants, hard hat, rubber work gloves, cotton liner gloves, and a stiff pair of caulk boots stuffed with newspaper crowd around the woodburner. All the gear is streaked with mud except the boots, which are caked with an inch-thick mud sole covering the steel nails. The liner gloves hang stiff and brown, the curving fingers frozen, like a dismembered manikin's hand making an elegant but meaningless gesture.

Mornings are slow. It's hard to move quickly when your stomach is bloated, your body is stiff, and, despite the coffee, your mind is still fatigue-foggy. You have to move though or miss your ride and lose your job. You try an experimental belch, which doesn't bring up too much half-chewed food with it and relieves the pressure.

The laxative effect of the coffee would send you to the toilet but your ride to town is due soon, so you save it for later. Better to shit on company time anyway, squatting out in the brush. It gives you a pleasant break, a few minutes of hard-to-come-by privacy, and it pisses off Jimboy, the foreman, since, being a college boy and therefore trained to worry about what people think of him, he could never bring himself to actually complain about it.

Lester the Rat taught him that lesson the first week of the season. Les had just planted a seedling and straightened up and turned his back on the slope to empty his bladder. The foreman glanced back to see him standing there with his back turned, staring idly across to the opposite slope.

"Hey, Gaines, get back to work! Let's go!"

The Rat turned to face him and shook the last golden drops off. He smiled pleasantly, showing a mouth full of crooked snoose-stained teeth. "Sure thing, Jim," he said mildly. "You bet." None of the professors up at the university had ever mentioned anything like that, and Jimboy blushed delicately while all up and down the line the crew snickered.

Jimboy makes more money than you do and doesn't work as hard, which is bad enough. But he's also afraid. It's his first winter on the slopes and he's not used to riding herd on a gang of brush apes. He also wants to make a good impression on his boss, the head forester, so he tries to push his crew into ever greater production. He sees himself as a leader of men, a rugged scientist overseeing the great work of industrial progress.

Everyone tries to get his goat so that, with any luck, he'll amuse us some day by breaking out in tears like Tommyboy, the last foreman, did. "You guys are just animals," Tommyboy had sobbed, setting off a delighted chorus of wolf howls and coyote yelps. It was the high point of the planting season and a considerable source of pride for the whole crew.

KAMIKAZES

There's a flash of headlights and the crunch of gravel in the driveway. Mighty Mouth awaits in his battered old Ford. You pull up your suspenders and start slapping your pockets: tobacco pouch and rolling papers, matches, bandanna, wad of toilet paper, pocket watch, jackknife, store-stop money—all there. You put on a baseball cap and a plaid woolen overshirt and gather up your gear: caulks, extra socks, rubber gloves, cotton liners, hard hat, rain gear, coffee thermos, and feed bucket. Then you step out into the rain.

There's nothing to talk about on the half-hour drive down the creek and downriver to the mill. You know each other too well by now, riding and working together twelve to fourteen hours a day—two moonlit rides and a picnic lunch every day— for three winters. The Mouth holds a beer bottle between his thighs and spits his chew as he drives.

You roll a cigarette and listen to the radio and peer out through the windshield, watching for the twin reflection of deer eyes ahead. The road is narrow and winding, the roadside brush thick, and you never know just when a deer will step out or leap, windshield-high, in front of you. Every day, somewhere on the drive, you see at least one fresh deer carcass on the road. Headlights dazzle the deer, and usually they stand frozen in their tracks before leaping aside at the last moment. Sometimes they leap toward the headlights though—always a suicidal move for the deer—but, like a kamikaze pilot, they can kill too.

CRUMMY TIME

The mercury-arc lamps light up the mill with a weird, hellish orange glow. Steam rises from the boilers and there's a sour rotting smell everywhere. The huge metal buildings bristle with an improbable-looking tangle of chains and belts and pipes. There's a constant whistling, clanging, and screaming of saws and machinery coming from them. Bug-eyed forklifts and log loaders crawl around the half-lit yards, mechanical insects scurrying to keep up.

Through the huge open doorways you can see the mill-hands at work in their T-shirts, sorting out an unending river of lumber and veneer into neat stacks. The mill workers sweat like desperate dwarves. They make more money than you and stay dry, but you feel pity and contempt for them. The poor bastards stand in one spot all night, moving to the computerized lightning rhythm of conveyors instead of their own human speed. The cavernous interiors of the mill sheds seem as cramped as closets compared to the open mountain slopes.

You work for the mill but not in the mill, on a company reforestation crew. Most of the company land is planted by contract crews, but the mill runs a crew that plants land the contractors won't touch—too steep or too ravaged, too old or too brushy.

Acres away, beyond the log pond, past the five-story-tall walls of stacked logs, next to the hangar-sized heavy equipment repair shop, is a small refrigerated trailer full of seedling trees in waxed boxes. Each box contains six hundred trees in bundles of fifty.

Mudflap and Sluggo are helping Jimboy load tree boxes into the back of a four-wheel-drive crew-cab pickup. They are young, straight out of high school, and eager to get a promised job in the mill come spring—if they "work hard and show up every day," of course. So they help load trees and ride with the foreman every morning.

You transfer your gear over to a mud-covered Chevy Suburban crummy. If you've ever ridden in one, you know why they're called crummies. The rig is a mess, both inside and outside. The seats are torn, the headliner is gone, the ceiling often drips from the condensed breath of its packed occupants. But you have a great fondness for the ugly thing. It is an oasis of comfort compared to the slopes.

We spend a large part of our lives roaring up and down-river, powered by the Suburban's monster 454 V-8. Of course, none of this travel, or crummy time, as it's called, is paid time. Only the forty hours per week on the slopes earn us money. The other ten to twenty hours of crummy tedium are not the company's concern. Together with the half-hour lunch, also unpaid, we spend eleven to thirteen hours a day together for our eight hours' pay. All winter long we see each other more than we see our wives and children. We know each other intimately after so many cramped hours. We bicker and tease each other halfheartedly, like an old bitter couple, out of habit more than need.

ARITHMETIC

The ten of us plant about 7,000 seedling trees every day, or about 700 "binos" apiece, enough to cover a little over an acre of logged-off mountainside each. It gets depressing when you start adding it up: planting 700 trees per day comes to 3,500 per week or 14,000 per month, which amounts to 56,000 trees in a season for one man planting one tree at a time.

Maybe you've seen the TV commercials put out by the company: helicopter panoramas of snow-capped mountains, silvery lakes and rivers, close-ups of cute critters frolicking, thirty-year-old stands of second growth all green and even as a manicured lawn, and a square-jawed handsome woodsman tenderly planting a seedling. The commercials make reforestation seem heartwarming, wholesome, and benevolent, like watching a Disney flick where a scroungy mutt plays the role of a wild coyote.

Get out a calculator and start figuring it: 700 trees in eight hours means 87.5 trees per hour, or 1.458 trees per minute—a tree punched in every 41 seconds. How much tenderness can a man give a small green seedling in 41 seconds?

Planting is done with an improbable-looking tool called a hoedag. Imagine a heavy metal plate fourteen inches long and four inches wide, maybe five pounds of steel, mounted on a single-bit ax handle. Two or three sideways hacking strokes scalp a foot-square patch of ground, three or four stabs with the tip and the blade is buried up to the haft. (Six blows 700 times amounts to 4,200 per day. At five pounds each, that comes to 21,000 pounds of lifting per diem, and many planters put in 900 to 1200 trees per day.)

You pump up and down on the handle, breaking up the soil, open the hole, dangle the roots down there, and pull the hoedag out. The dirt pulls the roots down to the bottom of the hole, maybe ten or twelve inches deep. You give it a little tug to pull the root collar even with the ground and tamp the soil around it with your foot. Generally, what's left of the topsoil isn't deep enough to sink a 'dag in, so you punch through whatever subsoil, rocks, or roots lie hidden by the veneer of dirt.

The next tree goes in eight feet away from the last one and eight feet from the tree planted by the next man in line. Two steps and you're there. It's a sort of rigorous dance, all day long—scalp, stab, stuff, stomp, and split; scalp, stab, stuff, stomp, and split—every 41 seconds or less, 700 or more times a day.

The ground itself is never really clear, even on the most carefully charred reforestation unit. Stumps, old logs, boulders, and brush have to be gone over or through or around with almost every slash-hampered step. Two watertight tree bags, about the size and shape of brown paper grocery bags, hang on your hips, rubbing them raw under the weight of the thirty to forty pounds of muddy seedlings stuffed inside.

Seven hundred trees eight feet apart comes to a line of seedlings 5,600 feet long—a mile and some change. Of course, the ground is never level. You march up and down mountains all day—straight up and straight down. Although nature never made a straight line, forestry professors and their students are quite fond of them. So you climb a quarter-mile straight down and back up. Then you eat lunch and do it again.

It's best not to think about it all. The proper attitude is to consider yourself as eternally damned, with no yesterday or tomorrow—just the unavoidable present to endure. Besides, you tell yourself, it's not so bad once you get used to it.

OUTLAWS

Tree planting is done by outcasts and outlaws—winos and wetbacks, hillbillies and hippies for the most part. It is brutal, mind-numbing, underpaid stoop labor. Down there in Hades, Sisyphus thinks about the tree planters and thanks his lucky star every day because he has such a soft gig.

Being at the bottom of the Northwest social order and the top of the local ass-busting order gives you an exaggerated pride in what you do. You invade a small grocery store like a biker gang, taking the uneasy stares of lesser beings as your natural due. It's easy to mistake fear for a higher form of respect, and as a planter you might as well. In a once rugged society gone docile, you have inherited a vanishing tradition of ornery individualism. The ghosts of drunken bullwhackers, miners, rowdy cowpunchers, and bomb-tossing Wobblies count on you to keep alive the 120-proof spirit of irreverence toward civilization that built the West.

A good foreman, one who rises from the crew by virtue of outworking everybody else, understands this and uses it like a Marine DI to build his crew and drive them to gladly work harder than necessary. A foreman who is uncomfortable with the underlying violence of his crew becomes their target. It is rare for a crew to actually beat up a foreman, but it has happened. There are many ways to get around a weak foreman, most of which involve either goldbricking or baiting. After all, why work hard for someone you don't respect and why bother to conceal your contempt?

BAG-UP

The long, smelly ride ends on a torn-up moonscape of gravel where last summer's logging ended. No one stirs. You look out the foggy windows of the crummy through a gray mist of Oregon dew at the unit. You wonder what shape it's in, how steep, how brushy, how rocky, whether it's red sticky clay or yellow doughy clay, freshly cut or decades old, a partial replanting or a first attempt. The answers lie hidden behind a curtain of rain, and you're not eager to find out.

The foreman steps out and with a few mutterings the crummies empty. Ten men jostle for their equipment in the back of the crummies. The hoedags and tree bags are in a jumbled pile. Most planters aren't particular about which bag they use, provided it doesn't leak muddy water down their legs all day, but each man has a favorite 'dag that is rightfully his. A greenhorn soon learns not to grab the wrong one when its owner comes around, cursing and threatening.

It's an odd but understandable relationship between a planter and his main tool. You develop a fondness for it over time. You get used to the feel of it, the weight and balance and grip of it in your hand. Some guys would rather hand over their wife.

The hoedag is a climbing tool, like a mountaineer's ice ax, on steeper ground. It clears the way through heavy brush like a machete. You can lean on it like a cane to help straighten your sore back, and it is the weapon of choice when self-defense (or a threat) is needed. It allows you to open up stumps and logs in search of the dark gold pitch, which will start a fire in a cold downpour, and to dig a quick fire trail if your break fire runs off up the hill.

The foreman hands out the big, waxed cardboard boxes full of seedling trees. The boxes are ripped open with a hoedag blade and the planters carry double handfuls of trees, wired up in bundles of fifty, over to the handiest puddle to wet down their roots. Dry roots will kill a tree before it can get into the ground, so the idea isn't purely a matter of adding extra weight to make the job harder—though that's the inevitable result.

Three to four hundred trees get stuffed into the double bags, depending on their size and the length of the morning's run. If the nursery hasn't washed the roots properly before bundling and packing, the mud, added water, and trees can make for a load that is literally staggering.

No one puts on their bags until the boxes are burned. It is an essential ritual, and depriving a crew of their morning fire is, by ancient custom, held to be justifiable grounds for mutiny by crummy lawyers everywhere. Some argue that homicide in such a case would be ruled self-defense, but so far no one has ever tested it.

The waxed cardboard burns wonderfully bright and warm. A column of flame fifteen feet high lights up the road, and everyone gathers around to take a little warmth and a lot of courage. Steam clouds rise from your rain gear as you rotate before the fire, like a planet drawing heat from its sun. It feels great and you need it, because once the flames turn to ashes you're going over the roadbank.

"Okay. Everybody get loaded and space out," the Mouth calls out. You strap on your bag, tilt your tin hat, and grab your 'dag. You shuffle over to the edge of the road and line up eight feet from the man on either side.

IN THE HOLE

The redoubtable Mighty Mouth, the third-fastest planter, plants in the lead spot, and the men behind him work in order from the fourth- to the eighth-fastest man. It is a shameful thing to plant slower than the guy behind you. If he's impatient, or out to score some Brownie points with the boss, he'll jump your line and you plant in his position, sinking lower in the Bull-of-the-Woods standings. Slow planters get fired, and competition is demanded by the foreman.

There are many tricks to appearing to be faster than you really are—stashing trees, widening your spacing, pushing the man behind you into the rougher parts while you widen or narrow your line to stay in the gravy—but all of these will get you in trouble one way or another, if not with the boss, then worse still, with the crew.

The idea is to cover the ground with an eight-foot by eight-foot grid of trees. If mountains were graph paper this would be easy, but instead, each slope has its own peculiar contours and obstacles, which throw the line off. Each pass, if it follows a ragged line, will be more irregular than the last pass, harder to find and follow. It is difficult enough to coordinate a crew strung out over a hillside, each planter working at a different rate, going around obstacles such as stumps, boulders, cliffs, and heavy brush, without compounding it by leaving a ragged unmarked line behind for the next pass.

The two fastest planters, the tail men, float behind the crew, planting two to ten lines apiece, straightening out the tree line for the next pass. They tie a bit of blue plastic surveyor's tape to brush and sticks to mark the way for the lead man when he brings the crew back up from the bottom.

CUMULATIVE IMPACT

It's best not to look at the clear-cut itself. You stay busy with whatever is immediately in front of you because, like all industrial processes, there is beauty in the details and ugliness in the larger view. Oil film on a rain puddle has an iridescent sheen that is lovely in a way that the junkyard it's part of is not.

Forests are beautiful on every level, whether seen from a distance or standing beneath the trees or studying a small patch of ground. Clear-cuts contain many wonderful tiny things—jasper, agate, petrified wood, sun-bleached bits of wood, bone, and antler, wildflowers. But the sum of these finely wrought details adds up to a grim landscape, charred, eroded, and sterile.

Although tree planting is part of something called reforestation, clear-cutting is never called deforestation—at least not by its practitioners. The semantics of forestry don't allow that. The mountain slope is a "unit," the forest a "timber stand," logging is "harvest" and repeated logging "rotation."

On the work sheets used by foresters, a pair of numbers tracks the layers of canopy, the covering of branches and leaves that the living trees have spread out above the soil. The top layer is called the overstory, and beneath it is a second layer, the understory. An old-growth forest, for example, may have an overstory averaging 180 feet and an understory 75 feet. Clear-cuts are designated by the phrase "Overstory: Zero."

In the language (and therefore the thinking) of industrial silviculture, a clear-cut is a forest. The system does not recognize any depletion at all. The company is fond of talking about trees as a renewable resource, and the official line is that timber harvest, followed by reforestation, results in a net gain. "Old-growth forests are dying, unproductive forests—biological deserts full of diseased and decaying trees. By harvesting and replanting we turn them into vigorous, productive stands. We will never run out of trees," the company forester will tell you. But ask if he's willing to trade company-owned old-growth forestland for a reforestation unit of the same acreage and the answer is always, "No, of course not."

You listen and tell yourself that it's the company that treats the land shabbily. You see your frenzied work as a life-giving dance in the ashes of a plundered world. You think of the future and the green legacy you leave behind you. But you know that your work also makes the plunder seem rational and is, at its core, just another part of the destruction.

More than the physical exhaustion, this effort to not see the world around you tires you. It takes a lot of effort not to notice, not to care. You can go crazy from lack of sleep because you must dream in order to sort out everything you see and hear and feel during the day. But you can also get sick from not being truly awake, not seeing, feeling, and touching the real world.

When the world around you is painful and ugly, that pain and ugliness seeps into you, no matter how hard you try to keep it out. It builds up like a slowly accumulating poison. Sometimes the poison turns to venom and you strike out, at work or at home, as quick as any rattlesnake but without the honest rattler's humane fair warning.

So you bitch and bicker with the guys on the crew, argue with the foreman, and snap at your wife and kids. You do violent work in a world where the evidence of violence is all around you. You see it in the scorched earth and the muddy streams. You feel it when you step out from the living forest into the barren clear-cut. It rings in your ears with the clink of steel on rock. It jars your arm with every stab of your hoedag.

THE LONG MARCH

"War is hell," General William Tecumseh Sherman said, because, unlike a Pentagon spokesman, he was in the midst of it and could not conceive of something so abstract as "collateral damage."

"Planting sucks," we say, because unlike the mill owner who signs our paychecks, we slog through the mud and bend our backs on mountain slopes instead of reading progress reports on reforestation units. Like infantry, we only know weariness and hopelessness in the face of insanity.

"The millions of trees that the timber industry plants every year are enough to plant a strip four miles wide from here to New York," the foreman tells us.

Our hearts sink at the thought of that much clear-cutting, but Madman Phil, the poet, sees a vision. "Forward, men!" he cries. "Shoulder to shoulder we march on New York. The American Tree Planter! Ever onward!"

Someone starts it and then the whole crew is humming "The Battle Hymn of the Republic," while in our minds we cross the Cascades, the Snake River Valley, the Rockies, the Great Plains, and onward, ever onward, a teeming, faceless coolie army led by Walt Whitman, Sasquatch, and Mao Tse-Tung, a barbarian horde leaving a swath of green behind us "from sea to shining sea."

"Oh God!" Jimboy moans. "You guys are crazy."

Cynthia Ozick

A Drugstore Eden

In 1929, my parents sold their drugstore in Yorkville—a neighborhood comprising Manhattan's East Eighties—and bought a pharmacy in Pelham Bay, in the northeast corner of the Bronx. It was a move from dense city to almost country. Pelham Bay was at the very end of a relatively new stretch of elevated train track that extended from the subway of the true city all the way out to a small-town enclave of little houses and a single row of local shops: shoemaker's, greengrocer, drugstore, grocery, bait store. There was even a miniature five-and-ten where you could buy pots, housedresses, and thick lisle stockings for winter. Three stops down the line was the more populous Westchester Square, with its bank and post office, which old-timers still called "the village"—Pelham Bay had once lain outside the city limits, in Westchester County.

This lost little finger of the borough was named for the broad but mild body of water that rippled across Long Island Sound to a blurry opposite shore. All the paths of Pelham Bay Park led down to a narrow beach of rough pebbles, and all the surrounding streets led, sooner or later, to the park, wild and generally deserted. Along many of these streets there were

empty lots that resembled meadows, overgrown with Queen
Anne's lace and waist-high weeds glistening with what the children termed "snake spit"; poison ivy crowded between the toes
of clumps of sky-tall oaks. The snake spit was a sort of bubbly
botanical excretion, but there were real snakes in those lots,
with luminescent skins, brownish-greenish, crisscrossed with
white lines. There were real meadows, too: acres of downhill
grasses, in the middle of which you might suddenly come on a
set of rusty old swings—wooden slats on chains—or a broken
red brick wall left over from some ruined and forgotten Westchester estate.

The Park View Pharmacy—the drugstore my parents
bought—stood on Colonial Avenue between Continental and
Burr: Burr for Aaron Burr, the Vice-President who killed Alexander Hamilton in a duel. The neighborhood had a somewhat
bloodthirsty Revolutionary flavor. You could still visit Spy Oak,
the venerable tree, not far away, on which some captured Red-
coats had been hanged; and now and then Revolutionary bul-
lets were churned up a foot or so beneath the front lawn of the
old O'Keefe house, directly across the street from the Park
View Pharmacy. George Washington had watered his horses, it
was believed, in the ancient sheds beyond Ye Olde Homestead,
a local tavern that well after Prohibition was still referred to as
"the speakeasy." All the same, there were no Daughters of the
American Revolution here: Pelham Bay was populated by the
children of German, Irish, Swedish, Scottish, and Italian immigrants, and by a handful of the original immigrants themselves.
The greenhorn Italians, from Naples and Sicily, kept goats and
pigs in their back yards, and pigeons on their roofs. Pelham
Bay's single Communist—you could tell from the election results that there was such a rare bird—was the Scotsman who
lived around the corner, though only my parents knew this.
They were privy to the neighborhood's opinions, ailments, and
family secrets.

In those years, the drugstore seemed one of the world's
permanent institutions. Who could have imagined that it would
one day vanish into an aisle in the supermarket, or reëmerge as

a kind of supermarket itself? What passes for a pharmacy nowadays is all open shelves and ceiling racks of brilliant white neon suggesting perpetual indoor sunshine. The Park View, by contrast, was a dark cavern lined with polished wood cabinets rubbed nearly black and equipped with sliding glass doors and mirrored backs. The counters were heaped with towering ziggurats of lotions, potions, and packets, and under them ran glassed-in showcases of the same sober wood. There was a post office (designated a "substation") that sold penny postcards and stamps and money orders. The prescription area was in the rear, closed off from view: here were scores of labelled drawers of all sizes, and rows of oddly shaped brown bottles. In one of those drawers traditional rock candy was stored, in two flavors, plain and maple; it dangled on long strings. And finally there was the prescription desk itself, a sloping, lecternlike affair on which the current prescription ledger always lay, like some sacred text.

There was also a soda fountain. A pull at a long black handle spurted out carbonated water; a push at a tiny silver spout drew forth curly drifts of whipped cream. The air in this part of the drugstore was steamy with a deep coffee fragrance, and on wintry Friday afternoons the librarians from the Travelling Library, a green truck that arrived once a week, would linger, sipping and gossiping on the high-backed fountain chairs, or else at the little glass-topped tables nearby, with their small three-cornered seats. Everything was fashioned of the same burnished chocolate-colored wood, except the fountain counters, which were heavy marble. Above the prescription area, sovereign over all, rose a symbolic pair of pharmacy globes, one filled with red fluid, the other with blue. My father's diploma, Class of 1917, was mounted on a wall; next to it hung a picture of the graduates. There was my very young father, with his round pale eyes and widow's peak—a fleck in a mass of black gowns.

Sometime around 1937, my mother said to my father, "Willie, if we don't do it now we'll never do it."

It was the trough of the Great Depression. In the comics, Pete the Tramp was swiping freshly baked pies set out to cool on windowsills; and in real life tramps (as the homeless were then called) were turning up in the Park View nearly every day. Sometimes they were city drunks—"Bowery bums"—who had fallen asleep downtown on the subway and ended up in Pelham Bay. Sometimes they were exhausted Midwesterners who had been riding the rails and had rolled off into the cattails of the Baychester marsh. But always my father sat them down at the fountain and fed them a sandwich and soup. They smelled bad, and their eyes were red and rheumy; often, they were very polite. They never left without a meal and a nickel for carfare.

No one was worse off than the tramps, or more desolate than the family who lived in an old freight car on the way to Westchester Square; but no one escaped the Depression. Seven days a week, the Park View opened at 9 A.M. and closed at two the next morning. My mother scurried from counter to counter, tended the fountain, unpacked cartons, climbed ladders; her varicose veins oozed through their strappings. My father patiently ground powders and folded the white dust into translucent paper squares with elegantly efficient motions. The drugstore was, besides, a public resource: my father bandaged cuts, took specks out of strangers' eyes, and once removed a fishhook from a man's cheek—though he sent him off to the hospital, on the other side of the Bronx, immediately afterward. My quiet father had cronies and clients, grim women and voluble men who flooded his understanding ears with the stories of their sufferings, of flesh or psyche. My father murmured and comforted, and later my parents would whisper sadly about who had "the big C," or, with an ominous gleam, they would smile over a geezer certain to have a heart attack: the geezer would be newly married to a sweet young thing. (And usually they were right about the heart attack.)

Yet, no matter how hard they toiled, they were always in peril. There were notes to pay off: they had bought the Park View from a pharmacist named Robbins, and every month, relentlessly, a note came due. They never fell behind, and never

missed a payment (and in fact were eventually awarded a certif-
icate attesting to this feat); but the effort—the unremitting
pressure, the endless anxiety—ground them down. "The note,
the note," I would hear, a refrain that shadowed my childhood,
though I had no notion of what it meant.

What it meant was that the Depression, which had already crushed so many, was about to crush my mother and
father: suddenly their troubles intensified. The Park View was
housed in a building owned by a woman my parents habitually
referred to, whether out of familiarity or resentment, only as
Tessie. The pharmacy's lease was soon to expire, and at this
moment, in the cruellest hour of the Depression, Tessie chose
to raise the rent. Her tiger's eyes narrowed to slits; no appeal
could soften her.

It was because of those adamant tiger's eyes that my
mother said, "Willie, if we don't do it now we'll never do it."

My mother was aflame with ambition, emotion, struggle.
My father was reticent, and far more resigned to the world as
given. Once, when the days of the Travelling Library were over
and a real library had been constructed at Westchester
Square—you reached it by trolley—I came home elated, carrying a pair of books I had found side by side. One was called
"My Mother Is a Violent Woman"; the other was "My Father Is
a Timid Man." These seemed a comic revelation of my parents'
temperaments. My mother was all heat and enthusiasm. My
father was all logic and reserve. My mother, unrestrained, could
have run an empire of drugstores. My father was satisfied with
one.

Together they decided to do something revolutionary,
something virtually impossible in those raw and merciless
times. One street over—past McCardle's sunbaked gas station,
where there was always a Model A Ford with its hood open for
repair, and past the gloomy bait store, ruled over by Mr. Isaacs,
a dour and reclusive veteran of the Spanish-American War, who
sat reading military histories all day under a mastless sailboat
suspended from the ceiling—lay an empty lot in the shape of an
elongated lozenge. My parents' daring plan—for young people

without means it was beyond daring—was to buy that lot and build on it, from scratch, a brand-new Park View Pharmacy.

They might as well have been dreaming of taking off in Buck Rogers' twenty-fifth-century rocket ship. The cost of the lot was a stratospheric thirteen thousand five hundred dollars, unchanged from the boom of 1928, just before the national wretchedness descended; and that figure was only for the land. Then would come the digging of a foundation and the construction of a building. What was needed was a miracle.

One sad winter afternoon, my mother was standing on a ladder, concentrating on setting out some newly arrived drug items on a high shelf. (Although a typical drugstore stocked several thousand articles, the Park View's unit-by-unit inventory was never ample. At the end of every week, I would hear my father's melodious, impecunious chant on the telephone, as he ordered goods from the jobber: "A sixth of a dozen, a twelfth of a dozen . . .") A stranger wearing a brown fedora and a long overcoat entered, looked around, and appeared not at all interested in making a purchase; instead, he went wandering from case to case, picking things up and putting them down again, trying to be inconspicuous, asking an occasional question or two, all the while scrupulously observing my diligent parents. The stranger turned out to be a mortgage officer from the American Bible Society, and what he saw, he explained afterward, was a conscientious application of the work ethic; so it was the American Bible Society that supplied the financial foundation of my parents' Eden, the new Park View. They had entertained an angel unawares.

The actual foundation, the one to be dug out of the ground, ran into instant Biblical trouble: flood. An unemployed civil engineer named Levinson presided over the excavation; he was unemployed partly because the Depression had dried up much of the job market but mostly because engineering firms in those years were notorious for their unwillingness to hire Jews. Poor Levinson! The vast hole in the earth that was to become the Park View's cellar filled up overnight with water; the bay was near, and the water table was higher than the hapless Levinson had expected. The work halted. Along came Finnegan and rescued Levinson: Finnegan the plumber, who for a painful fee of fifty dollars (somehow squeezed out of Levinson's mainly empty pockets) pumped out the sea.

After the Park View's exultant move, in 1939, the shell of Tessie's old place on Colonial Avenue remained vacant for years. No one took it over; the plate-glass windows grew murkier and murkier. Dead moths were heaped in decaying mounds on the inner sills. Tessie had lost more than the heartless increase she had demanded, and more than the monthly rent the renewed lease would have brought: there was something ignominious and luckless—tramplike—about that fly-specked empty space, now dimmer than ever. But, within its freshly risen walls, the Park View redux gleamed. Overhead, fluorescent tubes—an indoor innovation—shed a steady white glow, and a big square skylight poured down shifting shafts of brilliance. Familiar objects appeared clarified in the new light: the chocolate-colored fixtures, arranged in unaccustomed configurations, were all at once thrillingly revivified. Nothing from the original Park View had been left behind—everything was just the same, yet zanily out of order: the two crystal urns with their magical red and blue fluids suggestive of alchemy; the entire stock of syrups, pills, tablets, powders, pastes, capsules; tubes and bottles by the hundred; the fountain, with its marble top; the prescription desk and its sacrosanct ledger; the stacks of invaluable cigar boxes stuffed with masses of expired prescriptions; the locked and well-guarded narcotics cabinet; the post office and the safe in which the post-office receipts were kept. Even the great, weighty, monosyllabically blunt hanging sign— "Drugs"—had been brought over and rehung, and it, too, looked different now. In the summer heat it dropped its black rectangular shadow over Mr. Isaacs' already shadowy headquarters, where vials of live worms were crowded side by side with vials of nails and screws.

At around this time, my mother's youngest brother, my uncle Rubin, had come to stay with us—no one knew for how long—in our little house on St. Paul Avenue, a short walk from the Park View. Five of us lived in that house: my parents, my grandmother, my brother, and I. Rubin, who was called Ruby, was now the sixth. He was a bachelor and something of a family conundrum. He was both bitter and cheerful; effervescence would give way to lassitude. He taught me how to draw babies and bunnies, and could draw anything himself; he wrote ingenious comic jingles, which he illustrated as adroitly, it struck me, as Edward Lear; he cooked up mouthwatering corn fritters and designed fruit salads in the shape of ravishing unearthly blossoms. When now and then it fell to him to put me to bed, he always sang the same heartbreaking lullaby—"Sometimes I fee-eel like a motherless child, a long, long way-ay from ho-ome"—in a deep and sweet quaver. In those days, he was mostly jobless; on occasion, he would crank up his tin lizzie and drive out to upper Westchester to prune trees. Once, he was stopped at a police roadblock, under suspicion of being the Lindbergh-baby kidnapper—the back seat of his messy old Ford was strewn with ropes, hooks, and my discarded baby bottles.

Ruby had been disappointed in love, and was somehow a disappointment to everyone around him. When he was melancholy or resentful, the melancholy was irritable and the resentment acrid. As a very young man, he had been single-minded in a way that none of his immigrant relations, or the snobbish mother of the girlfriend who had been coerced into jilting him, could understand or sympathize with. In czarist Russia's restricted Pale of Settlement, a pharmacist was the highest vocation a Jew could attain to. In a family of pharmacists, Ruby wanted to be a farmer. Against opposition, he had gone off to a farm school in New Jersey—one of several Jewish agricultural projects sponsored by the German philanthropist Baron Maurice de Hirsch. Ruby was always dreaming up one sort of horticultural improvement or another, and sometimes took me with him to visit a certain Dr. McClean, at the New York Botanical Garden, whom he was trying to interest in one of his inventions. He was kindly received, but nothing came of it. Despite his energy and originality, all Ruby's hopes and strivings collapsed in futility.

His presence now was fortuitous: he could assist in the move from Tessie's place to the new location. But his ingenuity, it would soon develop, was benison from the goddess Flora. The Park View occupied all the width but not the entire depth of the lot on which it was built. It had, of course, a welcoming front door, through which customers passed; but there was also a back door, past a little aisle adjoining the prescription room in the rear of the store, and well out of sight. When you walked out this back door, you were confronted by an untamed patch of weeds and stones, some of them as thick as boulders. At the very end of it lay a large flat rock, in the center of which someone had scratched a mysterious X. The X, it turned out, was a surveyor's sign; it had been there long before my parents bought the lot. It meant that the property extended to that point and no farther.

I was no stranger either to the lot or to its big rock. It was where the neighborhood children played—a sparse group in that sparsely populated place. Sometimes the rock was a pirate ship; sometimes it was a pretty room in a pretty house; in January it held a snow fort. But early one summer evening, when the red ball of the sun was very low, a little girl named Theresa, whose hair was as red as the sun's red ball, discovered the surveyor's X and warned me against stamping on it. If you stamp on a cross, she said, the Devil's helpers climb right out from inside the earth and grab you and take you away to be tortured. "I don't believe that," I said, and stamped on the X as hard as I could. Instantly, Theresa sent out a terrified shriek; chased by the red-gold zigzag of her hair, she fled. I stood there abandoned—suppose it was true? In the silence all around, the wavering green weeds seemed taller than ever before.

Looking out from the back door at those same high weeds, my mother, like Theresa, saw hallucinatory shapes rising out of the ground. But it was not the Devil's minions that she imagined streaming upward; it was their very opposite—a vision of celestial growths and fragrances, brilliant botanical hues, golden pears and yellow sunflower faces, fruitful vines and dreaming gourds. She imagined an enchanted garden. She imagined a secret Eden.

What she did not imagine was that Ruby, himself so unpeaceable, would turn out to be the viceroy of her peaceable kingdom. Ruby was angry at my mother; he was angry at everyone but me—I was too young to be held responsible for his lost loves and aspirations. But he could not be separated from his love of fecund dirt. Dirt—the brown dirt of the earth—inspired him; the feel and smell of dirt uplifted him; he took an artist's pleasure in the soil and all its generative properties. And though he claimed to scorn my mother, he became the subaltern of her passion. Like some wizard commander of the stones—they were scattered everywhere in a wild jumble—he swept them into orderliness. A pack of stones was marshalled into a low wall. Five stones were transformed into a perfect set of stairs. Seven stones surrounded what was to become a flower bed. Stones were borders, stones were pathways, stones— placed just so—were natural sculptures. And, finally, Ruby commanded the stones to settle in a circle in the very center of the lot. Inside the circle there was to be a green serenity of grass, invaded only by the blunders of violets and wandering buttercups. Outside the circle, the earth would be a fructifying engine. It was a dreamer's circle, like the moon or the sun, or a fairy ring, or a mystical small Stonehenge, miniaturized by a spell.

The back yard was cleared, but it was not yet a garden. Like a merman combing a mermaid's weedy hair, my uncle Ruby had unravelled primeval tangles and brambles. He had set up two tall metal poles to accommodate a rough canvas hammock, with a wire strung from the top of one pole to the other. Over this wire a rain-faded old shop awning had been flung, so that the hammock became a tent or cave or darkened den. A back-yard hammock! I had encountered such things only in storybooks.

And then my uncle was gone—drafted before the garden could be dug. German tanks were biting into Europe. Weeping, my grandmother pounded her breast with her fist: the British White Paper of 1939 had declared that ships packed with Jewish refugees would be barred from the beaches of Haifa and Tel Aviv, and returned to a Nazi doom. In P.S. 71, our neighborhood school, the boys were drawing cannons and warplanes; the girls were drawing figure skaters in tutus; both boys and girls were drawing the Trylon and the Perisphere. The Trylon was a three-sided pyramid. The Perisphere was a shining globe. They were already as sublimely legendary as the Taj Mahal. The "official" colors of the 1939 World's Fair were orange and blue: everyone knew this; everyone had ridden in the noiselessly moving armchairs of the Futurama into the Fair's City of Tomorrow, where the elevated highways of the impossibly futuristic nineteen-sixties materialized among inconceivable suburbs. In the magical lanes of Flushing, you could watch yourself grin on a television screen as round and small as the mouth of a teacup. My grandmother, in that frail year of her dying, was taken to see the Jewish Palestine Pavilion.

Ruby sent a photograph of himself in Army uniform, and a muffled recording of his voice, all songs and jolly jingles, from a honky-tonk arcade in an unnamed Caribbean town. It was left to my mother to dig the garden. I have no inkling of when or how. I lived inside the hammock all that time, under the awning, enclosed; I read and read. Sometimes, for a treat, I would be given two nickels for carfare and a pair of quarters, and then I would climb the double staircase to the train and go all the way to Fifty-ninth Street: you could enter Bloomingdale's directly from the subway, without ever glimpsing daylight. I would run up the steps to the book department, on the mezzanine, moon over the Nancy Drew series in an agony of choosing ("Password to Larkspur Lane," "The Whispering Statue," each for fifty cents), and run down to the subway again, with my lucky treasure. An hour and a half later, I would be back in the hammock, under the awning, while the afternoon sun broiled on. But such a trip was rare. Mostly, the books came from the Travelling Library; inside my hammock cave the melting glue of new bindings sent out a blissful redolence. And now my mother would emerge from the back door of the Park View, carrying—because it was so hot under the awning—half a cantaloupe, with a hillock of vanilla ice cream in its scooped-out center. (Have I ever been so safe, so happy, since? Has consciousness ever felt so steady, so unimperilled, so immortal?)

Across the ocean, synagogues were being torched, refugees were in flight. On American movie screens Ginger Rogers and Fred Astaire whirled in and out of the March of Time's grim newsreels—Chamberlain with his defeatist umbrella, the Sudetenland devoured, Poland invaded. Meanwhile, my mother's garden grew. The wild raw field Ruby had regimented was ripening now into a luxuriant and powerful fertility: all around my uncle's talismanic ring of stones the ground swelled with thick, savory smells. Corn tassels hung down over the shut green-leaf lids of pearly young cobs. Fat tomatoes reddened on sticks. The bumpy scalps of cucumbers poked up. And flowers! First, as tall as the hammock poles, a flock of hunchbacked sunflowers, their heads too weighty for their shoulders—huge, heavy heads of seeds, and a ruff of yellow petals. At their feet, rows of zinnias and marigolds, with tiny violets and the weedy pink buds of clover sidling between.

Now and then a praying mantis—a stiffly marching fake leaf—would rub its skinny forelegs together and stare at you with two stern black dots. Or there would be a sudden blizzard of butterflies—mostly white and mothlike; but sometimes a great black-veined monarch would alight on a stone, in perfect stillness. Year by year, the shade of a trio of pear trees widened and deepened.

Did it rain? It must have rained—it must have thundered—in those successive summers of my mother's garden; but I remember a perpetual sunlight, hot and honeyed, and the airless boil under the awning, and the heart-piercing scalliony odor of library glue (so explicit that I can this minute re-create it in my very tear ducts, as a kind of mourning), and the fear of bees.

No one knew the garden was there. It was utterly hidden. You could not see it, or suspect it, inside the Park View, and, because it was nested in a wilderness of empty lots, it was altogether invisible from any surrounding street. It was a small secluded paradise.

And what vegetable chargings, what ferocities of growth, the turbulent earth pushed out! Buzzings and dapplings. Birds dipping their beaks in an orgy of seed-lust. It was as if the ground itself were crying peace, peace; and the war roared on. In Europe, the German death factories were pumping out smoke and human ash from a poisoned orchard of chimneys. In Pelham Bay, among bees and white-wing flutterings, the sweet brown dirt pumped ears of corn.

Though I was mostly alone there, I was never lonely in the garden. But, on the other side of the door, inside the Park View, an unfamiliar churning had begun—a raucous teeming, the world turning on its hinge. In the aftermath of Pearl Harbor, there was all at once a job for nearly everyone, and money to spend in any cranny of wartime leisure. The Depression was receding. On weekends, the subway spilled out mobs of city picnickers into the green fields of Pelham Bay Park, bringing a tentative prosperity to the neighborhood—especially on Sundays. I dreaded and hated this new Sunday frenzy, when the Park View seemed less a pharmacy than a carnival stand, and my isolation grew bleak. Open shelves sprouted in the aisles, laden with anomalous racks of sunglasses, ice coolers, tubes of mosquito repellent and suntan lotion, paper cups, colorful towers of hats—sailors' and fishermen's caps, celluloid visors, straw topis and sombreros, headgear of every conceivable shape. Thirsty picnickers stood three deep at the fountain, clamoring for ice-cream cones or sodas. The low, serious drugstore voices that accompanied the Park View's weekday decorum were swept away by revolving, laughing crowds—carnival crowds. And at the close of these frenetic summer Sundays my parents would anxiously count up the cash register in the worn night of their exhaustion, and I would hear their joyful disbelief: unimaginable riches, almost seventy-five dollars in a single day! Then, when the safe was locked up, and the long cords of the fluorescent lights pulled, they would drift in the dimness into the garden, to breathe the cool fragrance. At this starry hour, the katydids were screaming in chorus, and fireflies bleeped like errant semaphores. In the enigmatic dark, my mother and father, with their heads together in silhouette, looked just then as I pictured them looking on the Albany night boat, on June 19, 1921, their wedding day. There was a serial photo from that long-ago time I often gazed at—a strip taken in an automatic photo booth in fabled, faraway Albany. It showed them leaning close, my young father quizzical, my young mother trying to smile, or else trying not to; the corners of her lips wandered toward one loveliness or the other. They had brought back a honeymoon souvenir: three sandstone monkeys joined at the elbows—see no evil, hear no evil, speak no evil. And now, in their struggling forties, standing in Ruby's circle of stones, they breathed in the night smells of the garden, onion grass and honeysuckle, and felt their private triumph. Seventy-five dollars in seventeen hours!

Nearly all the drugstores of the old kind are gone, in Pelham Bay and elsewhere. The Park View Pharmacy lives only in a secret Eden behind my eyes. Gone are Bernardini, Pressman, Weiss, the rival druggists on the way to Westchester Square. They all, like my father, rolled suppositories on glass slabs and ground powders with brass pestles. My mother's garden has returned to its beginning: a wild patch, though enclosed now by brick house after brick house. The houses have high stoops; they are city houses. The meadows are striped with highways. Spy Oak gave up its many ghosts long ago.

But under a matting of decayed pear pits and thriving ragweed back of what used to be the Park View, Ruby's circle of stones stands frozen. The earth, I suppose, has covered them over, as—far off, in an overgrown old cemetery on Staten Island—it covers my dreaming mother, my father, my grandmother, my resourceful and embittered farmer uncle.

Edward Hoagland

Aging

We age at different rates, just as our pacing in adolescence and later is different. Hampered by a stutter, for instance, I was instead precocious as a writer and published my first novel before I had lost my virginity. In fact, the publisher had to fly me east for a last-minute consultation because their lawyer in reading the proofs of the book discovered a passage where I seemed to be describing a sexual act which could not be legally depicted in 1955—only to realize in interrogating me, of course, that I had never heard of or even conceived of the practice of cunnilingus. He forbore explaining, and I was drafted into the army, and my twenties then became like other people's teens as far as sexual experimentation was concerned. Thus my thirties probably corresponded to their twenties, and my forties were naturally rather like their thirties: in that aspect of life perhaps my prime. It seems to make it easier now to be in my sixties, because I don't have to look back in memory very far to uncommon adventures.

Sex is hardly the only form love takes, however, and most of us become better parents, better friends as we mature. The

ripening thirties and forties bring some patience and perspective. You learn to make the most of an hour with your daughter
at the zoo, or lunch with an old classmate who's resettling and
needs to find a job. Dawn in June, when you're my age, sixty-
three, with the songbirds singing, and a mother merganser flying over, an otter swimming ahead of your canoe suddenly
dodges as a duck hawk sweeps out of the trees. She had been
decoying you away from her knot of half a dozen bobbing babies; but down she splashes into the river, immediately diving
to escape the falcon, and succeeds. Great swamp maples and
willows; a wood turtle; a mallard family that appears to have
eluded the falcon's notice—he's gone after a blue jay. You're
with a friend who is saddled with heart trouble, and this is just
the kind of spectacle that concentrates your minds. Not only
the glee that you two felt when you were young and predatory
like the otter and the falcon, or the mercurial delight of being
alive with the sun and a breeze on the water, but the wistful
awe of knowing you won't always be outdoors in a canoe during
the spring in what looks awfully like God's best heaven. If it
isn't, then what is?

Summer won't be endless now; nor episodes of drama and
romance. The well takes longer to refill. Even walking, I pant
when going uphill—a nice healthy sort of pant in my case, I
hope, because I think that, in our day, our life spans, unless we
drive like maniacs, are determined by our genes. My father
died at just sixty-three, my mother is ninety-four, and I've always felt closer to her. People tend to gain in tolerance and
grow more generous-spirited as they get older, but on the other
hand, we often lose connectedness and some degree of interest
in what's going on. So our generosity or tolerance is not all that
expensive to us. Bring a cruel conundrum to our attention and
we will certainly sympathize, but we are quite inured to the
impossibility of combating injustice and to the corruption of the
sort of powerful people who otherwise might try. And much as
our backs slip out of whack at some small sidewise tug, so do
our minds skid off the point when fatigued a little or short-
circuited by a spark. I've been publishing books for forty years

and I don't have a fastball anymore, just a knuckleball, spitball, and other Satchel Paigey stuff.

You're only as old as you feel, is a refrain one hears enough that it must have some truth in it, though your oncologist might disagree. The remissions he sees uplift the spirits of so many dying people a week short of death, when they think they are going to live on for years, could be interpreted as the exuberance of fetal angels confused by a passage toward ecstasy, or as an aspect of the anesthetic that commonly tranquilizes creatures that are being engulfed by death, whether a wildebeest in the jaws of a lion or a frog in the mouth of a snake. While in the army, I worked in a morgue and noticed that most dead people smile.

And we are, indeed, in some respects as young as we feel. Life is moments, day by day, not a chronometer or a contractual commitment by God. The digits of one's age do not correspond to the arrhythmia of one's heart or to the secret chemistry in our lymph nodes that, mysteriously going rancid, can betray us despite all of the surgery, dentistry, and other codger-friendly amenities that money buys. Good works don't keep you off the undertaker's slab, either. But cheeriness, maybe yes. Cheery, lean, little guys do seem to squeeze an extra decade out of the miser up above, as if feeling young were not as important as having a peppy metabolism and appreciating being alive.

Blurry eyesight, fragile knees, broken sleep, the need to pee a dozen times a day (when somebody honks at my car, parked at the side of the interstate, I assume it's a man my own age) are not inherently fun, however, though the smoothing-out of temperament does help you cope. Your ingenuity, your curiosity must find a new focus, not simply exploring the world as a kid does. When I watched from my canoe a tall blue heron stalking field mice through the grass, then washing them down with minnows and tadpoles, I didn't experience the surge of ambition to be a zoologist I would have felt when I was fifteen. I just wanted to go on seeing these intricate things, in July, and next year.

Among my friends who have been notified that they were terminally ill, those who died least miserably, or most gracefully, were people who could be intrigued and mentally absorbed by the peculiar changes their bodies underwent. They didn't stop observing the incongruous handicaps, the bemusing treatments that they were subjected to. The music they loved, snatches from books that had meant a lot, the news of friends who stopped in to visit, the total novelty of dying, the civil war afflicting their bodies—comprehending such a crush of sensations took all their waking time (a last hearing of *The Children's Corner Suite!*) and emotional resilience. It was a voyage they stayed on deck for.

During a spell of semiblindness a few years ago, I found myself, too, registering the dismally curious stages of what was happening to me, as I gave up driving, lost the capacity to see birds in the sky, then gradually the crowns of the loveliest trees, and my friends' faces close at hand, a fascinating catastrophe. Surgery saved and rejuvenated me; I felt like Lazarus. But I learned how life itemizes exactly what you are losing. With binoculars around my neck, and then a telescope at the window, I put off curtain time. (The moon you can watch endlessly, or a lilac branch bounce in the wind, but people object to being gazed at.) As my daughter dropped in, and the leaves outside turned yellow, I was scrambling to improvise solutions: how to get a particular errand done, how to read three paragraphs by closing one eye and focusing the other ever closer. But would I see her face again? I was reviewing a day at the beach I had had ten years before in San Francisco with the love of my life, stripping the rubber band out of her hair and kissing a pimple she tried to hide with her free hand, as the purple underbelly of a rainstorm rolled in, but reminded myself that since things hadn't worked out, she wasn't really the love of my life. Or was she?

Life is minutiae, and aging progresses by two steps forward and then one back, jerky as one's legs become. And though, for instance, I was rejuvenated by millennium-type eye surgery (when Nature had had it fixed for aeons that people my age should quietly go blind or have heart attacks without by-passes, thus decently getting offstage and leaving enough space for younger people and other mammalians), my memory kept slipping out of gear, as if a cog was chipped, at the same time that I had more to remember in a lengthening life, and my temper grew crankier, though in fact my true balance was becoming more benign. While less in a hurry to get places, I drove worse because my mind was absent. My eyesight had been sharpened with plastic implants, but my mind coughed like an old car's motor and I would pull out into traffic without using them.

My chest ached afterward a little when this happened, as it does when my waking dreams go wandering into uncataloged drawers of my memory where they have no pleasant business being. Yet I don't glance back and notice missed opportunities. Wanting so passionately to be a writer, I grabbed what I saw as the main chance at every turn, avoiding offers to become a tenured professor or media editorialist in favor of staying free-lance. Living frugally came naturally to me as a stutterer who had wondered how it would be possible to earn a living anyway, and as a price to pay. The only regret that accompanied this choice was not feeling free to have and educate more than one child, instead of the three or four I would have liked to raise if I had had more income. I've never been treated scurvily, at least by my lights, and don't experience chagrin of that sort, looking back. But of course I debate my two marriages and the crossed wires that sometimes threw sparks, or other friendships that lived or lapsed. At parties, you recognize why old-fashioned women tended to be matchmakers. Couples seem so much happier than single people, above a certain age. You rarely meet a widow or a widower who is sighing with relief.

Marriage as the long-term pairing of men and women is such a hunter-gatherer sort of idea that its durability testifies to how primeval we still are, despite the voltage and velocities of our compression-chamber days. Our guns and murders do too, and the over-the-mountain infidelities that entertain us, our greed for swapping stacks of greenbacks ("frogskins," they used to be called) for goodies, and the special appetite for travel that seizes us, young and old. We hit the road as kids, and then again as old scouts furloughed from the city, retire to cruise ships or Winnebagos forty years later, feeling we've been bottled up, and forage in foreign markets, roaming for the sake of roving, watching the sun's progress as immemorial theater across the sky.

My work enabled me to travel even during my breadwinning years, in Europe or close to the Arctic or below the Sahara. I found the more you do, the more you're up to doing. Camping in the Rockies prepares you for Alaska, and Alaska for Africa. As you grow relaxed about the procedures of distant travel, you get resourceful about the details, locating a tuning fork within yourself that hears the same note in other people wherever you go. Even in war or famine or dictatorship—because we are not speaking of pollyanna travel—your intuitions are valid because all of us have a rendezvous with death, however humble and anticlimactic that may finally be, and exotic disasters should not be incomprehensible. Like Mobutu or Mussolini, we've been cruel and grandiose, have strutted, lied, and postured, known sneaky lust and shifty theft and opportunistic betrayal. The spectrum of behavior we witness in going abroad is seldom all that foreign to us.

The eye surgeon had warned me in 1992 that my blindness was going to recur and I should see whatever of the world I wanted to take in rather soon. So, at around sixty, I visited India and Antarctica, each for the first time, and returned to Africa twice. It was different because in the first two cases I was treated to blue-ribbon, well-financed wilderness tours of sights I could never have reached when my legs were young and strong. And in Africa I was already known for a book I had written there sixteen years before. The day after arriving in Nairobi, I got a call at the New Stanley Hotel from a stranger named Rob Rose, who was with the Catholic Relief Services agency and asked if I would like to accompany him tomorrow on a ten-day trip into guerrilla territory in the civil war raging in the southern Sudan, where roughly two million people have died. During the 1970s, in peacetime (and when I was twice as fit for hard travel), it had required months for me to win permission from the Sudanese government to visit the same high wild tribal redoubt on the upper White Nile.

We set off by Land-Rover for Kampala, in Uganda, spent a night, then ventured quickly through disputed territory in that country's own separate simmering civil war, up to the town of Gulu, with only one car breakdown. Next morning, we continued north through the hamlet of Atiak and choppy, evacuated grasslands and acacia forests and two military posts to no-man's-land and finally the Sudanese village of Nimule. Famine country was just beyond. The Dinka and Nuer had been allied against the Arab government in Khartoum, but now, alas, were fighting against each other as well. Their positions had consequently been shattered, their cattle and grain supplies destroyed. They'd fled to Ethiopia, been defeated there again, and retreated in a starving condition back to the Nile. But the aid agencies that had been feeding them, frightened by the lethal infighting—in which three UN workers and a journalist had been shot—had pulled out.

I felt sheepish for not having foreseen more than a hint of these developments during my previous trip. Yet I was white-haired now, which changed the character of my reception, even allowing for the impact of the emergency. One elder thought I must be a "King." When I said America didn't have kings, he amended that to "Millionaire," looking at my hiking boots; he was barefoot. A white-haired white man, to have come so far, must be at least a high official of the United Nations, who had heard a hundred thousand people here were starving. Pathetic, short, hand-shaped little mounds paralleled the networks of footpaths where we walked the next day. Each was marked by ragged tokens of the famished body newly buried, a broken doll, a tiny skirt or holey sweater that had been laid on top. Dysentery or pneumonia might have abbreviated the child's suffering, but surely a senior figure like me, beholding such a tragedy, might intervene potently.

My friend Rob, half my age, by dint of sleepless and dynamic initiatives, had indeed brought fifty-eight truckloads of corn from the Catholic Relief Services warehouse in the Kenyan port of Mombasa, the first food delivery in a couple of months to the refugee encampments we visited. In my eyes, he was a genuine hero, braving the dangers here and the UN's tacit boycott. But at Aswa, Amei, and Ateppi, smiling desperate children by the many hundreds ran to me, a mere itinerant journalist, to touch my hands and cheer me in the Dinka language as the godfather or patriarch who seemed to have arrived to save their lives. If only more food came!—it may have been the most pointed moment of my life. Some of them, boys and girls of six or twelve, had already shrunk to skeletal wraiths, monkey-faced from malnutrition, and I saw newborns who would die without ever tasting milk. Their mothers, stretched beside them on the ground, were themselves dying and, prompted by our guides, partly raised their bodies to show me their flat breasts.

Seven women were said to have been grabbed by crocodiles on the bank of the Nile, where they had gone to try to harvest lily roots or fetch water or spear a fish. Wild dates and nuts and the tufts of ricey wild plants had long since been exhausted; the rats smoked from their holes, the grasshoppers roasted. The local streams had been finger-sieved for shiners and crustaceans, and every songbird slingshotted. The very air smelt burnt. And inevitably, we Americans ate only sparingly, twice a day, whisked out of sight of the Dinka to a church compound at Loa, on a hilltop ten miles away. Africa doesn't get any prettier or more pristine than this mountainous region of the southern Sudan because its splendid forests have not been logged—or even the gold lode sought, whose nuggets you could buy in the village of Opari, near us—due to the guerrilla wars subsurface here ever since the middle 1950s, when the British left. Driving, you may pass a man dead of a bullet hole on the road; and just while we were there, Amnesty International later reported, the Dinka leadership had executed twenty-two of their own soldiers at Nimule, and were torturing other out-of-favor commanders near Loa, nailing one man's foot to the floor. Rob became disillusioned the next year, when he moved to Nimule with his wife to be helpful and guerrilla soldiers clubbed to death the African who was guarding his house. In 1995, I went briefly back and lost some illusions too.

But lives were being saved by our trip. Even divided among a hundred thousand souls, fifty-eight truckloads of corn staved off the agony of hunger pangs awhile, and my white pate was winning me more credit than I deserved. The hospital was the worst place, ringed by hungry irregular troops, the famished patients lying bedless on concrete, rationed to one cup of cornmeal per day. The nurses were so weakened they could scarcely function and were distracted by their own children's frantic straits. It seemed shameful for a well-fed man from Vermont to be touring this furnace unscathed, with boys and women rushing to him to intercede in Washington, perhaps, and bring it to an end. I did write about what I had seen, and did at the time shout at the guerrilla general who was thought to have helped precipitate this immediate calamity by setting up the killing of the UN workers (not realizing that white people are as tribal as anybody else), as I would not have had the confidence to do when I was young. At roadblocks I was more at ease when ordered out of the car by teenagers with Kalashnikovs to be checked; less edgy when we broke down in Uganda in lion and bandit country. As on the more ambitious journey in 1995, I knew that mines are more of a danger than lions, and malaria more than mortar shells, or the kids at a roadblock, who are looking for other African teenagers to kill, not a cautious and courteous white man.

Aging is not a serene occupation. You stumble physically and tire quickly, maybe even indoors, and your mind can be tricked by threadbare circuitry into surreal or simple confusions, like the proverbial second childhood, when for a moment you don't know where you are. Not in Africa, though; you're on your toes. And I don't think of travel as a vacation, or of retirement. I'd love to see Venice again, but doubt I have anything to say about it that hasn't been better said. So I turn to the new phenomena of the Third World for trips, barely scratched by various hassled travel writers. I want to work out toward the brink of what I think is going to happen—the widespread death of nature, the approaching holocaust of famines, while Westerners retreat in veiled panic into what they will prefer to regard as the realer world of cyberspace. Old age will not be an enemy, in that event.

The distractions, ruses, nostrums you used to employ to foil depression, such as sexual flings or mountain climbing, are not in the repertoire of most old guys; and their suicide rate can nearly approximate the febrile teens'. But they're also freer of sexual unease and self-esteem or money compulsions. They may lack money, yet not care as much; can better do without. And "seniors," after all, are living on borrowed time—borrowed from the unborn whose world they're using up. I'm almost twice as old as an average American's life expectancy in colonial times. Just a hundred years ago, I'd be blind, crippled with hernias, if not already dead from asthma, appendicitis, or parathyroid disease and other stuff I've had before.

And money can be an equalizer. On a ferryboat from Martha's Vineyard to Cape Cod last summer, I noticed with some sympathy an oldish man standing on the deck, who the whole way across the water and as if for dear life, hugged a sturdy, gaunt, blond, young-fortyish woman. Balancing uncomfortably against the boat's rock, she patiently allowed him to do as he wished, nursely in manner if not in fact. The two young boys traveling with them looked on, amused or embarrassed, though it was not clear whose kids they originally were, his or hers. From his clinging hunger and needy passion—stock-still on the deck hugging her for forty-five minutes, except when she excused herself once to go to the bathroom—she was a new and important acquisition for him. He felt thankful and lucky. Though of normal build, he looked frail and unsteady, as if he might have just had a major health scare, and was not making her a spectacle for our sake—the other passengers—but his own. Though she didn't care for the compulsive, public part, on the other hand, like a good sport and with a kind of good-hearted, working-class honesty, she appeared to recognize that it was part of the deal. If you become the third wife of an ailing businessman twenty-five years older and very much richer than you, and he's recuperating from surgery at his summer home, you let him hug you round the clock, with or without an audience.

In my fifties, I had a sizable love affair with a woman seventeen years younger than me, a nurse who took me all over Alaska on her supervisory rounds. In chartered Cessnas, we flew to remote Eskimo or Indian villages, sleeping on the floor of the health clinic or school gym in each of these while she consulted with patients and the local nurse. Frigid, wild places where in January my eyelids sometimes froze shut and I would not have gone by myself, but with her felt both bold and safe, knowing that whatever happened to me, I would not be alone. And somehow, like the Eskimos', her eyelids did not get sealed by the frosts. Nor was she winded or chilled on our strenuous walks. Whatever risks we met, surely she could wiggle me out. I remember hugging her intensely for her sex and youth, and like a lifeline to safety and my own youth. Sometimes she would pull my head next to hers and look in the mirror to see how others visualized us—was I conspicuously wrinkly and gray?—but decided no. We made love extensively every night for weeks, and the age disparity seemed to add spice. A tutor indoors, a dependent outside, I clung and pumped as if doubling my luck, my vanishing span on earth; and if I died I would be in her arms, which would make it all right. Now, I couldn't possibly do the things we did, in bed or out, flying all over Alaska, landing on rivers at hamlets where a white man was not welcome unless he couldn't be ejected because he was with the head nurse. It was delicious to bask in my friend's protection, a further frisson to fanciful sex. And chums who are eighty tell me how much more I'll lose by seventy, not to mention at their age, of the physical capacity I had at fifty-three.

But did we (we wonder) catch the spirit of our time? Did

we grasp a piece of it and participate? You know how a composer like George Gershwin captured the expatriate zest of the 1920s with *An American in Paris* and then in the democratic 1930s wrote *Porgy and Bess.* Aaron Copland, too, not a weathervane, spoke for the thumb-your-nose 1930s with *Billy the Kid* and then did *Appalachian Spring* in the patriotic, heal-the-wounds mid-1940s. Our telescoping century, from the Edwardians through two world wars to cyberspace—my mother, who is still alive, saw the first electric lights and automobiles come to her town—has made it hard to keep current. One wouldn't even want to have been a flapper in 1929, a Red-hunter a quarter-century later, and a bond salesman in the fabulous 1980s.

I left the city for the country in the 1980s, preferring at that point, I guess, to watch the carnival at one remove, and haven't shifted from typewriting essays to word-processing screenplays, as so many good folks have. Indeed my politics and style of dress (both shabby-Ivy) have scarcely changed since I left college. I pounded cross-country during the 1950s; heard Martin Luther King deliver his radiant speech at the Lincoln Memorial in 1963; protested against Vietnam; and saw ticker tape parades for FDR, Truman, Eisenhower, Kennedy, Johnson, and Nixon, plus King George VI and Charles de Gaulle. Didn't do drugs, but saw action enough, and didn't drop out of the domestic brouhaha until ten years ago.

I wanted to know shadbush from elderberry, dogwood from chokecherry, bluebirds from indigo buntings, yellowthroats from yellow warblers, the French horn from an English horn, a trombone from a sousaphone, Red Grange from Red Barber, and Newt Gingrich from Joe McCarthy. We opt for what we want as daily conversation in the privacy of our minds, and whether on most days we get to watch the sunrise and listen to a snatch of the genius of Bach. It's not expensive to pay attention to the phases of the moon, to transplant lemon lilies and watch a garter snake birthing forty babies and a catbird grabbing some, or listen to the itchy-britches of the Canada geese as autumn waxes. We will be motes in the ocean again soon, leached out of the soil of some graveyard, and everlastingly rocking. That is my sense of an afterlife and my comfort. The hurly-burly of streambed turmoil will be our last rush-hour traffic—thocketting through boulders, past perch pools and drift logs. Enough, we will say, reaching tidewater. We saw enough.

Contributors' Notes

Emily Fox Gordon lives in Houston, Texas. Her fiction and essays have appeared in *The Gettysburg Review, Boulevard, Salmagundi,* and *Southwest Review*. She is working on a collection of essays tentatively titled *From the Pisgah Mount*.

Margaret Talbot is a Senior Editor at *The New Republic* magazine in Washington, D.C. She was formerly editor of *Lingua Franca,* and has written for a number of publications, including *The Washington Post, Slate,* and *Vogue*.

"I wrote this essay in the first place because Leon Wieseltier, the literary editor of *The New Republic,* had the lovely idea of assigning it to me. But I think I enjoyed writing it as much as I did because I was very pregnant with my first child at the time and thinking a lot about the perils and pleasures of domesticity."

David Mamet's plays include *Sexual Perversity in Chicago, Speed-the-Plow, Oleanna,* and *Glengarry Glen Ross,* for which he received the Pulitzer Prize. He has also written and directed several motion pictures, including *House of Games, Things Change,* and *Homicide,* and written screenplays for *The Untouchables, The Verdict, Hoffa,* and other movies. His previous books include *The Village,* a novel, and the essay collections *Writing in Restaurants, Some Freaks,* and *The Cabin*. He lives in Massachusetts and Vermont.

Vivian Gornick is the author, most recently, of *Fierce Attachments* (a memoir) and *Approaching Eye Level* (a collection of personal essays). *The End of the Novel of Love* (a collection of critical essays) will be published by Beacon Press in the fall of 1997. She lives in New York City.

"For years I thought 'The Catskills Remembered' was a short story. It was only when I realized it was a memoir that my memories clarified and 'the story' fell into place."

Mary Gaitskill's books include *Bad Behavior* (Vintage), a book of stories, and *Two Girls, Fat and Thin* (Bantam), a novel. She lives in Houston.

Christopher Hitchens writes a monthly column for *Vanity Fair* and also contributes the "Minority Report" column to *The Nation.* He has published two collections of essays, *Prepared for the Worst* and *For the Sake of Argument,* and is working on a third. His most recent book is *The Missionary Position: Mother Teresa in Theory and Practice.* In 1997, in a visiting capacity, he was Andrew W. Mellon Professor of English Literature at the University of Pittsburgh.

"I also taught a course on the history of free expression in America, and had to explain to my students that, while the United States Constitution doesn't mandate an opposition party, it does give the press the right, and in a sense the duty, of untrammeled liberty. I have been depressed for some time at the scant use that is made of this privilege. During the especially dispiriting election campaign of 1996, I also became fed up with the way that so-called public intellectuals invented apologetics for the mediocre status quo. 'Against Lesser Evilism' is a polemic against the practical consequences of such a style, but also, I hope, an attack on the wretched reasoning that underlies it."

Diana Trilling was one of America's foremost essayists, reviewers, and cultural critics. Among her writing credits are five books: *Reviewing the Forties, We Must My Darlings, A Visit to Camelot, The Beginning of the Journey,* and *Mrs. Harris: The Death of the Scarsdale Diet Doctor.* Her work has appeared in *The New Yorker, The Atlantic, Harper's, The Nation,* and *The Partisan Review.* Diana Trilling died in October of 1996.

Jean Baudrillard was born in Reims in 1929 and now lives in Paris. From 1966 to 1987 he taught sociology at the University of Nanterre.

His books include *America, Cool Memories I, The Transparency of Evil, The System of Objects,* and *The Perfect Crime,* all published by Verso.

Daniel Harris is the author of *The Rise and Fall of Gay Culture.* His work appears in *Harper's* and *Salmagundi.* He lives in Brooklyn, N.Y.

Bob Shacochis's first novel, *Swimming in the Volcano,* was shortlisted in 1994 for the National Book Award. His short story collections are *Easy in the Islands,* which received a National Book Award in 1985, and *The Next New World,* which was awarded the Prix de Rome by the American Academy of Arts and Letters. In 1994 he also published *Domesticity,* a collection of essays about food and love. Mr. Shacochis has worked in the Peace Corps, has taught at the University of Iowa, as well as many other writing programs, and is a contributing editor to *Harper's, Outside,* and *GQ.* Shacochis is currently working on *The Immaculate Invasion,* a nonfiction book about the military intervention in Haiti.

Hubert Butler was born in 1900 at Maidenhall, County Kilkenny. After school and university education in England, he worked in Ireland for several years before spending much of the 1920s and 1930s in Egypt, Russia, the Balkans, and the Baltic countries. Upon his father's death in 1941, he returned to Maidenhall, where he lived for the next half-century. Butler's essays were first published in book form in Dublin in 1985–86 in four successive volumes, which later formed the basis of *Independent Spirit: Essays,* from which "Little K" is drawn.

Hilton Als writes most frequently for *The New Yorker* and *Grand Street* magazines. He lives in New York City. *The Women* is his first book.

William T. Vollmann's books include *You Bright and Risen Angels, The Rainbow Stories, Whores for Gloria, An Afghanistan Picture Show, Thirteen Stories and Thirteen Epitaphs, Butterfly Stories,* and three of the projected seven novels in his "Seven Dreams" series: *The Ice-Shirt, Fathers and Crows,* and *The Rifles.* The recipient of a Whiting Foundation Award, he lives in California.

"I am pleased and flattered to have 'The Prophet of the Road' appear in this collection. Mr. Lopate's *Art of the Personal Essay* is one of my bedside companions.

When writing makes its last stand, I imagine that it will do so (without surrender) on the battlefield of exposition. The succubi and incubi of the film studios can tell stories; sometimes, like that great Satan called television, they can even talk about them; but only the written word can truly explain them."

Aldo Buzzi is the author of *Journey to the Land of the Flies* (Random House) from which the essay here published was selected. Born in Italy, on the shore of the Lake of Como, he trained as an architect in Milan, where he now lives.

"Someone asked me if all my travels were real travels. Well . . . this is not the point. I'm a mix of mobile traveler and still traveler, and that is the result."

Thomas Larson's "Freshman Comp, 1967" is one of a dozen pieces he is collecting for a volume of personal essays about his classroom experiences as student and teacher from kindergarten learner to college professor. He has written a memoir, *River of Fathers*, about his father and his sons, and he teaches writing at San Diego City College.

"One of the most transformative periods of my life was my freshman semester at the University of Missouri. The idealism about literature and writing with which I entered college was immediately challenged by the kinky egotism of the local poetry scene. To grasp why the eccentricity of these poets so affected me, I rushed their antics into a composition for my English teacher, Mr. Marquard. Reading my work, he suggested that if I was to become an essayist, my eagerness to disclose the truth about others would stay with me forever yet to disclose the same about myself would take much longer. After years spent crafting this essay, I'm beginning to understand his point."

Richard Howard is a poet, translator, and critic who teaches at the arts school at Columbia University. His "essay" was originally a talk given to the PEN–American Center in the spring of 1996. His eleventh book of poems, *Trappings*, will appear in 1998 from Counterpoint.

Lynne Sharon Schwartz's essay is taken from *Ruined by Reading: A Life in Books*, published by Beacon. Her novels include *The Fatigue Artist*, *Leaving Brooklyn* (nominated for the 1990 PEN Faulkner Award for Fiction), *Disturbances in the Field*, *Balancing Acts*, and *Rough Strife* (nominated for a National Book Award and PEN/Hemingway First Novel Award). Her essays as well as stories from her two short fiction collections have been widely anthologized.

Leonard Michaels is the author of two story collections, *Going Places* and *I Would Have Saved Them If I Could,* a novel, *The Men's Club,* a memoir, *Sylvia,* and various essays. Some of his essays and recent stories are in his collection, *To Feel These Things.* He lives in Berkeley, California, and in Italy, in Umbria.

"My essay is about the movie *Pulp Fiction* and very generally about the way we talk in America. By 'talk' I mean mainly entertainment-talk, what you hear in movies and television, but you can hear that kind of talk in a lot of other places, too, and it's such a weird American reality that I wrote my essay about it. I know that an essay is only another kind of talk, but mine is supposed to be personal, and very different from the kind of talk I'm talking about."

James Allen McPherson is the author of *Hue and Cry, Railroad, Elbow Room,* and the forthcoming *Crabcakes.* Among his many awards are a Guggenheim Fellowship, a MacArthur Prize Fellows Award, and the Pulitzer Prize for Fiction in 1978. A member of the American Academy of Arts and Sciences, Mr. McPherson has published stories and essays in newspapers and magazines around the world, including *The Atlantic, The Nation, The New York Times, World Literature Today, Double-Take,* and *The Chiba Review* (Japan).

"This piece is a small part of a letter written to a Japanese friend as a kind of apology, one that was required to take into account events leading up to a certain rudeness. The Japanese man had no other way of understanding the life of black Americans, and so the letter about the background of the rudeness was the only way the writer could 'explain' why a certain thing happened. The full letter will be in *Crabcakes* this fall."

Richard Rodriguez, a contributing editor to *Harper's* and *U.S. News and World Report,* is the author of *Hunger of Memory: The Education of Richard Rodriguez* and *Days of Obligation: An Argument with My Mexican Father.* He has won a Fulbright Fellowship, an NEA grant, the Christopher Prize for autobiography, and was a finalist for the Pulitzer Prize for general nonfiction in 1993. Among the magazines that have featured his work are *Harper's, The American Scholar, The New Republic,* and *Time.*

Pascal Bruckner has served as visiting professor at New York University and San Diego State University in the United States, and l'Institut d'Études Politiques de Paris in France. His works published in English include *Evil Angels* (Grove Press), *The Tears of the White Man: Cooperation as Contempt* (Free Press), *The Divine Child* (Little, Brown), and the film *Bitter Moon*. He lives in Paris.

Andrei Codrescu was born in Sibiu, Romania, in 1946. Since emigrating to the United States in 1966, he has published poetry, memoirs, fiction, and essays. He is a regular commentator on National Public Radio, and has written and starred in the Peabody award-winning movie *Road Scholar*. In 1989 he returned to his native country to cover the collapse of communism for NPR and ABC's *Nightline*. The book describing these experiences was *The Hole in the Flag* (Morrow), which was a New York Times Notable Book of the Year. His novel *The Blood Countess* (Simon & Schuster) was a national bestseller. He teaches writing at Louisiana State University in Baton Rouge, Louisiana, and edits *Exquisite Corpse: A Journal of Letters and Life*. He lives in New Orleans. His latest books are *The Dog With the Chip in His Neck: Essays from NPR and Elsewhere* (St. Martin's Press) and *Alien Candor: Selected Poems 1970–1996* (Black Sparrow Press).

" 'Intelligent Electronics' is one of a number of essays investigating cyberspace and attendant phenomena. A one-hour radio documentary, *Hacking Toward Utopia*, was broadcast in April 1997."

Kai Maristed is the author of two novels, *Fall* and *Out After Dark*. Born in Chicago, she studied political science and economics in Munich and at MIT, has worked as a broadcast journalist and playwright in Germany, and currently teaches literature and writing in Boston. Her collection of stories, *When the Strange Horses Come*, will be published by Random House in the winter of 1998.

"The genesis of 'Nicotine: An Autobiography,' is self-evident. Along with loss of concentration, one of the most powerful goblins for some cigarette addicts is the fear of not ever again being able to string words together without smoke. This essay began as a test; it's a message after a period of silence, the first one I found I could write."

Robert Leo Heilman lives in the Umpqua country of southern Oregon and writes full-time, earning an income that amounts to half the prevailing minimum wage. His collected essays, *Overstory: Zero, Real Life in Timber Country*, earned the 1996 Andres Berger Award for creative nonfiction by a Pacific Northwest author and was chosen as a finalist for the 1996 Oregon Book Award.

Cynthia Ozick is the author of short stories, novels, essays, and a play. Her most recent collection of essays, *Fame and Folly,* is the recipient of the 1997 PEN/Spielvogel-Diamondstein Award for the Art of the Essay. *Best American Essays,* an annual, has included five of her essays. Her newest novel is entitled *The Puttermesser Papers.* She is a member of the American Academy of Arts and Letters.

"I have come tentatively and late to the memoir, since for many years I was seriously unable to write autobiographically. 'A Drugstore Eden' is my third such venture. Memory, I have learned, is a secret cave where nothing ever evaporates and everything is preserved. Once entered, tunnel opens into tunnel, and one discovers a surfeit of disclosure, even without Proust's madeleine. Or put it that the madeleine is found in taking the dare to nibble on one's own history."

Edward Hoagland has published fifteen books in a career stretching back over forty years. About half have been collections of essays, and in 1982 he was elected to the American Academy and Institute of Arts and Letters.

"I believe in 'seizing the day,' as this essay makes clear. Also in taking advantage, as a writer, of one's handicaps—in my case, a bad stutter, and for a while, legal blindness. Insight through vertigo; insight through improvising."

Acknowledgments

Grateful acknowledgment is made for permission to reprint copyrighted material, as follows:

"Mockingbird Years" by Emily Fox Gordon. Copyright © 1996 by Emily Fox Gordon. Originally appeared in *Boulevard,* Volume II, Numbers 1 and 2. Reprinted by permission of *Boulevard.*

"Les Très Riches Heures de Martha Stewart" by Margaret Talbot. Reprinted by permission of *The New Republic,* copyright © 1996, *The New Republic,* Inc.

"The Diner" from *Make-Believe Town* by David Mamet. Copyright © 1996 by David Mamet. Reprinted by permission of Little, Brown and Company.

"The Catskills Remembered" by Vivian Gornick from *Approaching Eye Level.* Copyright © 1996 by Vivian Gornick. Reprinted by permission of Beacon Press, Boston.

"Revelation" by Mary Gaitskill from *Communion,* edited by David Rosenberg. Copyright © 1996 by Mary Gaitskill. Reprinted by permission of the author and Doubleday.